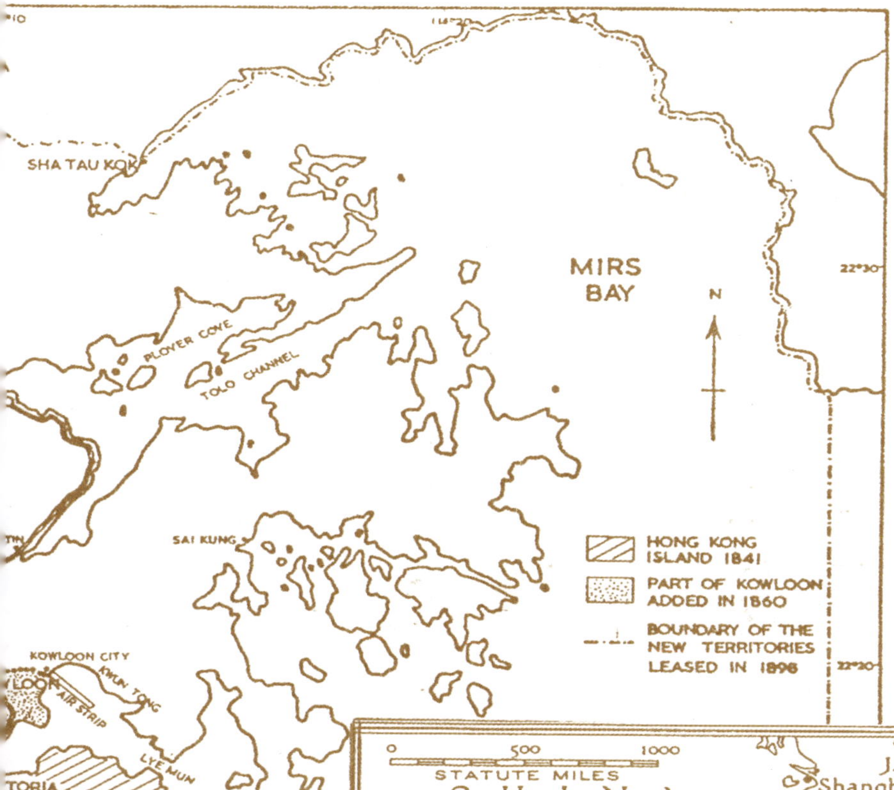
SHA TAU KOK
MIRS BAY
N
22°30'
PLOVER COVE
TOLO CHANNEL
SAI KUNG
HONG KONG ISLAND 1841
PART OF KOWLOON ADDED IN 1860
BOUNDARY OF THE NEW TERRITORIES LEASED IN 1898
22°20'
KOWLOON CITY
KWUN TONG
AIR STRIP
LYE MUN
SAI WAN
CAPE COLLINSON
TYTAM
STANLEY (CHEKCHU)
CAPE D'AGUILAR
WAGLAN ISLAND

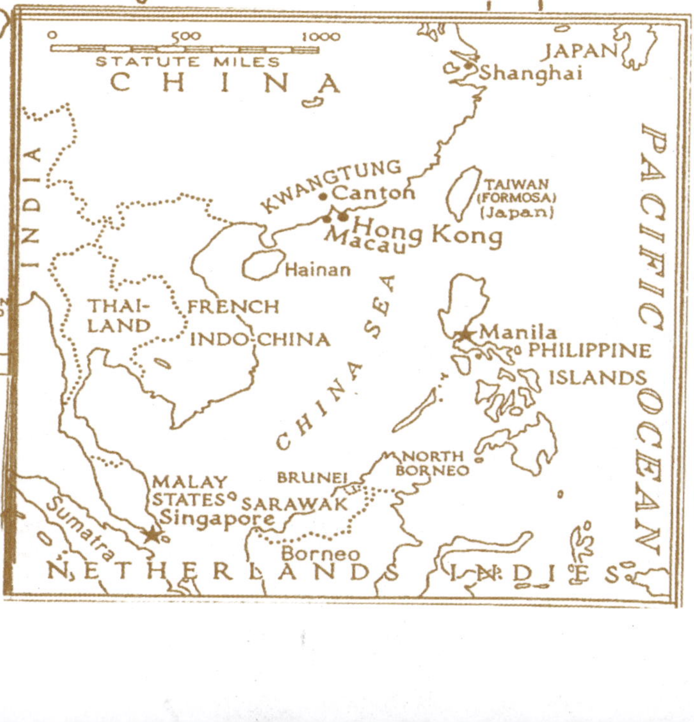
0 500 1000
STATUTE MILES
CHINA
JAPAN
Shanghai
PACIFIC OCEAN
INDIA
KWANGTUNG
Canton
TAIWAN (FORMOSA) (Japan)
Hong Kong
Macau
Hainan
THAI-LAND
FRENCH INDO-CHINA
CHINA SEA
Manila
PHILIPPINE ISLANDS
NORTH BORNEO
BRUNEI
MALAY STATES
SARAWAK
Singapore
Sumatra
Borneo
NETHERLANDS INDIES

AIRPORT OF THE NINE DRAGONS
KAI TAK, KOWLOON

MY APPROACH – *Recollections of Aviation at and around Hong Kong's International Airport.*

Capt. Charles *Chic* Eather
Author of *Syd's Pirates*
We Flew In Burma

ChingChic PUBLISHERS – SURFERS PARADISE, AUSTRALIA

ChingChic Publishers – Surfers Paradise
Copyright (C) Eather, Charles Edward James, 1920 -
EATHER, CHARLES EDWARD JAMES, 1920 -
AIRPORT OF THE NINE DRAGONS – KAI TAK, KOWLOON
ISBN 0 9586746 0 4

1. Eather, Charles Edward James, 1920 -
2. Aviation
3. Airlines – Aviation – Hong Kong
4. Air Pilots – Civil Aviation Department – Biography. 1 Title.
1996

First published 1996.
Reprinted 1997.

Typeset by Ocean Graphics Pty Ltd, Gold Coast.
Printed and bound by: Merino Lithographics Pty Ltd, Queensland.
Cover Design by: Ocean Graphics Pty Ltd, Gold Coast.
Wholly designed and set up in Australia by ChingChic Publishers.

This book is sold subject to the condition that it shall not, by way of trade or otherwise be lent, resold, hired out or otherwise circulated without the Publisher's prior consent in any form of binding or cover other than that which is published and without a similar condition including this condition being imposed on the subsequent purchaser.

CONTENTS

	Page
DEDICATION	v
FOREWORD	vi
ACKNOWLEDGEMENTS	vii
PREFACE	viii

CHAPTER:

1.	HONG KONG TAKES TO THE AIR – 1891-1919	1
2.	CRAZY HARRY – THE FIRST TENANT – 1920-1930	5
3.	THE LONG-RANGE PIONEERS – 1924-1929	9
4.	WEANING & GROWING PAINS – 1930-1935	20
5.	AGE OF CONSENT – 1936-1938	31
6.	UNCERTAINTY RULES – 1939-1940	40
7.	AIRPORT OF THE NINE DRAGONS OVERRUN – 1941	43
8.	UNDER THE CONQUEROR'S HEEL – 1942-1945	47
9.	THE FIRST YEAR OF RECOVERY – 1946	53
10.	FREEBOOTERS OF THE SKY – 1947	62
11.	ENTER THE BUTTERFIELD & SWIRE HONG – 1948	71
12.	THE KUOMINTANG RETREATS – 1949	82
13.	AN UNEASY BRITISH COLONY – 1950	91
14.	A NEW RUNWAY MOOTED – 1951-1953	98
15.	MURDER ON THE WING – 1954-1955	105
16.	KAI TAK AIRPORT MARKS TIME – 1956-1957	115
17.	THE MIRACLE STRIP	121
18.	THOSE TRAUMATIC BUILDING YEARS – 1959-1962	140
19.	KAI TAK'S THICKENING WAISTLINE – 1963-1967	150
20.	THE DAYS OF ADVENTURE DECLINE – 1968-1973	158
21.	KAI TAK TAKEN FOR GRANTED – 1974-1975	168
22.	EPILOGUE – TWILIGHT OF THE NINE DRAGONS – MIDNIGHT 30 JUNE 1997	174

APPENDICES:

1. CIVIL AVIATION DEPARTMENT – HONG KONG. PERSONNEL 178
2. AIRCRAFT ON HONG KONG REGISTER 179
3. KAI TAK AIRPORT – CONTROL TOWERS, TERMINALS,
   & DCA LOCATIONS 190
4. HONG KONG AVIATION CORPORATIONS – BRIEF NOTES 192
5. PIONEER FLIGHTS TO THE FAR EAST 198
   - LIEUTENANT GEORGES PELLETIER d'OISY 198
   - THE AMERICAN ROUND-THE-WORLD FLIERS – 1924 199
   - THE BRITISH WORLD FLIGHT ATTEMPT – 1924 202
   - MAJOR PEDRO ZANNI 204
   - THE SPANISH RAID – MADRID TO MANILA – 1926 206
   - THE PRIDE OF DETROIT – SCHLEE & BROCK – 1927 208
   - THE RAF'S FAR EAST FLIGHT – 1927-1928 209
   - MARGA von ETZDORF – 1931 210
   - THE FLYING HONEYMOONERS – MR & MRS C H DAY – 1931 211
   - CAPTAIN FERNANDO REIN LORING – 1932 211
   - WOLFGANG von GRONAU – 1932 213
   - THE AMERICAN FLYING HEIRESS – MISS BESSIE OWEN – 1937 ... 214
   - MAURICE NOGUES – 1932 215
   - MARIE-ANTOINETTE MARYSE HILSZ – 1933 216
   - VICOMTE DE SIBOUR – 1933 218
6. TRIPPE'S PAN AMERICAN AIRWAYS SYSTEM 219
7. THE MOUNT CAMERON MONSTROSITY 222
8. THE PENINSULA HOTEL & LEOPOLD GADDI 224
9. PIRACY – SCOURGE OF THE CHINA COAST 228
10. THE SECOND & THIRD OPIUM WARS – 1856-1860 230
11. THE SACRED HILL – SUNG WONG TOI 237
12. THE LOCKHEED ELECTRA L188 – PROBLEMS & RECTIFICATION 241
13. AFTERMATH OF MURDER ON THE WING – 23 JULY, 1954 243
14. CHEK LAP KOK – THE ULTIMATE AIRPORT 244

GLOSSARY OF ABBREVIATIONS & MEANING OF WORDS 245

PRINCIPAL WORKS CONSULTED 247

INDEX 249

JUDY

My dearest wife and life companion — I dedicate this book. Concurrently, my sternest critic and most ardent fan — a Cathay Air Hostess who shared the dangers that lurked in the circuit of the Airport of the Nine Dragons.

FOREWORD

Kai Tak Airport has become such a household name in world aviation for squeezing a quart into a pint pot. The traffic throughout has exceeded the wildest expectations of anyone, including all my predecessors thrice removed and more.

With the single runway involving an unorthodox approach from one direction, to put it mildly, one tiny passenger terminal of about 27,000 square metres, a two-unit high-tech terminal and 69 aircraft parking bays, it was handling as of January 1995 25.45 million passengers and 1.30 million tonnes of cargo, through some 144,000 international aircraft movements in a year. What a far cry from the day 31 August 1958 when the old Kai Tak cross-runways had to be closed down prematurely and the present runway pressed into action with its unpainted asphalt surface still warm to the touch!

What happened on that fateful day was that a C-54 (DC-4), coming over the then barren hills on the shores of the then unpolluted and unreclaimed Kowloon Bay, to land on the then runway 31, struck the sea wall with its main gears on the undershoot, and slid to a stop at exactly the intersection with runway 07/25. It burnt out, but not before all on board clambered to safety. After that, a DC-3 gracefully glided in to land on the remainder of runway 07 and stopped well short of the wreckage. The first aircraft to land on the brand-new runway was a search-and-rescue amphibian type which loitered around for about four hours until everybody else holding had to divert. The nearest diversion aerodrome in those days was in south Taiwan. The first commercial aircraft to depart from the new runway was, not surprisingly, a Cathay Pacific aircraft. No, no turbo props yet on the Cathay inventory. But those transitional days to the first turbine-powered aircraft types were to my mind the most glamorous days of civil aviation.

Kai Tak has served Hong Kong well, and since 1978 the rest of China. In the 10 years up to 1993, passenger traffic grew at almost 11 per cent per annum whereas the world average was just under 7 per cent. Too bad that in 1994, Kai Tak's passenger traffic growth dropped to 3.1 per cent whereas the world average was 5 per cent, due to Kai Tak's many times stretched capacity being reached, and as many as 300 flights a week having to be turned away. One can only wait with bated breath for the opening of the new grandiose Chek Lap Kok airport, some time in 1997.

From its humble 3390-metre runway, non-stop flights serve destinations in Europe and the west coast of North America. It used to take as long for the Sunderland flying boats to get from Kowloon Bay to Singapore, non stop. Yes, Kai Tak has served us well.

PETER K. N. LOK
Director of Civil Aviation
Hong Kong. 1988 – 1995

ACKNOWLEDGEMENTS

Appreciation is a strong word but falls short of my grateful thanks to the following aviation enthusiasts. I have recorded their names in alphabetical order. Perhaps I have overlooked your name, if so, please accept my sincerest apology.

Dick Barton, Ray Bull, Phil Burfurd.

Leon Callaghan, John Chetwynd-Chatwin, Grace & CC Chien, Stuart Clarkson, Kit Cumings.

Bill Darragh, Derek Davis, Buji Dhabher, Ian Diamond, Roy Downing, Roger Draper, Cliff Dunnaway.

Rod Eddington.

Roberto Fernandez.

John Gardner, Peter Gautschi, Arthur Gomes.

Al Hausske, Betty and Len Hill, Warwick Hobart, Geoff Holland, Trevor Hollingsbee, Leslie Howard, Andrew Huige.

Russell Keirnan, Heather Kelsall, *Marimill* Fernandez-Kerr, Ted Kidner, Ron Knight.

Mabel & Cliff Large, Norm Latham, May Lillywhite, Henley Lo, Sir Roger Lobo, Peter Lok.

Neil McPherson, Carl Myatt.

Desmond Naismith, Aad Neeven.

Norman Oei, Peter Onions.

Lester Padman, Diana Patten, Val & Ross Penlington, Ralph Pixton.

Nick Rhodes, Sir Denys Roberts, Jean Irvine Robertson.

Saw Puay-Lim, Dick Siegel, Terry Smith, Tony Smith, Lorna & Dave Smith, Jim Stonier, Peter Sutch, Sir Adrian Swire.

Reg Thatcher, Trevor Thorpe, Tommy Tomkins.

Fanny Tse.

Arianne Wasserman, Martin Willing, Cyril Wray.

Susana Yuen.

* * *

Air France Museum – Jean Lasserre, Curator.

Musee de l'air et de l'espace, Le Bourget, Paris. le General de BA (CPN) J.-Paul Siffre, Directeur.

Royal Air Force Museum – Dr Michael A. Fopp, Ray Funnell.

PREFACE

ESTABLISHMENT OF HONG KONG – A FESTERING PIMPLE

Hong Kong was born out of aggression, unreasonable demands and distrust. Its main purpose was to appease merchants with a secure trading base, and the Royal Navy with a deep-water port.

These avaricious merchants perpetuated the opium trade in China. The three wars that established the Crown Colony were to safeguard their trade.

The treaties that resulted from the Three Opium Wars brought a restless peace. They were one-sided and made little pretence of the powerful dictating to the weak. This is not extraordinary for it is the way of the conqueror. Where time has healed the wounds of others, the Chinese mind has festered over these humiliations. On July 1, 1997, China will regain her pride and Hong Kong will cease to exist as we know it today.

In Confucian society scholars head the list with peasants, artisans, and the military in that order. This ancient society considers the merchant or trader just a smidgen higher than an outcast.

Mixing in the politics of China has brought success to some individuals. For many, this success was a temporary illusion and the harbinger to downfall and historical obscurity. Even once loving and close-knit families have not escaped China's capriciousness.

***

Probably, the earliest traders to visit China were Nicolo and Maffeo Polo. They befriended the Mongol ruler Kublai Khan. The great Khan was sorry to see them leave but they left with an invitation to come back. They arrived back in Venice in 1269. In 1271, accompanied by Nicolo's son Marco, they made another expedition. Their return to Venice in 1295 marked an absence of 24 years. A generous Kublai Khan had given them great riches of ivory, jade, jewels, porcelain, silk and other treasures.

They arrived in Venice to find it at war with Genoa. When the Genoese captured the city they jailed Marco Polo. From a cell he wrote *Description of the World*, an account of his travels through China – then known as Cathay. In it he described the Khan's postal service, his mining and burning of coal as fuel, the widespread use of paper money and the Chinese inventions of the compass, paper-making, and printing. It became the most widely read book in Europe and historians believe it may have influenced many explorers, including Christopher Columbus.

Early in the 16th century the Portuguese discovered the direct sea route to China. In 1514 their trading vessels berthed at Canton's seaport of Whampao, some 12 miles from the city. There *they behaved more like pirates and hooligans than honest traders*. Though the authorities gave them a condescending welcome they would not allow them to live on China's soil.

This restriction forced them to seek solace at Macau. It lies about 40 miles (64 kilometres) west of Hong Kong at the mouth of the Pearl River. The Portuguese first settled Macau in 1557 and paid China for that privilege. It was not until 1887 that China recognised Macau as a Portuguese enclave.

In 1715 the Chinese granted the British East India Company the right to establish a permanent base at Canton. There they had to deal through appointed Chinese merchants known as *Co-hongs*. This favoured group fixed prices and determined import and export quotas. Graft and corruption existed on an enormous scale. Each Co-hong had a private money-tree!

It is wrong to assume that opium was the limit of imports. The available merchandise was wide-ranging. They included Manchester goods, whiskey, seal skins, and the quaint trade in *singsongs*. Yet most of these goods were difficult to sell, for the Chinese considered themselves self-sufficient. The West, attempting to impress Peking, sent a steel needle with a hole drilled through the point. The Chinese returned the needle with a hole drilled along the centre of the shank!

In 1782, John Henry *Squire* Cox arrived in Canton to sell his stock of English *singsongs*. These were musical clocks, watches, and mechanical toys. His range included a snuff box – lifting the lid revealed a brightly hued bird that sang.

At this time there were no Chinese watches so the singsongs proved an instant success. They made ideal presents, and customers ranged from mandarins to merchants. Already a quaint trade, it became quainter, and doubly profitable, when the Chinese began to wear watches in pairs. They figured that when one went to *sleep* the other would be *awake!*

There were few fortunes made by the importer of traditional goods. They soon left the scene, but the *singsongs* trade remained profitable for decades.

By the year 1820 French, Dutch, British and U.S. ships packed Macau's muddy, shallow harbour. There they trans-shipped their cargoes up the Pearl River to Canton where they traded opium for tea, silk and cotton goods. A trade imbalance resulted favouring the Co-hongs.

A western European delegation went to Peking seeking more favourable terms. Their approach was tactless and their demeanour superior. This attitude confirmed to the Sun of Heaven their barbarian status and their *entreaty* met with disdain. He refused to relax the ruling on foreign mixing and prohibited the teaching of the Chinese language to foreigners. Here was proof that both sides were arrogant and unencumbered by humility.

Lord Napier became the first *superintendent* of British trade in Canton in 1834, but Chinese officialdom refused to deal with him as an equal. This brought further friction and Great Britain took the initiative to force changes. Her merchants insisted on more conditions than the Chinese would concede. Armed conflict was inevitable. Meanwhile, Lord Napier returned to Macau, where broken in spirit he died on October 11, 1834.

John Francis Davis succeeded Lord Napier. Davis' successor was Sir George Robinson. The year 1836 ended with Sir George replaced by Captain Charles Elliot, Royal Navy. **This appointment marks the historical beginning of British Hong Kong.**

The Chinese Government blamed the British for introducing opium into their land. This is wrong, for the Portuguese, Dutch, French, American and others also traded the drug. Yet, there is little doubt that the British was the front runner in its illegal importation. They had the inside track for the tons of opium produced in Bengal, British India.

The dried narcotic juice of the Eurasian poppy was available in China long before the foreign merchants brought it to the masses. Opium-smoking is soothing, but dangerous when over-indulged. The Chinese became easy prey and its addicts were called *hippies* for they reclined on their hips while smoking. Great fortunes came to the traders. Finally, the drain on the silver holdings of his treasury forced the Emperor to ban the traffic. He sent a special commissioner to stamp out the trade.

Lin Tse-hsu arrived at Canton in 1839 and issued an edict to the foreign traders to surrender their stocks of opium for destruction. He seized and destroyed thousands of chests of opium and demanded their word that they would not bring in further stocks. The British objected to his high-handed methods, and sought compensation. Lin ignored their demands and the final straw came when a drunken brawl resulted in the killing of a Chinese national. Captain Elliot tried and imprisoned the seamen responsible for the death. His actions did not appease Commissioner Lin who demanded he hand over the culprits. Elliot refused.

Elliot's defiance came from an infamous incident in 1784. Under threat of a stoppage of trade, the Company (the Honourable John Company or East India Company) had handed over to the Chinese a gunner from the *Lady Hughes*. When the gunner fired a salute, he accidentally killed a Chinese boatman nearby. The court sentenced him to death following a secret trial. He was strangled.

Elliot would not repeat that spineless mistake. Lin Tse-hsu went into a rage and occupied Macau, the opium traders' operational base. The traders demanded protection and Lord Palmerston, then Prime Minister of Great Britain, sent the Chinese an ultimatum demanding compensation and a secure venue for future British trade. The Chinese ignored his ultimatum and the British Government dispatched 15 warships and 5,000 troops to enforce the demands.

In November 1839, fighting started and so began the First Opium War. The British inflicted repeated defeats on the Chinese forces and overran Canton. The 1840 conference at Chusan produced the Convention of Chuenpi that ceded the island of Hong Kong and its harbour to Great Britain.

The Mandarin Kishen, Governor of Hopeh, was the Manchu negotiator and Captain Charles Elliot RN represented Great Britain. Elliot made his decision to nominate Hong Kong Island from advice received from James Matheson. This decision brought Elliot's downfall for it raised the ire of Lord Palmerston. Britain's crusty Prime Minister called it a *barren island with scarcely a house on it*. The Chinese translation for Hong Kong is *Fragrant Harbour*, but to many this is a distortion of fact.

CAPTAIN CHARLES ELLIOT, RN
(1801-75).

British Superintendent of Trade in China
1836 – 1842

(Photo: Ian Diamond, Hong Kong Archivist)

CONFERENCE AT CHUSAN, 1840.
Captain Elliot negotiating the Convention of Chuenpi with the Mandarin Kishen, Governor of Hopeh.
(Photo: Ian Diamond, Hong Kong Archivist)

The once-powerful Kishen was returned to Peking in disgrace. His jailers dragged him before his Emperor bedraggled and shackled in chains. History records nothing further of his fate!

Elliot's Naval Commodore, Sir Gordon Bremer, proclaimed British sovereignty over Hong Kong in a flag-raising ceremony at Possession Point on January 26, 1841. This he did on the strength of the Convention of Chuenpi, **a document never ratified!**

Under Capt. Elliot's enthusiastic administration the Colony was a hive of activity with excavations for house sites and roads. The disturbed earth, when exposed to rain and sun, produced a virulent form of fever that took a heavy toll of life. The Government hastily built hospitals, and established a cemetery.

Queenstown soon had 50 European-owned buildings scattered along Queen's Road, its main street. At the eastern end of this road Jardine and Matheson established its headquarters. Its founding was the result of the opium trade and it was the peer of the British trading companies. The two partners became Hong Kong's first *Tai Pans*, or great managers, and their company – *The Princely Hong*.

Dr. William Jardine, who had studied medicine, was the doer and therefore obvious. On one occasion, someone struck him on the head while petitioning a local authority. He shrugged off the attack and continued his negotiations. From that time he was the *Iron-Headed Old Rat*. While James Matheson was the more dangerous, being the thinker. Both these men were principals in founding the Crown Colony of Hong Kong.

Another firm of the time was the trading house of Davidson. Two brothers, Lancelot and Wilkinson Dent, owned the company that later became known as *Dent's*. Their customers considered them more respectable and reliable than their more flamboyant competitors.

On July 21, 1841, a *killer* typhoon slammed the Colony. She was severe on the jerrybuilt hospitals and unroofed almost every house. It decimated the Chinese boat population, and destroyed six foreign ships.

A second typhoon hit four days later but was not as intense as the first. It did endanger Captain Elliot and Commodore Bremer for it caught them between Hong Kong and Macau in the cutter *Louisa*. Elliot assumed control of the ship and showed great seamanship in beaching it on an island. The screaming wind and pounding waves reduced the cutter to kindling. At this time the mandarins had a price of $100,000 on Elliot's head. When the typhoon abated, the crew of a Chinese vessel found the castaways who swayed their rescuers to take them to Macau for $3,000. Their troubles seemed over until a war-junk ordered their vessel to heave-to for inspection. There were some minutes of breathless suspense but the search didn't find the two Englishmen hidden under a cover of matting.

Captain Elliot could handle treacherous mandarins, deadly epidemic disease, and even the vagaries of nature. Yet, it was Westminster politicians that brought his downfall. Palmerston ordered his negotiator back to England. Elliot ended his public career as the Governor of the obscure island of St. Helena. Hong Kong had begun its toll on public figures. Lord Palmerston also became a casualty when he resigned as Prime Minister in 1858 over his China policy. Unlike Elliot, he was a more consummate survivor, and recovered again to lead his nation.

Some historians considered that Elliot had lived a wasted life. This is not my impression of the man. Beside his timely service in China, he was charge d'affaires in Texas 1842-46, Governor of Bermuda 1846-54, of Trinidad 1854-56, and, as stated earlier, Governor of St. Helena 1863-69. In 1856 he became a civil knight-of-the-realm. As a retired officer his naval promotions continued as honorary ranks. He became admiral on September 12, 1865. Admiral Sir Charles Elliot died at Witteycombe, Exeteron, September 12, 1875. His was not a wasted life by any yardstick!

Elliot's replacement was Sir Henry Pottinger – the first governor of the Crown Colony of Hong Kong (1842-1844). His highly respected Chinese Secretary was J. R. Morrison. Sir Henry's mandate protected 12,000 souls spread over about 20 villages. When he took office he changed the town's name from Queenstown to Victoria. Then he gathered his forces and reopened hostilities against the Chinese. Again they defeated the Chinese and finally captured the city of Chen-chiang at the intersection of the Yangtze and the Grand Canal. A frightened Imperial court agreed to Sir Henry's demands, and on August 29, 1842, they signed the Treaty of Nanking.

The Treaty opened the five ports of Canton, Amoy, Foochow, Ningpo and Shanghai to free commerce and allowed foreigners to reside there. These cities became known as the Treaty Ports. The Treaty abolished the one-sided Co-hong arrangement and henceforth trade would be conducted between officials on a basis of equality.

Arising from the Treaty of Nanking was the Treaty of the Bogue. This gave reciprocal rights for Chinese Nationals from the five *Treaty Ports* to trade with Hong Kong on payment of Customs duties to Canton. Certain clauses that appeared in the Chinese version of the Treaty were not included in the Hong Kong copy. When the British traders' discovered these missing parts Governor Pottinger was reviled.

Sir John Davis (1844-1848) replaced Sir Henry and then Sir George Bonham (1848-1854) replaced Sir John Davis. During their tenure there was a building boom that included two hotels. The consecration in 1849 of the Cathedral of St. John brought the Colony's newspapers an increased circulation. The Army extended their barracks at Chek Chu (Stanley), and a Chinese business community flourished along Bonham Strand.

Governor Sir John Bowring (1854-1859) presided over a more troubled period. He arrived in Hong Kong with his wife and youngest daughter, the vivacious Emily. The Bowring family was of staunch Church of England stock, yet his son went over to Rome and entered its priesthood.

Sir John was not the best choice to respond to that touchy time in Sino-British relations. He was a martinet with a high conception of Britain's place in the world, and like his friend Lord Palmerston demanded respect for his country from other nations. Some of Sir John's detractors said he was a clone of that self-opinionated Peer.

The Treaty of Nanking satisfied neither side. The foreigners argued that it did not grant enough, while the Chinese believed it conceded too much. The Chinese reverted to treating foreigners as inferiors and barbarians. The treaty had skirted the hoary question of opium importation and the Chinese again used this as their main forum for objection. This brought friction and frequent clashes. It was during these hostilities that the mandarins put a price on Sir John Bowring's head.

In January 1857, Cheong A. Lum a Chinese baker, obeying his mandarin's orders, laced his bread with arsenic. Lum, the proprietor of the E. Sing Bakery, had premises in the Wanchai district. His vile crime had only limited success. He had overdosed his dough and his innocent consumers' sufferings were mainly acute vomiting. The Governor and his family were more serious victims – Lady Bowring, never in robust health, was dead within a year. Sir John's constitution was stronger, yet it took three years to get the arsenic residue out of his system. There are no reports on how the other 500 bread consumers fared.

Police raided the bakery and arrested everyone. They then brought Lum back from Macau, where he had fled on the morning of the crime. The authorities charged Lum and 50 others with the outrage. Racial hatred fermented to where the foreign community demanded the accused be hanged without trial. The Governor, to his credit, resisted their demands. A British jury found Lum not guilty from lack of evidence. This verdict enraged the foreign community, but British justice gained in reputation.

The detention of Lum's employees dragged on until February. The authorities dropped charges against them and ordered their release on condition they leave Hong Kong. Within a few days Cheong A. Lum also left the Colony. His departure closed the unsavoury case of the *Queen vs. the Poisoners* and another incident of Hong Kong's lusty history became a shadowy archival statistic.

The Governor never recovered from the death of Lady Bowring, but Emily was his tower-of-strength. As the first lady her social obligations were strenuous, yet she always found the time to visit the sick. Much of the esteem Sir John received from the poorer Chinese was because of his daughter's charitable work.

Sir John's administration ended in May 1859, and in a painful scene Emily told him she would not be returning with him to England. She would remain in Hong Kong to take the veil. He left the Colony in utter despair.

Just 11 years later, on August 20, 1870, Canossian Daughter of Charity Sister Aloysia (Emily) of Hong Kong's Italian Convent died. She was just 37. Her legacy was the first headmistress of the first English school for girls in the Colony.

SISTER ALOYSIA (EMILY) BOWRING 1833-1870
Headmistress of Sacred Heart Canossian School, Hong Kong. 1860-1870
(Photo: Courtesy School Archivist)

Sir John Bowring was a complex enigma, a greatly misunderstood individual. He made little effort to seek popularity. It probably saddened him when Lord Palmerston sent Lord Elgin to Hong Kong. Palmerston was under great pressure from Cabinet members to take this action. No doubt he also realised Bowring had limits as a statesman, yet he never abandoned support and patronage to his friend.

Is Sir John Bowring (1792-1872) watching over Hong Kong with a wry smile? When other more flamboyant people of his era are historical relics he still enjoys universal fame. A very devout Christian, his glorious hymn *In the Cross Of Christ I Glory* still is a periodic part of Anglican church services.

The Second Opium War began on October 8, 1856, over a comparatively minor incident. The Chinese violated the British flag flying on a Chinese-owned but British-registered lorcha. This assault on the *Arrow* was the catalyst that started the Second Opium War of 1856-60. Historians call it the Arrow War. The French, then an ally of the British in the Crimean War, used the murder of a Roman Catholic missionary in Kwangsi to join forces with the British. For a time the allies did not force the pace; for the Crimea, the Persian problem and the Indian Mutiny occupied the British.

In late 1857 the British and French captured Canton. Their forces moved on Tientsin. The Taku forts, the last line of protection for Peking, were overrun. To save their capital the Chinese capitulated and they initialled the Treaty of Tientsin in 1858.

The treaty gave increased terms in the foreigners' favour. When, in 1859, the allied envoys came to ratify the treaty, they found the way to Tientsin blocked. They failed in attempting to force their way past the Taku forts and suffered great loss of life and equipment.

The Third Opium War followed. In 1860, the allies reopened hostilities and forced their way into Tientsin and then captured Peking. The former violation of the flag of truce and the death of some of its bearers brought severe retribution on the Chinese. The allies looted and torched the summer palace, and destroyed the Taku forts. The Chinese, to prevent further retribution, ratified treaties with additional conditions. The French gained freedom for movement of their missionaries, other world powers, who had *sat-on-the-fence*, gained favourably, with the British ceded the peninsula of Kowloon and Stonecutter's Island. The British now controlled Kowloon to Boundary Street.

The once great Cathay was now in decay and easy pickings for the foreign powers to grab chunks of her territory. The British seized Upper Burma, and the French – Annam. Then, in 1894, the Japanese forced China to her knees and drove her out of Korea and Formosa. The foreign powers, rutting like squealing pigs, grabbed other choice fragments. In November 1897 German forces seized Tsingtao. In March 1898, China formally leased Tsingtao and its associated bay Kaiochow to Germany. Russia, using the German seizure of Tsingtao as an excuse, occupied Port Arthur. In counter-action, Wei-Hai-Wei fell under British control *while Russia held Port Arthur*. Imperial China's slide into chaos gathered speed. In this uncertain atmosphere the British Government, in 1897, leased a large area north of Boundary Road that became the New Territories. This final addition took place during the tenure of the Colony's 11th governor, Sir William Robinson, 1892-1898.

This, then, is a condensed historical sequence of the origin of the British Crown Colony of Hong Kong. For those who wish to read more of the Second and Third Opium Wars I include a few more details, still greatly abridged, in the Appendices.

It is an over-simplification to suggest that opium brought down the Manchu dynasty – other factors contributed. These were arrogance, intransigence, an inability to recognise the winds-of-change, an overbearing attitude of self-importance, and an effete Imperial Court. These when combined led to its decay. Yet the importation of opium was probably the prime catalyst.

(Left): HOWQUA
All foreign business was transacted through 13 Chinese merchant companies – called co-Hongs. Howqua was the leader of this Group.

(Photo: Ian Diamond, Hong Kong Archivist)

(Below): THE CANTON FACTORIES – c. 1835
The trading countries' flags fly above the factories.

(Photo: Ian Diamond, Hong Kong Archivist)

THE CHINESE BAKERY – E. SING
Under orders from the Canton mandarins the proprietor laced his bread with arsenic.

THE EXAMINATION OF CHEONG A. LUM
The accused (in profile) supported by his father (full face). (Photos: Courtesy The Royal Hong Kong Police Archives)

THE HARBOUR & KOWLOON PENINSULA – 1859-1865.
(Photo: Shell Company of Hong Kong)

VICTORIA, HONG KONG c. 1855.
(Unknown French artist)

CHAPTER 1

HONG KONG TAKES TO THE AIR – 1891-1919

In January 1891, the *China Mail* published details of a coming event. Mr Thomas Baldwin, helped by his younger brother, would ascend by hot-air balloon from Happy Valley. Their exhibition was to conclude with a parachute descent by the young man.

On the third of January, a vast crowd gathered at Happy Valley. They applauded enthusiastically when the balloon rose majestically into the air. Then gasped when a small object left the gondola. They sighed with relief when a white canopy opened checking the parachutist's sickening speed, then broke in to thunderous applause as he touched the earth as light as a feather. Buoyed by success they repeated their performance on January 18 at Macau. There the crowds were equally demonstrative and treated the Baldwins as demigods.

In an interview, Baldwin humbly claimed to have invented the parachute. This was untrue for the first successful parachute jump, from a balloon, was by Andre-Jacques Garnerin (1768-1823). The Frenchman jumped from 2,230 feet over Monceau Park, Paris, on October 22, 1797. This was 100 years or so before the modest Baldwin's claim.

Senor Leo Hernandez chose November 9, 1892, to give a balloon demonstration from the West Point Praya. *The Acrobat and Aeronaut*, a term used in *The Hongkong Telegraph* newspaper, would ascend in his brilliantly illuminated balloon. From amid the clouds he would fire signal rockets and then float to the ground clutching the shroud-lines of a fiery parachute.

The evening was one of menacing gun-metal clouds deranged by blustery winds. As he stepped into the gondola his balloon exploded in a sheet of flame. *Mexican Bill* emerged, *burned and blackened,* and apologised for his failure. His audience, in appreciation of his savoir-faire, took up a collection to buy him another balloon.

The year of 1910 found Hong Kong again embracing the balloon adventurer. Baldwin returned in January with his huge balloon *Mogul* to repeat his 1891 triumphs. Then on June 1, the *SCMP* advertised the Chinese Aeronaut Hee Chong would help P. H. Hilborne with a balloon and parachute exhibition. Arranged for the following day bad weather forced a deferment. In the early afternoon of June 7, a vast crowd witnessed Hilborne's balloon rise from Happy Retreat. At 5,000 feet an easterly breeze drifted the balloon over the Happy Valley Race Course. The crowd watched entranced as a budlike object dropped away. Then they roared with excitement as it became the support for the figure swaying beneath. Hilborne's successful parachute jump finished on a sparsely wooded hillside near *The Calvery*. On October 31, 1910, Baldwin got permission to use an open space opposite Victoria View. This is the current site of the Peninsula Hotel. Nearby Signal Hill and Holt's godown, both splendid vantage points, swarmed with enthusiastic viewers. Baldwin's parachute jump ended in the harbour. He emerged soaked but uninjured and clearly elated.

This Baldwin demonstration effectively ended Hong Kong's balloon era. The Colony revived this interest in the 1970s when Cathay Pacific Airways sponsored a balloon in its distinctive Brunswick-green livery. It attracted worldwide publicity and thousands of dollars worth of business. It also brought a world altitude record to Captain Geoff Green, a Cathay Pacific Boeing 747 pilot.

Captain Baldwin's attraction for the Colony brought him back in 1911. This time with two aeroplane pilots and three Red Devil pusher biplanes. They were en route to a carnival at Manila. On January 28, 1911, he sought permission to give an *exhibition of flying* from Happy Valley. The authorities refused this venue but approved an alternative site – a field in the Taipo marshes. The difficult access had Baldwin abandon the idea and his group left for Manila.

* * *

The conquest of the air has been the dream of the visionary from ancient times. The 1972 *Guinness Book of Records* states the first man-carrying powered aeroplane to fly was not entirely under its own power for the take-off was down a steep incline. This occurred about 1874 at Brest, France.

It also mentions that Clement Ader flew his *Eole* for about 164 feet at Armainvilliers, France on October 9, 1890. There were no witnesses to confirm the flight. His claim lost further credence when later, with officials present, his plane did not leave the ground.

Early in December 1903, a journalist from a New York paper came to Kitty Hawk, North Carolina. From the protection of a hedge he saw something that sent him running to the nearest telegraph office. Part of his vividly-worded cable described a track 70 feet long that carried a trolley to support a flying machine. To obtain initial acceleration, a cord connected the trolley to a releasable weight at the top of a portable tower. The fall of the weight with the thrust of the propellers produced the speed to lift the machine into the air. (The Wright Brothers abandoned this catapult-type device before the successful first flight.)

The editor threw the cable into the trash-basket and suspended his journalist for having put such fantastic stuff on the wire. That disbelieving editor lost the scoop of the century.

On December 12, 1903, a toss of a coin decided that Wilbur, the older of the Wright brothers, should try first. His *Flyer* clattered down the track, rose too steeply, stalled, and fell back into the sand. The steep climb came from an unexpected gust of wind.

Four days later, Orville succeeded where his brother had failed. His triumph had the significance of being the *world's first controlled flight* by a man-carrying, power-driven aeroplane, and *landing at a point as high as the take-off point*. That day, for 12 seconds, he turned years of dreams and heartbreak into reality.

Later that day Wilbur regained some lost pride. He made a flight that lasted 59 seconds and covered a distance of 582 feet. It was a record that lasted for four years.

Wilbur died of typhoid fever in 1912. In the 36 years that Orville survived his brother he saw aeroplanes evolve to commercial airliners and couriers of devastation. What were his thoughts of the London blitz and of Hiroshima and Nagasaki?

* * *

HONG KONG TAKES TO THE AIR – 1891-1919

As the shadows lengthened in Yuen Chau Kok and Tsang Tai Uk, at Sha Tin, the village folk expected a restful evening. The strong, gusty wind that had whipped the sand of their Tolo Harbour beach into stinging projectiles had become a gentle cooling breeze. Suddenly a screeching shattered the peace of their quiet haven. They had heard the Colony's first heavier-than-air flight.

The exact time was 5:10 p.m. on March 18, 1911. The intrepid airman was the Belgian Charles Van den Born – a Henry Farman Company test pilot and instructor. His plane was a Farman Mark II named *Wanda*. The *Winged Walloon's* plane had two-wings (biplane), equipped with a *Gnome* motor that drove the standard propeller of the time. Van den Born claimed the *Gnome* the first motor to support flight in the Far East.

Van den Born arrived by the steamer *Donai* with three aeroplanes. His planes were easy to transport – they could be dismantled into eight separate segments.

His arrival date is at variance. One report stated this as February 27, 1911. Another is 20 February calculated from a letter he wrote board the *Donai* steaming in the Gulf of Siam.

After lengthy negotiations the Hong Kong authorities approved his application to fly. They chose the Sha Tin area doubtless satisfied that he could not spy on the Colony's defences from there! Some months earlier they refused an American aviator a similar approval. I wonder why the Colonial authorities considered a Belgian less a security risk than an American!

Van den Born was no stranger to the plaudits of the thousands – he was a former Belgian cycling champion. (Here is an interesting parallel – the Wright Brothers also had an association with bicycles.) Yet on March 18, 1911, just a few hardy visitors from town and some passing villagers applauded his momentous achievement. Another report gave his

1911

The Belgian pilot Charles Van den Born at controls of Farman biplane with joy-rider precariously perched behind. (Photo: SCMP 4 November 1962)

audience as *a few despondent water buffaloes and a handful of Hakka peasants.* Yet, this was not the way the promoters planned it!

For days display flags gave directions how one could get to the venue. The newly completed Kowloon-Canton railway to Sha Tin was the most convenient travel mode. The cost to witness the flight ranged from 50 cents to $3 – a ride would cost the fearless $75.

The daring Belgian had attracted Vice-Regal patronage. On that historic day hundreds left the comfort of the Hong Kong Hotel, and less opulent *watering-holes*, on special trains for Sha Tin. The Rajput band kept the visitors entertained. The Major-General Commanding the Garrison escorted His Excellency Governor Sir Frederick Lugard and Lady Lugard. They were looking forward to the exhibition.

The main event was not a success as His Excellency's party was late. When they arrived a 30-knot wind had arisen that prevented a take-off. Sir Frederick's disappointment turned to impatience and resulted in his party leaving the scene. His decision was a signal for a mass exodus. The Kowloon train, scheduled for a 5:10 p.m. departure, left early and as it puffed out of Sha Tin Station the Farman took to the sky. This proved the Belgian's ability to fly, *a question much debated during the afternoon.*

About a week later Van den Born provided another demonstration at Sha Tin. His final flight showed he was both a consummate airman and survivor. Those who came to see him also witnessed Hong Kong's first plane crash. Avoiding a crowd of Queen's College students, playing on his landing area, he hit the ground with a sickening thud. Although shaken he had escaped serious injury.

With a repaired *Wanda* Van den Born left for Canton. There the Tartar General Fu Chi, the *Guardian of the Cantonese*, applauded each dive and turn. His successful flight turned to tragedy when a republican gunman assassinated the general. This led to the cancellation of further flying in Canton.

Did Van den Born go into the interior of China? His intention was to do so but plague was rampant. Another of his letters stated he expected to sell his planes there. I have no information on the outcome of this plan!

On August 4, 1914, the First World War began. The Hong Kong Government, as with the Boxer uprising that besieged Peking in 1900, saw there was no serious threat but brought the Colony to a semi war footing.

The expatriates initially viewed the outbreak of the War with mixed feelings. These businessmen were a close-knit community and local events took precedent over those half a world away. Anyhow few doubted that the war would be over within six months!

Aviation in Hong Kong lapsed during the war years. The only aerial event occurred in 1915 when a Chinese aviator, Captain Tom Gunn, gave a hydroplane (seaplane) exhibition at Shatin.

Another of the Colony's pioneer aviators also used the Happy Valley Racecourse. Mr. Lim On was a successful Canadian-Chinese businessman who learned to fly in Canada. Mr. Lim bought a *Jenny* JN-4C built by Glen Hammond Curtiss, an American.

In 1919 he shipped his plane to Hong Kong to continue his exhilarating hobby. One blustery day, high above the racecourse, a downdraft caught him napping and he finished in a tree. Another report of the time states he crashed in a timber yard. Whatever the sudden stop, he staggered from the accident in better shape than his beloved *Jenny*. She was a mangled wreck that he unceremoniously dumped in a gloomy godown. That godown was not to be her final resting place for another enthusiast found her. He restored her and in 1924 she climbed into the skies again.

CHAPTER 2

CRAZY HARRY – THE FIRST TENANT – 1920-1930

The airport of Kai Tak has for its backdrop a range of hills with a serrated crest that resembles a giant cross-cut saw. The Chinese are sure these higher points resemble dragons. They call them, from East to West, Razor Hill, Hebe Hill, Kau Lung Peak, Temple Hill, Crown Point, Lion Rock, Beacon Hill, Eagle's Nest, and Tai Mo Shan. These then are the *Nine Dragons of Kau Lung* (Kowloon).

Most pilots know that Tai Mo Shan is 3,140 feet and is the highest point in the Colony. The name means: Tai, big; mo, hat; shan, mountain – *The Mountain Capped with Mist*.

Messrs. Kai and Tak were citizens of the time and greatly respected. Mr. Au Tak was the owner of a thriving photographic business. Doctor Kai Ho Kai qualified in medicine at Aberdeen University. Later he was called to the Bar at Lincoln's Inn. Doctor Kai returned to Hong Kong where he practised medicine then, in 1882, he turned his attention to the law.

He founded the Alice Memorial Hospital in memory of his English wife. A Knighthood followed in 1912 for his part in founding the Chinese Medical College, the forerunner of the University.

In 1924, only a dusty track separated Kowloon City from Kowloon Bay. Kai and Tak decided to reclaim land from the shallow waters of the Bay. Their sole interest was to develop the area for a housing estate. The Kai Tak Land Development and Investment Company failed and they filed for bankruptcy. The reclamation came under the control of the Crown and subsequently became a flying area.

The first name given to the landing area was the Kowloon Aviation Field. Some pilots considered it *as postage stamp size* while others felt that definition an exaggeration. The lard factory and the raw sewage floating in the adjacent nullah produced a *fragrance* that defied description.

Many early travellers still remember this olfactory welcome. A story has an English-born comedian taking a deep breath at the plane's door. In disgust he gasped – "What is that terrible stench?" A friend replied that it was shit. The comedian observed – "That I realise but what have they done to it?"

Long before seaplanes used the cluttered waters of Kowloon Bay pilots were using other water areas.

AIRPORT OF THE NINE DRAGONS, KAI TAK, KOWLOON

1870s – DR KAI HO KAI

Knighted in 1912. With Mr Au Tak he reclaimed a portion of Kowloon Harbour to develop a garden city. The development failed and in time the reclaimed area became the nucleus of Kai Tak Airport.

(Photo: Ian Diamond – Hong Kong Archivist)

In 1921, the Colony attracted a group of intrepid American aviators. Captain Charles E.W. de Ricou (Recoux), a French World War I pilot, was their leader. His fleet of seaplanes, bought as World War I surplus, assessed operating conditions at Tsin Shui Wan (Repulse Bay) on Hong Kong Island and Lai Chi Kok on the mainland. They decided to make their base at Repulse Bay. There the water was clear with few sampans and the palatial Repulse Bay Hotel made splendid headquarters.

The *Macau Aerial Transport Company* proposed providing a service linking Canton, Macau, and Haiphong with Hong Kong. Captain de Ricou's first submission was modest – return flights to Macau. The Hong Kong authorities granted their request but set harsh conditions.

Based at Repulse Bay their source of income would come from Hong Kong's capital city Victoria. Their terminal was the Statue Square Bund next to the Star Ferry.

The authorities restricted their flights to 150 feet or less over the busy harbour. The restriction resulted as none of the de Ricou team was a British subject. The Government reasoned that any flight by a foreign national above this height might lead to potential espionage – the Colony was a fortified place! These bureaucrats conveniently forgot that a couple of years earlier the French and Americans bled beside their British brothers in defeating a common enemy.

CRAZY HARRY – THE FIRST TENANT – 1920-1930

Captain de Ricou's men got past this ridiculous restriction. They landed at the entrance of the Harbour and then taxied to the Bund. The journey took over 20 minutes compared with the flight time of just under 20 minutes to Macau. This handicap proved too much for the budding airline. It disbanded with several pilots taking flying jobs in China.

Civilian flying began on the Kai and Tak reclamation in 1924. Its diminutive size did little to curtail the vigorous activity that soon flourished.

In April of that year, a 24-year-old American soldier-of-fortune leased part of the reclamation. Lt. Col. Harry W. Abbott called his portion the Kowloon Aviation Field and there founded the Commercial Air Company.

Colonel Abbott was a far-sighted pilot who saw an opportunity to become an aviation entrepreneur. Reginald Earnshaw, a friend of long standing and a gifted aircraft mechanical engineer, shared his dream.

They had arrived without planes and while casting around heard of Mr. Lim On's derelict *Jenny*. With a minimum of haggling they bought the wreck for 2,000 Hong Kong dollars. Working round-the-clock Reg Earnshaw soon had it serviceable. Harry Abbott test flew the rebuilt Curtiss *Jenny* JN-4C on April 24, 1924. Their Company was in business.

They gained the confidence of aviation enthusiasts and many locals became pupils. Soon a Curtiss *Jenny* JN-4D and a Curtiss Oriole enlarged their fleet.

With an expanded fleet Harry Abbott increased his staff. High above the racecourse and the harbour his group gained respect for their courageous wing-walking. The *piece de resistance* was Harry calmly stepping from wing to wing as his planes flew in close formation. A *South China Morning Post* reporter called it *the best show in town*, and tagged him *Crazy Harry*.

In 1925, the Chinese Lunar New Year fell on January 25, beginning the *Year of the Ox*. Harry decided this would be an auspicious date to dedicate the *Abbott School of Aviation*. His way of celebrating this occasion was to fasten firecrackers to the *Jenny's* tail skid. As Reg Earnshaw lit the string Harry applied take-off power. The strong slipstream extinguished the spluttering flame. Harry returned to silence – the failed display was *bad joss! Worse joss* lay ahead.

1924 – ABBOTT'S KOWLOON AVIATION FIELD

L. to R. *The hapless Reg Earnshaw, Claude his brother, Mr Sales, Harry's wife Dolly, and ground crew. The mangled Jenny JN-4, found in Mr Lim On's dusty godown, is restored and ready to fly. In the front cockpit sits Harry Abbott and in the rear Lim On.*

(Photo: Dan-San Abbott)

AIRPORT OF THE NINE DRAGONS, KAI TAK, KOWLOON

1924 – THE ABBOTT SCHOOL OF AVIATION

L. to R. Instructor Harry Abbott, Dolly his wife (Mary Alice Cecilia Abbott), and Mr O'Brian (student). The plane is a Curtiss Oriole – note the highly inflammable matshed hangar. (Photo: Dan-San Abbott)

Shrugging off his disappointment, Abbott proceeded with a planned parachute descent. At the last moment, the parachutist refused to do the stunt, so Harry asked his mechanic to jump. Reg was not keen but Harry swayed him with the reminder that it would be a soft water-landing with his brother Claude commanding the pick-up launch. The still reluctant mechanic climbed from the cockpit and then faltered. When he finally released his hold he was past his best jump point. He splashed safely into the water, but his inexperience made no allowance for the parachute canopy. It collapsed around him and dragged him under the surface. When Claude's launch got to the new position Reg had drowned.

On August 22, 1930, page thirteen of the *SCMP* established an air of mystery with the words *a strange coincidence* – the Obituary of Harry Abbott followed that of Claude Earnshaw. For the past six years Claude had managed the Palace Hotel in Kowloon – he died following a fit. Harry crashed while making a speed trial in a baby pursuit plane at Berkeley, California.

The stories are endless about Harry Abbott – a man with great aeronautical gifts. Why did he name his Curtiss plane *Felix the Cat*? How did he get such a frightfully scarred face? His affable son Dan-San now resides in the States – who gave him that name? Each story has an interesting background and other writers have done them justice. Yet, my final thoughts about Harry Abbott, the first tenant of what became Kai Tak Airport, takes a different tack.

Why Kai Tak Airport and not Abbott Airport? The Colonel had a splendid aviation background whereas Messrs Kai and Tak had none!

CHAPTER 3

THE LONG-RANGE PIONEERS
1924-1929

An airfield, airport, aerodrome, waterdrome, call it what you will, attracts the public as iron-fillings to a magnet. One sure draw-card is an air carnival and the associated display of classical planes with a sprinkling of modern giants.

In earlier days it was the arrival or departure of the long-distance flyer. For these were the men and women whose courage surpasses the norm, knowing and accepting the odds stacked against them. They were the true heroes of the formative years of airline operation.

Several pioneer aviators visited the Colony during 1924. These were from the American and the British *round-the-world* flights. The Portuguese airmen Sarmento, de Beires and a mechanic, the Frenchman Lieutenant d'Oisy and Argentina's Major Zanni.

The air forces of the United States and Britain, ever the friendly rivals, determined their country would be first round-the-world. The Americans chose to fly east to west while the British west to east. Their plan was to meet at Hong Kong and compare route details. This was not to be!

Under the leadership of Major Frederick L. Martin, four *Douglas World Cruisers* (DWC) left Santa Monica, California, on 17 March. Squadron Leader MacLaren, commanding a crew of two, left Calshot (Southampton Water) on 25 March. MacLaren's plane was a Vickers-Napier *Vulture* amphibian.

A few minutes after noon, on June 8, three DWC's flew through Lei Yue Mun Pass and touched down in Kowloon Harbour, Hong Kong. On 25 June, while refuelling at the Burmese airfield of Akyab, MacLaren saw the American planes passing overhead.

The British plane touched down in Kowloon Harbour at 1700 hours on 30 June. The following day, Squadron Leader MacLaren and his crew, Flying Officer Plenderleith and Flight Sergeant Andrews, lunched with the Members of the Hong Kong Club. That evening they dined with Governor Sir Reginald Stubbs KCMG, and Georges Pelletier d'Oisy (now Capitaine). This distinguished French aviator had, on 9 June, captured the record from Paris to Tokyo.

In April, three Portuguese Air Force Officers left Sines (150 kms south of Lisbon) to secure the record from Lisbon to Macau. They were de Beires (Brito) Pais, Sarmento de Pais (pilots), and Manuel Gouveia (mechanic). Their plane, a Breguet 14 bomber baptised *Patria*,

AIRPORT OF THE NINE DRAGONS, KAI TAK, KOWLOON

THE AMERICAN ROUND-THE-WORLD FLIGHT (Arrived in Hong Kong – June 8, 1924)

A painting of the two World Cruisers that completed the round-the-world flight. The Chicago (Number 2) was flown by Lieutenant Smith. The Number 4 DWC New Orleans *flown by Lieutenant Nelson fills the foreground. The World Flight badge, painted on the fuselage of each plane, is visible on* New Orleans. (Painting: US Air Force Central Museum, Ohio)

THE BRITISH ROUND-THE-WORLD FLIGHT (Arrived in Hong Kong – June 30, 1924)

Lord Thomson, the Air Minister, wishes the British crew good luck. Left to Right: Flight Sergeant Andrews, Flying Officer Plenderleith, Squadron Leader MacLaren and Lord Thomson. (Photo: Royal Air Force Museum)

crashed in India after an adventurous journey. The replacement plane was a two-seater deHavilland 9A, the *Patria* II – the mechanic finished the voyage by land.

During the night of July 20 they approached Macau in very bad weather. Unable to land they diverted to Hong Kong where the weather was marginally better and finally crash landed near the Kowloon railway. Their plane was a write-off but they miraculously escaped injury.

In September 1924, the Argentine airman Major Pedro Zanni landed in Hong Kong on his flight round the world. Unable to get permission to land in Shanghai the Major kicked-his-heels around the Colony until the Chinese relented and he left on 27 September.

On November 3, 1924, the seaplane carrier HMS *Pegasus* steamed into Hong Kong's harbour. A part of her company was a RAF contingent with four Fairey 111 D seaplanes powered by 450hp Napier Lion engines. The planes – equipped with vertical air cameras – provided the first aerial survey of the Colony.

The following day Flight Lieutenant G. *Gerry* E. Livock DFC AFC, a noted cricketer, taxied plane N9634 through the dirty waters of Kowloon Bay. His take-off was nerve-racking for the Bay swarmed with junks. He made several landings and take-offs then reported the Bay too hazardous for seaplane operation. They accepted his recommendation to use Tolo Harbour and completed the aerial survey from there.

RAF FIRST AIR SURVEY FLIGHT – HONG KONG, NOVEMBER 4, 1924

Pilots of the special 'air survey flight' that made the first RAF flights into Hong Kong. Photographed on board the seaplane carrier HMS Pegasus. L to R: Flt Lt (later Gp Capt) G. E. Livock DFC, AFC; Fg Off (later Air Cdre) A. J. Rankin AFC, Sqn Ldr (later Gp Capt) E. L. Tomkinson; Fg Off (later Wg Cdr) F. H. Isaac DFC and Flt Lt (later Gp Capt) E. P. M. Davis AFC, AM. The aircraft is the Fairey 111D No. N9634 that made the first flight – Flt Lt Livock pilot.

(Photo: *Gau Lung* – RAF 50th Anniversary Souvenir Booklet – 1977)

AIRPORT OF THE NINE DRAGONS, KAI TAK, KOWLOON

Then the Governor, Sir Reginald Stubbs (1919-1925), requested a reconnaissance of pirate hide-outs in Mirs Bay and Taya Wan (Bias Bay). This expedition was illegal for they had no permission from the Chinese Government to fly in its airspace. The patrol disclosed vital information of pirate infestation throughout the area. Sir Reginald was the first Governor to fly in a seaplane around his domain.

In December 1924, HMS *Pegasus* steamed out of Hong Kong Harbour arriving at Singapore in January 1925. Four years later Flight Lieutenant (now Squadron Leader) Livock, who had made the first RAF flight in the Colony's skies, would return to these waters.

Within a month of the *Pegasus* departure, an aerodrome at Kowloon opened. Yet it would be two years before the RAF established a permanent base there. This was the result of the 1921-22 Treaties of Washington. The Conference resulted in seven agreements. The first, and the one that concerns us, was a pact between the USA, the British Empire, France and Japan, restricting Great Britain from building a military base east of Singapore. The British Government overcame this by designating Kai Tak a civilian aerodrome. As a civilian aerodrome there would be no restriction on any aircraft, service or otherwise, using its facilities. This flimsy ruse met with no objection from the other signatories, so the British established an aerodrome at Kai Tak.

The Spanish Government decided their Air Force should join other nations in long-range flights (raids). On 5 April 1926, three Breguet X1X bombers left Madrid (Cuatro Vientos) bound for faraway Manila. The pilots were Esteve, Gallarza and Loriga – their mechanics were Arozamen, Calvo and Perez.

Although the flight did not enter Hong Kong air-space the Colony had a role in the expedition's success.

On 1 May, two Breguets left Hanoi for Macau. (Esteve and Calvo had withdrawn from the raid after force-landing in the desert.) Loriga landed at Macau on a tree-enclosed football field with a seized motor. Gallarza overshot the field and finished in the branches of a tree. The Macanese gave the Spanish airmen unfettered use of their workshops but their engineers lacked aeronautical experience. The British Army dispatched Lieutenant Maud, with two ex-RAF mechanics, in the Hong Kong mail boat. They could do little with Loriga's useless engine but repaired Gallarza's plane.

A single Breguet X1X commanded by Gallarza, with Loriga his observer, left Macau on 11 May. They landed in Manila two days later. They had flown 17,100km, at an average speed of 161km/hr, in 106 flying hours.

In 1927, the first Service aircraft flew into Kai Tak aerodrome. They were Fairey 111D, Fairey 111F, and Fairey Flycatcher types. The formal commissioning of RAF Base Kai Tak occurred on March 10, 1927. Its strength was 24 officers from three flights of the Fleet Air Arm and one accountant officer. Of the three flights, only No. 442 Fleet Fighter Flight was to be based at Kai Tak and equipped with Fairey 111D aircraft. One week later Squadron Leader R. B. Munday, the first CO, arrived – he held this position for eight days. Squadron Leader C. E. MacPherson succeeded him.

The RAF base began as a complex of matshed buildings on the western perimeter of the airfield. (The site is now the aircraft movement area fronting HAEC.) The Officers' and Sergeants' Messes formed part of that complex. The Airmen's quarters were in a rickety building, an old rope factory, about a mile away in Ma Tau Kok.

At the rear of the matsheds a nullah flowed into Kowloon Bay from San Po Kong. A crane, near to the nullah's discharge point, lifted seaplanes out of the water. Other matsheds housed a maintenance section strategically placed near the crane. Traffic crossed the nullah on concrete-slabs to narrow streets that separated weathered stone buildings.

During August a typhoon played havoc with the matsheds. Falling debris destroyed several aeroplanes. With his base in shambles, the CO arranged temporary quarters in the unfinished shell of The Peninsula Hotel.

THE LONG-RANGE PIONEERS – 1924-1929

11 MARCH 1926
The three Spanish Captains at Heliopolis. L to R. Esteve, Gallarza and Loriga.
(Photo: Aad Neeven)

A VICIOUS VISITOR... AUGUST 1927
A typhoon plays havoc with the matshed hangars. (Photo: Hong Kong Airport. DCA booklet.)

AIRPORT OF THE NINE DRAGONS, KAI TAK, KOWLOON

THE AFTERMATH OF A VICIOUS VISITOR – AUGUST 1927
As the wind unroofed the matshed hangars, falling debris damaged several planes.   (Photo: Fl/Lt Noel Hitching, RAF Kai Tak)

The airmen returned to a sturdy building just across the nullah. It was in the fourth street from the water's edge. (That street is the current site of the airport's fuel farm.) The Officers' Mess moved across the airfield to a turreted house on the eastern perimeter.

The contamination of the nullah had not become the problem of later years, but a nauseating stench came from the lard factory nearby. This, when added to the humidity of summer, made Kai Tak less than a salubrious posting!

Two American aviators, William Brock and Edward Schlee, honoured Hong Kong by dropping in at 3:25 p.m. on September 9, 1927. Their *Pride of Detroit* was a high-wing monoplane built by Eddie Stinson and designated the SM-1 Detroiter. The adventurers were on the downhill part of a flight that began on August 22 from Detroit's Ford Airport. Their flight had taken them across the Atlantic Ocean to England through the near East and the sub-continent of India.

In faraway England another great adventure was beginning. On October 17, 1927, four RAF Southampton flying-boats left Plymouth Sound. The commander of this, the Far East Flight, was Group Captain H. M. Cave-Brown-Cave DSO DFC. His second-in-command was Squadron Leader Gerry Livock DFC AFC. Cave-Brown-Cave's mandate was to open an air route to Australia and the Far East.

Fourteen months later Southamptons had shown the flag over 43,450km (27,000 miles) of the world. They proved that air travel was not only feasible but reliable. Their splash-down in Kowloon Bay on November 18, 1928, seemed to belie this for the residents' reception was lukewarm.

Although the Hong Kong public showed little interest the authorities did! This interest led to the Government taking control of airport operations and upkeep in 1930. Meanwhile, in 1928, the Government made plans to reclaim more of Kowloon Bay's foreshore. The cost of this operation was too great to be borne out of revenue so they

THE LONG-RANGE PIONEERS – 1924-1929

FLEET AIR ARM (FAA) FAIREY 3F ON CRANE.
(Photo: Hong Kong Airport. DCA booklet.)

floated a six per cent loan issued at a premium of three per cent. The public instantly oversubscribed the loan. This reclamation, filled to a height of two feet below formation level, came from harbour dredgings. A sea-wall stabilised the fill. On June 7, 1929, a concrete slipway replaced the tedious method of lifting float-planes ashore by steam crane.

Hong Kong in the spring of 1929 experienced extreme drought. A radical therapy had the RAF bombing the clouds with silver nitrate dust. An Australian engineer claimed the procedure had brought rain relief during a Queensland big-dry. Squadron Leader Freeman dropped the bombs with the same result as another attempt by the Far East Flying Training School in 1948. Both sorties failed and Nature continued with her timetable.

Hong Kong was slow to emulate the enthusiasm for heavier-than-air flight then sweeping Europe. Far-sighted pioneers spoke of flying Hong Kong to London in about eight days but they were few. Civil aviation at Kai Tak, historically, began its growth with the Hong Kong Flying Club's formation.

In mid-1929, Wing Commander R. Vaughan Fowler rented part of the reclamation from the Government. He was a man with a single-purpose drive and strong views. His intransigence would lead to controversy in the months ahead.

The Hong Kong Flying Club shared the diminutive field with the petite RAF establishment. They shared a cluster of matsheds built beside the nullah that drained into

AIRPORT OF THE NINE DRAGONS, KAI TAK, KOWLOON

THE HONG KONG FLYING CLUB – 1929

The founders – Mr F. C. Smith and Wing Commander R. Vaughan Fowler.

KAI TAK AIRFIELD – 1930

The airfield showing the matshed buildings alongside the nullah. The crane in the bottom left-hand corner lifted seaplanes out of the water. The white building at the far right is the officers' mess that stood roughly where the airmen's married quarters now stand. The aircraft are probably Fairy Flycatchers of the Fleet Air Arm. (Photo: *Gau Lung* – RAF 50th Anniversary Souvenir Booklet – 1977)

THE LONG-RANGE PIONEERS – 1924-1929

Kowloon Bay from San Po Kong. The thriving lard business across the nullah let one's olfactory organ fix the wind direction.

The club started with two Avro Avian 594 MK 1V/M planes. They held the Colony's initial registrations. The Department of Civil Aviation list VR-HAA as first registered March 10, 1930, and de-registered on September 11, 1930. The other Avian became VR-HAB, first registered on August 19, 1930, and de-registered December 10, 1931.

Club membership was steady without being spectacular. This changed when Governor Sir Cecil Clementi became an active supporter. He rarely missed an opportunity to urge people to join the Club. His intervention became so vocal that in 1930 the Legislative Council voted the club $60,000 and an annual subsidy of $30,000. These sums were more than generous for the times.

In October of 1929, the RAF received a reminder of its mortality. During a routine patrol Flight Lieutenant A. R. Ward of 442 Flight lost his life. His Fairey 3D disintegrated as it crashed into Victoria Harbour.

When 1929 drew to its close Kai Tak had a total aerodrome area of 205 acres. An impressive achievement on the 25 acres (400 yards by 300 yards) that existed five years previously.

Kai Tak had tasted the explosive expansion that lay ahead.

The Argentine Air Service's Major Pedro Zanni began a round-the-world flight on July 26, 1924. On 24 September, 1924, he landed his Fokker biplane (450hp Napier Lion engine) in Kowloon Harbour. (Photo: Courtesy Royal Air Force Museum)

AIRPORT OF THE NINE DRAGONS, KAI TAK, KOWLOON

Mijnheer Anthony Fokker poses between Major Pedro Zanni and his engineer, Mr Beltrame, just before they left Amsterdam. Paradoxically, the Argentine Air Service chose a Dutch machine, powered by a British engine, to carry their flag.

(Photo: Courtesy Royal Air Force Museum)

THE PRIDE OF DETROIT CREW
(Arrived in Hong Kong – September 9, 1927)

William Brock (left) and Edward Schlee at Croydon on 28/8/27. Pose before the Stinson monoplane they flew from Newfoundland to Tokyo. (Photo: Fred Lillywhite)

Group Captain Cave-Brown-Cave, leader of the Far East Flight. (Photo: Royal Air Force Museum)

THE LONG-RANGE PIONEERS – 1924-1929

THE RAF FAR EAST FLIGHT (Arrived in Hong Kong – November 18, 1928)

Supermarine Southamptons of the Far East Flight. (Photo: Royal Air Force Museum)

CHAPTER 4

WEANING & GROWING PAINS
1930-1935

In 1930, Commander George Francis Hole was the Director of the Harbour Department. A retiree from the Royal Navy he made a splendid Harbour Master. With the planes of the day using the waters of Kowloon Bay the Governor increased Hole's responsibilities, but not his salary, to directing Air Services. Later, when the aviation scene moved on to the land reclaimed by Messrs. Kai and Tak, he continued to control the *raucous infant*.

Commander Hole remained Director of Air Services until 1940. On November 14, 1940, James Jolly, CBE, RD (CMG) replaced him as Harbour Master and Director of Air Services.

Later the Government separated these departments under a full-time director. Meanwhile, the Home Government had eased Hole's task by appointing a man with an aviation background. This was Mr Albert James Robert Moss. Born on November 21, 1898, *Papa* Moss had served in the Royal Air Force. Moss, appointed on August 9, 1930, arrived in Hong Kong during September as Aerodrome Superintendent.

Moss immediately brought relief to the harassed Harbour Master. In March 1930 a fatality had occurred involving a service plane. LAC Jarvis, a RAF air-gunner, fell from a Fairey 3F of 440 Flight – his parachute didn't open. The RAF insisted this was a service matter – the Director of Air Services thought otherwise. Commander Hole compromised by suggesting a combined inquiry.

ALBERT JAMES ROBERT *PAPA* MOSS – 1951
Appointed Aerodrome Superintendent August 9, 1930
Director of Air Services 1946-48
Director of Civil Aviation 1948-52

(Photo: Fred Lillywhite)

WEANING & GROWING PAINS – 1930-1935

The RAF refused these terms and rancour developed between the department and the service.

Papa Moss, with his RAF credentials, approaching the service on common ground, finalised the matter in a few days. This was the only fatality that needed Moss's attention until July 1939. Yet a spate of minor accidents on Kai Tak's Lilliputian landing area kept him busy.

1931

Commander Hole's report for 1931 was one of personal satisfaction. His staff levelled the aerodrome's surface and began spot turfing. During the year civil aircraft made 1,100 flights totalling 300 hours. The Hong Kong Flying Club was the principal user. The Club ended the year in a strong position with 52 flying members and 15 associates. Against this bustling activity only one accident occurred when a student made a heavy landing. His pride suffered more than his plane.

The airfield continued to attract pioneer flyers. French pilots Brutin (Burlin) and Moench landed in *Alsa*, a Farman 190, on their flight from Paris to Tokyo. Mr and Mrs C. H. Day, blending the complexities of domesticity with the lesser hazard of flying, landed on their way from London to Shanghai. They left Hong Kong on October 9, bound for Amoy. Meanwhire, a Mr Brophy, made a *shortie* from Amoy to Canton, stopping by for fuel.

Japan's invasion of Manchuria began with a clash between Japanese and Chinese troops near Mukden. On September 18, 1931, the Japanese forcibly took control of the city from the Chinese authorities. This reckless action started a conflict that lasted for 14 years and ended with an atomic bomb

The Mukden *incident*, the historians' blithe idiom, led to violent anti-Japanese riots in Kowloon. Although rioting did not spread to the airfield the Flying Club set guards on their

FRENCHMEN – BRUTIN (BURLIN) & MOENCH

The pioneer aviators landed at Kai Tak in 1931, on their record-breaking flight from Paris to Tokyo and return in 250 hours. Their plane was a Farman 190 dubbed Alsa. (Photo: Courtesy Musee de l'air et de l'espace, Le Bourget.)

AIRPORT OF THE NINE DRAGONS, KAI TAK, KOWLOON

RAF BASE KAI TAK – 1931
Fire gutting a matshed hangar of 440 Fleet Fighter Flight. (Photo: Fl/Lt Noel Hitching, RAF)

planes and the RAF cancelled leave. These precautions proved a blessing when a fire, starting in the office of the Officer Commanding 440 Flight, quickly gutted the matshed hangars. There was no shortage of men to push the planes from danger. Other than the easily replaceable matsheds the Club and the RAF suffered trifling losses.

1932

With the passing months the Civil Air Services' dreams evolved into reality. A voted $800,000 for development meant a long overdue hangar and allied office accommodation. The draftsmen had the installation positioned just behind the lard factory and stretching into a market garden. This meant demolishing the old RAF airmen's quarters and several other private buildings. James Robertson & Company of Glasgow won the contract for the building's sheeting.

Early in 1932, another matshed fire convinced the RAF they needed more durable structures. They first built a substantial hangar on the eastern perimeter near to the southern sea-wall. Later they concentrated on several stone structures straddling the Officers' Mess. The RAF base gradually developed into a splendid installation. Access to the base was a pitted dirt track (that became Kwun Tong Road) that rambled from Kowloon City.

A total of 1,785 flights carried 1,185 passengers. The curse of aeroplane operators was the introduction of Landing Fees. Revenue jumped from the meagre annual $40 to $14,000. This affluence had floodlighting of the whole airfield mooted for the following year.

WEANING & GROWING PAINS – 1930-1935

The pioneer flyers continued to attract public hero-worship. Six pilots took advantage of the safe haven of Kai Tak and its improved facilities. These were Fernando Rein Loring, Madrid to Manila (31 May); Fraulein Marga von Erzdorf, Japan to Surabaya (April); and the legendary Wolfgang von Gronau on his round-the-world attempt (27 September). Others were Captain Dickson, Shanghai to South Africa; Captain Maurice Nogues, who commanded the flight that carried the first air mail between Hong Kong and Paris (1 November), and Mr Smith-Reynolds, Egypt to Hong Kong.

The year of 1932 finished with a rebellion from the members of the Hong Kong Flying Club. No longer would they yield to Wing Commander Vaughan Fowler's overbearing directives. The Club suspended operations, with Vaughan Fowler advising the Government of *a conflict of interests*.

1933

During 1933, Aerodrome Superintendent *Papa* Moss continued his professionalism at Kai Tak Airfield. His friendly welcome charmed several visiting aviation enthusiasts. They included Mademoiselle Marie-Antoinette (Maryse) Hilsz, Paris to Tokyo (14 April); Captain Bremer on a World Tour, and Viscount de Sibour, Paris to Hong Kong (December) and return. Spaniard Fernando Rein Loring made a second visit (10 April).

Another visitor that year was Harold M. Bixby. Moss considered him a kindred spirit and gave him VIP attention. Bixby, representing Pacific American Airways (an offshoot of Pan American Airways) was en-route to Shanghai, the headquarters of the China National Aviation Corporation (CNAC).

The CNAC was an airline without directional drive. Its balance sheet clearly reflected this ruinous trend, and coupled to this its planes were obsolete! On paper CNAC was a company with little future. In this gloomy corporate setting Pan American Airways saw an opportunity to establish themselves in China.

PanAm began operating CNAC on July 3, 1933, using Sikorsky S-38 Amphibians. On August 14, Bixby and Chief Pilot William S. Grooch skipped their amphibian on to Kowloon Bay. On the following day they landed in Lingayen Gulf before continuing to Manila. On August 29, they were back in Hong Kong having completed the first round flight trip ever made between Hong Kong and Manila.

CNAC had a towering part in arguably the greatest of the flying adventures – *The Hump*. CNAC employed many competent pilots of the day. Among them were Sydney *Syd* deKantzow, a founder of Cathay Pacific Airways, and Royal Leonard – both personal pilots to Generalissimo Chiang Kai-shek.

Our main interest in CNAC is the work they did when the Japanese advanced on Hong Kong. In the few days before the Colony fell the pilots of CNAC proved their courage and professional dedication to those in distress.

The Director of Air Services recorded 1933 as an accident-free 12 months. His records show civilian planes made 1,455 flights totalling 950 hours that carried 567 passengers. The decrease in the number of flights was the loss of the Flying Club's activities.

The year was one of soul-searching for the members of the inactive Hong Kong Flying Club. Although his intentions were well meaning, Vaughan Fowler had brought the *never questioned* service attitude into a civilian environment. There he found his directives questioned at every turn.

Vaughan Fowler, without consulting the former members, approached Government. He proposed that the Far East Aviation Company Limited, of which he was a director, should form a subsidiary company to be known as the Far East Flying Training School Limited. He also proposed the transfer of the subsidies enjoyed by the old club to the new school.

AIRPORT OF THE NINE DRAGONS, KAI TAK, KOWLOON

Negotiations went on until November when the Government backed Vaughan Fowler. Government support was not without trepidation but it made the final decision based on *the devil you know!* The intransigent Vaughan Fowler did not get everything his way. Government demanded that another director of the Far Eastern Aviation Company Limited should run the School. Meanwhile, the Government agreed that Mr Vere Harvey, the demonstration pilot for the parent company, should manage the School.

The Far East Flying Training School, incorporated as a limited company on November 7, 1933. George G. N. Tinson, Solicitor, A. Ritchie, Chartered Accountant, and D. S. Scott, Merchant, were the subscribers. A capital of HK$500,000 got it started at 26 Nathan Road, Kowloon.

Finally, Mr W. F. Murray became Commandant with Lord Malcolm Douglas-Hamilton his Chief Instructor. The new commandant controlled the capricious ex-Wing Commander with little difficulty and Vaughan Fowler gradually lost interest in the School. He gave his energy to the Far East Aviation Company Limited, the company that held the area franchise for A. V. Roe's *avroplanes*. From 1930 to 1935 the Hong Kong Register records over 50 planes registered to that company.

1934

The School commenced aviation activities at Kai Tak in February 1934. It began with a single Avro Trainer 626 (VR-HCO) and two Avro Cadet 631s (VR-HCM and VR-HCN). Almost immediately the School enrolled 20 student pilots, 10 Chinese, and the same number of Europeans. The engineering courses under Chief Engineer E. Waldron and Ground Instructor W. Wilcocks attracted 42 applicants. It was a profitable business right from the start. In August another Avro Cadet (VR-HCS) joined the fleet, and an Autogiro C3OA (VR-HCT) followed in December.

KAI TAK AIRFIELD – 1934

Building activity within the RAF installation in foreground. The large hangar, left foreground, was shared by the RAF and the Far East Aviation Company. At the western boundary only one matshed hangar remains, and a jetty and slipway supports the crane. (Photo: *Gau Lung* – RAF 50th Anniversary Souvenir Booklet – 1977)

WEANING & GROWING PAINS – 1930-1935

KAI TAK AIRFIELD – LATE 1934

The RAF technical stores and workshops are completed. The Civil Air Services hangar, on the right western boundary, is also completed. The RAF and civil traffic have become separate entities. (Photo: *Gau Lung* – RAF 50th Anniversary Souvenir Booklet – 1977)

The return of pilot training boosted airfield activity. In the 11 months that remained in 1934, the Air Service recorded an increase in flying hours and passengers carried. There were four accidents involving serious structural damage during this time, doubtless a product of the increased usage. Mr Moss's investigating staff adjudged each as errors in judgment.

The only long-distance visitor of the year was Lieutenant da Crux of the Portuguese Air Force. His flight originated in Lisbon with Macau his destination. He dropped by Kai Tak to observe the airfield's improvements and to *show the flag*. He returned to Lisbon by the same route.

1935

By late 1934, the Director of Air Services had taken possession of a modern hangar floodlit for round-the-clock utilisation. A concrete control-tower, attached to the hangar, enhanced the facilities. Locally employed personnel quickly occupied the offices and workshop annexes. The workmen had completed the protection pier for the slipway and the perimeter fencing. Several fuel companies had established themselves in solid structures.

Mr Erik Nelson arrived in this hive of activity as First Assistant Aerodrome Superintendent. *Papa* Moss could now relax for Nelson was a splendid addition to his staff. Erik answered his mobilisation orders and left Hong Kong soon after the declaration of World War II.

AIRPORT OF THE NINE DRAGONS, KAI TAK, KOWLOON

Forty-five years later Richard A. Siegel, the current Director of Civil Aviation, met Erik at Kai Tak. Then, *Dick* Siegel held the position of Assistant General Manager. He recalls Erik's incessant chatter about the old days and his disbelief at the airport's magnitude. In 1986, Erik again returned to Kai Tak courtesy of British Airways. He helped celebrate the 50th Anniversary of their first flight from Penang to Hong Kong. Erik Nelson, in his early 80s, then lived in Maryland, U.S.A.

On April 1, 1935, *RAF Kai Tak* became *RAF Station Kai Tak*. Then, Squadron Leader C. R. Keary commanded the Station. His opinion of the Royal Navy ranged from apathetic to contempt. The Station's rescue launches came back from a naval dockyard overhaul with *RAF Base Kai "Tack"* stencilled on the life belts. The unit's change in designation allowed the dockyard to correct this glaring error. Keary was inconsolable at the loss of that visual proof of Royal Navy inefficiency.

During June three Supermarine *Southampton* flying-boats of No. 205 Squadron attached to RAF Singapore landed in Kowloon Bay. They were en-route to Japan on a courtesy visit. This exercise in public relations was a disaster – one plane became unserviceable at Kai Tak, and a second at Shanghai. Only one *showed-the-flag* in Tokyo – hardly an impressive show!

In November 1935, a Fairey 3F, returning from patrol, and doubtless a sweep or two along Chatham Road, made a hot landing and wiped-off the undercarriage. The plane skidded to a stop just short of the newly finished barrack block. It is likely the pilot had other things on his mind. Then, Chatham Road boasted the headquarters of a thriving nudist club. On the lawn of a spacious mansion the members paid homage to *sol* draped mostly in skin.

During the Air Service's development the RAF had allowed civilian use of their new hangar. Some private owners, including the Far East Aviation Company and Imperial Airways, accepted the RAF's generosity.

The occupation of the Air Service's premises meant the end of civilian and service interdependence. The RAF had tacit control of the eastern side of the airfield and civilian traffic the western side. There had been contrasts in operational procedures but they had co-existed remarkably well and parted congenially.

In this relaxed atmosphere the following long-distance flyers passed through the Colony. The Japanese airman Mr K. Ano, arrived from London en route to Tokyo flying a German Klemm *Eagle*. Commander Scaroni was delivering an Italian Savoia Machetti S.72 to Marshal Chiang Kai Shek at Nanking. Mr H. L. Farquhar, chose an American Beechcraft to fly to London. Granted leave from the British Embassy in Mexico City, he picked this novel mode of transport. In September 1935, Herr Kaspar and Herr Kruger landed at Kai Tak en-route to Shanghai. They were ferrying two Junkers Ju-52s for the Eurasia Aviation Corporation.

During August 1930, German Lufthansa and the Chinese Government signed a contract for a commercial air venture. This became Eurasia Aviation Corporation. With a two-thirds interest, the Chinese administered but Lufthansa controlled flight operations.

Eurasia had problems from the outset. Following the successful inauguration flight from Shanghai-Berlin on May 30, 1931, the Soviets withdrew over-flight rights. They suspected the Germans of gathering intelligence.

The Soviets offered an alternative that proved clumsy and uneconomical. It suggested three round trips weekly to the border city of Manchuli. The trip would continue by train to Irkutsk and finally to Berlin by Soviet aircraft. Beginning in June 1931, it utilised single-engine Junker monoplanes. The lack of passenger interest forced a cutback to two flights each week. Then Mongolian bandits shot down and imprisoned a crew. Eurasia cancelled its international ambition and concentrated on the domestic market. By 1935 it owned four

WEANING & GROWING PAINS – 1930-1935

KAI TAK AIRFIELD 1934-1935

The northerly aspect of the RAF establishment. The Officers' Mess is at the right border, foreground. The Mess and the complex is separated by a dusty, pitted track (to become Kwun Tong Road) that meandered from Kowloon City. In the left background is the Civil Air Services' hangar. The field resembles an obstacle course! (Photo: Fl/Lt Noel Hitching, RAF Kai Tak)

NOVEMBER 1935 – IMPERIAL AIRWAYS SURVEY

Captain William Armstrong surveyed Kai Tak in a DH86A. The plane, named Dorado, was one of Imperial Airways' fleet of 12 DH86As. With the class name Diana, the plane could carry 10 passengers, cruising at 145mph with a range of 764 miles. Four 200hp Gipsy Six engines provided the power. (Photo: Courtesy Shell-Mex Company)

AIRPORT OF THE NINE DRAGONS, KAI TAK, KOWLOON

SPANIARD – CAPTAIN FERNANDO REIN LORING

1st Raid (flight) Madrid-Manila – April to July, 1932. Posing with Loring E-II EC-ASA built by his uncle Jorge. His la Pepa (Josephine) was powered by a Kinner K5 of 100hp. He landed at Kai Tak 31 May. (Photo: Felipe E. Ezquerro)

Wolfgang von Gronau and his crew stand on the forward deck of the Dornier WAL – (Whale). N-25, once owned by Roald Amundsen, had been refitted with German BMW V1 tandem engines. L to R. Funker Albrecht (radio operator), Flugzeugfuhrer Zimmer, Wolfgang von Gronau, Bordmonteur Hack (fitter/mechanic). (Photo: Courtesy Luftwaffenmuseum, Berlin)

WEANING & GROWING PAINS – 1930-1935

FRAULEIN MARGA von ERZDORF (ETZDORF)

The German aviatrix landed at Kai Tak in April 1932 en route Japan to Surabaya. Her plane was a Junkers Junior dubbed Kiek in die Welt (Jump into the World) powered by a 80hp Genet-Motor. (Photo: Courtesy Luftwaffenmuseum, Berlin)

In 1930 and 1931, von Gronau made two round trips to New York in the WAL – then carrying the German registration D-1422. The following year, he flew it westward around the world landing in Kowloon Harbour on September 27, 1932. An Allied air raid, in 1944, destroyed the Deutsches Museum in Munich, and this aviation treasure. It is possible to read the fuselage registration and near the mooring station – German Traffic Flying School. (Photo: Courtesy Luftwaffenmuseum, Berlin)

AIRPORT OF THE NINE DRAGONS, KAI TAK, KOWLOON

tri-motor Junkers Ju-52s and used these splendid planes to serve a widespread network in China. Eurasia flew the inaugural service Hong Kong to Peiping on June 29, 1937.

The Germans withdrew from China in 1941 but Eurasia continued flying. On March 1, 1943, Eurasia Aviation Corporation ceased operations and from its ashes came Central Air Transport (CAT).

In November 1935, Captain William Armstrong arrived at Kai Tak as airfield surveyor for Imperial Airways. The report of his approach to Hong Kong remains a public-relation dream. He waxed lyrical with the *fantastic panorama unfolding before my eyes*. His plane was a then state-of-the-art de Havilland DH86A named *Dorado*. His description of Kai Tak is worth repeating.

> *"Here we landed and found it to be a good hard ground. What an incredible situation! Bounded on one side by sea, it had the steep Lion Rock on the other, and rocky obstructions at each end."*

CHAPTER 5

AGE OF CONSENT
1936-1938

Aviation in Hong Kong came of age in 1936. From the laid-back setting of club and service flying it shifted to the prelude of professionalism. In the years ahead Kai Tak's success eclipsed the vision of the most ardent optimist.

Throughout 1936, the Air Services continued to improve their operation. An all-wave W/T receiving station, located on the top floor of the administration block, and remote control to the Hung Hom W/T transmitter, handled traffic movements. A powerful floodlight, installed on the tower's roof, gave shadow-bar assistance for night-landings. The installation of special mooring buoys for flying boats, and a pontoon built near the slip-way aided embarking and disembarking. Anticipating an influx of passengers the police established a control post. Kai Tak had every basic facility to begin its move into the future.

Captain John Lock, of Imperial Airways, continued Captain Armstrong's work. He made 10 further survey flights assessing airfields at Hue, Tourane, the French enclave at Fort Bayard (Chanchiang) for emergency, and Saigon. Imperial chose a weekly service from Penang to Hong Kong. They made intermediate landings at Saigon (Ho Chi Minh City) and Tourane (Da Nang).

The flight that heralded the Hong Kong service left London on March 14, 1936. A sleek DH86A, the RMA *Dorado* (G-ACWD), inaugurated the Penang to Hong Kong section. Captain Lock's landing at Kai Tak on March 23 forged another link between cities of the far-flung Empire.

The Governor, Sir Andrew Caldecott (December 1935-April 1937), led the welcoming party supported by the Director of Air Services Commander Hole. Erik Nelson represented the Superintendent of Kai Tak Airport, *Papa* Moss.

The honour of being the first regular air service passenger to land at Kai Tak goes to Mr Ong Eee-lim. Ong, an enthusiastic private pilot from Kuala Lumpur, reclined throughout the trip on 16 bags of mail. Then the mail took precedence over passengers, who flew at their own risk!

Imperial Airways' first regular air service left Kai Tak on March 27. The fare from Hong Kong to Penang was £30. For the remainder of 1936, Imperial made 84 trips between

AIRPORT OF THE NINE DRAGONS, KAI TAK, KOWLOON

KAI TAK HANGAR/CONTROL BUILDING – 1936

Imperial Airways' sleek DH86A RMA Dorado *on hard-standing. The* Dorado's *(G-ACWD) inaugural flight to Hong Kong was March 23, 1936. Mr Ong Eee-lim was Imperial's first passenger. Among the light planes, in the background, is a rare picture of the FEFTS's Autogiro C30A (VR-HCT).* (Photo: Courtesy James Robertson & Company, Glasgow through Derek Davis)

Penang and Hong Kong. The DH86A flew those 130,200 miles with hardly a hiccup carrying 77 passengers and 9.3 tons of mail and freight.

At Penang the passengers made connecting flights to England or Australia. From Hong Kong to London a fare of £175 offered 10 days of exciting travel.

On October 26, 1936, the first Martin M-130 skimmed on to Kowloon Bay. The Philippine Clipper's pilot was Juan Terry Trippe. Some 4,000 spectators, crowding the Bay's foreshore, applauded his arrival. How many in that cheering throng knew the diplomatic manoeuvres that preceded this momentous milestone?

The British Government, unable to get reciprocal landing rights in China, refused PanAm landing rights in the Colony. Trippe solved his problem by signing an agreement with Portugal in January 1936. This was for the transport of mail between Macau and the United States by way of the Philippines. At Macau, PanAm set up the terminus for its trans-Pacific route. The British had second thoughts and on June 11, 1936, withdrew its objection and gave Hong Kong landing-rights to PanAm and CNAC. The Director of Air Services issued an operating permit from September 17, 1936.

There remained one final stumbling-block. The Chinese had to sign an international contract for air-mail exchange between China and the States. Bixby had been working on this for some years and each time he raised the matter received a polite rebuff. Finally, Bixby, with some fancy semantic sashaying, convinced the Director of Chinese Posts of the value of an agreement – both signed the document on January 19, 1937.

CNAC taking advantage of Trippe's adroitness extended the Shanghai-Canton flights. On November 5, 1936, it inaugurated a thrice-weekly mail and passenger service to the Crown Colony. It used Condor and DC2 planes – a combination of the old and the new.

AGE OF CONSENT – 1936-1938

During the remainder of the year the company thrived. It made 106 trips, carried 171 passengers, and flew a total of 53,070 miles. The freight figures (0.6 tons of mail and freight) being the only disappointment.

A disturbing event, and one recurring in the years ahead, occurred in June. Several Chinese Air Force officers deserted. Four planes disobeyed the tower's instructions and landed at Kai Tak. A fifth pilot, losing his bearings, force-landed on the emergency strip at Fanling. The Government ordered the return of men and planes to the Chinese authorities the following month. One can only ponder their fate!

The RAF's aircraft strength remained an unimpressive deterrent. There were three Hawker Horsleys and two Tiger Moths. Their prime task was drogue-towing for anti-aircraft predictor practice.

The Director of Air Services ended his report for 1936 on a congratulatory note. Not one to squander words, Commander Hole praised, at some length, the work of the Far East Flying Training School. Commandant Murray had brought the training syllabus to a professional level. The number of student enquiries and the acceptance rate forced him to expand the premises.

1937

In February, the RAF replaced the aged Hawker Horsleys with an obsolete Vicker type. The Vildebeeste, originally designed as a torpedo bomber, had a top speed of 140 knots. Besides the Vildebeestes and Tiger Moths, the Station was responsible for maintaining three Walrus amphibians and two Fairey Swordfishs of the Fleet Air Arm. The Station used the Vildebeestes and Walrus amphibians for reconnaissance work. The performance of these planes brought no anxiety to the Japanese warmongers.

On April 23, PanAm inaugurated a new service from San Francisco to Manila. This weekly flight subsequently increased to a bi-weekly service. Five days later, PanAm extended the San Francisco-Manila service to Hong Kong. The first regular passenger flight, by Sikorsky S-42B (NC16734) Hong Kong Clipper, arrived at the Kai Tak marine terminal on 6 May. The S-42B carried 28 passengers at a cruising speed of 163 mph.

PAN AMERICAN AIRWAYS
The first regular passenger flight, by the Sikorsky S-42B (NC16734) Hong Kong Clipper *landed in Kowloon Harbour on May 6, 1937.*   (Photo: *Papa* Moss)

AIRPORT OF THE NINE DRAGONS, KAI TAK, KOWLOON

On June 29, Eurasia Aviation Corporation extended their Peiping-Canton passenger service to Hong Kong. Eurasia increased this to three services a week to deal with the growing traffic. Eurasia used the splendid Junkers Ju52s and Ju34s on this service.

During the year, a petite girl breezed in and created a sensation. Like the flick of a brush her red Waco caressed Kai Tak's landing surface. Heiress to a wealthy doting grandfather, Miss Bessie Owen shrewdly brought no competition to the labour market. The well-informed aviatrix candidly talked about everything except her age. In despair, the news snoopers made their decision – she must be in her mid-20s!

On September 2, a tai fung (typhoon) or big wind screamed into the Colony and screamed out again. It left in its wake 11,000 dead and vast property losses. It decommissioned Kai Tak for several days demolishing, in its fury, the mooring pontoon, marine terminal and seriously damaged the slipway. The wind destroyed the shadow-bar floodlight and brought the D/F mast through the roof of the hangar. A faceless statistician lamented it the most vicious since the 1906 killer.

I first met *Papa* Moss in early 1947. He had just endured 52 months of Japanese hospitality at Stanley Camp. I found him a man with a useful gift of informality; he also lacked a sense of self-importance, a quality of great rarity, especially within our aviation fraternity.

He was a treasure-chest of the Colony's early aviators. He told me how he helped Captain Royal Leonard, Chiang Kai-shek's personal pilot, outwit an obstinate bureaucrat. This was Howard Donovan, the acting American consul at Hong Kong.

At Nanking during October 1937, Captain Leonard received instructions to fly the Generalissimo's plane from Canton to Kai Tak. There he was to supervise its servicing, and then fly it to Hankow.

Chiang Kai-shek's *Flying Palace* was a beautifully appointed DC2 and famous throughout China. On the outside it was simply a silver-skinned, twin-engined monoplane. The interior was another matter! A lining of black-wood veneer sheathed in red-plush cloaked a luxurious red floor carpet. It had two full-length lounges and upholstered chairs complete with seat belts. There also was an ornate writing desk, a small radio, and a food box. Heavy-duty bolts secured everything to the deck.

Captain Leonard's troubles started in Nanking. He found the airlines were no longer running to a schedule, but a friend got him a seat on the last CNAC plane to leave the city. Arriving in Shanghai he learned he had a 12-hour layover before there was a plane for Hong Kong.

The sound of exploding bombs awoke him the next morning. The glass from windows showered him as the concussion tossed him out of bed. The *Broadway Mansions*, his home in Shanghai, was on the opposite side of the street from the Japanese Concession. The *Idzuma* was not more than 100 yards away and Chinese bombers had targeted the Japanese flagship. Deciding that this was no place for him he was stuffing clothes into a suitcase as the next stick of Chinese bombs bracketed the *Idzuma*. His frantic phone call to CNAC found all flying suspended. How was he going to get to Hong Kong? At the height of this uncertainty a CNAC official phoned. Would he fly one of their planes to Hankow?

He rushed to Shanghai's Lung Wah airfield and found the Japanese retaliating. Their bombers had reduced most of the buildings to rubble but one hangar stood unscarred. A bomb had come through its roof but it was a dud. He gingerly walked around the bomb and climbed aboard the plane he was to fly.

Droning overhead, Japanese planes bombed and strafed anything that moved. He started the engines inside the hangar, and without a warm-up, slammed open the throttles. The plane screamed out of the hangar, skidded around two bomb craters, and zoomed up into a 500-foot cloud ceiling. Safe in cloud he set course for Hankow, where he got a flight to Hong Kong.

There he arranged with the authorities the permit to bring the *Flying Palace* to Hong Kong. Then a coastal boat took him to Canton, where he found the Douglas DC2 gassed and ready to go. He was back at Kai Tak that evening.

The next morning a phone call ordered him to report to the office of the acting American consul. Howard Donovan demanded that he leave China immediately. Leonard told him he would do so but first must deliver the Generalissimo's plane to Hankow. Donovan shouted that he would not authorise such a flight. Captain Leonard spent the rest of that day getting affidavits. One signed by *Papa* Moss, the British Kowloon airport superintendent, certified:

My inspection show there is no ammunition or arms aboard. The plane's fittings are for the private transportation of personnel.

A. J. Moss, Superintendent of Airport.

Armed with this and other evidence he returned to Donovan's office. Donovan pushed his documents aside and again forbade him to leave Hong Kong. Leonard's apparent acceptance of this edict relaxed Donovan and when he asked for permission to continue maintaining the plane he grudgingly agreed. Later Moss phoned Donovan and found Leonard had permission to make any necessary test flights. Leonard made two test flights and found everything working perfectly. After the second one he asked Moss if he could arrange a weather report. He pointed out the cloud and fog had thickened and with another scheduled test flight he didn't want to get caught without a diversion field. Moss, described as a little sparrow of a man, cocking his head to one side and as he slowly lifting an eyebrow agreed this was a wise precaution. He was back in a flash with a report that included a forecast for Hankow. Leonard thanked Moss who said "Good-bye – visit us again sometime." Releasing that Moss had seen through his scheme the American's wry smile broke into a wide grin.

Captain Royal Leonard roared away into the overcast and, some hours later, landed the *Flying Palace* at Hankow.

The month of October brought the arrival of Governor Sir Geoffrey Northcote. He came into an atmosphere of grave incertitude. The previous month Japanese warships had bombarded Bias Bay. During December, his concern deepened as Japanese war-planes bombed Sham Chun (Shenzhen), a town just north of the Hong Kong border. That attack signalled a landing by a small force of Japanese troops at Bias Bay.

As the Japanese rolled through North China their victories began to affect the internal carriers. CNAC abandoned services to Shanghai when, in November, Japanese troops captured the city. Their rolling victories then forced the Nazi-controlled Eurasia to revise its routes. Hong Kong's Kai Tak became a haven in a mad world of uncertainty.

On December 12, the Imperial Airways' UK-Australia connection became Bangkok. The revised route was Bangkok-Udorn-Hanoi-Fort Bayard-Hong Kong. One week later, the DH86 *Delphinus* (G-ACPL) left Bangkok for Hong Kong. Simultaneously the *Dorado* (G-ACWD) left Hong Kong for Bangkok.

As the year of 1937 ended, the Japanese had practically encircled the Crown Colony of Hong Kong. Yet this did not deter Commander Hole. With true British aplomb he spurned the Japanese heavy breathing and finished his annual report with a revenue and expenditure table. What panache!

1938

Imperial Airways' nervousness increased as Japan swallowed large tracts of China. It had the DH86As painted with large Union Jacks on the upper wing, also on the sides. Quaintly,

AIRPORT OF THE NINE DRAGONS, KAI TAK, KOWLOON

IMPERIAL AIRWAYS

The sister plane Delphinus *(G-ACPL) joined the* Dorado *on the Bangkok-Hong Kong sector on 19 December, 1937. Imperial named its DH86s from the heavens;* DORADO: *Doradus, a southern constellation between Carina and Phenix, the site of the larger of the two Magellanic Clouds.* DELPHINUS: *genitive Delphini, a northern constellation near Pegasus*

RAF KAI TAK 1938

Fairey Swordfish planes of 804 Squadron from HMS Eagle. (Photo: Fl/Lt Noel Hitching, RAF Kai Tak)

they considered this gave protection against the Japanese whose forces had overrun parts of the southern coastal strip. Several of these pockets were on the DH86A's route. The Jacks did nothing! In February, shrapnel peppered the *Dorado*, but caused no injury. The plane landed safely at Kai Tak.

Owen FitzWilliam Hamilton, MBE, arrived in Hong Kong an expatriate appointee under the Director of Air Services. On June 1, he assumed the duty of Marine Supervisor. *Hammy*, born on June 10, 1900, enhanced his office with dignity and common sense. He gained his nautical experience from the Merchant Navy. *Hammy's* internment, at Stanley, followed Hong Kong's surrender on Christmas Day 1941.

When he retired in 1962, he had served the civil aviation authority for 24 years. He held the positions of Assistant Airport Manager, and Acting Director of Civil Aviation. In 1952, he became Airport Manager, with a title change in 1958 to Airport Commandant. In 1973, in Middlesex, he died. *Hammy*, this most generous of gentlemen, remains in the memory of his legion of friends.

During August, Air France extended the Far East route from Hanoi to Hong Kong. For two years they served this route with the superb Tri-motor Fokkers and dependable Dewoitines. Its last service, by a Dewoitine D338, left Kai Tak on June 7, 1940.

On August 25, a CNAC flight, under the command of American H.L. Woods, left Hong Kong for Chungking. *Woody's* plane, a DC2, carried the name *City of Kweilin*. Soon after he cleared the Colony's border a gaggle of Japanese fighters intercepted his plane. With bullets tearing through the fuselage he ditched in the Pearl River. As his passengers struggled from the doomed plane the enemy strafed them. Each pass killed more of the survivors until just *Woody*, his radio-operator and one passenger, with a bullet wound in the neck, remained. They had managed this by ducking under the water each time the fighters' swooped down. That day 14 innocent people died under the guns of barbarians.

It had been a well-planned operation. Another group of Japanese fighters circled 50 miles further along his track – just in case! This significant operation came from intelligence that Dr Sun Fo, son of Dr Sun Yat-sen, the father of modern China, was aboard. Dr Sun had shrewdly left earlier on a Eurasia plane.

The attack brought the cessation of China's commercial airlines. The Nazi-controlled Eurasia resumed later when the Japanese allowed them a tacit immunity. Yet, some Japanese pilots were trigger-happy and Eurasia planes had some close calls.

On September 5, Japanese fighter planes intercepted a Eurasia Ju52 between Hong Kong and Luchow. Ten bullets struck the cabin, but caused no injury. The attack led to a temporary suspension of Eurasia's operations.

The Hong Kong Air Services responded by introducing night flying. This brought a resumption of CNAC and Eurasia services but only during the hours of sunset to sunrise.

Maxwell Norman Oxford arrived from London in September. Max, born on May 3, 1905, became Second Assistant Superintendent of Aerodrome effective September 28. World War II interrupted his civilian career. Following his return, he became Deputy Director of Civil Aviation and Airport Manager. In late 1950, he transferred to Malaya as Director General of Civil Aviation.

On October 9, CNAC began a night service from Hong Kong to China's temporary capital Chungking. This night flight had just one intermediate landing field at Liuchow. For 770 miles, with no airway beacons, unreliable radio communication, meaningless weather reports and stalking Japanese fighters kept the crew interested! As a pilot approached Hong Kong his route crossed Japanese bases so most held altitude until over Kai Tak then spiralled down like a turning phonograph record.

Delays to departures took on a new meaning. Clear moonlit nights caused delays – even cancellations. The black, stormy nights became the pilots' salvation. The following weather

AIRPORT OF THE NINE DRAGONS, KAI TAK, KOWLOON

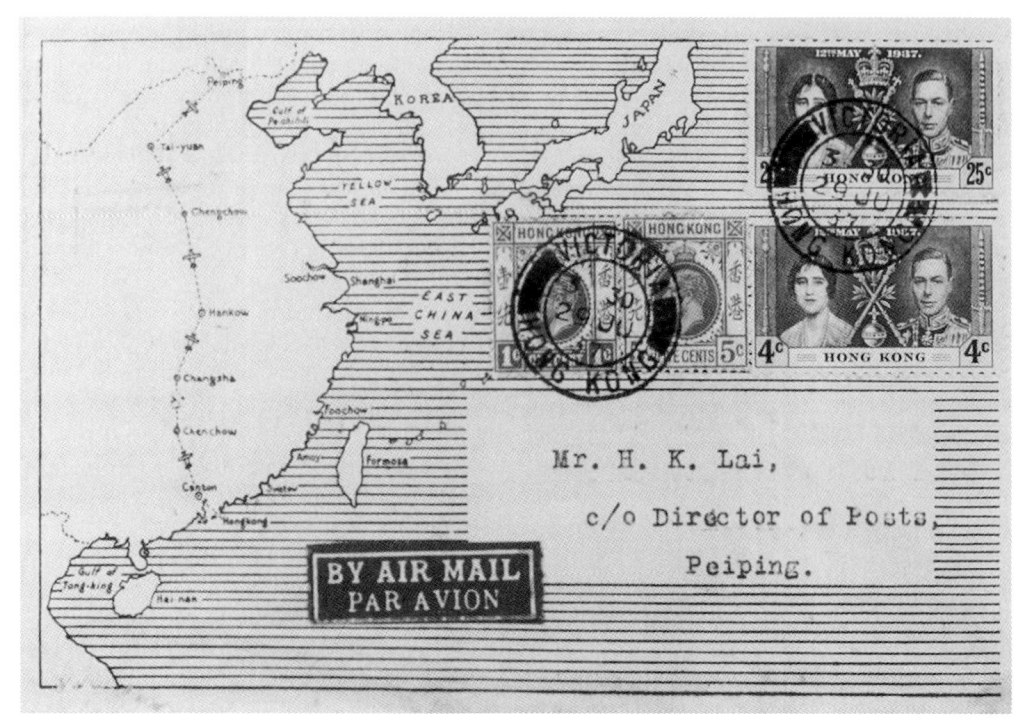

EURASIA AVIATION CORPORATION
First Day Cover celebrating the Hong Kong extension to its Peiping (Beijing) route structure. (Photo: Terry Pile)

EURASIA AVIATION CORPORATION
On June 19, 1937, Eurasia extended its Peiping-Canton (Beijing-Guangzhou) passenger service to Hong Kong. Passengers and well-wishers surround the Junkers Ju-52. The Tower is just off the port wing-tip. (Photo: *Papa* Moss)

report, interpreted by a Chinese forecaster, eased many a furrowed brow. *Dark – Mist – Gloom. Ceiling not known. Visibility not known. Stars no shine. Moon no beam.*

For a short time in October, CNAC abandoned Kai Tak to evacuate the city of Hangkow. Flights from the doomed city continued at a frenzied pace, but the dawning of October 24 found 1,000 Chinese officials still to be evacuated. The Generalissimo planned to abandon Hangkow the next day, but had he left his departure too close? With the enemy closing the trap and their guns pounding the doomed city he and his staff faced capture. Captain Walther Stennes, the Prussian head of the Generalissimo's personal bodyguard, approached Eric Just. Captain Just, a German ace in Richthofen's famous fighting squadron of World War I, was a skilful pilot but lacked night-flying experience. Stennes then turned to Captain E. M. Allison, an American air-mail pilot with 4,000 hours' night experience, who accepted the job. Allison left in his rickety plane with the Generalissimo and his party. On reaching cruising height his plane had a complete electrical failure and he had to creep back to a hairy landing at Hankow. When all seemed lost, CNAC's Chief Pilot Charles L. Sharp materialised out of a blinding snowstorm. Without cutting his engines he loaded the Generalissimo, Madame Chiang Kai-shek, Captain Stennes and their staff and had them in Henyang within three hours. The Generalissimo immediately established his headquarters just 250 miles south of the lost Hangkow.

Royal Leonard's was the last plane to leave Hangkow. He had landed in the midst of an unruly crowd. They swamped his DC2 and refused to budge. With enemy shells creeping closer he crawled over a mass of terrified people, scrambled on to his flight deck and opened the throttles. A red lantern waved him to a stop. The Chinese in charge of the field yelled not to depart in that direction. His men had sown mines to delay the Japanese. Leonard pointed to another direction. A vigorous shake of the head indicated it had received the same treatment. Leonard screamed out when had they done that! The harassed official yelled two weeks ago – nobody had bothered to tell the CNAC pilots who had been using all directions for days. Leonard slammed open the throttles and crossed the strip's threshold as the Japanese streamed from the darkness. When he landed he counted 40 people instead of the 15 the plane's licence allowed.

Also in October, enemy activity forced the closure of the Kowloon-Guangzhou (Canton) road, and soon after Canton fell. During November, the Japanese cruiser *Myoko* made an arrogant *courtesy* call to the Colony. The cruiser was returning after bombarding Canton into submission from the Pearl River. On November 26, the people of Hong Kong awoke to the news that Japanese troops had occupied Sham Chun (Shenzhen), the town just across their border.

The loss of the cities of Hankow and Canton did not effect passengers and mail continued moving between cities still in Chinese hands. The records for December show 9,969 passengers passed through Kai Tak, tripling that of the previous year. These were mainly refugees staying one step ahead of the Japanese juggernaut.

The net was tightening!

CHAPTER 6

UNCERTAINTY RULES
1939-1940

1939

In January, following a massive naval bombardment, the island of Hainan fell to the rubber-shod *monkey* men. The next month, Japanese bombs killed 12 civilians at Lo Wu, New Territories.

The inevitable student demonstration in June produced the inevitable result – noisy bluster and broken shop windows. As usual with such conduct, it brought anxiety to policemen, also with dependants, as they kept the peace. The Government used the demonstration to introduce conscription and strengthen the volunteer forces. The strengthening Japanese presence caused the Governor to declare a state-of-emergency on August 24, and ordered the registration of British women and children. The flood of refugees moving across the border became a trickle.

On September 1, the first drops of blood splattered the tapestry of *cultured* Europe as the Nazis let loose the *blitzkrieg* (lightning war) on Poland. Two days later, Britain and France supported Poland by declaring war on Germany. Churchill refused to increase the military presence in Hong Kong. His words – *We must avoid frittering away our resources on untenable positions*. Then out of character, during November, he sent 44 Vickers tanks to Hong Kong!

Five airline companies still maintained services from the airport but the enemy on Hong Kong's doorstep had its effect. The main losers were Imperial Airways and Air France. With fewer passengers travelling to and from Europe and the cancellation of all-up postal rates their profits were small.

PanAm's route to the new world had minor disruptions, but again the loss of the postal incentive caused concern. CNAC's and Eurasia's profits, in contrast, rose dramatically. CNACs' coverage of Chungking, Hanoi and Rangoon attracted a bumper-crop of passengers. Eurasia's night operation to Chungking through Kweilin brought increased loadings.

In May, Deutsche Lufthansa introduced a service from Berlin to Tokyo through Hong Kong. With the tension Herr Hitler had strewn in Europe and the Japanese incursions in China few people overlooked the obvious.

UNCERTAINTY RULES – 1939-1940

The first service used a Junker Ju52 (D-ANJH) and carried 11 passengers. The second plane – D-AGAK – touched down in August with four passengers. On the way back it avoided internment in Hong Kong by a hair's breadth, but when it got to Bangkok there it stayed. The declaration of war by the French and British against the Nazis, coupled to the plane's restrictive range, gave it no place to go!

On May 20, three Japanese planes of the 24th Sentai (group) destroyed a Russian L.Z. reconnaissance plane. The U.S.S.R. border at Nomenkan, south-west of Hailar, exploded into a wall of flame. Air action intensified with the fighting edge going to the Nakajima KI-27 type 97 Fighters.

On July 1, the 84th Independent Flying Chutai (squadron) took over patrol of the Canton area. The squadron had a nucleus of aces from the 64th Sentai.

In this atmosphere, Royal Leonard got a special flight from Hong Kong to Kunming. Before signing his load sheet he noted the 10 chests jammed between the seats. The chests, impressively sealed, contained 10 million Mexican silver dollars.

That stormy night, Leonard followed his usual departure. In the entrails of turbulent clouds he circled for height. At 16,000 feet he levelled off his darkened plane and headed north. By following this heading for 80 miles he could avoid the dangerous zones. To the north of Canton he set course for Kunming.

At Kunming, waiting for a return load, he stayed with Colonel Chennault. One evening several members of the Generalissimo's secret service took Chennault aside. He came back looking worried and disturbed. Without preamble he told Leonard that he must land at Kweilin. Leonard refused! He reminded Chennault that the Japanese bombed the strip all day and the coolies spent all night filling in the craters. Chennault, waving aside these arguments, told him it was crucial he take the Kweilin flight. He must take a general there without delay. Leonard continued to argue until he saw the look in Chennault's eyes.

At the Kunming field he submitted a flight plan for Kai Tak and then waited for his passengers. The mysterious passengers were a middle-aged Chinese, an elderly bearded Chinese and a beautiful Chinese girl. Two grim-faced Chinese dressed in blue followed closely behind, their hands hidden in voluminous sleeves.

On the way to Kweilin, Leonard got madder and madder. With no general aboard he felt cheated! Several times he decided to overfly Kweilin and continue to Hong Kong. It was fortunate he did not for that action would have caused murder. This only came to light much later.

The partly deaf Chennault greeted him with the roar – "How did you like the spies?" He then explained that the passengers were three famous espionage agents of the Japanese captured in Kunming. They were friends of the local war-lord who forbade their execution in his city. Similarly, the British would have frowned on their execution in Hong Kong! Kweilin alone suited the spies' date with destiny. The Chinese guards had orders to kill them immediately if Captain Leonard didn't land there.

The Far East Flying Training School continued to give a fine service. The mobilisation of its instructors affected the training and output began to wind back. Missing the expertise of key personnel two of the School's five planes came to disaster. The Volunteer Air Arm increased its usage and other flying members improved their ability. In the engineering section 10 students passed the examinations for Government certificates.

The daily meteorological flights continued unabated until the observatory staff learned a disturbing fact. Their most grateful *customers*, the Japanese, copied the weather broadcasts from ZBW (Radio Hong Kong) and devoured them with avid interest!

In this uncertain atmosphere Kai Tak Airport continued to update its facilities. To cope with a building demand, five stores were under construction. The hangar got an extensive rewiring, allowing round-the-clock work on the planes of CNAC and Eurasia – now Kai Tak's primary tenants.

Meanwhile, the Government decided to expand Kai Tak and build another military airfield. Work started at a site near Pat Heung, now known as Sek Kong. Work stopped as the invader brought the site within range of its artillery.

The Kai Tak plans were to lay a 500-yard tarmac runway that started at the RAF hangar near the southern coastline to bear 310°. In June, the contractor, Fook Lee and Company Limited, dismantled the RAF hangar and stockpiled the framework at the southern end of the RAF Station. It remained stockpiled throughout the occupation and then re-erected near the present engineering area.

During this crucial period RAF Walruses kept up a daily reconnaissance of Japanese shipping. They gave specific attention to the Mirs Bay area and the mouth of the Pearl River. On July 13, a Walrus patrol ended in disaster. It crashed into Tai Tam Bay with the loss of pilot and observer.

On September 16, Japan and the U.S.S.R. concluded a truce, and so ended the Nomenkan Incident. This truce increased CNAC's and Eurasia's flying hazards for it allowed more Japanese planes to patrol.

1940

The people of Hong Kong got on with their daily tasks, but the passing months brought increased anxiety. Their gloom deepened as air links with Europe were severed as gangrenous limbs.

On June 7, a Dewoitine D388 of Air France left Kai Tak on its last service. Two weeks later, France and Germany signed an armistice at Compiegne – on the conqueror's terms.

The British Overseas Airways Corporation (BOAC), established in November 1939, had taken over Imperial Airways on April 1. On September 15, it suspended the service to Hong Kong. The DH86s kept operating until October, when the French prohibited BOAC the use of Indo-China air-space. PanAm kept Hong Kong in touch with the Americas. CNAC and Eurasia continued to serve free China.

Meanwhile, by May, Hong Kong's Governor Sir Geoffrey Northcote's health had worsened and he returned to England. Sir Geoffrey appointed Lieutenant General E.F. Norton, commander of British forces, as Acting Governor of the Colony.

In November, CNAC's indefatigable operations manager left on the night service from Kai Tak. William L. Bond had taken the first step on a vital mission – a future *lifeline*.

Arriving at Lashio, the Burmese terminal of the Burma Road, he assigned Captain Hugh Woods to fly him to Myitkyina, in upper Burma. Circling the sprawling town, *Woody* chose a site for an airfield.

A northerly course brought them to Burma's Fort Hertz (Putao). Over the tiny settlement Woods climbed his DC3 to 15,000 feet. In an uncharacteristic cloudless sky, he swung eastwards over the Naga Hills. As they parallelled the Himalayan Range he made notations of several uncharted passes. He correctly recorded the heights of the Likiang and Tali mountains. They flew over the Chinese towns of Chikiang and Suifu, then landed at Chungking. Although he did not know it then, he had flown the first trip over what became known as *the Hump*. His flight had found a route beyond the then range of Japanese fighter planes based in Burma.

This great achievement had a down-side. It showed that Hong Kong had almost reached its *use-by* date. Yet, despite his personal feelings, William Langhorne Bond looked to the future. His was a direct philosophy – **With the wall at your back, the only way out – is forward!**

CHAPTER 7

AIRPORT OF THE NINE DRAGONS OVERRUN – 1941

In February, a patrolling Walrus reported a Japanese aircraft carrier in Bias Bay. Other RAF planes reported a general increase in Japanese shipping in the Pearl River. In April a Royal Scots Bren Gun platoon moved into position on Kai Tak Airport. This insignificant force had the duty of defending the entire eastern wing of the Kowloon Peninsula. In June the Japanese, in overwhelming strength, occupied the Hong Kong border – an attack was imminent, but when.

Meanwhile, in April, Major Tateo Kato assumed command of the 64th Sentai (group), based at Canton. His top pilots flew with the 3rd Chutai (squadron) led by Captain Katsumi Anma. These were Lieutenant Shogo Takeuchi, Lieutenant Shungji Takaashi, and Sergeant Major Yoshito Yasuda.

Throughout March and July, CNAC used Kai Tak Airport to take urgently needed freight to cities still in Chinese hands. A surprise came on August 1, when Eurasia sacked the staff of the German operations department. Their arrogant attitude, nurtured by their Nazi masters, forced the Chinese Government to take this drastic step.

The month of September marked the arrival of the Colony's new governor, Sir Mark Young. Major General Christopher M. Maltby, General Officer Commanding (GoC) accompanied him. These men had accepted the most onerous appointments ever made. It was significant that their families did not accompany them!

General Maltby appointed Max Oxford, the Assistant Superintendent of Airport, his liaison officer. *Hammy* Hamilton replaced Squadron Leader Oxford as *Papa* Moss's assistant.

The Colony's air-space had the protection of three ancient Vildebeeste torpedo bombers (without torpedo racks). There were two Walrus amphibians for patrol duty. These five planes formed the Station's aerial strength, hardly assets to promote over-confidence in any commander-in-chief! The Japanese squadrons based at Canton had proven planes piloted by battle-seasoned aces.

On 7 December, Wing Commander H. G. *Ginger* Sullivan assumed command of RAF Station Kai Tak. Was this the shortest appointment in air force history? Within hours of his arrival the Japanese task-force admiral received the signal to *Climb Mt. Niitaka*. Japan had

AIRPORT OF THE NINE DRAGONS, KAI TAK, KOWLOON

DECEMBER 8, 1941
Japanese bombers attacking Hong Kong. Within a few minutes the RAF had lost control of the air.
(Photo: Carl Myatt, SCMP Archives)

begun her day of infamy – Sunday, 7 December. In Hong Kong, West of the International Date Line, it was the 8th – a Monday.

At his Repulse Bay apartment, William Bond, CNAC's general manager, answered the telephone. Fred S. Ralph, skipper of PanAm's *Hong Kong Clipper* (NC16735), wanted advice. The Superintendent of Kai Tak had ordered Ralph to get his flying-boat out of the Colony. Bond could not think why Moss should be that direct but advised Ralph to obey him. A few minutes later Captain Ralph phoned again with the news that Kai Tak was on full alert. Bond left his Repulse Bay apartment immediately.

Just after daybreak, on the 8th, planes of the resident squadrons left Canton. The 45th was equipped with Tachikawa Ida Ki-36's, used as light bombers and reconnaissance. The 10th flew the splendid Nakajima Ki-27 *Nate (Abdul)* fighters.

At 08:00 hours some 36 Japanese planes crossed the border following the route marked by the Colony's *fifth column* (the Wang Ching Wei-ites). The white sheets billowing from strategic rooftops blazed an easy path.

The first wave attacked RAF station headquarters and hit one Vildebeeste that exploded in a plume of black smoke. Succeeding strafing waves left many civilian planes burning furiously.

Finally, the airport, now completely obscured by oily smoke, forced the raiders to other targets. They turned their attention to two Supermarine Walruses and a big flying-boat moored in Kowloon Bay.

That day, PanAm lost a Sikorsky S-42B. Exploding fuel tanks accounted for three of Eurasia's four Ju-52/3M's. The Hong Kong Volunteer Defence Corps ceased to exist with the loss of its Tutor, Hornet Moths and Cadets. The Far East Flying Training School lost most of its planes and equipment. Commandant Murray's years of striving had become heartbreak within minutes.

The airport had taken a severe battering, but the smoke saved two Vildebeeste planes parked away from the RAF buildings. Japan had gained control of the Colony's air space in a matter of minutes.

Meanwhile, Bond got to the Star Ferry just as the air-raid sirens sounded. Finding the ferry service inoperative he commandeered a sampan. At Kai Tak he found half his fleet in ashes. The bombers had destroyed two DC-2s and three Condors – two DC-3s and a DC-2 had escaped damage. Expecting more raids, Bond bulldozed a passage through the perimeter fence and camouflaged his priceless planes in a vegetable garden.

The planes of Bond's CNAC began evacuating people that evening. His pilots operated without lights, feeling their way between freshly filled bomb craters. The first aircraft, a DC3 piloted by Frank L. Higgs, roared off Kai Tak's runway at 19:00 hours for Namyung, a small field about 200 miles north of Hong Kong. Higgs had gained notoriety as *Dude Hennick* in *Terry and the Pirates*. This was a popular syndicated cartoon series of the day. Frank like the *Dude* had one continuous thick black eyebrow right across his eyes – a feature to gladden the heart of caricatures.

Captain Harold Sweet took off in a DC3 15 minutes later, followed by Paul W. Kessler in a DC2. All three aircraft carried the airline's staff, families, and equipment.

With his planes in the air, Bond drove to the Peninsula Hotel to arrange for the evacuation of Chinese officials. Some could not leave that night, those that could returned with him to Kai Tak.

Captain Higgs was the first back from Namyung. As he crossed the airport, the British anti-aircraft gunners mistook his plane for a Japanese bomber and sounded an air-raid alarm. Higgs turned on his lights establishing his identity. The refuelling staff fled at the sound of the alarm so the planes had to be refuelled by hand pump. Kessler, landing after Higgs, told Bond that Harold Sweet had engine trouble at Namyung. Higgs and Kessler refuelled, loaded passengers and left again for Namyung.

Captain William McDonald then arrived from Chungking. Bond directed the loading and the plane returned to Chungking. Then, Higgs and Kessler returned from their second flight to Namyung. They refuelled, loaded civilians, and followed McDonald to Chungking. Bond dragged himself to the Peninsula Hotel. He had been awake for 53 hours but frequent air-raid sirens allowed him little sleep.

Bond spent Tuesday morning the 9th sorting company documents and contacting those he had to evacuate. Many resisted crossing to the mainland; they thought the Island was the safer place! In late afternoon Bond returned to Kai Tak to prepare for his planes that would come with the night.

At Kai Tak, it had been a quiet day, and now the evening shadows were lengthening. The two Vildebeestes were fully serviceable, though General Maltby had grounded them.

Flight Lieutenant D. S. *Sammy* Hill and Flying Officer H. B. *Dolly* Gray had cooked-up a scheme to night-bomb Canton. When Wing Commander Sullivan presented the plan Maltby refused permission.

That night Maltby ordered the evacuation of Kai Tak. Wing Commander Sullivan then asked for authority to evacuate his two planes to Kwei Lin with a minor diversion to bomb Nam Tan on the way. Again Maltby refused and ordered Sullivan to destroy the planes.

About 22:00 hours the CNAC planes arrived. Bond quickly had them refuelled, loaded passengers, and off they went to Chungking. With one plane waiting for the last of the evacuees, Bond hurried to answer a ringing phone. *Papa* Moss, wasting no words, told him the airport would be blown up the next day. Bond asked Moss to leave a short strip for his planes to operate the next night – there were still people to evacuate. Moss agreed! Bond, now tired in spirit and body, struggled aboard the last plane. His pilot was the legendary Captain Moon Chin.

As the dark enveloped Hong Kong that Wednesday the 10th, CNAC evacuation planes were closing on Kai Tak. An hour out McDonald and Higgs received a message withdrawing their operating permission. They diverted to Namyung. Later that night Moss ordered the demolition of his beloved field.

In two desperate days, the airline had flown 16 trips and evacuated 275 souls from the doomed Colony. There was some criticism that CNAC showed preference to its staff above others. It would be useless to discuss that claim. On such an emotional issue how could there be consensus.

Bond had handled the CNAC evacuation splendidly. Captains Higgs and McDonald did most of the flying. Captains Kessler, Moon Chin, Robert S. Angle and Harold Sweet played their part. Hugh Chen, CNAC's first native-born Chinese captain, flew a single-engine trainer to Namyung. Was this the Far East Flying Training School's sole surviving plane?

On Christmas Day the Crown Colony of Hong Kong surrendered to Japan. The order to surrender relieved Squadron-Leader Max Oxford, Maltby's RAF liaison officer, of duty. With Admiral Chan Tak, head of the Nationalist Chinese Defence Mission in Hong Kong, he escaped in a Motor Torpedo Boat. Admiral Chan and Oxford came ashore on a deserted beach. They spent weeks avoiding capture and living off the land finally to arrive in Chungking.

It would be over four years before civilian traffic again used the *Airport of the Nine Dragons*.

CHAPTER 8

UNDER THE CONQUEROR'S HEEL – 1942-1945

1942

The Japanese interned the civilian expatriates primarily in Stanley camp. Among them were *Papa* Moss and *Hammy* Hamilton. They caged the defenders at various locations throughout the Colony. The Japanese held most of the Royal Air Force survivors at the Sham Shui Po camp.

The Sham Shui Po camp commandant made *Dolly* Gray (now a Flying Officer) responsible for the Kai Tak work-parties. Tony Weller, a 17-year-old volunteer siege gunner, remembers those days.

"An old Star ferry picked us up from Sham Shui Po camp and took us to Kai Tak. At first we fetched and carried, cutting grass and moving bricks. Then in July we began to build a runway. We worked from pre-dawn to dusk levelling a hill at San Po Kong – it was hard *yakka!*

"We had four-wheeled bogies to carry the rubble. Being young and foolish we would jump on the load and ride to the bottom. One day it hurled out of control and jumped the track. Geoff Sloss, son of the Hong Kong University's vice-chancellor, and I escaped without a scratch but one of our mates broke his leg. That ended our *horsing-around*, the Japanese guards saw to that. Other prisoners hauled stone and rubble taken from Kowloon's Walled City.

"As concrete runway builders we were a total loss. The first runway we built had a compass direction of 13/31. It wasn't much good, we badly tamped the foundation and the mix of cement to sand and rubble was a joke. We even kept loaded wheelbarrows off it. Yet, this was the idea. Even the destruction of one Japanese plane would be a victory!

"Endless day followed endless day with our main diversion hurling ourselves into ditches to escape strafing attacks from Allied planes. American high-level bombers also took an interest in our work but we escaped injury."

AIRPORT OF THE NINE DRAGONS, KAI TAK, KOWLOON

THE JAPANESE RADAR SITE ON TAI MO SHAN – 1942-43
Built by prisoner of war labour, the site, on Hong Kong's highest mountain, provided admirable coverage. The receiving heads were near the mountain's crest. The operators occupied well-concealed barracks. Lion Rock, in left background, seems to dwarf all!

(Photo: Fl/Lt Noel Hitching, RAF Kai Tak)

1943

The Japanese also used POWs to prepare the site for a radar station on Tai Mo Shan, but the Kai Tak expansion remained their priority. The decision to add an east-west runway (07/25) involved the provision of a safe flight path. This required the demolition of tenements and *Papa* Moss's civil aviation complex. The rubble from these sources, even when combined with that from Diamond Hill, was not sufficient. They turned their attention to the nearby Sacred Hill.

The superstitious Japanese, careful not to insult the resident spirits, brought 50 white-clad monks to appease them. This exorcism, beginning on 9 January, lasted for three days. An added incentive to *depart peacefully* came from bribes of rice, pork, and sweetmeats. Convinced their monks knew their catechism the Japanese went ahead with their demolition.

A blasting charge broke the great Sung rock into three but one part retained the original inscription intact. What a bizarre scene – modern bulldozers scurrying between mediaeval robed monks busy expelling ghosts.

The war's end prevented the complete removal of the Sung Emperor's Terrace and the Sacred Hill. That epilogue came during the construction of Kai Tak's water-tongued miracle.

1944

This year speeded Japan's down-slide. Their dream of a Greater East Asia Co-Prosperity Sphere was in tatters, with American forces advancing towards their home islands. The

UNDER THE CONQUEROR'S HEEL – 1942-1945

14th USAAF had isolated their armies in Southern China and controlled their supply ports. The defeats inflicted on their once invincible German ally added to their despondency.

The Japanese still had one desperate card to play – the kamikaze (*Divine Wind*) suicide pilots. On October 25, 1944, the first kamikaze attack took place. At dawn six planes left Davao, in the southern Philippines, and damaged three escort carriers.

To the very end the *Divine Wind* wrought severe damage to Allied shipping.

Hong Kong experienced its first concentrated air bombing in December. The bombers of the 118th Tactical Reconnaissance Squadron hammered shipping, harbour installations – and Kai Tak.

A week of bad weather brought the Japanese some respite, but on the 19th the 118th returned in great strength. That day 45 Japanese fighters climbed from Kai Tak to battle them. The Americans lost eight Mustangs but the Japanese lost many more. The next day's strafing accounted for many Oscars and Zeros scattered around the field. Although the Americans continued their raids they encountered no further fighter opposition.

They had bombed Kai Tak out of commission.

1945

This would be a year of historical moment. A year that would defeat psychopaths bent on enslavement, and the emergence of the atomic bomb – the ultimate weapon of horror. Yet the year began *normally* – waging traditional techniques of destruction and slaughter.

The American bombers kept up their attacks preventing any useful repair work on the airport. With things going badly for Japan the USAAF were careful in their choice of targets. Unnecessary damage to civilian property was a top priority.

Throughout their strikes the Americans had avoided Macau. Yet, PanAm's store of oil and fuel there must not fall into the hands of a now resource-starved enemy.

THE KOWLOON DOCKS GET WORKED OVER BY USAAF BOMBERS – 1945

Smoke billows from exploding "eggs" laid by China-based United States bombers. A Japanese Zeke screams to the attack above the Peninsula Hotel. Just west of the Kowloon Peninusula enemy ships burn while near North Point a tanker streams an oil slick. The Kai Tak complex is clearly visible showing the extensive demolition of private property and the civil hangar that extended the airfield. (Photo: Fl/Lt Noel Hitching, RAF Kai Tak)

AIRPORT OF THE NINE DRAGONS, KAI TAK, KOWLOON

THE SURRENDER FORCE ARRIVES – 30 AUGUST, 1945

HMS Swiftsure *abeam of North Point after entering the harbour to take the Japanese surrender. Rear-Admiral C. J. Harcourt (Sir Cecil) landed from* Swiftsure *at the naval dockyard in central Victoria. The Japanese Memorial is visible on Mount Cameron.*
(Photo: Ian Diamond, Hong Kong Archivist)

On January 16, ignoring Portuguese neutrality, American bombers *targeted* the depot. PanAm's last base on mainland China became a site of desolation.

On the diplomatic scene, Generalissimo Chiang pressed for new negotiations over the Colony's future. Churchill had been unable to get Roosevelt to support Britain's claim – Roosevelt was loath to restore a Colonial power on the China coast. The best Churchill could expect was an international body to control Hong Kong.

On August 14, President Harry S. Truman, who had replaced the dead Roosevelt, announced Japan's capitulation. Yet, Hong Kong's future remained in limbo. Prime Minister Attlee managed to get Truman's tentative support for Hong Kong's return to the British Crown. This was a coup for Truman held Chiang Kai-shek in high regard but suspected deep-rooted corruption among his advisers. A suspicion that became reality in the years ahead.

Finally, Truman gave Attlee his unqualified agreement. This cleared Rear Admiral Sir Cecil Harcourt's squadron to approach Hong Kong.

On August 29, a flight of Hellcats and an Avenger approached Kai Tak. The Avenger was to bring senior Japanese officers back to the HMS *Indomitable* for surrender talks. The Avenger made a heavy landing and burst a tyre.

On August 30, a fortnight after Japan's capitulation, Harcourt's ships inched through the mine-suspected waters of Lei Yue Mun Pass to accept the Japanese surrender. On September 1, the 3rd Royal Marine Commando formally reoccupied Kai Tak and hoisted the White Ensign. Four days later Wing Commander R. C. Haine took command of RAF Station Kai Tak.

The Royal Navy followed by establishing a repair depot for its Corsair planes – HMS *Nabcatcher*. This location was west of the runways' intersection – roughly the current site of the vast HAEC complex.

UNDER THE CONQUEROR'S HEEL – 1942-1945

KAI TAK – NOVEMBER 10, 1945

A rare aerial photograph taken by the RAF from 20,000 feet shows the erstwhile Japanese establishment. The worn track from the Kowloon Hills that crosses the San Po Kong nullah and Kwun Tong Road to the turning-pan of runway 13 was used by the British prisoners of war to haul the mined rubble for the runways. (Photo: Fl/Lt Noel Hitching, RAF Kai Tak)

AIRPORT OF THE NINE DRAGONS, KAI TAK, KOWLOON

On September 7, a DC3 arrived from Kunming. It was to repatriate British prisoners-of-war to India. Later that month, Spitfires of 132 (Bombay) Squadron arrived at Kai Tak from the aircraft carrier HMS *Smiter*.

The local Japanese commanders surrendered to Sir Cecil on 15 September. This formal ceremony took place in Government House.

On October 9, Spitfires of 132 Squadron celebrated Victory Day with a fly-past in *good formation*. Spitfires of 681 should have taken part but the squadron could only muster one plane!

By December, Kai Tak had two fully operational Spitfire squadrons, three Sunderland flying boats and several DC3s of 219 Squadron RAF Transport Command. The Transport Command's passengers checked in at the Peninsula Hotel in downtown Tsim Sha Tsui. At Kai Tak they boarded their plane from a hut near the southern water perimeter of the RAF installation.

Corsairs and Spitfires began anti-piracy patrols. The Station increased the sweeps when more pilots arriving by the S.S. *Monarch*.

A combined Spitfire and Royal Naval operation captured a fleet of pirate junks in Deep Bay. A newspaper report of this incident brought relief to its readers. The emergence of the pirate scourge meant that their life style was gradually returning to a semblance of normality.

A DOWNED ZEKE AT KAI TAK – DECEMBER 1944

Probably a A6M5 Model 52 Zero-Sen with the stronger non-folding wings and ejector-stack exhausts. The Zero was a single-seat carrier-based fighter. Mitsubishi Jukogyo KK built models A6M1 to A6M8c. Nakajima Hikoki KK built models A6M2-N.

(Photo: Fl/Lt Noel Hitching, RAF Kai Tak)

CHAPTER 9

THE FIRST YEAR OF RECOVERY – 1946

The occupation had brought dramatic changes to Kai Tak Airport. From a grass field of 171 acres the Japanese more than doubled it to 376 acres and added two concrete runways. The busiest runway – 13/31 – was the shortest, 4580 feet, but widest with 321 feet. The 07/25 runway was 4730 feet long by 221 feet wide.

The runways had a maximum calculated load factor of 70,000lbs. The largest planes allowed were Skymasters and Lancastrians.

The prisoners-of-war scheme to sabotage the runways now *came home to roost*. No-one knew the strength of the concrete or where the weaknesses were likely to occur! Yet, there were no disasters.

With the end of hostilities the service and civil authorities took control of Kai Tak. The common flying area was 181 acres. The RAF controlled 110 acres with the Royal Navy sprawling over 52 acres. The civil aviation authority was the poor-relation with just 33 acres.

Without buildings on the civilian site it made necessary the erection of tents near the end of runway 25. The Air Services used these for administration, Customs, Immigration and radio facilities. The RAF proved co-operative by lending equipment and taking responsibility for Air Traffic Control, Aeradio and Air Traffic Handling Services.

The month of January was one of changes and accidents. It began with 681 Squadron's posting to Malaya and ended with a return of air-mail to China.

On the 4th an Aeradio watch received a distress message. A Dakota of RAF Air Transport Command had earlier left Kai Tak for Saigon. The plane had a crew of four plus five service passengers. The plane's commander, Flight Lieutenant Handle, radioed an uncontrollable engine fire had spread to the wing. He was about to ditch near Hainan Island.

Hong Kong Search and Rescue sprang into action. Two destroyers, a frigate, three Sunderlands and two Dakotas left for the area.

The search planes returned to Hong Kong at dusk without any sighting. About 2100 hours the HMS *Tenacious*, racing to investigate red flares, found a dinghy with six survivors.

AIRPORT OF THE NINE DRAGONS, KAI TAK, KOWLOON

Three days later an American Dakota that had used Kai Tak as a check-point, crashed 140 miles north of Canton. As the plane screamed towards the ground nine parachutes blossomed from the stricken plane.

This was a service operated by the United States Army to ferry officials between Manila, Hong Kong and Canton. A similar service operated from the USS *Tangier* in Kowloon Bay that used flying boats.

The distance from Kai Tak to Canton is less than 100 miles – it's extraordinary they could have drifted 140 miles off track in 40 minutes! Perhaps they were on a covert mission.

Spitfires of 132 Squadron and a FAA Corsair, on the 10th, responded to a distress call from a Hong Kong fishing fleet near Ping Chau. The planes' strafing broke up a pirate attack. As an armed air-sea rescue launch joined the melee the pirates fled into Chinese territorial waters.

The CNAC was the first post-war civil aviation company back into the Colony. In September 1945, it revived the Chungking, Kweilin, Hong Kong service.

In January the Colony's post-master negotiated with CNAC to reopen mail flights into China. On the 29, CNAC restored the air-mail to Chungking, Canton and Shanghai. The cost was 50 cents plus a postage of 8 cents for a half-ounce letter.

April 15 saw the disbandment of 132 Squadron. Spitfire spares had become scarce as *hen's teeth* and most of its planes were grounded.

The departure of 209's Sunderlands for Seletar left RAF Kai Tak with 1000 personnel but few planes. The station's Flight totalled three Beaufighters, and two Sentinels.

The Sentinels had restrictions on usage because of a lend-lease agreement. The Beaufighters alone carried the fight to an increased piracy threat. Group Captain Horner, the current Station Commander, had few resources, but this was to change.

On May 1, the Air Services separated from the Harbour Department's control with a full-time director. Max Oxford, returning with the relieving forces, had become the Acting Director of Air Services.

A fortnight later the Air Services took over the responsibility for booking civilian priority passengers. The appointment of a Passages Officer kept things running smoothly.

THE RAF's POST-WAR CONTROL TOWER – 1946/47

It was located on the southern seawall, slightly east of the tent city. Ben Hewson assumed civilian control of it during October 1947. (Photo: Roy Downing, DCA)

The late Captain Pat Armstrong came to Kai Tak in April as a member of 96 Squadron. This was a squadron of 35 Dakotas formerly based at Hmawbi, a satellite field of Mingaladon, the airport of Rangoon, Burma.

Pat said the squadron linked BOAC's flying boats then terminating at Calcutta to major cities in South-East Asia. The 96 Squadron carried priority passengers from Hong Kong to Shanghai, Iwakuni and Tokyo. They also brought passengers to Saigon, Bangkok, Singapore and Calcutta.

The 96 Squadron, now the resident Kai Tak squadron, was in reality operating as a regional passenger carrier. On June 15, Pat's squadron became 110 (Hydrabad) Squadron.

Early in the morning of July 18, Pat awoke to the sinister atmosphere that predicts a typhoon. It was a feeling once

THE FIRST YEAR OF RECOVERY – 1946

TYPHOON TANTRUMS – JULY 18, 1946

In 1946, Nature spawned a vicious tiffy in the South China Sea. Her eye passed directly over Kai Tak. She treated giant planes as miniature toys and devastated the Nissen huts of HMS Nabcatcher. Her 150mph winds left Kai Tak a field of desolation.

A C47 of the U.S. Air Force, with engines running, tried to ride-the-storm. When the undercarriage collapsed the blades of the port propeller left a gaping tear in the fuselage. (Photo: Harry Smith, HAECO)

An unserviceable Royal Air Force Sunderland flying-boat fared no better. (Photo: Fl/Lt Noel Hitching, RAF Kai Tak)

experienced that remains in the memory. His nerves were raw, the air hung heavy yet his lungs laboured to find a breath, his body itched yet scratching brought no relief! The rain started as a slight shower, and the wind a gentle breeze.

The *killer's* approach started the evacuation of the serviceable planes. The last wobbled through Lie Yue Mun pass in severe turbulence.

Frantically, work continued on the five unserviceable Dakotas and two visiting Sunderlands. The engineer-officer decided to remove an engine from one Sunderland to get the other airworthy. The deteriorating conditions were making work on the wings hazardous. Time had run out for remaining planes. They were tied-down with heavy concrete weights and abandoned to the elements. Within minutes the showers became a downpour and the wind a fury.

By the early afternoon the 150-mph wind was flattening everything in its path. The rain was sweeping horizontally to the ground. The Nissan huts of HMS *Nabcatcher* and the Air Services' temporary structures imploded as though a giant hand had crushed them.

Without warning there came an unreal silence. The wind and rain stopped. Pat Armstrong, looking above saw a large funnel-shaped hole capped by a few wisps of cirrus clouds floating in a tranquil blue sky. Yet, an impenetrable wall of boiling clouds ringed the Colony. Hong Kong was in the eye of the typhoon!

This was when most people died. Thinking the typhoon had passed they ventured out to survey the damage. Without a second's warning the wind renewed its fury – this time from the opposite direction.

Farmers who had scurried back to shelter died in each other's arms. Their huts, weakened by a wind from one direction, could not withstand an opposite attack. Others unable to find shelter had died in the flooded paddy-fields they had tended for decades – and would need no more! The concrete-anchored planes were a mess of twisted metal. The typhoon left Kai Tak Airport a grim scene of desolation.

Pat Armstrong, while convalescing from an attack of jaundice, became Senior Air Traffic Control Officer. This appointment lasted for about six months when he returned to flying duties. His minute tower was slightly west of a line of tents that became the departure and arrival facilities.

Police Inspector Frank Indge-Buckingham remembers the *tent city* and even the site before that! The earlier site was near the end of runway 25. His *office* was a table under the verandah of the RAF Passenger and Freight office.

In June 1946, the Directorate moved from the Colonial Secretariat to a temporary structure beside the Supreme Court. The superb location compensated for the austere office accommodation, with plenty of free parking in Statue Square, and a short stroll to the Star Ferry.

Papa Moss returned thoroughly rested to become Director of Civil Aviation. His home-side briefing included the aeronautical advances that flowed from the war. *Hammy* Hamilton arrived soon after to become Max Oxford's assistant. These three splendid men faced the daunting task of reorganising civil air operations on an almost faceless airport.

Although Viscount Knollys, Chairman of BOAC, had in January announced the return of services to the Far East in the *immediate future* it was not until August that it materialised. On August 24, BOAC began a weekly schedule from the United Kingdom (Poole) to Hong Kong.

This *Dragon* service, through Bangkok, used Hythe flying-boats. The Short Brothers had converted their successful war-time Sunderland for the purpose. The journey took six days with each night comfortably spent in a top-class hotel.

The first schedule by G-AGIA *Haslemere* ended at Karachi. The *Hunter* (G-AGLA) flew the Hong Kong sector. The *Harwick* (G-AGKZ) operated the entire westbound flight.

THE FIRST YEAR OF RECOVERY – 1946

BOAC supplemented the Hythe service with the improved Plymouth class Sandringhams. These flying-boats flew a weekly route from Poole through Augusta (Sicily) and Cairo. They continued to Bahrein, Karachi, Calcutta, Rangoon, terminating at Bangkok.

The Roy Farrell Export-Import Company (RFEIC) was the result of men seeking civilian stability from years of service flying. Roy Clinton Farrell organised men he had befriended during the *Hump* adventure. Their combined flying expertise and financial backing formed the company. The chief engineer was Bill *Hokum* Harris.

Advertised – *The First International AIRMERCHANDISE Service in the World* – the RFEIC flew its first direct service between China (Shanghai) and Australia (Sydney) on 4 February. Roy Farrell was in command with Robert Stanley Russell his co-pilot. Their plane was a C47 with the American registration NC 58093 that they named *Betsy*.

On March 11, the RFEIC registered under the NSW Business Names Act, 1934. It operated from Rooms 21-22 in the Prudential Building, Martin Place, Sydney. The astute Harry deLeuil was the Sydney manager.

A booming business forced them to recruit more air-crew. John Aubrey *Pinky* Wawn, Neville Gerald Hemsworth and Robert Donovan joined in April. They also hired *Vic* Leslie as a co-pilot and Lyell William *Mum* Louttit as radio officer. With these men the company flew the first direct air service between Hong Kong and Australia on 12 July.

The Roy Farrell Export-Import Company (HK) Limited was registered on 28 August. Its business address was Room 311, Prince's Building, and in November changed to Rooms 402-403 in York Building, Chater Road, Hong Kong.

The initial directors were Farrell, William Geddes Brown, Syd deKantzow, Millard Kadot Nasholds, Neil Buchanan and Robert Stanley Russell. Henry Streit and Floyd McClennan also had holdings in the company.

CATHAY PACIFIC'S FIRST AEROPLANE

The legendary Betsy *(VR-HDB) parked at Kai Tak in December 1946. She arrived in Asian skies in February 1946, as NC58093, carrying the Roy Farrell Export-Import Company's logo.* (Photo: *Papa* Moss)

AIRPORT OF THE NINE DRAGONS, KAI TAK, KOWLOON

With ships returning to the China coast the RFEIC business was in decline. The directors saw their survival lay in regular air-line routes. The Hong Kong Government had sympathy with their aspirations but there were obstacles to overcome.

BOAC, learning of RFEIC's interest, decided its monopoly should include the Far East – an area they had mainly ignored. The Hong Kong Government saw through BOAC's sudden interest and manfully supported the company that had the faith to get in early. This was the Farrell enterprise, yet the company's composition tied the Government's hands. There were too many foreign nationals directing the company for it to get British route rights. A company with fewer foreign directors had a better chance to get governmental support.

In September a brash new company burst upon the South East Asian scene. On the 24th, Cathay Pacific Airways Limited incorporated in Hong Kong with an authorised capital of HK$5,000,000. Its original subscribers were Roy Farrell and Syd deKantzow.

Cathay Pacific began operating from the P. J. Lobo and Company premises in Chater Road. From this location Rogerio Hyndman Lobo, the eldest son, began an association with Cathay that mutually flourished.

CPA began with two DC3s – VR-HDB *Betsy* and VR-HDA *Niki*. These were the first two planes recorded on the post-war Hong Kong Register dated 3 October.

My records suggest that *Betsy* left Hong Kong for Sydney before the official change of business name still carrying the NC 58093 registration. In Sydney a sign-writer changed the registration to VR-HDB.

The return flight left Mascot, Sydney, on 25 September under the command of Captain George Peter Hoskins, with Captain deKantzow his co-pilot and Alexander *Alex* William Stewart his radio-officer.

My association with Captain Hoskins came in 1943 when I was a young first-officer with Ansett Airways. He was the chief pilot.

At 0935 hours on September 25, a RAF Dakota departed Kai Tak towards the north-west on runway 31. The weather at the time gave good visibility with gusty winds blowing from the north-west. Four minutes later the plane appeared to be in difficulties. There was a screech of power then the wobbling plane crashed into foot-hills between Lion Rock and Beacon Hill. The exact point of impact was a few yards above the end of Waterloo Road, Kowloon Tong. The plane immediately burst into flames that destroyed 1,500lbs of mail and all but one wing. From the meagre evidence it seemed the plane flew into a *mountain wave* from the north-westerly wind swirling over the hills that spoiled its angle-of-attack. The roar of the engines was the pilot slamming on full power to counteract his descent but attempting to turn away from the hills had lost flying speed, stalled and crashed.

Being a service aircraft (Transport Command) and knowing that two passengers carried sensitive documents the RAF ordered heavy security. Within minutes Director of Air Services Moss and the AOC (Air Commodore Webster) arrived. The police supported by RAF personnel threw a cordon around the crash. They searched all sightseers and confiscated films from cameras. Yet these precautions were unnecessary. An urgent memo to the Hon. Colonial Secretary, from Papa Moss, stated: *The flames have caused such severe damage it is doubtful whether any further examination of the wreckage would give a possible clue to any failure that may have occurred during the flight.*

The Colony's newspapers had a field day. *Nineteen Die In Hong Kong's Worst Air Disaster.* This was the banner headline of the *China Mail* of Thursday, 26 September. In a smaller font – *Prominent Officials, Civilians Lose Their Lives in "Dakota" Crash.* The Mail stated – *not only the worst disaster in the history of Hong Kong aviation but also the first to involve the death of passengers at the Colony's airport.*

The five crew members were W/O A. Christie, Commander; W/O R.N. Blackmore, co-pilot; F/Sgt. J.W. Holden, navigator; F/Sgt. R.S. Bond, Wireless Operator; and F/Sgt. J.K.

THE FIRST YEAR OF RECOVERY – 1946

Hazeldean, the stand-by pilot. Of the 14 passengers – five were for Saigon with the rest going to Singapore. Among those bound for the Lion City were Colonel Cyril Wild, War Crimes Liaison Officer, and Mr. Davis, Chief British Prosecutor at the trials of the major Japanese war criminals.

An inquest held on October 21, 1946, received in evidence copy of a Gross Weight Manifest prepared by Capt. W. D. Tucker of PI-C141 Dakota. It showed the Philippine Airways plane weighed 24,755lbs when it left Kai Tak at 0830 hours the same day as the RAF plane. The PIC plane, bound for Bangkok, also used runway 31 and found no operating difficulty.

With no tangible evidence to consider the Chairman closed the hearing. The Court of Enquiry made no recommendations or apportioned blame.

Following the liberation William Forrest *Bill* Dudman moved to reactivate the Far East Flying Training School. He had to start from scratch for nothing remained of the buildings or equipment.

By November 22, his school was in business with nine students. The Hong Kong Register records the School had three Stinson L5 type planes, registered VR-HDD and -HDE and -HDF. His technical superintendent was Hew Kui Watt and his flying instructor was Robert Tai.

Late on the afternoon of December 20, 1946, I arrived in Hong Kong for the first time – a *sprog* first-officer with Cathay Pacific Airways. In command was Captain *Pinky* Wawn. We had touched down following a tropical downpour and water was draining away in torrents. Sydney deKantzow and Bill Dobson, Cathay's P.R. man, were on hand to meet VR-HDA. *Syd* to greet his partner Roy Farrell, and Bill for the story of our forced landing at Libby. This was an abandoned Japanese airstrip near Davao City on the Philippine island of Mindanao.

KAI TAK'S FIRST POST-WAR TERMINAL – DECEMBER 1946

Port Health, Immigration and Customs cleared passengers through a tent-city near the south sea-wall. Inspector Frank Buck Indge-Buckingham (right) commanded the police presence. (Photo: Buck Indge-Buckingham)

AIRPORT OF THE NINE DRAGONS, KAI TAK, KOWLOON

THE AIR SERVICES TEMPORARY ACCOMMODATION

In June 1946, the fledgling Air Services moved from the Colonial Secretariat to huts beside the Supreme Court in Statue Square.

A southerly aspect taken from a Fleet Air Arm Sea Otter. (Photo: A. W. Alex Hill, FAA)

View shows the Air Services' huts in the mid-foreground. (Photo: Courtesy Hong Kong & Shanghai Bank Archives)

THE FIRST YEAR OF RECOVERY – 1946

Syd decided to give me a briefing on the topography of Kai Tak. He pointed out the rugged hills that encircled the field to the east and north. His finger moved to the west where the ground was lower but still presented hazards to the unwary pilot. Our eyes moved to the smoke pouring from the stack of the Green Island Cement Works at Hung Hum. He said the smoke was a problem when it mixed with drifting fog from the Western Harbour and Lei Yue Mun pass that quickly reduced visibility to a memory! He pointed at the Japanese Monument on Mount Cameron. It reflected the sun from about midday and its rays were visible from Pratas Reef, a Chinese meteorology station, 90 miles away in the China Sea. Other than on the cloudiest days it was a helpful navigation check-point.

Syd's friendly voice suddenly took a serious tone. Looking me straight in the eye he said I must never agree to a departure on 31 – the runway towards Lion Rock. A RAF Dakota, using that direction, had recently crashed after takeoff, with no survivors. His gory rendition left little to the imagination – he made his point.

Finally, it was time to complete arrival requirements. The officers of Customs, Immigration, and Port Health worked in tents loaned by the Royal Navy. This *canvas city* was a few yards from the southern seawall of Kowloon Bay. Their working environment was Spartan with duck boards randomly floating from the earlier downpour.

Neither did they spoil the passengers. A tent set aside for their use lacked electricity and plumbing. There was no catering and water had to be trucked from the RAF site in drums.

The whole set-up did nothing to raise the spirits of a new boy. I rallied when I learned that the building activity a couple of hundred yards further west, next to the flying-boat slipway, would be the new terminal facility. The building seemed small and squat but anything was better than the ordeal of the tents.

Although I was weary the excitement of new surroundings kept me alert. Syd deKantzow drove the five miles to our lodgings in as many minutes. The same trip today takes almost half-an-hour. Syd screeched to a stop outside an imposing Peninsula Hotel – that we called *the upholstered sewer*.

CHAPTER 10

FREEBOOTERS OF THE SKY – 1947

While waiting for Lisbon and London to approve a schedule service to Macau, Cathay Pacific Airways decided to accept temporary non-schedule status. On January 5, Cathay's Chief Pilot *Pinky* Wawn approached the tiny grass field at Macau. Captain Syd deKantzow was his co-pilot and their plane was Dakota VR-HDA *Nikki*. A few seconds before they crossed the retaining wall of the Reservatorio de Aqua an observer scrambled back to the cabin. Standing at the flight-deck door his nerve broke with the flatness of the approach. His action upset the delicate balance and the undercarriage clipped the retaining wall. *Nikki* continued to skid across the grass with the propellers tearing up divots and stopped – perfectly aligned with a red-carpet.

The sheepish crew emerged to a trumpet proclamation and applause from the crowd. The Macanese officials continued with their ceremony of welcome as if nothing untoward had happened!

The accident to *Nikki*, the company's plush aircraft, was a serious revenue loss. *Hokum* Harris, Neil Norquay, and *Pouch* Williams took several months to get it serviceable. *Pinky* Wawn and radio-officer Bill Carew flew it back to Kai Tak.

Cathay temporarily abandoned its thoughts of a land-operated service to the Portuguese Enclave of Macau.

On January 25, a Philippine Airlines Dakota PI-C12 lost radio contact with Kai Tak. The weather had deteriorated rapidly and visibility was down to a minimum. Darkness fell with the belief that the plane had crashed in pirate-infested waters outside the harbour. Destroyers and launches spent the night scouring the sea.

The next morning an aerial search found PI-C12 strewn over Devil's Peak on Mt. Parker. A grisly exhibit gave the exact time of the crash. At 1503 hours the impact stopped Captain O. T. Weymouth's watch. This they learned when they pried his severed hand from the control column.

The plane carried a crew of four and 50 boxes containing gold coins and bars valued at HK$15,000,000. When Police Inspector W. Kinlock got to the site he found the bullion spewed over a quarter-of-a-mile area.

FREEBOOTERS OF THE SKY – 1947

COMMUNIST GROUND FIRE HITS FEFTS PLANE AT MACAU

On 13 April, 1947, while on a training flight, ground fire hit a Far East Flying Training School's plane, in Portuguese air space. Aboard were Sel Halls, the School's CFI, and Cathay Pacific's Public Relations Officer, Bill Dobson. At Macau, an angry Sel poses before his damaged Stinson L-5.

(Photo: Carl Myatt, SCMP Archives)

Although the police threw a cordon around the site and searched those leaving the scene a million dollars of bullion escaped detection. The cunning peasants buried their booty and returned to their cache days later. It is very difficult to outsmart a Chinese!

Although the BOAC management was not having things their way they continued to press their claim for Hong Kong regional rights. Throughout February and March, they intrigued with Jardine Matheson & Company to form Hong Kong Airways Limited. This company was to operate feeder services connecting the main Chinese centres with the BOAC trunk route at Hong Kong.

On March 4, with a capital of HK$1,200,00 and a newly framed Certificate of Incorporation it opened for business. Its office was in the Jardine Matheson & Company building at 18 Pedder Street. Arthur Donald *Don* Bennett, Manager, Far East Area, BOAC, sat luxuriously ensconced in that office. It mattered little that he lacked both aeroplanes or pilots.

When Chinese troops opened fire on a Hong Kong plane the Far East Flying Training School made the headlines. A few seconds after 0915 hours on April 13, the Chief Instructor Sel Halls left Kai Tak in a Stinson L5 on a training flight to Macau. His pupil was Cathay Pacific's public-relations officer Bill Dobson.

At 400 feet on final approach to the Macau landing field their plane seemed to back-fire yet there was no power loss. Then they saw wicked flicks from a Nationalist Chinese machine-gun post and small holes appearing in the starboard wing. The firing continued until they touched-down in Portuguese territory.

The British Consul in Macau arrived on the scene to be greeted by the enraged pilots. Mr Hill Murray assured them he would be in immediate touch with the Home Office. The newspapers joined in calling for action, but both the Hong Kong and Macau governments quietly dropped the matter.

AIRPORT OF THE NINE DRAGONS, KAI TAK, KOWLOON

THE SEA-WALL TERMINAL BUILDING
In June 1947, the Civil Aviation Department occupied a substantial building adjacent to the sea-wall. It replaced the tent-city.
(Photo: Fred Lillywhite)

Drama of a different kind occurred later that month. On the 27, a BOAC flying boat arrived overhead with visibility below the company's minima. The Hong Kong authorities diverted it to Hainan Island.

In fading light the flying boat landed in the open sea, some 25 miles from the seadrome at Hoihow. It spent the night wallowing in a gentle swell and at first-light slowly taxied to Hoihow. The Chinese authorities held it for two days then allowed it to refuel and go to the Colony. Even with the Chinese Ambassador to Poland aboard bureaucracy had moved with the rapidity of glacial creep!

In June the airport's terminal building opened for business. It had a restaurant, a friendly though Spartan bar, and the usual areas for processing arriving and departing travellers. The Royal Navy got back its tents, and although the tents had formed an admirable stop-gap nobody missed them.

A vital addition was the new service road that obviated passing through the RAF area. The one remaining source of irritation was the Royal Navy. The planes of HMS *Flycatcher*, the former HMS *Nabcatcher*, still *shared* the tarmac terminal apron.

That month *Papa* Moss became Director of Civil Aviation, a more realistic title for the position.

On 23 June, BOAC began weekly Poole, Augusta, Cairo, Bahrein, Karachi, Calcutta, Rangoon, Bangkok, Hong Kong schedules. BOAC supplemented their Hythes with the Short Plymouth class Sandringham flying-boats.

The Colony's navigational aids continued to be up-graded. There was a high and very high frequency (VHF) direction finder. Combined with a medium frequency, a beam approach and radar beacons the aids were comparable to other South East Asian airports. The radar aids mainly benefited BOAC for only they had the equipment for its use.

FREEBOOTERS OF THE SKY – 1947

The difficult approaches restricted night operation at the Airport. There was emergency lighting available and it got a work-out on 3 July.

A U.S. Navy air-sea rescue Consolidated *Privateer* left Okinawa at 1100 hours. It was to search South China waters for a missing ship. At dusk, Lieutenant Barker arrived overhead with intermittent radio reception and limited fuel reserves.

Pat Armstrong assumed command of the RAF Control Tower and impressed the station's lorries and jeeps into service to supplement the airport's emergency lighting. For two hours the four-engined plane circled trying to make radio contact. Finally Lieutenant Barker abandoned these attempts and used Morse Code with his signalling lamp. With emergency lighting, vehicular headlights and a friendly moon the skipper made a skilful landing.

The next morning Lieutenant Barker looked around Kai Tak. He stated that had he known the airport's terrain he would have thought twice before choosing to land there. Although he liked the place never again would he arrive after dark! His crew of six vigorously nodded their agreement.

A British delegation had gone to Nanking on 5 February to discuss an air agreement between the governments of His Britannic Majesty and China. The leader was a senior official from the Ministry of Civil Aviation, London. He had admirable support from Hong Kong's knowledgeable Director of Air Services A. J. R. Moss. A BOAC representative went along to grind the corporation's axe.

On July 19, China and the United Kingdom signed a bi-lateral agreement. Under the agreement, His Majesty's Government could nominate British airlines' passenger route-rights to and from four Chinese airports. These were Kunming, Canton, Shanghai and Tientsin. Chinese aircraft got reciprocal rights with Hong Kong.

The two British nominees were BOAC and Hong Kong Airways. The Chinese companies were the China National Aviation Corporation (CNAC) and the Central Air Transport Corporation (CATC) that had evolved from Eurasia.

A similar agreement was in train with the Philippines. The negotiators initialled it in Manila during December and confirmed it on January 7, 1948.

Hong Kong Airways Limited got schedule routes to Shanghai and Canton. The company's first two Dakotas (C47/DC3) appeared on the Hong Kong Register on 9 October. They were VR-HDN and VR-HDP. On December 2, with seconded BOAC pilots, the first British scheduled service to China arrived in Shanghai.

On September 1, Squadron Leader Heinbush's 88 Squadron came to Kai Tak. His Sunderland 1V flying boats worked beside the Dakotas of 110 Squadron. Heinbushe's planes provided bi-weekly flights to Iwakuni.

An early flight carried several Japanese war criminals to Japan for trial, with Gurkha troops forming the guard. The Gurkhas presented the Sunderland crew with kukris when they returned to Kai Tak. With the kukri practically a religious artifact this was a signal honour.

The Sunderlands gradually replaced the Dakotas until in April 1948 just one Dakota remained on station. The station reserved this plane for the Governor's use.

Following the disbandment of 110 Squadron Pat Armstrong accepted a local discharge. He joined Cathay Pacific Airways on April 6, 1948. Meanwhile the reduction of the British Army of Occupation in Japan halted the Sunderland bi-weekly Iwakuni flights.

A PanAm Clipper flying-boat skimmed the waters of Kowloon Bay on 28 October. PanAm had come back! It returned to find a worthy challenger in the BOAC Hythe. PanAm soon realised its once monopolistic hold on flying-boat service had died with British equipment advances made during the war.

Even before Cathay Pacific's aircraft engineering aspirations the Jardine *Hong* saw such a need. On October 3, the Jardine Aircraft Maintenance Company Limited (JAMCO)

AIRPORT OF THE NINE DRAGONS, KAI TAK, KOWLOON

JARDINE AIRCRAFT MAINTENANCE COMPANY LIMITED – JAMCO

On October 3, 1947, JAMCO was incorporated. It would be established on land vacated by H.M.S. Flycatcher. *The above photograph was taken in 1949 and shows how the company has extended its presence.* (Photo: Harry Smith, HAECO Archives)

became a reality. With a Certificate of Incorporation and a registered office at 18 Pedder Street they became an aircraft engineering force of note. The directors, David Fortune Landale and Robert Gordon, had HK$10,000,000 to spend and they did this with astuteness and business acumen.

During the latter part of the year Air Traffic Control Services remained under the control of the Royal Air Force. The Government Telecommunication Department continued to be maintained and jointly operated by the Aeradio Services and the Royal Air Force.

On October 10, Ernest Sunley *Ben* Hewson arrived as Air Traffic Control Officer, Grade 1. With charm he evicted Pat Armstrong from the Control Tower and installed himself. A few days later George S. R. Cannon took control of Aeradio Services and on December 6, Roy Evans Downing, Air Traffic Control Officer, Class II, arrived to help Ben Hewson.

The control of the airport was in splendid hands.

Meanwhile the vagaries of Hong Kong's weather claimed another victim. On November 12, a Far Eastern Air Transport Skymaster, the *Miss Luzon*, circled over Hung Hum. She had a crew of 12 commanded by Captain Noel Worley. The flight originated from Shanghai with 28 of the 30 passengers to disembark at Kai Tak.

The weather showed no signs of improving and the *Miss Luzon* diverted to Laoag, on northern Luzon. Later Aeradio intercepted a distress message of the *Miss Luzon* ditching about 80 miles short of Laoag.

FREEBOOTERS OF THE SKY – 1947

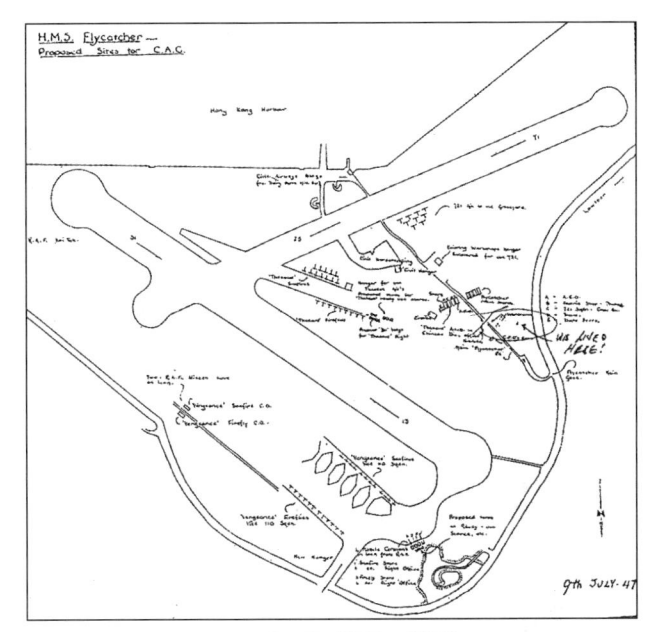

H.M.S. FLYCATCHER SITE – JULY 9, 1947

(Courtesy A. W. Alex Hill, FAA)

THE KAI TAK PANORAMA – 1947
A view of Clearwater Bay Road winding around the threshold of Runway 13 with Runway 07/25 in the middle distance.

(Photo: Sir Denys Roberts)

AIRPORT OF THE NINE DRAGONS, KAI TAK, KOWLOON

A FAA Tiger Moth on base-leg for Runway 07.

KAI TAK AIRPORT – 1947
Looking east along Runway 07. The access road from Kowloon City alleviated passing through the RAF installation. Cathay Pacific's engineering complex sprawls in the right foreground. The complex lies roughly at the threshold of the current runway. The Sacred Hill crests about 50 yards to starboard.

(Photo: Author)

FREEBOOTERS OF THE SKY – 1947

KAI TAK – JULY 1947

On base-leg for Runway 13. Runway 07/25 is just under the starboard wing. (Photo: A. W. *Alex* Hill, FAA)

How the field looks from 6,000 feet through broken cumulus clouds. (Photo: A. W. *Alex* Hill, FAA)

AIRPORT OF THE NINE DRAGONS, KAI TAK, KOWLOON

An air-sea rescue plane sighted five life rafts and directed the USS *General Collins* to the area. The ship picked up 36 survivors, but reported six missing – presumed dead.

The Hong Kong air fares were high when compared with Europe and America but competition brought discounts. A trip to Manila that cost $800 became $300. The Shanghai sector sold at $380, a saving of $320 on the January fare.

Kai Tak Airport was host to six scheduled carriers. BOAC, PanAm and Air France were the international operators. Hong Kong Airways Limited, CATC and CNAC flew into China with Curtiss Commandos, Skymasters and Dakotas. The CATC and CNAC handled 63 per cent of the Colony's traffic.

There were seven carriers operating non-scheduled and charter flights. Cathay Pacific Airways used Dakotas and Skyways (UK) Limited a Lancastrian. The Philippine Air Lines Incorporated (PAL) operated Dakotas and Skymasters, while Trans-Asiatic Airlines Inc. (TAA) and Commercial Air Lines Inc. (CALI) used Dakotas. Braathens SAFE Airtransport A/S (Norwegian) and Trans-Asiatic Airlines (Siam) Limited were the other Kai Tak users.

By the end of the year the Airport had become a busy place – a precursor of the future! The Department of Civil Aviation recorded 5,486 aircraft movements during the year carrying 81,815 passengers. The operators moved 1,036 tons of mail and freight compared with 236 tons the previous year.

Airport fees remained at the same level as in 1937!

CHAPTER 11

ENTER THE BUTTERFIELD & SWIRE HONG – 1948

Cathay Pacific's accident to *Nikki* at Macau caught the attention of an Australian entrepreneur. On November 30, 1947, Eric McIllree and another crew flew two Avro Ansons into Kai Tak.

This was of personal interest for these planes I had ferried to Camden, a private airfield near Sydney, from RAAF disposal units in Australia. This was a splendid time to buy aeroplanes. Eric paid £250 Australian for each Anson and then spent over £1,000 Australian modifying the centre-sections to civil standards.

Eric's brochure described the Anson as a de luxe 10-place feeder-liner. Farrell and deKantzow were in the market for a plane with short-field capability.

With a maximum load Eric left Kai Tak the next day landing at Macau with space to spare. He topped up his fuel tanks and at maximum take-off weight returned to Kai Tak. This impressed Cathay yet deKantzow demanded further tests at Macau. Finally, deKantzow closed the deal making one further stipulation – that Eric meet the full cost of ferrying the planes to Rangoon, Burma. They agreed and the Ansons came on the Hong Kong Register as VR-HDU (VH-BFK) on January 5, and VR-HDX (VH-BFL) 16 days later.

The Ansons were not a success in Burma. On February 9, VR-HDX came to grief when *Morrie* Lothian wrote-it-off at Sandoway, an airfield on Burma's western coastline. The other Anson, VR-HDU, became the property of Major A. S. *John* Cannon in November 1950 and is an ever-green adventure story – the famous *midnight-flit!*

Meanwhile, Cathay Pacific remained interested in Macau, and the gold charters came from this interest. Besides renting office space to Cathay Pacific the P. J. Lobo company acted as agents for the Banco Nacional Ultramarino.

Then an agreement existed between the International Monetary Fund and signatory countries. The agreement controlled the importation and dealing in gold.

Several countries refused to sign the Bretton-Woods, New Hampshire agreement. Macau was one of them. With no constraints the Lobo company and Farrell and deKantzow's Cathay formed an alliance to handle the precious metal. Roger (now Sir Roger) Lobo tells of the early *gold-runs:*

AIRPORT OF THE NINE DRAGONS, KAI TAK, KOWLOON

"We made the first delivery with a Dakota flying along the Macau racecourse. With no horses since the Pacific War it was a light aircraft training field and unsuitable for bigger planes – shown when *Betsy* hung her landing gear on the reservoir wall.

"With landing gear extended and half flap we approached low and slow. On a pre-arranged signal we shoved 50-pound bags of gold through the rear door on to the muddy field. The plan was not a success! The bags burst on impact – we spent days digging our loot out of the mud.

"We then tried sealing our load in 44-gallon gasoline drums. This seemed the solution until on the second run we almost squashed some of our bank coolies. This was too dangerous to continue.

"Then we considered fitting floats to a Dakota, a proven method in Canada and Alaska. This appeared to suit our purpose until we learned how floats would restrict our payload, so we abandoned that as well. These setbacks led us to the splendid Catalina PBY/5A amphibious planes."

Cathay's first Catalina was PI-C258 and entered on the Register as VR-HDS on July 30, 1947. The next was the ill-fated VR-HDT that began Cathay service on December 5, 1947. The CAD registered the third VR-HDH in February 1948.

My first flight on the *gold run* was January 24, with Don Teeters as skipper. We left Kai Tak for Saigon using VR-HDS. A Banque de l'Indo-Chine official supervised the loading of 30 wooden boxes containing gold bars. They were about 14 inches long by nine wide and nine deep. The next day we landed in the breakwater at Macau, taxied up the abandoned PanAm slipway, and off loaded our cargo. We were back at Kai Tak just as the sun set. Other gold charters took us to and from Djakarta.

THE MACAU GOLD-RUN – JANUARY 24, 1948
Macau Bank officials supervise unloading the gold boxes from Saigon into a truck – heavily armed! The location is the erstwhile PanAm site. A U.S. bombing raid demolished the site during the dying days of WW II – a girl sits among the rubble. Captain Don Teeters and F/O Chic Eather rest under the fuselage. (Photo: Ken Wolinski, CPA Radio Officer)

ENTER THE BUTTERFIELD & SWIRE HONG – 1948

In January, the CAD again reminded Cathay Pacific that allocation of official franchises was approaching. If Cathay expected consideration it must reduce its American interest to 10 per cent. Farrell and deKantzow, the main shareholders, began looking for a British company to buy out the American interest.

The Chairman of Skyways Limited, Brigadier-General Critchley, had previously approached deKantzow on this matter. Skyways had interested the Far East Aviation Company in a mutual bid for Cathay Pacific. Critchley arrived in the Colony expecting to find a despondent deKantzow ready to sell his assets for a pittance. He found a man confident and aware of the value of his business. They came close to a sale but Critchley's bully-boy tactics and deKantzow's brassy temperament prevented further negotiations.

The Skyways' manager was M. H. Curtis, who operated from the Jardine Matheson & Company building. Skyways, in the autumn of 1947, transferred its agency from Jardine to Butterfield and Swire. When Curtis got a *seat* in Cathay's office he disclosed particulars of Skyways' negotiations with Jardines.

Soon John Swire and Sons, the parent company of Butterfield and Swire, began discussions in London with Skyways. Their talks centred on starting an air repair company at Kai Tak and reopening discussions with deKantzow.

In February 1948, a period of intense negotiation began with Cathay Pacific when John Kidston *Jock* Swire arrived in Hong Kong. These negotiations culminated in a *Basis of Agreement* initialled on 5 May. The agreement was the formation of a new Hong Kong company to be called Cathay Pacific Airways (1948) Limited. This led to a company called Cathay Pacific Holdings Limited filing for registration on 5 May – it had a nominal value of HK$10,000,000.

The Swire Group confirmed the Agreement on 1 June. Although operations started on July 1, they did not register the company until 18 October. They dropped the *1948* portion and retained the original name.

John Swire & Sons had realised its ambition of entering *Air* in Hong Kong for the value of Cathay's assets. They made no consideration for goodwill. The new company took over seven DC3s for HK$1,462,621 and one Catalina – the *Miss Macau* – for HK$173,400.

When the Swire influence bought Cathay Pacific Airways there were two segments making high profits. One was the Burma operation that they continued. The other was the gold charters. The latter made Swire's uncomfortable and they would have no part of it. This led to the entry of Macau Air Transport (MATCO) on 8 July.

The Civil Aviation Department, anticipating an increased work-load, began recruiting more expatriate staff. This proved a wise precaution when on 10 January Hong Kong Airways started a twice daily service to Canton.

On March 19, BOAC extended the United Kingdom-Hong Kong flying-boat service to Iwakuni, Japan. BOAC transferred the Japanese terminal to Tokyo on 20 November.

Meanwhile some newly appointed Civil Aviation Department (CAD) staff arrived. Frederick Richard John *Fred* Lillywhite reported for duty on 19 January, followed by Ronald Stanley *Tommy* Tomkins, on 9 February. James Fleming *Pip* Pickering joined them on 3 August. These splendid men had RAF training and joined as Air Traffic Control Officers, Class II.

April continued to bring rapid changes. On the 9th, a Friday, Macau's Governor Albano Rodrigues de Oliveira greeted Cathay Pacific's inaugural Catalina passenger service. Syd deKantzow ended his speech with a toast to the Governor, who broke a bottle of champagne against the hull of VR-HDT the *Miss Macau*. The fare was HK$40 single or HK$75 return.

April also removed an irritant. The Royal Navy's HMS *Flycatcher* withdrew from the airport. The CAD rented the vacated area to two aircraft maintenance organisations. These

AIRPORT OF THE NINE DRAGONS, KAI TAK, KOWLOON

CATHAY'S INAUGURAL CATALINA FLIGHT TO MACAU APRIL 9, 1948

The Miss Macau waits at Kai Tak for her inaugural passenger flight to Macau. The Miss Macau was a Catalina PBY/5A registered VR-HDT. The official party – L/R: Fred Gallian (Proprietor of Macau Electric Company Ltd.); Mr Ian Grab Grabowsky (General Manager, CPA); Mrs Angela deKantzow; Captain Syd deKantzow; Mr Fletcher (Manager, Macau Water Works); Mr Y. C. Liang (Banker) and Mr P. J. Lobo (Banker/Tycoon).

The Miss Macau touched down in the Macau breakwater. She slowly taxies to the old PanAm slipway. Macau's Governor Albano Rodrigues de Oliveira led the welcoming party.

(Photos: Courtesy Cathay Pacific Airways)

were Pacific Air Maintenance and Supply Company Limited (PAMAS) and Jardine Aircraft Maintenance Co. Limited (JAMCO).

JAMCO purchased en bloc its overhaul shop from the States. Zigmund *Sol* Soldinsky arrived in the Colony with 12 American aviation engineers.

The late Harry Smith, a HAEC executive, remembers the Soldinsky group with affection. They were a gregarious lot forever holding parties in their Humphrey's Avenue mess in Kowloon. Their propeller specialist was Eddie Walsh, a teetotal non-womaniser, whose main interest was photography.

Horsing around one evening his mates slipped him a *Mickey Finn*. They stripped him, called in a local *pro* and photographed them in comprising positions. *Sol* called Eddie into his office, tossed the revealing snaps on to the desk, and demanded an explanation. *Sol*, up to his eyebrows in the scheme, gave him a stern lecture on morality, adding if he didn't change his ways he would be shipped-out. The words were prophetic for it wasn't long before they all left the Colony.

Sol Soldinsky had gained respect as CNAC's chief mechanic in China. His reputation became enhanced when he fitted a DC2 wing to a bomb-damaged DC3 at Suifu in 1941. The result was the legendary DC2½.

The man who flew the DC2 wing from Kai Tak to Suifu was Captain Harold A. Sweet. He was a CNAC pilot who flew civilians from Kai Tak in unarmed transports as the Japanese approached. With 16,000 hours flying time and aged 43 years he collapsed and died on a golf course on April 11, 1948.

The Civil Aviation Department (CAD) occupied their new Kai Tak premises on 31 May. This was a Nissen hut, with brick walls, 125 feet long by 36 feet wide. This centralised Area

PACIFIC AIR MAINTENANCE & SUPPLY CO. LTD.

PAMAS was incorporated 4 November, 1948. This photo was taken in 1949. (Photo: Harry Smith, HAEC Archives)

AIRPORT OF THE NINE DRAGONS, KAI TAK, KOWLOON

Control, Flight Information, Aeradio Services, Meteorological Services and Administration for the first time.

The CAD built a new Control Tower on the roof of the Jardine building. It provided better airport coverage than the old RAF Tower further to the East. The complex occupied the site where once stood the *tent city*.

An invitation found Hong Kong represented at an International Civil Aviation Conference for the first time. Other Asian countries had finally recognised the emergence of a strongly controlled local authority. This important event was in New Delhi with *Papa* Moss and *Ben* Hewson representing the Colony.

In early June, Cathay Pacific took part in a crucial South-East Asian event. The *Miss Macau* left Kai Tak on 6 June under the command of Captain *Dick* Hunt. His principal passenger was Ex-Emperor Bao Dai of Annam to witness a provisional agreement granting independence to the French Indo-China possessions.

About two hours later they landed beside a French cruiser in the Baie d'Along, near the city of Haiphong.

On November 4, Pacific Air Maintenance & Supply Co. Ltd. (PAMAS) incorporated. With a registered office in the Butterfield & Swire building it began with a capital of HK$5,000,000.

CATHAY PACIFIC'S FIRST ENGINEERING STORE – 1947

The Union Jack flutters above Cathay's first engineering store. Bill Hokum Harris, Chief Engineer, proudly surveys his kingdom.

(Photo: Author)

CATHAY PACIFIC'S FIRST HANGAR – 1947

Workshop facilities – a canvas awning was strung between two Japanese revetments to provide protection from the elements and sea spray. Ground engineer Geoff Arnold leans against his bike. His assistants changed over to PAMAS when it was established in November 1948.

(Photo: Bob Smith)

ENTER THE BUTTERFIELD & SWIRE HONG – 1948

The original site of Cathay Pacific's engineering *facilities* was on the southern side of runway 07/25. It occupied an area between the road and the seawall – just left of the current threshold of runway 13.

Cathay maintained its planes from *Hokum* Harris's flag-poled Quonset hut. Geoff Arnold and his men worked on engines protected from rain and sea-spray by a dirty tarpaulin strung between old Japanese revetments. With no hangar facilities all other work had to be done on the hard-standing. The Swire interest moved most of this Spartan installation, including the aircraft spares, to the new PAMAS site. They sold the Quonset hut for HK$5,717.

The spares that helped established PAMAS came from a Manila aviation *dump* that Roy Farrell bought in January. Several of us wandered around with Farrell that day. It was a treasure trove of aeroplane parts. There were dozens of aviation engines that had not run since their static check. Scattered around were complete Curtis Commandos and Dakotas that only needed the engines uninhibited and fuelled to fly away. There also were hundreds of angry black snakes. One plump sleek reptile showed an unnatural interest in me. Even when I put myself behind others she ignored them and pursued me! My *friends* were beside themselves with delight until Farrell blew her head off with the hand-gun he packed.

This was the year a band of aviation enthusiasts revived a name that had fallen into disuse following the Vaughan Fowler fiasco of the early thirties. The Hong Kong Flying Club Limited reactivated with the purchase of a Piper Super Cruiser Cub registered as VR-HDZ on 15 September. They bought a Tiger Moth, VR-HEL, the following year.

On November 14, a Dodwell employee left Kai Tak in FEFTS's Piper L4J registered VR-HDY. Above the fishing village of Aberdeen pilot Cedric Slater's engine stalled. He dived hoping to catch the engine with an impact start but failed and ditched in Telegraph Bay. A launch rescued pilot and passenger just as the plane slipped beneath the surface. They salvaged the plane but sea-water immersion led to its deregistration.

Soon after I arrived in Hong Kong I met, and liked, the aeronautically dedicated Bill Dudman. My offer to instruct in an honorary capacity found Sel Halls checking me out on the Piper and Ryan on 11 December.

On December 21, Bill Dudman assigned me a Chinese pupil named Wong G. Bun. This was his first flight and I climbed above the airport to show the *effect of controls*. We had departed in reasonable visibility but in a few minutes conditions had clamped in. The Tower controller, *Roy* Downing, advised me to land on the old pre-war field at Pat Heung (later called Sek Kong). Approaching Pat Heung the weather seemed no better, but directly overhead appeared a well-defined break. I spiralled down to a landing. Wong Bun and I had a hair-raising ride back to Kai Tak with a taxi driver who operated solely by Braille. Years later Val Penlington, in her splendid manuscript about the HKAAF, called that circular break in the clouds the *Sek Kong Duty Hole*.

Meanwhile a CNAC Skymaster approached Kai Tak with all souls marked for death. That morning Captain Charles Sunby's plane had departed Shanghai with a crew of seven and 28 passengers.

Captain Sunby made an early descent over Bias Bay for a contact approach to an airport where visibility was low and decreasing by the minute. Picking his way past sampans an island appeared out of the murk. This was the remote Basalt Island, about 11 miles east of Kai Tak.

Although the media dutifully published the names of the victims they concentrated on the newsworthy Quentin Roosevelt. He was CNAC's vice-president, grandson of the late United States President Theodore Roosevelt, and son of the late Brig-General Theodore Roosevelt, Jr.

AIRPORT OF THE NINE DRAGONS, KAI TAK, KOWLOON

FAR EAST FLYING TRAINING SCHOOL LIMITED

The FEFTS's sleek Ryan ST-M VR-HDK. The Ryan ST-M was a splendid plane for a trained pilot yet difficult for a trainee to handle. This photo is matchless – the Sacred Hill fills the background. (Photo: Hew Kui Watt, FEFTS – Director & Vice-Principal)

The FEFTS's installation. This photo was taken in 1956 from the crest of the Sacred Hill and shows preliminary dredging work for the new runway, also some early demolition activity on the Sacred Hill site. (Photo: Fred Lillywhite, CAD)

ENTER THE BUTTERFIELD & SWIRE HONG – 1948

The 30-year-old Quentin's ashes are buried on Basalt Island. This follows the family tradition that a man should stay where he met death.

The crash had an aftermath of pathos. Roy Downing tells this story.

"Mrs. Anna *Eleanor* Roosevelt, widow of the 32nd President of the United States, served with the UN Human Rights Commission. The duties associated with this body frequently brought her through Hong Kong. She always asked the PanAm captain to circle Quentin's grave. Basalt Island is in a Prohibited Area but we never refused her Captain's request. Mrs. Roosevelt followed this ritual until her death in 1962."

A few day's later BOAC began a Hong Kong-Shanghai service using the Plymouth flying boats. It was a short-lived service for political difficulties forced its withdrawal.

BOAC's subsidiary, Hong Kong Airways, continued to press its advantage with the Ministry of Civil Aviation. A series of proving flights to Manila led to the grant of schedule rights to the Philippine capital.

Jardine, Matheson & Company spent most of the year negotiating with BOAC to purchase the controlling interest in Hong Kong Airways Limited. They succeeded towards the end of the year.

Meanwhile, the Hong Kong Government manfully supported Cathay Pacific, now a 90 per cent British-owned company. Yet found its hands tied! It made a partial solution by offering unofficial schedules renewable periodically. It would be two years before Cathay received sanctioned routes.

The year slipped away as one of Hong Kong's more eventful ones. Yet, an event that made the front page of almost every newspaper in the world, remains to be told. It was the first air piracy for monetary gain ever recorded.

The pirating of Cathay Pacific's Catalina developed in the minds of three villagers of Nam Mun, in the Seong Chao region near Macau. They were Chio Tok, Chio Kei Mun and Chio Cheong. Tok, the leader, would take control of the Catalina when they subdued the pilots. He had learned to control flying-boats when he lived in Manila. Kei Mun, an opium addict, proved a liability and Tok replaced him with Chio Choi. Tok then approached Wong Yu, a rice farmer. Wong was to choose a secluded bay where the passengers could be held during ransom negotiations.

Then Cathay's Catalina was on charter to MATCO with schedule departures twice a day. Captain Dick Hunt commanded the morning flight but was developing an ear infection. The dispatch officer called the standby to take the afternoon flight.

The Macau service had proved a bonanza with every seat booked. One was the late Alan Marshall, author of *I Can Jump Puddles*. Cathay had commissioned Alan to prepare a brochure on the flight and his round-trip was for local colour. Sitting at the departure bar he cancelled his trip, pleading that his crippled legs were causing him severe pain. Our Sales and Traffic Manager, Robert Lowich *Bob* Frost grabbed his seat. *Bob,* a new bridegroom, was at a loose end. His wife was at the hairdresser.

At 1724 hours on 16 July the Catalina *Miss Macau* left Kai Tak for Macau. The captain was Dale Cramer, an American, with Australian co-pilot Keith Stewart *Ken* McDuff and Delca da Costa the hostess.

Dale chose the fair-weather route that passed on the west side of Lantau Island crossing Chek Lap Kok Island. He climbed to 1,000 feet for the short hop and within 30 minutes the Catalina bobbed at its buoy inside the Macau breakwater.

The 23 return passengers entered through the port blister. There was no seat allotment on the short hop – passengers sat where they liked. It was a normal takeoff and a shallow turn headed the plane towards Hong Kong. McDuff unfastened his seat-belt to climb the *tower* – the engineer's post when we carried one. This was the only point where the wing-floats could be raised or lowered. As he stepped from the flight deck he found two Chinese

AIRPORT OF THE NINE DRAGONS, KAI TAK, KOWLOON

CATALINA PBY5A – VR-HDT

The Miss Macau *makes a smooth landing on Runway 31 on February 6, 1948. The white buildings form the Administration part of the RAF complex. In one section was the Medical Officer authorised to handle flight crew licence renewals.*

(Photo: Ken Wolinski)

CATALINA PBY5A – VR-HDT

The distressing remains of the once beautiful Miss Macau *following the air piracy of July 16, 1948.* (Photo: *Papa* Moss)

80

men holding guns on him. One then ordered Cramer to surrender his command – Cramer refused. During this short altercation McDuff struck one pirate with the light-weight flag staff. This had practically no effect but caused the man to reel and bump into the one accosting Cramer. The man's finger pressed the trigger and Cramer slumped over the controls putting the *Miss Macau* into a fatal dive that ended in the muddy Pearl River estuary.

A fisherman who had seen the crash hastened to the scene and rescued a man clinging to a seat cushion. There were no other survivors. He took Wong Yu to the Saint Januario Hospital at Macau.

Cathay Pacific raised the wreck and barged it to Macau. During inspection they found spent shells and bullets. The Macau Commissioner of Police, Luis Augusto de Matos Paletti, Captain of Infantry, questioned the survivor who revealed nothing. Then Paletti installed a spy in the next bed to Wong Yu. The spy after gaining Wong's confidence learned the details of the scheme.

Hong Kong and Macau lacked legislation that dealt with air-piracy. Neither authority could try Wong Yu. The Macau Government held him without trial for three years. On release he returned to China where he died in a contrived accident.

The Chinese authorities detest piracy in any form – aerial of otherwise!

CHAPTER 12

THE KUOMINTANG RETREATS – 1949

In the early morning of February 11, Flight Lieutenant George Francis, AFC, left Saigon in RAF Vampire F-3 VG703. *Kiwi* Francis was responsible for the tropical trials of the graceful wooden-framed de Havilland fighter. His flight kit had maps for the 900-mile flight and a meteorology report compiled from surface data. The forecaster did not know a severe upper air trough was advancing on the Colony.

About an hour out of Hong Kong *Kiwi* entered thunder-heads and squalls – static blanketed his radio. When the controller finally made contact he was 100 miles past his landing point. The controller gave him a vector but while short of Colony waters he ran out of fuel. As he broke out of the overcast he just missed a Sunderland of 88 Squadron on anti-piracy patrol. *Kiwi* saw a crescent-shaped beach and made a splendid dead-stick landing. The Sunderland radioed Kai Tak that plane and pilot were safe – then landed in Bias Bay.

CATHAY PACIFIC DC-3s AT KAI TAK
Betsy *is in the background with* Nikki's *nose protruding at right. The ill-fated VR-HDG is in the foreground.* (Photo: Author)

THE KUOMINTANG RETREATS – 1949

KAI TAK AIRPORT – INTERIOR OF CAD TOWER – MAY 1949

On December 6, 1947, Roy Downing joined the fledging Civil Aviation Department as Air Traffic Control Officer, Class II. Roy Evans Downing became Director of Civil Aviation (1972-78). (Photo: Fred Lillywhite)

Bias Bay was the headquarters of a band of pirates whose ruthlessness could not match that of their leader. This was the attractive Madame Wong (Chung Lo-Yu). The Madame inherited the business when her husband kept an unexpected appointment with the local axe-man.

Lance Westlake, the de Havilland's resident engineer at Singapore, continues the story.

"I had arrived at Kai Tak in a Transport Command Dakota to be on hand for the Vampire's arrival. Learning of *Kiwi's* misfortune F/Lieut J. Stanley flew his Sunderland, with the Vampire's ground crew and myself, to Bias Bay. As we landed beside the other Sunderland we saw a large band of men advancing on the hapless pilot but our presence warned them away. Our inspection found the Vampire had only been superficially damaged – *Kiwi* had made a miraculous landing.

"During the night the H.M.S. *Belfast* anchored and put ashore a company of Royal Marines. About six o'clock in the morning a landing craft careened on to the beach, lowered its ramp, and dispersed a detachment of the *Buffs* who immediately dug-in. The beach had become a busy place!

"We removed the Vampire's drop tanks and ballast and considered flying her off. This was abandoned when the tide was wrong. Our attempt to lift the plane eight feet over a pair of horns on the bows of the landing craft failed miserably. We then cut off the horns and after much exertion lifted 703 aboard. The landing craft made a strange sight!

"When we attempted to close the ramp we realised the horns were necessary to secure the doors. We jury rigged the amputated horns and picked up our freezing protectors. We were ready to leave.

"Meanwhile the sea beyond the bay had increased to a long, dangerous swell. The landing craft, unbalanced by the protruding Vampire's wings, was unstable. We hoisted the plane aboard H.M.S. *Belfast* secured her and returned to Hong Kong. JAMCO gave us full use of its engineering facilities.

"A careful check, that included several undercarriage actuations, showed the Vampire was fully serviceable. That afternoon F/Lieut Francis completed his delayed demonstration – the first jet plane to take-off and land in Hong Kong."

February 24 was a day dreaded by aviators and air traffic controllers. A day when the best mixing-breeze was a fraction high and fog density changed by the minute. Then objects took a ghostly shape – become identifiable – then quickly faded.

Roy Downing, on duty in the control tower, could see aeroplanes circling above at 5,000 feet, but not a yard horizontally. Should he recommend closing the field or not? Should a pilot who had glimpsed a runway continue his approach? An uncertain and dangerous time!

In these *iffy* conditions a Cathay Pacific Dakota approached the Colony from Manila. Captain John Paish, DFC, commanded with a crew of three and 19 Chinese passengers.

That day I was at the FEFTS explaining the Ryan's blind-flying instruments to a pupil, K. C. Lam. We stopped to watch as a Hong Kong Airways Dakota appeared out of the murk and make a perfect landing. This came as no surprise for David Lampard and his co-workers had developed a splendid stop-watch procedure that needed practically no forward visibility – albeit without official sanction. Did this landing contribute to the CPA crash?

John Paish heard the Hong Kong Airways plane land and its report that they had ample visibility for a safe approach. Paish then requested permission to approach. Roy Downing authorised it but only if Paish had a forward visibility of three miles.

The Air Registration Board recorded – *the aeroplane, attempting an overshoot, struck the hillside by Braemar Reservoir.* There were no survivors. Later, departmental findings apportioned the loss of VR-HDG to pilot error.

The Communist southwards surge brought an influx of charter companies to Kai Tak. They were on a moment's call to jump into beleaguered cities to evacuate personnel and other juicy missions. Cathay Pacific Airways got a goodly share of these charters.

On April 29, Captain Bob Donovan was returning from Shanghai with evacuees. Near Foochow he encountered a severe line-squall but pressed through it. He radioed Captain John Moxham, who had left Shanghai after him, how severe was the storm and suggested a diversion. On the high ground around Kai Tak the CAD had arranged to light guidance fires. They proved helpful and Donovan landed without difficulty. He had made the first civil night landing since the end of the war.

Meanwhile, Moxham and Radio Officer Ken Wolinski turned inland to parallel the line-squall. The lightning was a terrifying experience and, worse, there seemed no way around the storm. Moxham turned the cockpit lights full on to counteract a lightning strike, and with an extra hitch to his lap-strap ploughed into the storm. The severe turbulence and pelting rain was nerve-shattering. Suddenly they were through and the menacing forked lightning was left behind. The fuel they had used in parallelling the storm left them little in reserve. With the fuel needles registering a hair width from empty tanks the fire beacons appeared. Moxham tore through the south-east pass to thump his aeroplane on the strip.

As Jackie Williams taxied the plane to the hangar both engines cut. If Captain Moxham had to make a go-around . . .!

Against a background of ideological upheaval it seems incongruous that ordinary things could happen at tiny Kai Tak.

On April 12, the Hong Kong Air Advisory Board first met. The members would assemble nine times during the year.

The following day brought a North West Airlines DC4 Skymaster from Shanghai on a survey flight. Aboard were 14 senior personnel making route notes. In May, North West began three scheduled flights a week terminating at Kai Tak.

THE KUOMINTANG RETREATS – 1949

A WET, MISERABLE DAY AT KAI TAK – 1949

On August 23, BOAC began a weekly service from London using Canadair DC4M Argonaut planes. The Plymouth flying-boat service ended in September. This western aspect shows a QANTAS DC-4 Skymaster and three BOAC Argonauts. The Terminal building, the jetty and slipway are evident. (Photo: Fred Lillywhite)

On May 27, the Hong Kong Flying Club lost VR-HDZ, its Piper Super Cruiser Cub. An eye-witness saw it flying low near Foo Tau Mun when a wing-tip hit the water. The Cub spun as a top and sank. A nearby fisherman rescued George Wong and P. C. Lee but the pilot, Chiu Hoi-pin, had disappeared.

On June 26, QANTAS Empire Airways began a regular Sydney to Hong Kong service through Darwin and Labuan. The aeroplane was a Douglas DC4 Skymaster. Captain J. M. Hampshire commanded VH-EBM on that first flight.

That month Hong Kong Airways' commitment to interior evacuations exceeded its operational capability. The company wet-chartered a BOAC Plymouth flying-boat for the Hong Kong to Manila schedule.

The Communist advances prompted the Home Government to boost the RAF presence. Number 80 Squadron arrived at Kai Tak with Mark 24 Spitfires.

On July 11, a Dakota, VR-HDQ, owned by Hong Kong Airways Limited had a hydraulic failure during take-off. Captain R. G. Ballantyne aborted the take-off but a CNAC Skymaster moving towards the intersection prevented him turning off the runway. At five miles an hour Ballantyne's plane nosed into the harbour. There were no casualties. This was Hong Kong Airways' first accident in 4,500 flights between Hong Kong and Canton.

On August 23, BOAC began a weekly London to Hong Kong service using Canadair 4 Argonaut planes. The route called for landings at Rome, Cairo, Basra, Karachi, Calcutta and Bangkok. This was the first BOAC all-landplane service to the Far East and the first service flight of the Argonaut class.

That day, a Spitfire of 80 Squadron developed engine trouble. Flight Mechanic Stan Jones, attached to 88 Squadron, witnessed the loss. The Senior Aircraftsman saw the Spitfire clear Lion Rock and as the pilot tried to stretch the glide his plane lost airspeed and crashed. The plane burst into flames incinerating Flying Officer W. R. Pickering.

On a happier note Vyvyan Henry Anderson joined the CAD on 26 August. *Andy* gained his experience from the Civil Aviation Authority, China. He joined as Air Traffic Control Supervisor on temporary basis. Andy retired to San Francisco where he died on July 24, 1974.

Meanwhile, the incredible advances of Mao's troops brought disquiet to the Colony. The officials at Kai Tak Airport handled 1,300 passengers every day.

AIRPORT OF THE NINE DRAGONS, KAI TAK, KOWLOON

Cathay Pacific's Captain Bob Donovan and R/O Ken Wolinski again teamed to evacuate people from Kunming. Besides the radio Ken was the *navigator* and marked their route on a tattered road map. As they got closer to Kunming the clouds thickened and glazed ice covered the wings. About 20 minutes out they heard a faint voice calling Kunming. It was Dave Lampard of Hong Kong Airways. Through the static Bob Donovan copied the letdown procedure dictated by Lampard. They broke through the overcast at 400 feet to find the 6,240 foot above sea-level Kunming strip dead ahead.

The Kuomintang troops, receiving no pay, began defecting. The *Gimo*, Generalissimo Chiang Kai-Shek, tried to counter this by flying in boxes of Mexican silver dollars. Cathay Pacific brought the boxes from Manila and CATC flew them to the various trouble spots.

An old friend, Captain *Woody* Forte of CATC, was the last pilot to fly into Cheng-tu before the Communists overrun the field. He landed with the Communists holding one side and the Kuomintang holding the other with both sides blindly firing across the field. *Woody* had his loaders kick off the boxes and tore away just as the Communists streamed across the field. *Woody's* radio call stopped another CTAC plane from landing and they flew off to Kwangnan some 30 miles to the north-east.

During September the Plymouth flying boat made its last flight to Hong Kong. This ended an era of comfort and civilised flying. BOAC introduced the Canadair DC4M landplanes.

Late in the month Canadian Pacific Air Lines began a Vancouver to Hong Kong service. CPAL made intermediate stops at Tokyo, Anchorage and Shemya also using the Canadair.

Cathay Pacific bought KLM's Douglas Skymaster for HK$803,800. A colleague of my Ansett days, Captain John Presgrave, on loan from Australian National Airways, ferried the plane from Amsterdam. His crew was Cathay's Chief Pilot *Dick* Hunt and Senior R/O Lyell *Mum* Louttit. The plane came on the Hong Kong Register as VR-HEU and on September

CNAC & CATC PLANES DEFECT TO KAI TAK – 1949

Eighty Nationalist planes sought refuge at Kai Tak in November. This photograph shows DC-3s, a Curtiss Commando and a DC-4. Others were scattered throughout the airport. (Photo: Fred Lillywhite)

THE KUOMINTANG RETREATS – 1949

CATHAY'S DISASTER AT NORTH POINT

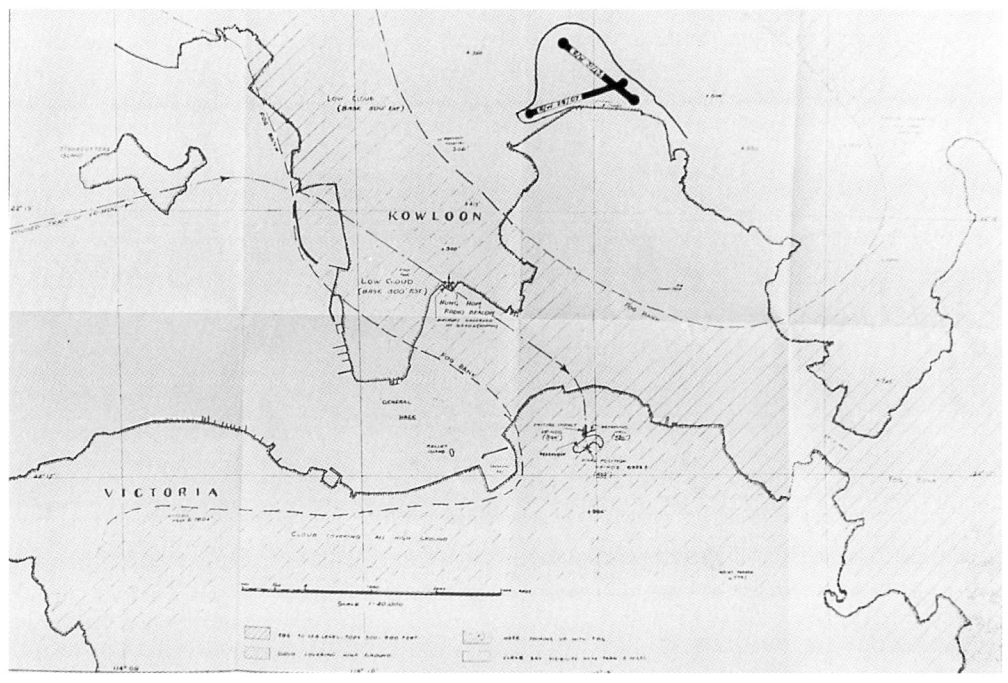

On February 24, 1949, Captain John Paish, DFC, followed this track to oblivion.

VR-HDG, a smouldering wreck on Braemar Reservoir. (Photos: Cyril Wray)

AIRPORT OF THE NINE DRAGONS, KAI TAK, KOWLOON

THE NOCTURNAL ADVENTURE OF 9 NOVEMBER, 1949

Colonel Liu Ching Yi, circled, with his wife, and the pilots who escaped with nine of the refugee planes to Peking.

(Photo: The *Courier Mail*, Brisbane)

PAPA MOSS ORDERS REFUGEE PLANES IMMOBILISED

On November 17, 1949, the Director of Civil Aviation instructed the immobilisation of the remaining refugee planes. Engineers removed wings and drained fuel tanks. This photograph, taken in 1951, shows some of the wings in the foreground and wingless planes south of the Terminal access road and others to the left of Runway 07.

(Photo: DCA Archives)

AERIAL VIEW OF KAI TAK AIRPORT

This superb photograph was taken in 1950. The black spots to the left and right of Runway 07 show the refugee CNAC & CATC planes.

(Photo: DCA Archives)

23 inaugurated the Bangkok and Singapore route. Captain Frank Smith, DFC, and Flight Engineer Leo Callaghan supplemented the ferry crew.

This Skymaster faced a terrible destiny, but this was in the future. Meanwhile she helped carry the *Gimo's* silver bars from Kunming to Kaitak.

On September 30, Mao Tse-tung became Chairman of the People's Republic of China.

In early November, with Kwangnan about to fall, the fleets of CNAC and CNAC reached Kai Tak. *Papa* Moss, with tongue-in-cheek, remarked those 80 planes scattered around his airport had it *bursting-at-the-seams*. Coming events eased his concern.

On November 9, Colonel C.Y. Liu, CNAC's managing director, and Colonel C.L. Chen, general manager of CATC, declared for the Communists. In an exciting nocturnal adventure Liu led the escape of nine planes and crews from Kai Tak to Peking. Chairman Mao and Premier Chou En-Lai declared them daring patriots. The Generalissimo branded them as defectors and put a price on their heads.

Mao asked Colonel Liu Ching Yi to stay in Peking in a high government post but he preferred his family life in Hong Kong. Peking put out a report that Colonel Liu lost his life in a plane crash at Lanchow in southern China. Liu returned secretly to his house in Prince Edward Road, Kowloon.

In 1971 the Liu family immigrated to Australia. Colonel Liu died of a stroke at Roseville, a Sydney suburb, in 1973.

November interposed events of magnitude with ordinary ones. Cathay's Skymaster made her inaugural Saigon flight.

A strengthening of the RAF at Kai Tak brought 80 Squadron to help 28 Squadron with border patrols. The H.M.S. *Triumph* hastening from Singapore joined an exercise to test the Colony's defences with a mock attack on the Colony.

Two Nationalist Ministers arrived on the 14th to discuss the fate of the CNAC and CATC planes. Then Major General Claire L. Chennault claimed ownership of some of them – the pot stayed on the boil!

The 17th found *Papa* Moss enforcing a court order to suspend the registration documents of the disputed planes. *Papa*, ever the realist, knew papers would not deter a desperate man. He ordered all the fuel tanks drained and the wings removed. As an afterthought he stored the wings on another part of the airport. Finally, he strengthened the boundary fence and appointed additional guards to patrol the area. These precautions defied anyone to *nick* the rest of *his* planes!

By December 8, just a few pockets of sporadic Kuomintang resistance remained. With the Communists firmly installed in Peking the *Gimo's* cause had petered out.

The Nationalist Government abandoned the mainland and shifted its capital to the off-shore island of Formosa. Generalissimo Chiang Kai-shek and his staff took control in Taipei on January 10, 1950.

At the Hong Kong border post of Lo Wu a huge Red Flag flew with arrogant pride. Around it massed an army flushed with victory while within the Colony Communist sympathisers lost no opportunity to spread discord. It was not surprising that Hong Kong faced the new year with trepidation – was it to be a repeat of the Japanese invasion?

CHAPTER 13

AN UNEASY BRITISH COLONY – 1950

The Hong Kong supporters of Peking and Taipei decided to probe the resolve of the British authorities. Demonstration followed demonstration, each becoming more impudent.

Meanwhile both ideological *camps* declared the detained planes, the offices and plant belonged to their respective governments. They picketed selective aeroplanes and occupied offices of CNAC in Gloucester Building and CATC in Shell House. The British authorities had armed police guarding the premises and planes but still the *patriots* evaded their net. They made sorties under cover of darkness, erasing or painting flags on the fuselage and wings of many planes.

The Nationalists (the term Kuomintang had become unfashionable) proceeded to sack the Peking-appointed directors and replaced them with its appointees. PanAm sold its interest in CNAC to the National Government for $1,250,000, the exact amount held by CNAC in American banks. The *Gimo* transferred this interest to General Chennault and his CAT co-proprietor Whiting Willauer.

Chennault then brought a legal action for ownership of the detained planes. Major-General William *Wild Bill* Donovan arrived in Hong Kong to head Chennault's legal assault. *Wild Bill* was the war-time head of the Office of Strategic Services (OSS) and directed a thriving New York law company.

The Governor, Sir Alexander Grantham, stated only full diplomatic recognition by Britain would release the planes to the Communist regime. This was a courageous statement for on 6 January Britain formalised relations with Maoist China. Meanwhile litigation made the matter subjudice.

The British Government's recognition of Communist China enraged the Nationalists on Formosa. British aeroplanes diverting to Taipei because of adverse weather at Kai Tak got a cool reception. I was on one diversion where authorities kept us aboard with drawn curtains and armed soldiers patrolling the aisle. They denied us sandwiches and water. Only the flight-engineer, under heavy guard, left the plane to refuel.

In this flash-point atmosphere Cathay Pacific Airways managed to retain its equilibrium. On January 10, it opened a new air link to Sandakan.

AIRPORT OF THE NINE DRAGONS, KAI TAK, KOWLOON

The agreement between Hong Kong Airways (HKA) and Cathay Pacific of May 11, 1949, clearly defined their operational areas. Cathay could exploit the area south of Hong Kong and Hong Kong Airways areas North. Any incursion by one company into the area of the other was by agreement on a reciprocal or other agreed basis. Macau was an exception where HKA already held the franchise. The other exception was Manila where both companies held equal rights. The Colonial Office and Ministry of Civil Aviation approved the document two days later.

On March 22, 1950, the Hong Kong Licensing Committee granted franchises to both companies. The main winner was Cathay, for Mao's control of the mainland negated most of HKA's expected routes.

At 0530 hours on April 2, Eric Aylward woke to a strident telephone and an explosion. He lived near the airport in College Road and was a staff engineer with PAMAS. *Hokum* Harris, his boss, screeched *they* were blowing up the detained planes. As *Hokum* ordered Eric to conduct a search of the remaining planes another bomb exploded. Eric told *Hokum* to go himself. *Hokum* screamed he was too busy – Eric hung-up and went back to sleep. The bombs, placed in empennage and engine cowls, destroyed seven planes. The Communists blamed the Nationals, the Nationals blamed the Communists – and both blamed the Hong Kong Government!

On April 23, the last Nationalist strongpoint fell to the Communist forces. Generalissimo Chiang ordered the evacuation of the island of Hainan.

On May 5, a Communist battery on Hainan Island fired on a Cathay plane. The Dakota carried the Hong Kong registration VRHDI and was under the command of John Furley.

The uncertainty created by the detained aeroplanes did not affect the running of the airport. The air defence radar, at the old Japanese site on Tai Mo Shan, had unacceptable limitations especially in the high winds of a typhoon. This prompted the authorities to move the radar equipment to Mount Davis on Hong Kong Island.

In October 1949 the RAF requisitioned several workshops vacated by H.M.S. *Flycatcher*. The CAD gave permission for the RAF to use its hangar. The Government Surveyor checked the height of several buildings around the airport. Those that affected the flight path lost their top storey.

The Police Commissioner established a station in a former Japanese block-house at Kai Tak. With the airport becoming a police responsibility the CAD retrenched the security guards.

THE EXTENSION TO RUNWAY 13

An additional 608 feet was gained by reclaiming land north of Clearwater Bay Road. The extension was fitted with gates that stopped traffic when a plane was about to land. (Photo: Sir Denys Roberts)

AN UNEASY BRITISH COLONY – 1950

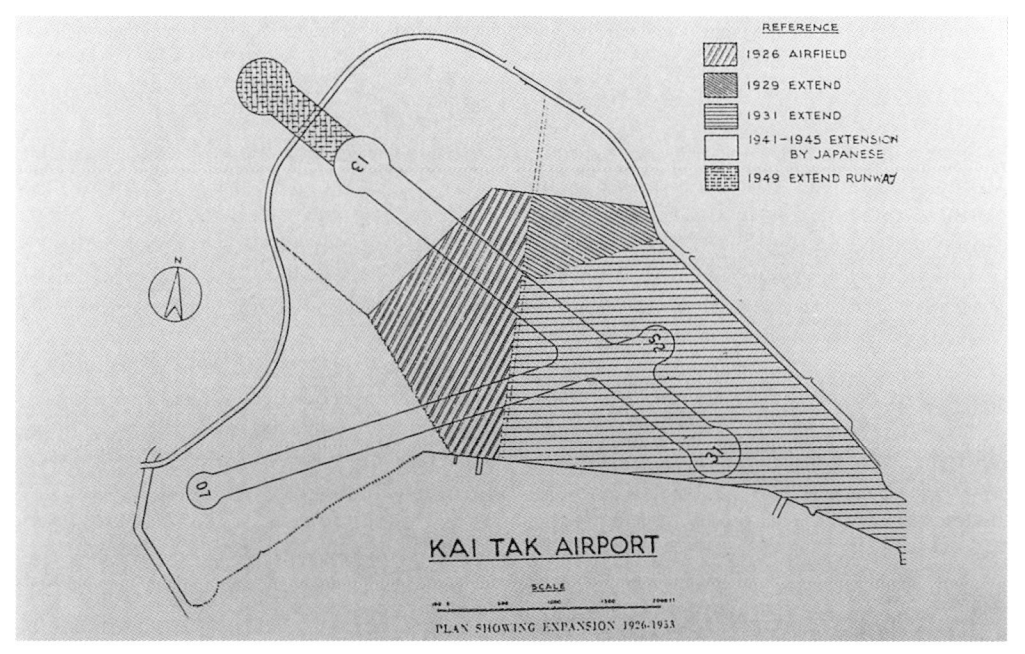

KAI TAK AIRPORT EXPANSION PLAN

The expansion marked 1949 was not operational until October 1950. (Photo: Courtesy DCA, Hong Kong)

In late 1950, Max Oxford transferred to Malaya as Director General of Civil Aviation. This appointment was a just reward for a splendid man but came at an inopportune time for *Papa* Moss.

The October change that impressed the pilots was the 608 feet that lengthened Runway 13. The Department gleaned that valuable addition by crossing the Clearwater Bay Road. To the West of the runway two police guards manned a small post. The clanging of a bell was their signal to press a switch that started two heavy metal gates moving on a recessed rail. The gate operation – taking 60 seconds – gave pedestrians time to complete their crossing. The bus and taxi drivers knew the operation time and many stretched their luck to the limit.

Roy Downing recalls pressing the bell as a long funeral procession wended its unhurried way across the extension. Suddenly the gates began to move. The solemnity of the occasion changed to one of bedlam. The pallbearers began to run and taxis, skidding between the mourners, added to the panic. As the gates narrowed the coffin swayed and the rear pallbearers abandoned their charge and scrambled back the way they had come. The bearers in front, realising ahead was the shortest route, sprinted with the rear of the coffin bumping and grinding. They scrambled through just as the gates clanged shut.

On another occasion I approached for a landing to find a *honey-truck* stalled on the intersection with the crew and guards trying to push it. Hearing my engines they abandoned their effort – considering the type of obstruction I over-shot!

In those days, especially in the New Territories, large black tankers collected night-soil in *honey-pots*. The drivers, careful to avoid a crumbling verge, drove down the centre of the road. A continuous horn-blast had them reluctantly move aside. Then the experienced road-user took a deep breath before passing. That *aroma* once experienced stayed in the memory forever!

In addition the Tower controlled lights that stopped traffic on Tam Kung Road which passed a few yards from the threshold of Runway 07. The Public Works Department installed them when pilots complained that buses and trucks caused a landing hazard. That light switch also controlled traffic using the Airport Terminal road.

In June a newspaper snippet advised the release of pirate Wong Yu. He left Macau for the interior of China; officially we never heard of him again.

The Chinese intervention in Korea and Britain's heavy military support against Communist North Korea was a time of unease for the Colony. A threatened invasion of Formosa combined with the CNAC and CATC bickering and the *hubris* of the Chinese troops massed on the border had the Hong Kong Government treading a tricky path.

On July 4, a Hong Kong Airways Dakota approached Swatow en route to Taipei. Captain Mike Harvey, F/O *Lawrie* G. King (later of Cathay Pacific), R/O Cowley and Hostess M. L. Wong were the crew.

Without warning one of two strange aeroplanes with stranger markings fired on their plane. The crew thought the attacker had the fuselage of a Thunderbolt and the wings of a Panther. Their markings conformed to no known country; half circles of blue and white on the fuselage and blue-white-blue stripes on the tail. They were uncertain if they were propeller-driven or jet – the attack happened too fast! The fighters had certain *Zero* characteristics of those the Russians captured in Manchuria when Japan capitulated. Whatever the type, was this the precursor of a Communist invasion of the Colony?

August at Kai Tak brought its quota of accidents. On 21, a privately-owned Tiger Moth making an emergency landing on a Lantao beach rolled over. Mr R. Cavill and his lady passenger, Mrs Stevenson, escaped injury. The water police brought the chastened pair back to Kai Tak.

A more serious accident befell a Catalina on a post major overhaul test flight. On the 29th, at 1630 hours, PK-AKR, owned by the Netherlands New Guinea Petroleum

HONG KONG AIRCRAFT ENGINEERING COMPANY – HAEC

HAECo came from merging JAMCo and PAMCo – their popular names. The SCMP reported these companies merged on 1 November, 1950, yet the Certificate of Incorporation is dated 23 November 1950. The JAMCo name is distinguishable beneath the over-paint, on the large right hangar, and plainly on the workshop group behind the hangar. This aerial photograph was taken in 1951. Just east of the old JAMCo hangar several wing-less refugee CNAC & CATC planes are visible. MATCo's service area was located behind the black-painted HAEC hangar. (Photo: Harry Smith, HAEC Archives)

AN UNEASY BRITISH COLONY – 1950

Company, took to the air. Captain Lee Murray checked the rate of descent, the hull feathered the water of Kowloon Bay, and the plane disintegrated.

A misalignment of the nose-wheel doors left them partly open. The bucking rudder pedals trapped one of Lee's feet and severed it. The left side of engineer Geoff Holland's face hit the bulkhead and caved-in. Of the remaining three crew members, two had superficial injuries and severe shock. George Cattanach, the other engineer, escaped without a scratch – his day of destiny lay four years in the future.

Julian Howe's team got them aboard the rescue launch and within half-an-hour they were in Kowloon Hospital. Leo Callaghan rushed to casualty to find Geoff, covered in blood, lying unattended on a stretcher. He grabbed the nurse and demanded why he was not in surgery only to be told he was dead. Leo angrily cried – *bullshit, he's alive!* The confusion brought the Chief Surgeon out of casualty. Leo demanded that Mr Cook should take another look. Australian Geoff Holland, other than a scar on his left forehead, made a full recovery. He lives in retirement near Sydney.

In October the Kai Tak RAF pulled out all stops to celebrate the Battle of Britain. Their hidden agenda had the ulterior motive of *showing the flag* by putting 28 Spitfires aloft. The two resident squadrons, 28 and 80, were the only squadrons left in the RAF with operational Spitfires.

PAMAS and JAMCO amalgamated on 1 November. The main change was a shuffling of the top executive and busy painters stencilling the hangar roofs with HAEC.

The year ended on a note of adventure, mystery and drama. At 0640 hours on the morning of December 15, Kai Tak Control copied this message:

> *Hello! Hong Kong approach. This is Catalina VR-HEV. My aircraft is sinking rapidly. Am being taken aboard a Communist gunboat. All crew safe.*

The Catalina's flight-plan lodged at Chittagong, East Pakistan (now Bangladesh), had it departing at 0228 hours Hong Kong time. The skipper estimated the direct flight to Kai Tak would be 13 hours. The tanks held sufficient fuel for 23 hours of flight endurance.

They encountered unexpectedly strong tail winds that brought the plane over Hong Kong *five hours* ahead of schedule. It circled over the Colony establishing contact on its auxiliary as the main transmitter had failed. Hong Kong Control accepted responsibility for its welfare. The skipper advised he would circle overhead until he had sufficient light to land.

The radio officer made periodic transmissions until his signal began to fade. The next signal received was the dramatic 0640 hours transmission. A RAF Sunderland scouting the area saw a Chinese gunboat towing the Catalina towards the Communist-controlled Wang Kam Island near Macau.

The background of this intriguing plot is worthy of the great Ian Fleming. Captain Ross Sandford Bohm, a pilot with MATCO, radio officer William Michael *Bill* James of Cathay Pacific Airways, and a MATCO flight engineer, John Francis *Dick* Richmond, formed the operating crew. A Mr Sun Chung-liang had bought the Catalina from MATCO and was aboard as supercargo.

The crew had agreed to make three flights to check fuel consumption graphs. They were to be paid £10,000 Australian for the first flight, then £12,000 Australian and £14,000 Australian for the remaining two. This seemed generous for work already documented world wide!

Following Hong Kong Control's acceptance the Catalina mysteriously left Hong Kong airspace and landing in the open sea damaged the hull. Ross managed to get it airborne again and landed in the sheltered waters of a bay. Soon after a gunboat sped around the bay's headland. Rumours circulated that as the gunboat approached the plane some fishermen saw people dumping bags over the side. Another rumour spread that sea-soaked opium could be bought in the criminal Chung-San area of Macau at discount rates.

AIRPORT OF THE NINE DRAGONS, KAI TAK, KOWLOON

THE END OF CATALINA PBY-5A . . . VR-HEV

On December 15, 1950, VR-HEV was landed at sea. She was taken under tow by a Chinese Communist gunboat to forever vanish behind the Curtain of Bamboo.
(Photo: Author)

VR-HEV'S CREW RELEASED

After 20 months of imprisonment her crew were pushed across the Hong Kong Border. L/R: Bill James, radio officer; Ross Bohm, captain; John Richmond, flight engineer.
(Photo: SCMP, HKG)

AN UNEASY BRITISH COLONY – 1950

The Chinese authorities took the crew to Skekki, a town near the Macau border, and placed them under house arrest. Certain Nationalist sympathisers planned a rescue bid, but the Communists got wind of it, and moved the airmen further inland to Canton.

Held in frightful conditions for 20 months their captors released them after they signed statements of smuggling prohibited drugs. The statements obtained under duress mentioned 40,000 taels (1260 kilograms) of opium loaded from an abandoned airstrip in Northern Burma.

As they pushed them across the Hong Kong border at Lo Wu, Bill James bid the Communist guards au revoir with that graceful Aussie two-fingered gesture. Although not broken in spirit they were in bad physical shape. They remained in the Queen Mary Hospital until they were strong enough to be *tossed* to the media piranhas.

Besides drug smuggling other imaginative theories surfaced. One had them transporting Nationalist spies to locations where they could infiltrate Communist China using the legendary Burma Road. I lean to this theory. Why would the Nationalists plan a rescue mission for drug smugglers?

I knew each of these men and dope trafficking was not a characteristic. In freedom neither did they admit that charge, nor did the Hong Kong police pursue that line of enquiry.

Will we ever learn the real story? Ross Bohm died still a young man, in April 1978. I traced Dick Richmond in 1982 but the privations of detention still lined his features. I understood his reluctance to talk of those days. Bill James worked in a sports shop in Sydney then slipped from sight. I have no idea the whereabouts of this likable man.

The *bamboo curtain* closed forever on Catalina VR-HEV. Perhaps the same happened to Mr Sun Chung-liang. I know nothing of his fate – whatever it was I wager it wasn't pleasant!

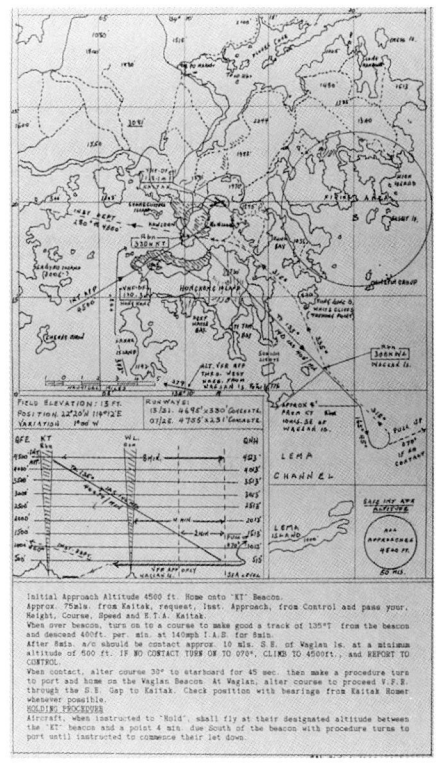

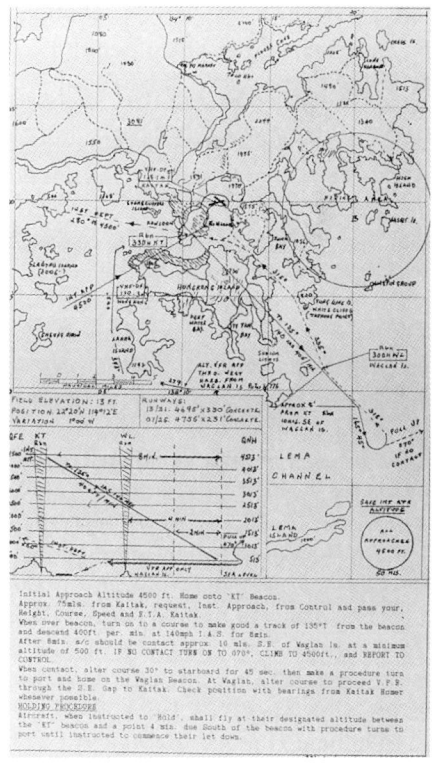

CATHAY PACIFIC AIRWAYS – APPROACH CHARTS

January 1, 1950. (Photos: Operations Manual issued to Author)

CHAPTER 14

A NEW RUNWAY MOOTED
1951-1953

1951

In January the *Bamboo Curtain* made Hong Kong Airways unviable. They sold their Dakota fleet but retained their identity using Cathay to operate their trades under charter. Hong Kong Airways remained in limbo until 1957 when they revitalised with the jet-prop Vickers Viscount.

A *Hong Kong Standard* article stated that Cathay Pacific Airways had become a major Far East airline after a modest beginning. The brief history ended with the catchy phrase *Our Wings Cover the Orient.*

That month 28 Squadron flew its last Spitfire sortie and re-equipped with Vampire 9s. The Spitfires transferred to 80 Squadron at Shek Kong.

In December, 80 Squadron flew a Spitfire for the last time. The planes, presumably, passed to the Hong Kong Auxiliary Air Force (HKAAF).

On March 2, *Hammy* Hamilton, Assistant Airport Manager, updated Security Identification Permits. This made it easier for the police to check those lurking around the detained aeroplanes.

The shortage of staff continued to impede the Department's plans. The loss of two dedicated Air Traffic Control Officers, J. Warne and J. F. Wills, curtailed the Briefing Service.

In June the Ministry of Civil Aviation dispatched a technical mission to Hong Kong to evaluate sites mooted for an international airport. The two sites at Deep Bay and Stanley Bay proved unacceptable for political and financial seasons. The mission presented their findings in a document known as the *Broadbent Report.*

The swirling mist hiding the rugged terrain trapped another victim. On March 11, a Pacific Overseas Airlines (Siam) Skymaster, with John R. Corey in command, originated in Tokyo through Taipei for Bangkok.

At 1030 hours the plane struck the saddle between Mt Parker and Mt Butler killing 26 people. When the police collected the pitiful personal belongings there were toys, golf clubs, watches, ladies' hats and a booklet on meteorology. On the book's fly leaf was the

A NEW RUNWAY MOOTED – 1951-1953

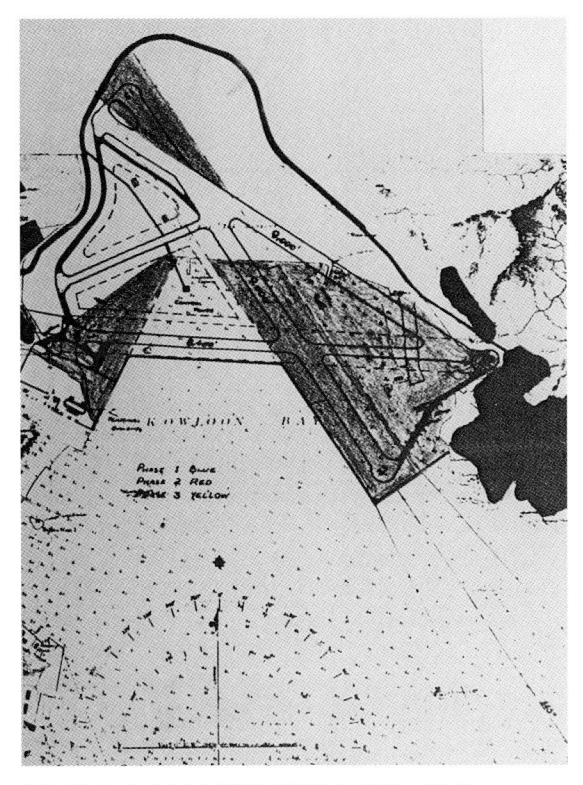

THE BROADBENT SURVEY REPORT – JUNE 14, 1951

The working drafts for extending Kai Tak Airport. Then favoured, the Broadbent scheme was superseded by the current single runway, claimed entirely from Kowloon Bay. (Drawings: Department of Civil Aviation, HKG)

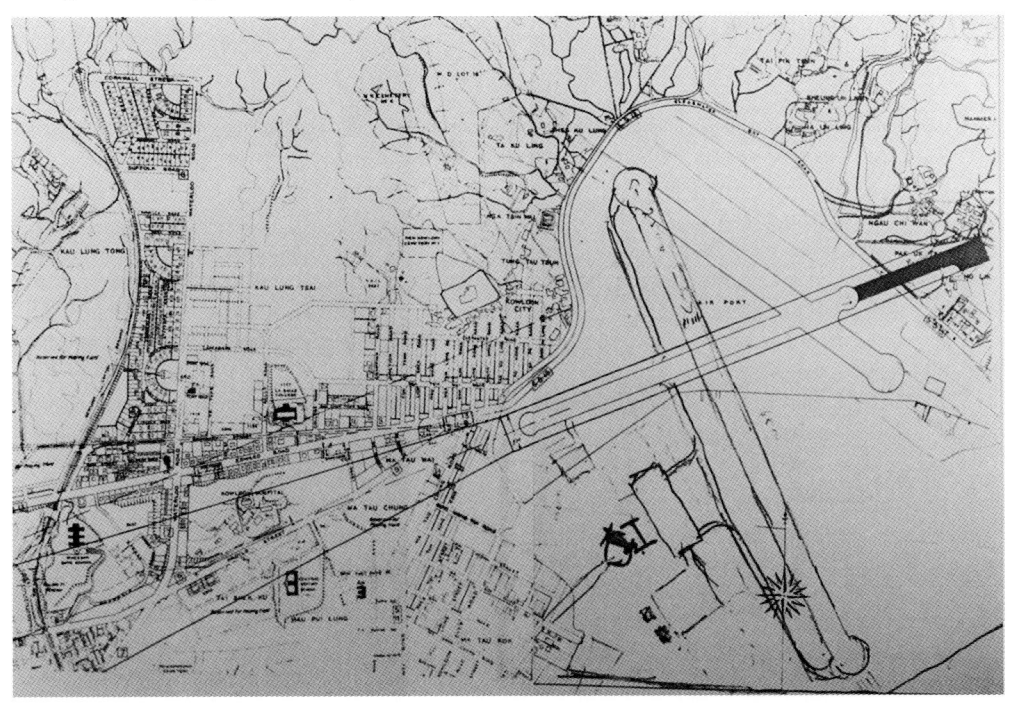

signature S. Indapunya, the co-pilot. His book had the chapter *The Warm Front* dog-eared – the weather phenomena that took his life.

The inquiry undertaken by the DCA Malaya, at the request of the Hong Kong Government, apportioned the blame to pilot error.

The weather during April continued to restrict visibility. On the 9th, HS-SAE, a Dakota of Siamese Airways, arrived over Kai Tak. With visibility below limits the plane diverted to Tainan, on Southern Formosa. A few minutes before arriving in the circuit a severe rain squall closed the airport. The captain decided to return to Kai Tak where the weather showed a slight improvement. Just before nightfall he made a pass at Kai Tak, lost visual contact, and made the instrument over-shoot. With little fuel left he got permission to let down over the sea near Waglan and make a visual approach. His last message – *Flying at 300 feet under visual flight conditions.*

A resident of Shek-O, Mrs J. Linstead, saw the plane hit the sea near Cape D'Aguilar. Sixteen people died in the crash.

Again the DCA Malaya handled the inquiry. This time the Hong Kong Government did not accept the findings and referred it to the Ministry. Air Commodore Vernon Brown, CB, CBE, Chief Inspector of Accident, Ministry of Civil Aviation, apportioned the cause to pilot error with faulty navigation a factor.

Captain Tayarn Timkul's choice of Tainan surprised me. When weather was bad at Kai Tak it usually was the same on Formosa, the reason Cathay Pacific's primary diversion was Manila. This meant carrying additional fuel but safety was the main consideration. Also, Luzon had several other airfields in case unexpected headwinds further reduced fuel reserves.

I included this snippet to show that a captain has opponents other than nature! One Saturday afternoon I diverted to Manila. The headwinds across the China Sea chewed into my reserves and, in failing light, I had the *temerity* to land at Clark AFB. The American Operations Officer was not bursting with brotherly love. It seemed my arrival interfered with a social event that evening. His attitude concerned me not at all – my passengers were safe – a skipper's first care.

1952

Most of the year was a patchwork of conventional incidents. The changes of departmental personnel coupled to the solution of the detained planes lifted it above the commonplace.

The types of planes using Kai Tak was a montage of old favourites and favourites to be. The splendid Dakotas shared *work-horse* duty with Curtiss Commandos. Skymasters, Argonauts, Douglas DC-6 and the Constellation handled the international passenger trade.

The Far East Flying Training School added an Airspeed AS40 Oxford to the fleet. The Department entered it on the Register as VR-HFC. This type possessed some fiendish traits and was hardly the best choice to promote pupil confidence.

On April 27, a chartered Bharat Airways plane landed at Kai Tak. The plane was the first arrival from behind the *Bamboo Curtain* since October 1949. The Skymaster came for a HAECO check after leaving an Indian Trade Mission in Canton.

HAECO started the major overhaul of Cathay Pacific's Skymaster on 4 May. Cathay, through Hong Kong Airways, *dry-chartered* a North West Airways Skymaster. For the first time in local aviation history an all British crew operated an American owned and registered airliner for regular commercial service.

Two other *firsts* soon followed. On 21 June an Italian Fiat owned by Societe Italiano per Transporte Aerci landed at Kai Tak. In September PanAm replaced the Constellation with the less graceful Douglas DC-6B, but PAL had shown us the type the previous month.

A NEW RUNWAY MOOTED – 1951-1953

The re-equipping of 80 Squadron with Hornets did not go smoothly. On December 6, 1951, four left Singapore on the first leg to Clark AFB but engine trouble forced one to return to Singapore. At Clark the weather had socked-in killing one pilot in a heavy landing. Another with fuel spent bailed-out breaking his leg – just one plane reached Kai Tak.

On December 24, 1951, four more Hornets arrived. In January the squadron was at full strength.

On the political scene it was not a tranquil period. A delegation from Canton attempting to bring relief for fire victims instead brought rioting.

Industrial disagreement in America between oil companies and employees restricted fuel supplies in Hong Kong. On May 12, 1952, the Aviation Spirit Control Order, 1952, affected international air traffic for a month.

The Hong Kong Court favoured Communist ownership of the CATC planes. The Privy Council overturned that ruling and awarded 40 CATC planes to Chennault's Civil Air Transport (CAT).

On the morning of 29 July the local government prohibited access to those planes. Anticipating Communist intervention the Government closed Kai Tak Airport to other than bona fide passengers but it was National supporters that caused the trouble. They mounted vicious attacks on Communist offices throughout the city.

Meanwhile, General Chennault forestalled Communist intervention by bringing in a L.S.T (Tank Landing Ship). He winched aboard every aircraft he could reach! Then he calmly sailed away to Formosa.

Chennault had bought the LST as war surplus from the Chinese Nationalist Government and converted it to a floating workshop. The escape of the H.M.S *Amethyst* in July 1949 had world press coverage, not so the Chennault LST escapade.

The General had kept his LST in the Whangpoo River until the Communists invaded Shanghai. When the city fell on May 25, 1949, his pilots flew the planes away. In the dead of night he slipped past extensive Communist positions and sailed L.S.T *Chung* to Canton reopening for business.

The removal of the planes suspended the security order and the public had entry to the airport from October.

The Department of Civil Aviation continued to attract competent individuals.

On 28 February, Ralph Winship took up his duties as Deputy Director of Civil Aviation. He had a RAF background and had spent four years as an Air Traffic Control Officer in East Africa. Ralph retired on October 13, 1964, accepting an appointment with ICAO – the International Civil Aviation Organisation. I held this man in warm esteem though his greatest joy was to grind me into a tennis court.

John Anthony Hallam had a Royal Navy background. His appointment, on 30 May, was Class II Air Traffic Control Officer. *Tony* gave 26 years' valuable service and retired on August 9, 1978, as Acting Deputy Director of Civil Aviation.

Albert James Robert *Papa* Moss departed the Colony on pre-retirement leave on 28 October. Like the fabulous bird of mythology *Papa* had led Kai Tak to its phoenix-like rejuvenation. I don't know who chose his apt nickname – Eric Aylward frequently used it.

Mervyn Jackson Muspratt-Williams, *Papa's* successor, began the war in the Army and ended it seconded to the RAF. His appointment as Director of Civil Aviation, Northern Rhodesia, began on August 28, 1946. He transferred to the equivalent position in Hong Kong on 20 October.

Muspratt-Williams was a reserved man dignifying his charge through its traumatic years of expansion. He left on pre-retirement leave on August 28, 1966, and died in Malta three years later.

AIRPORT OF THE NINE DRAGONS, KAI TAK, KOWLOON

1953

In February a USAF C54 (the military version of the Douglas DC-4 or Skymaster) crashed on landing at Kai Tak Airport and caught fire. The Fire Service extracted all the crew and brought the flames under control. Two men received serious injuries resulting from the impact. The United States authorities expressed their appreciation of the skill and praised the daring of the infant Kai Tak Fire Service.

This success brought pride tempered with relief to a Department concerned with the large-capacity planes regularly using Kai Tak. A well-equipped, highly trained Fire Service was that safety-valve.

During the year PanAm carried the largest number of passengers arriving and leaving Kai Tak. Cathay Pacific, the local airline, followed with BOAC relegated to third place.

On 20 February, Fred Lillywhite invited me to join him to welcome a de Havilland Dove plane. This was the first time a Dove had landed at Kai Tak. Fred knew I had flown the type in Burma and could advise him on its performance. I had nothing but praise for this magnificent *pilots'* plane and when the ferry pilot used reverse he had Fred *hooked*. The plane had come from England for a customer in Japan.

The UN embargo on trade with China introduced in February 1951 affected HAEC. With spare parts hard to secure some maintenance overhauls experienced extensive delays. Yet, HAEC managed to enhance its reputation with major repairs to a BOAC Argonaut. The plane had suffered extensive structural damage landing at Tokyo. BOAC arranged its transportation by sea and within hours of clearing Customs dozens of HAEC staff had swarmed to its succour.

A successful test flight in March confirmed the work and the plane flew off to England. This was a splendid achievement yet another gets my accolade.

The Burmese airfield at Pakokku nestles at the intersection of the Irrawaddy and Chindwin rivers. Captain Tin Tun had just started his take-off run when his Dakota triggered a land-mine. The explosion severely damaged the undercarriage, the centre-section and the starboard wing.

HAEC sent a team under Stephen Pao to repair the plane. With no mechanical equipment, and working under primitive conditions and flying bullets, they patched the plane with angle-iron (Dexion) supports.

Union of Burma's Captain K. T. Leong then flew the *meccano* plane to Hong Kong. His was a creditable feat of airmanship. The HAEC men responsible for the *jury rig* showed faith in their work by accompanying their hybrid.

The RAF extension work to runway 13/31 had proved a disappointment. The surface had collapsed in several places forcing its closure. The reduction in runway length reduced payloads and increased operating costs. Under a barrage from the airlines the Government directed the Public Works Department to solve the problem. The PWD evacuated the extension to a depth of 3 feet 6 inches and the relaid surface was in use by 31 March.

The year progressed with several accidents and other snippets of historical interest.

On May 22, a RAF Sunderland lost a wing-float during landing. There were no casualties.

July 8 brought the loss of a RAF plane. Two Vampires were practising in the Port Shelter Range. One plane didn't pull out of a strafing dive and plunged into the sea killing the pilot.

Later that month a Hastings of RAF Transport Command left Changi, Singapore, with a technical landing at Saigon. Approaching Kai Tak from the direction of Lion Rock it encountered a down-draft and touched short of the extension. One wing struck a farmer, Wong Leung, killing him instantly. Another farmer, Poon Ho, took a glancing blow that hurled him into the nullah. The plane hit the kerb, where Clearwater Bay Road crossed the

A NEW RUNWAY MOOTED – 1951-1953

KAI TAK AIRPORT 1952

From Tate's Cairn – looking west. The Green Island Cement Company pollutes the atmosphere. (Photo: Author)

intersection, and spun in a complete circle. The fuel tanks burst squirting high-octane gasoline on to the hot engines.

The Kai Tak Fire Service again proved their quality. Just before the plane exploded they had accounted for all 40 passengers and crew. The Kai Tak Fire Service, supported by RAF fire-tender and the Kowloon City Fire Brigade could not save the plane. The only part to escape the inferno was the tail that bore the numbers 564.

August brought a Spitfire loss to the Hong Kong Auxiliary Air Force. On the 17th, Flying Officer H. L. Mose's plane developed engine trouble that forced him to ditch in Kowloon Bay near Chakwoling. On hitting the water the plane turned turtle and sank but *Lou* struggled to the surface unhurt.

Lou Mose was co-pilot on my first command flight with Cathay Pacific. Lou, unwilling to wait for promotion in Cathay, resigned in 1954. His luck deserted him in October 1961. In command of a positioning flight from Leeds to Carlisle his Dakota crashed into a hill near Croglin Fell, Cumberland. There were no survivors.

On 9 September, two unarmed Hornets of 80 Squadron were on patrol in the Pearl River Estuary. They saw a Chinese gunboat shelling a British naval launch. The gunboat broke off the engagement when the Hornets dived to help the launch. Flight Sergeant Kearns, running the gauntlet of continuous fire, angrily buzzed the gunboat. He had the pleasure of driving it into a tree-covered river. He rejoined Flying Officer Phillips and they escorted the damaged launch as it limped back to Hong Kong with its dead and dying. This incident ended the dispatch of unarmed British planes.

AIRPORT OF THE NINE DRAGONS, KAI TAK, KOWLOON

The death of the six British ratings predicated a minor show of strength. A fortnight later the H.M.S. *Concord*, H.M.S. *Modeste* with a naval launch pugnaciously patrolled the Pearl River Estuary. Twelve Hornets, bristling with armaments, gave them top cover. The Chinese refused to take-the-bait and the force returned to the Colony.

October brought the Hong Kong Auxiliary Air Force back into the news. A Spitfire belly landed at Kai Tak when its undercarriage would not lock down. The pilot escaped injury but the plane suffered severe damage.

On 10 November, a RAF Vampire veered off the runway during landing. The pilot walked away from his slightly damaged plane.

During December a United States Navy Neptune (P2V) made an approach on Runway 13. The flight originating from Sangley Point, Philippines, carried 14 naval personnel. The pilot's heavy landing collapsed the undercarriage and tore off the port engine. The plane belly-skidded for 400 yards from the point of impact. All the occupants escaped, supporting three injured colleagues, just as the plane burst into flames. A few minutes later the once sleek Neptune was an unrecognisable heap of smouldering metal.

Kai Tak Airport remained a trap for the unwary!

CHAPTER 15

MURDER ON THE WING
1954-1955

1954

Mr Alan Lennox-Boyd, the Minister of Transport & Civil Aviation, proposed that Hong Kong should have a Regional Carrier. He invited Sir Miles Thomas of BOAC, Mr W. J. Keswick of HKA, and Mr J. K. Swire of Cathay, to open such a dialogue.

In February, Mr Lennox-Boyd called them to the House of Commons to discuss the progress of their deliberations. Keswick and Swire tabled their ideas but Sir Miles's plan was not ready for presentation.

Sir Miles had originally given lip service to the idea but Keswick and Swire doubted his resolve. They were right! In May, Sir Miles called the whole thing off pleading BOAC's loss of two Comets and a Constellation occupied his thoughts.

On January 6, a helicopter from the fleet carrier H.M.A.S. *Sydney* practised air-sea rescue procedures. A mechanical failure caused the *chopper* to crash into Kowloon Bay. The pilot and observer escaped without injury with the boom vessel H.M.S. *Barbain* salvaging the helicopter.

A fortnight later the harbour claimed another victim. The Tower reported the RAF Hornet appeared to make a normal take-off then without warning it plunged into the sea. The plane caught fire on impact but the pilot escaped injured.

The following day a BOAC Argonaut caused excitement when coolant fluid leaked on to an engine exhaust causing a cloud of steam. Captain P. W. E. Mayger cut his engines and ordered evacuation. The stewardess handled the situation with calmness although a group of Tibetans unable to understand English became panicky.

June 13 brought the loss of another HKAAF Spitfire in the Port Shelter Range. The pilot, aged 28, had joined the RAF in South Africa in 1942 and flew operational Mustangs over Italy. Squadron Leader E. J. G. Gauntlett was an employee of Cathay's managing company Butterfield & Swire. The month before his death he led the HKAAF Spitfire formation in the Colony's Centenary Fly-Past. The salvage operation did not recover his body. A wife and child survived him.

AIRPORT OF THE NINE DRAGONS, KAI TAK, KOWLOON

The following month tragedy again struck the HKAAF when a Harvard trainer crashed near Cheung Chau Island. This accident claimed Flight Lieutenant R. McConville, the Auxiliary's flight instructor. Fishermen pulled the unconscious cadet pilot from the plane just as it sank. The 18-year-old, Brian Bernard Farrell, son of the Manager of the Hong Kong Telephone Company, died on the way to hospital.

An hour later a RAF Sunderland flying boat combing the surface struck a submerged object. It tore off a wing-float and holed the hull. The Sunderland capsized and sank. A naval vessel picked up the crew.

Later in the month a RAF Hastings landed hot and crashed into a boat-house. There were no casualties but the plane and the boat-house suffered extensive damage.

In the remaining months of the year other accidents occurred to service aeroplanes. On August 27, a RAF Hornet crashed into the sea near Waglan Island at high speed. The troopship *Empire Halladale*, bound for Singapore, witnessed the crash and lowered a boat. There was no sign of the pilot.

A USN Neptune aircraft, on 14 October, made an approach on Runway 13. The landing was accompanied by a tyre bursting that caused the plane to swerve off the runway. A binding brake was the probable cause. There were no casualties.

That day a RAF Hornet suffered a similar failure. The starboard undercarriage collapsed as the tyre burst. The pilot escaped with mild shock.

A review of three serious accidents resulting in fierce fires brought disquiet to the Director. In each case the firemen controlled the flames long enough to rescue all aboard but the flames became uncontrollable within a short time. The Director established a committee to investigate the airport's fire-fighting procedures and make recommendations.

The Committee recommended upgrading equipment and appointing an officer specialising with foam. The Government approved the recommendations and instructed Chief Officer, Fire Brigade, to choose a man as a matter of urgency. In June, Mr A. S. *Steve* Henderson, a divisional Fire Officer, filled the newly created post of Airport Fire Officer.

When the Chief Officer, Fire Brigade, recommended Steve Henderson he had made a peerless choice. On the sporting field, 6 foot 4 inch Steve was an ungainly man. In charge of a fire his awkwardness vanished and he became as fluid as the means he used to fight his *enemy*.

The Department had located his Station just ahead of the Control Tower 100 yards east of the sea-wall Terminal Building. He was a stickler for practice drills yet found time to beautify the front of his station with immaculately groomed grass. Then he spoiled the scene with irritating signs to *Keep off the Grass*.

Throughout the year there were few changes to airline equipment. Hong Kong Airways continued to wet-charter a DC4 from Northwest Airlines for the Taipei route. On August 14, Air-India International introduced Lockheed Constellations for the Bombay-Calcutta-Hong Kong service. In December, Cathay Pacific bought a Douglas DC-6 from PanAm Grace Airways (Panagra). Cathay paid HK$5,699,663 – the greatest they had expended on a single plane. The sale included extensive spares, two engines and training for two crews. Its previous registration was N 90876 and became VR-HFG. Cathay sold it to Air Vietnam, Saigon, on December 20, 1962.

In view of the projected extension the Government decided that no major works would be done on the existing airport. Yet with the new facilities several years away some improvements were necessary. The congested conditions in the Terminal Building made it imperative to improve facilities by providing annexes to the existing buildings. In August this work began simultaneously with a large fenced visitors' enclosure and a traffic roundabout.

MURDER ON THE WING – 1954-1955

THE DEPARTURE & ARRIVAL SCENE – 1954
House flags proudly flutter at the sea-wall Terminal. Passengers arrive and depart with a minimum of bureaucratic control. Cars park at will – the atmosphere is relaxed and casual. These days were about to change! (Photo: Norm Latham, CAD)

THE DEPARTURE & ARRIVAL SCENE – 1955
A traffic roundabout and a secured visitors' area have been added. A police boom restricts entry to the tarmac, the CAD's admin. buildings, the Tower, the Fire Station and airline buildings. (Photo: Norm Latham, CAD)

AIRPORT OF THE NINE DRAGONS, KAI TAK, KOWLOON

In November the new building housed Immigration, Customs and Port Health. The space vacated by these departments became airline reception and booking offices, a money-changing kiosk, two shops and a comfortable restaurant. A covered walk-way connected the new building with the Terminal Building. The airlines contributed house flags to brighten the general appearance.

The roundabout improved vehicular flow and light metal tables with coloured umbrellas enhanced the visitors' enclosure. An occasional service band performance brought a festive atmosphere.

The excitement of the proposed new runway did not overawe the Department to ignore other matters. In February they build a radio mast on the roof of the Control Tower. The following month the installation of traffic lights on Tam Kung and Ma Tau Cheung Roads protected aircraft operating on Runway 07. The long lines of traffic that accumulated with the closing of the runway extension gates caused the police concern. They remedied this by banning the Clearwater Bay Road to learner drivers.

In May the Green Island Cement Co. Limited installed a precipitator they guaranteed would control smoke emissions. Only a person reduced to Braille conceded it an unqualified success!

The Department of Civil Aviation ended 1954 with 12 expatriates and 217 locally domiciled Officers. The administrative highlight was the transfer from Statue Square to the third floor of the New Secretariat Building.

The event of 1954 was a barbarous air attack on a civil airliner. It had sinister over-tones for it left the area balanced on the brink of another armed conflict.

Pip Pickering, the Kai Tak Duty Controller, scanned the message thrust into his hand by the radio operator.

Mayday! Mayday! VR-HEU going down, engine on fire, engine . . .

CATHAY PACIFIC'S DC-4 SKYMASTER . . . VR-HEU
Hong Kong Island forms the background – July 1, 1954.   (Photo: Cathay Pacific Archives)

MURDER ON THE WING – 1954-1955

The horizon was a lighter black as 12 passengers ambled across the tarmac of Bangkok's Don Maung Airport. They boarded the Cathay Skymaster VR-HEU for Hong Kong and the stewardesses, Esther Law and Rose Chen, made them comfortable. Captain Phil Blown and his co-pilot Captain Cedric Ced Carlton completed their check-list and waited *clearance to start*. Engines three and two started but the port outer engine would not mesh. The passengers returned to the departure lounge while the two pilots and Flight Engineer George Cattanach made a three-engine take-off, completed an impulse start, landed and reboarded the passengers. The logged departure was 0528 hours HKT (Hong Kong Time) and the date was 23 July.

The flight proceeded normally with Radio Officer Steven Wong transmitting regular position reports. His 0829 hours report:

Position 18°06'N, 110°06'E, 9,000 ft. VFR (visual flight rules), Track 042°, Ground Speed 207 knots, Wind 212°/19, Fuel remaining 8 hours.

Captain Blown waited for seven minutes then gently wound the auto-pilot, rolling on to the 070° heading. They were on the western side of *Airways Green 8* with Hainan Island visible to port.

Ced Carlton, checking the starboard engines, saw a cream-coloured fighter formatting on them. His report caused Phil Blown to check his side to find another fighter, with red markings, stationed there. As he disengaged the autopilot to turn further away from the Communist island both fighters attacked the plane. The cannon bursts set the port engines on fire. The skipper hurled the Skymaster around to evade and dived steeply. His indicated speed increased to 350 mph. This was 100 mph above the design speed for the wing yet the fighters kept his plane bracketed. The Number 4 engine now ran wild, its shriek abusing their overwrought nerves. Cedric managed to reduce the revs and pushed the CO_2 extinguisher. This brought the engine fire under control but the port wing was a sheet of flame. George Cattanach and Steve Wong eased the bullet-ridden body of Rose Chen on to a seat and then died helping Esther Law hand out life jackets to the passengers. Mr Peter S. Thatcher watched Leonard L. Parish kiss his two sons, Laurence 4, and Phillip 2, and cover their bodies with his massive frame.

At 5,000 feet the fighters shot away the rudder controls but Phil managed to regain some control reducing power on the port side. The Skymaster's 160 mph deceleration as it slammed into a 15-foot swell snapped the pilots' safety belts. Phil and Ced helped each other from the sinking plane. From the moment the attack had begun to their ditching 11 miles south-east of Tinosa Island the assault did not exceed 100 seconds.

On the surface they found a few survivors swimming aimlessly around. Phil told them to support themselves with mail bags while he got them into life jackets. Meanwhile Ced inflated a 20-man dinghy found floating among the debris and soon had the survivors on board.

In Hong Kong *Pip* Pickering scrambled the RAF Hornets and notified the 31st Air Rescue Squadron based at Clark AFB. Captain Jack Thompson Woodyard's Grumman Albatross was on the way within 20 minutes. Another Grumman commanded by Captain Dale R. Baker followed soon after. Laurence E. Rodrigues, Woodyard's radio officer, copied a message from the Communists prohibiting any military planes to approach the crash site. Woodyard shrugged and told Rodrigues to log the message.

About 75 miles from the calculated crash site Woodyard received a message from a French Privateer pilot that he had a dinghy in sight. The Privateer, based at Tourane, also had answered the distress call. Woodyard now descended to 1,500 feet and made a superb approach and landing beside the dinghy that the French pilot had marked with a drift signal. Getting the nine survivors aboard was a tricky operation because of the 12-foot swell. Captain Blown reported to Woodyard to be wary as fighters had downed his command. Woodyard instructed Rodrigues to tell the covering planes of this. Meanwhile Woodyard taxied to calmer water and took off avoiding a fleet of sampans that tried to intercept them. The covering planes escorted them to Hong Kong.

The French Privateer was the last to leave the scene. The news that the unarmed Skymaster was a victim of Communist fighters drove the commander into a frenzy. He told anyone who wanted to listen he had enough armament aboard to shoot down the entire *fornicating* Communist Air Force and only wanted a *petite* chance to prove it.

Captain Woodyard touched down at Kai Tak at 1715 hours by *Ced's* watch. There was no elation – passenger Miss Rita Cheng had died within sight of the Colony.

The French pilot's need for retribution had support from others! Three days later a squadron of American Douglas Sky Raiders, searching for survivors, came under attack from Communist LA-7 aircraft. The *dog-fight* took place over the high seas – the Communists lost two planes.

1955

A new Bilateral Agreement with the Philippine Government became effective in January. This allowed PAL an additional weekly Convair 340 service.

On 17 March, His Excellency the Governor paid an official visit to the airport. Sir Alexander Grantham's unconcealed enthusiasm ended with a tour of the Hong Kong Aircraft Engineering Company. HAEC's splendid work continued to attract clients from Thailand, Indo-China, Formosa, Burma, Malaya and the Philippines. During the year the Company overhauled many types including the *Marathon, Mallard, Tudor* and the *York*.

The long-haul foreign operators using Kai Tak Airport continued with few equipment changes. The newcomers were Japan Air Lines (with a DC-6B) and Korean National Airways. KNA's Seoul through Taipei service began on 5 February with a Skymaster. The Scandinavian countries replaced Braathans (SAFE) with Scandinavian Airlines System (SAS), using the weather radar DC-6B. The Constellation Connie (L-49) was the preferred type for Air France, the BOAC Majestic service, and Air India International.

The *Connie* did not prove a lucky plane for BOAC or Air India. A BOAC Constellation from Singapore, on 13 May, landing on Runway 07, clipped the nullah wall. The impact damaged the wall and tore a tyre from the port wheel. The pilot stopped the airliner on the grass verge about half-way along the runway.

Steve Henderson's firemen soon accounted for all personnel. A bemused male passenger said he was not aware of anything out of the ordinary! The Department replaced the nullah wall with a light wooden fence.

The Chinese political ideology again showed its intransigence on 11 April. A mechanic working on an Air India International plane fixed a time bomb in the inner starboard engine nacelle. With no remorse he watched the crew and passengers board the Constellation VT-DEP and take off. Then he *left town*.

The *Kashmir Princess*, chartered to carry delegates to the 29-nation Afro-Asian Bandung Conference in Djakarta, carried a crew of seven. There were 11 passengers – a Vietminh observer, two Eastern Bloc journalists and eight Peking officials. Mr Chou En-lai, the Chinese Prime Minister, was to lead this group but at the last moment changed his mind.

At 0930 GMT a distress report gave its position as 108 miles north-west of Kuching. The RAF Singapore dispatched a Sunderland to the area equipped with radar for a night search. Several hours passed before the searchers pin-pointed the crash.

There were six survivors. Captain M. C. Dixit, the co-pilot, Navigator J. C. Patak and Flight Engineer A. S. Karnik swam to an island while a passing ship rescued three unnamed passengers.

MURDER ON THE WING – 1954-1955

Peking charged that American supporters had hatched the scheme in the Colony. They further charged the Hong Kong authorities had been derelict in providing proper security. These charges brought an angry denial from Mr Humphrey Trevelyan, the British Charge d'Affairs in Peking. Mr Trevelyan assured the Chinese Foreign Minister that there would be a full probe.

Meanwhile, Commander Charles Roe, captain of the H.M.S. *Dampier*, a naval survey ship, arrived on the scene. Parts of the crash lay in 30 feet of water but most of the fuselage had slipped into very deep water at the reef's edge. He put down four divers whose grappling disturbed three bodies that floated to the surface. They recovered the bodies and hoisted aboard the wreckage.

Commander Roe's lookout saw people waving from a beach on Sidanau – an island in the rambling Natuna Group. He found three crew members draped in the *Mae Wests* that helped them swim to safety. The Commander took these men to Singapore.

The crash had occurred in Indonesian waters so he took the salvaged parts to Djakarta. Mr Muspratt-Williams, the Hong Kong Director of Civil Aviation, flew there to observe the investigation.

Some years later Roy Downing, the then Hong Kong DCA, attended a conference of Regional Directors of Civil Aviation. He found himself seated next to his Indian counterpart. Captain Dixit told him this story.

"Our plane cruised in a cloud-speckled sky above hundreds of tiny islands. This was my *leg* and I occupied the left-hand seat. A sudden explosion seriously injured Captain Jatar and he slumped over the controls. Flames billowed from the starboard wing and filled the plane with dense smoke. Someone opening an emergency exit in the cabin thickened the smoke in the cockpit. I pulled the unconscious skipper off the controls but the smoke prevented me from seeing the instrument panel. I opened the storm-window on my side and got some visibility. More by luck than skill I managed to bring the blazing plane to a *controlled crash* on the water.

"The crash had fractured my collarbone and I could not get through the window. The navigator squeezed through then eased me out. The flight engineer followed and got me into a life jacket. We watched the plane sink. There were several other survivors but we lost them battling a tide-rip for eight hours. Once ashore a village headman took me to the police post where I radioed the Indonesian authorities, who had reported the plane overdue but lacked knowledge of our fate. There had been no time to get out a *Mayday* call!

"The crash investigators' found parts of a clock with a timing mechanism still attached. That mindless act of sabotage cost 11 lives."

Captain Dixit's story varied with media reports. This account, from a trained participant, must have more credence than the dramatised mishmash of a journalist. You must make your decision!

The year brought accidents and fatalities to service and quasi-service planes using Kai Tak. In April the HKAAF trained for Her Majesty's Birthday celebration. It would be the last occasion the Auxiliary flew as an accredited fighter squadron. The fly-past that took place on the 21st provided a splendid spectacle. The precise formation of HKAAF's Harvards and Spitfires matched the Austers, Hornets and Vampires of the RAF.

The loss of fighter squadron status did not prevent the Auxiliary from giving the Colony sterling service. On June 12, two Harvards guided a launch to a disabled Dragon craft of the Hong Kong Yacht Club near Ping Chau. The Harvards circled while the five occupants were trans-shipped and the yacht taken under tow to Kellet Island.

That day the HKAAF lost a pilot and a Spitfire. The Port Shelter range had claimed another victim. The force of the crash broke the plane into fragments that sank without trace. They never recovered the pilot's body.

AIRPORT OF THE NINE DRAGONS, KAI TAK, KOWLOON

DARING RESCUE IN THE SOUTH CHINA SEA – 23 JULY 1954
Captain Jack Thompson Woodyard's SA-16 Grumman Albatross AF1009 churns through angry swells and aeroplane debris towards Cathay's survival dinghy. (Photo: U.S. Audio Visual Workshop)

CAPTAIN WOODYARD FOLLOWS THE MARSHALL'S BATS
Aboard were the survivors of the downed Skymaster. (Photo: Author)

MURDER ON THE WING – 1954-1955

CLARK AFB, PHILIPPINE ISLANDS – 26 AUGUST 1954
Major-General John W. Sessumus Jr. pins the Distinguished Flying Cross on Captain Jack Woodyard for his part in rescuing nine survivors from a downed Cathay Pacific airliner near Communist China's Hainan Island. Captain Frank Rohan, the General's aide, looks on. (Photo: U.S. Audio Visual Workshop)

DECORATING VR-HEU'S PILOTS – 15 JUNE 1955
His Excellency the Governor, Sir Alexander Grantham, has pinned the Badge of the Queen's Commendation for Valuable Services in the Air on Captain Phillip Blown and Captain Cedric Carlton. Ced and wife Irene stand behind his Excellency with Phil and wife Bunty in right foreground. (Photo: Ced Carlton)

AIRPORT OF THE NINE DRAGONS, KAI TAK, KOWLOON

A RAF Vampire crashed at Kai Tak on 16 July following a severe rain squall. The Vampire aquaplaned on the standing water. With ineffective braking it struck a Nissan hut killing the pilot and a Malayan airman.

Two days later a HKAAF Harvard struck the sea off Cheung Chau. The crash killed both occupants.

On September 6, a training Vampire came to grief when it overran the extension of Runway 31. It skipped the retaining wall and dropped into Clear Water Bay Road nullah. The plane had superficial damage and other than a little lost pride there were no injuries. The pupil under instruction was the Station Commander, Kai Tak, Group Captain J. F. Newman.

In October a RAF Harvard made a splendid landing on Runway 13. The pilot braked to starboard at the intersection but the high speed collapsed one leg of the undercarriage. Flight Lieutenant Humphrey's messmates chided him for days on his lapse of airmanship.

Later that month Kai Tak played host to a spectacular aviation exhibition. The programme included aerobatics, bombing, gunnery, and air-sea rescue procedures. The Meteor and Vampire jet fighters gave precision rocket attacks. Helicopters and Lincoln bombers kept the enthusiastic crowd interested. The United States Air Force, for the first time, joined in this annual exhibition. They restricted their participation to a static display with two Sabre jets and a Globemaster. The tremendous crowd showed their appreciation with a record contribution to the RAF Benevolent Fund.

Still later that month Flying Officer Huggett, of 28 Squadron, lowered his undercarriage for landing. The nose-wheel indicator of the Vampire jet showed an unsafe condition. He selected wheels-up and went around. Huggett made several trail lowerings and when his indicators showed safe he made a smooth landing. He held the nose off the runway until the plane slowed to a crawl then cut the engine. As the ground crew arrived to pin the undercarriage the nose wheel collapsed. Huggett showed he was a splendid airman.

The main excitement within the Department of Civil Aviation was the new runway.

CHAPTER 16

KAI TAK AIRPORT MARKS TIME – 1956-1957

1956

The spate of accidents to non-civilian aeroplanes continued to worry the Director. In January an Army observation Auster ditched in Tolo Harbour. The frigate H.M.S. *Comus* patrolling the area rescued the two occupants.

On February 1, a Taiwan-based Sabre landed at Kai Tak with engine trouble. Major Lee Shun-ling stepped from his silvery jet to find it surrounded by security guards. HAEC made the necessary adjustments and the 31-year-old pilot returned to Taiwan the following morning.

That day a RAF Vampire landing on Runway 13 had brake failure. The pilot, realising he could not stop in time, retracted the undercarriage. The jet came to rest in the overrun area with the nose protruding over the water. An uninjured but shaken pilot climbed out.

The following month another Vampire crashed three miles NE of Sek Kong. The impact killed the pilot.

Later that month two Royal Navy Sea Hawks struck fog-shrouded Devil's Peak. The crash tore the planes to fragments killing the pilots and an elderly Chinese lady.

On May 20, a HKAAF Harvard crashed on Aplichau Island. The pilot died.

On a less distressing note June allowed a sliver of light through the *Bamboo Curtain*. On the first the People's Republic of China resumed sending weather radio broadcasts. This was a welcome gesture after a silence of seven years. Any thoughts of increased goodwill lost momentum by events in mid-October.

On 6 October the RAF gave its annual flying display. The programme followed the usual pattern and, as usual, was a success. During the interval Mr E. B. David, the Officer Administering the Government, flew in and out by helicopter from the aircraft carrier US *Lexington*. This departure from the norm proved a splendid PR stratagem.

The festivities continued into the following day when several local operators made their planes available for sight-seeing. Seven hundred people each paid HK$20 to see their Colony from the air. Every cent collected went to the RAF Benevolent Fund.

The Department of Civil Aviation recorded a marked increase in charter flights. In the main, they carried Chinese seamen joining and leaving ships trapped either side of the Suez Canal.

On October 29, Israel had invaded Egypt. Two days later Great Britain and France attacked Egypt to restore international control of the waterway. United Nations action ended the fighting on November 6. The Canal remained closed until March 1957 when it reopened under Egyptian management.

Bill Dudman's Far East Flying Training School continued to fulfil a worthy need. His Link Trainer A13/28 proved a signal success. Often I worked in its claustrophobic sauna-like entrails under the indifferent guidance of Captain Tony *Pontius the Pilot* Rignall – a Cathay colleague. Each of Tony's debriefings was an anti-climax of brevity. I never learned if he thought me efficient or beyond improvement. I suspect the latter for he seemed relieved when I departed – allowing him to *wash his hands!*

The Department kept airport work to a minimum. The main addition was a VIP lounge decorated and furnished in contemporary style. Mr Horace Kadoorie, OBE, donated a carpet, locally woven, carrying the Colony's Coat-of-Arms. On November 18, Haile Selassie, Emperor of Ethiopia, was the first to use the facilities.

Several staff appointments strengthened the Department's staff albeit the loss of a dedicated man. Mr G. S. R. *George* Cannon, Chief Signals Officer, resigned after serving nine years. As usual other splendid men waited an opportunity to show their mettle. Phil Wood and R. G. *Reg* Heron both moved up a notch in the Signals Division.

Mr J. H. D. Bell, Assistant Airport Fire Officer, took over when Steve Henderson, Airport Fire Officer, enjoyed a vacation. Mr R. K. K. Yuen competently handled the duties of Assistant Airport Fire Officer.

The two unfilled Briefing Office posts brought Mr R. J. *Ron* Capern in mid-April and Mr J. T. *Trev* Thorpe in early August. The vacant Air Traffic Control Officer Grade II post attracted Mr D. Falgate DFC, in May.

The total establishment of the Department stood at 18 expatriates and 249 locally domiciled officers. This showed an increase of four officers over the previous year.

Among this last group was 20-year-old Peter Lok. Peter joined as a Traffic Control Officer Cadet. He would become the first Chinese to hold the office of Director of Civil Aviation.

1957

In the space of five weeks the airport authorities faced two civil plane emergencies. Each had the potential for disaster.

On the last day of 1956 a Thai Airways DC-4 advised the Tower of a total loss of hydraulics. The plane would have to make a landing without flaps, the undercarriage lowered by *free-fall*, and emergency braking used. The airport came to full alert with a FEFTS training plane ordered to land immediately.

The DC-4 came into sight over Stonecutters Island with wheels extended. As the pilot lined up on Runway 13 he applied full power and thundered through Lie Yue Mun Pass. The pilot told the Tower he suspected the port undercarriage had not locked safely. He advised he would climb to 4000 feet then dive to lock the wheel down *pulling G force*. His plan was a success.

The pilot made an excellent landing but emergency braking burst all four tyres. HAEC engineers *pinned* the undercarriage and after changing the wheels towed the plane away.

On 5 February, an Air Laos passenger DC-3 left Kai Tak. About 20 minutes into the flight the pilot reported a severe fire in the port engine and was returning. The crew followed the emergency drill – as the prop feathered they used the CO_2 charge. The flames

KAI TAK AIRPORT MARKS TIME – 1956-1957

resisted for a moment then went out. The plane landed on one engine. An inspection showed the engine a ruined mess with extensive scorching around the oil tank . . .!

In both incidents the crews showed their professionalism – nobody suffered a scratch.

On March 1, Thomas Russell Thomson joined the Department of Civil Aviation as Airport Commandant. He had a RAF background in East Africa and was Chief of Kenyan Air Navigational Services from 1952 to 1957. He replaced Mr Muspratt-Williams as Director on August 28, 1966. Mr Thomson, OBE, went on pre-retirement leave on May 2, 1973.

In late April, Cathay's DC-4 (VR-HFF) completed her HAEC overhaul. From February to May a dry-chartered DC-4 from Korean National Airways flew its schedules. My log book records my first flight on HL-108 was April 22 – my final flight in her was 4 May.

Saturday, April 27, North West Airlines proudly showed the first DC-7C to land at Kai Tak. A large crowd thronged the viewing enclosure at the Terminal Building.

The jet-prop Vickers Viscount 760 made its maiden flight early in December 1956. Her power came from a Rolls-Royce Dart gas turbine engine that drove a propeller. Each engine developed 1,780 equivalent horse-power on take-off. The plane seated 44 passengers and cruised at 325 mph at 20,000 feet and had a range of 2,250 miles. She was a superb piece of machinery even with a price tag of £350,000 Sterling.

On 10 February, the first (VR-HFI) touched down at Kai Tak with a second (VR-HFJ) following on 8 March. The planes arrived to considerable public interest – they heralded the remodelled Hong Kong Airways (HKA).

The Chief Pilot was Walter Burman. His support came from Captains John Fawdon and David Lampard – a long-time Hong Kong aviation identity. The First Officers were John Muir and Neville Hall. Nev Hall would make his mark in Cathay Pacific Airways.

The Viscount's introduction broke trip records between several cities. The most impressive was Captain Lampard's flight from Hong Kong to Seoul. *Dave* covered the 1,600 miles in five hours 20 minutes at an average speed of 300 miles-per-hour. Normal scheduled time for the flight was nine hours.

Cathay Pacific found no joy in their return. They considered BOAC and Jardine Matheson & Company Limited had formed a Regional Company under the *cloak* of HKA. Their argument – the paid-up ordinary capital of HKA appeared to be only HK$3,200,000 subscribed equally by BOAC and HKA. The purchase of the two Viscounts must have come entirely from BOAC coffers!

APRIL 27, 1957
Northwest Orient Airlines displays a Douglas DC-7C, its newest plane at Kai Tak Airport. (Photo: Leon Callaghan)

AIRPORT OF THE NINE DRAGONS, KAI TAK, KOWLOON

With Hong Kong Airways reactivating its franchises North West Airlines (NWA) began making waves. NWA showed unwillingness to cancel the 1951 arrangement where it operated between Taipei and Tokyo under HKA colours. The Hong Kong Government decided the arrangement was a commercial one between the two companies and instructed NWA to withdraw.

In July an irritated Mr Bensceter, vice-president for NWA in the Far East, approached Cathay Pacific. His suggestion was to permit him to hang a Cathay charter plate on his DC-6B aircraft between Manila and Hong Kong, giving him a through service from the States. Cathay's violent criticism of HKA when they played the same game between Taipei and Hong Kong would not allow them to do the same between Manila and Hong Kong. The plans of North West Airlines came to nothing.

Then Civil Air Transport (CAT) tried its hand at the franchise intrigue. The Company submitted an application to play the old HKA game between Taipei and Hong Kong. Their hidden agenda was an extension to the Hong Kong – Bangkok route. The Hong Kong Licensing Committee turned down their application.

With *Merdeka* (Independence), BOAC bought a controlling interest in Malayan Airways (MAL). Cathay saw this as an additional danger to its regional trades and realised the choice of future aircraft was a vital priority.

Therefore, Cathay's Captain Ken Steele, Captain Dave Smith and Engineering Director Jack Gething went to London. There they joined Bill Knowles the Butterfield & Swire (B&S) Managing Director who was on leave. They carried out trials on the de Havilland Comet 1VB and assessed the future Vickers Vanguard. Cathay decided that no British built aeroplane suited their trade but the superb Lockheed Electra L188, costing HK$11,546,657, fulfilled every requirement. In April 1959, VR-HFO entered CX service and in June VR-HFN joined her.

Meanwhile, Jardines continued to make full use of their nuisance value by harassing Cathay to join in a Regional Company. Cathay's Managing Director *Bill* Knowles rejected this move as *incipient suicide.*

At the spring 1958 Annual General Meeting, BOAC's accounts showed losses of over half-a-million pounds for their associated and subsidiary companies. In respect of Hong Kong Airways its loss was £167,000 Sterling. These losses perturbed the Board of BOAC who decided their Regional Companies should be managed locally and operate with outside finance. BOAC would retain as much influence as possible by retaining a seat on their respective Boards.

BOAC's Lord Rennell found his corporate machinations matched by the guile of *Jock* Swire. In July 1958 he approached Swire with the plan that BOAC would buy the Jardine portion of Hong Kong Airways. Then merge Hong Kong Airways with Cathay and take a substantial shareholding themselves. He asked if Cathay would buy HKA with payment by a share issue to BOAC. Swire told Lord Rennell that Cathay considered HKA *not only worthless but a liability*, but agreed to consider the matter.

Lord Rennell left London for a tour of the Far East in October 1958. *Jock* Swire decided to be in Hong Kong during his Lordship's visit. This was a wise move for in the relaxed atmosphere they agreed. They returned to London and signed a Letter of Intent that did not include the Viscounts and that BOAC assumed responsibility for the HKA staff.

With this agreement Cathay formed a new Company *Cathay Holdings Limited*. This called for a complicated share manipulation. *Holdings* bought the current Cathay from the existing shareholders giving them one share in *Holdings* for every Cathay share. Cathay then made a bonus issue of 1,500 shares to *Holdings* and bought the entire share capital of HKA from BOAC with Cathay ordinary shares.

Meanwhile *Jock* Swire received a letter from Mr Hugh Barton, Chairman of Jardines. His letter proposed he offer Jardines a token holding and a seat on its Board. Barton further undertook that after three years Jardines would resign from the Board and sell back the shares to *Holdings* at the same price, if so requested. After discussion with Lord Rennell, Swire offered Jardines 500 shares at HK$167 per HK$100 share and a seat on the B&S Board on the stipulations given in Barton's letter.

To give a smooth hand-over Cathay also undertook to manage HKA for the account of BOAC from February 1, 1959, until 30 June, on a flat fee basis. With the expected arrival of the Cathay Electras this made good sense. The astute Swire also had nullified the possibility of HKA and Malayan Airways forming an alliance – a risk Cathay could not afford to take!

Jock Swire's guile had retained the Cathay name, kept the Company under Butterfield & Swire control, and eliminated its regional competitor. This ended *the Battle of Hong Kong Airways* – a battle that had lasted for eight years.

Not all the intrigue radiated from board-rooms. On April 24, the front page of the *South China Morning Post* told a stirring tale.

DARING RESCUE REVEALED
Americans Fly Into China To Save Boy
EIGHT-HOUR ADVENTURE IN HUNAN PROVINCE
PLANNED IN H.K.

American Henry Peter Bush was a pilot on leave from the Government-owned Venezuelan Airline, Linea Aeropostal Venezolana. The report described him as a 42-year-old mild-spoken greying man with 19 years' flying experience. Captain Bush told the *Post* how he and another American flew deep into Red China's Hunan Province and rescued a 12-year-old boy.

The other American, who he refused to identify, was in Phnom Penh, Cambodia, when a well-dressed Chinese offered him US$10,000 to fly a rescue mission. He produced a plane ticket to Hong Kong and hotel reservations. If the project interested the American further details waited him in a certain Chinese restaurant near Kai Tak Airport. The American took the ticket and went!

In the negotiations a beautiful Chinese girl was the intermediary. She impressed the American with her sincerity. Returning to his hotel he bumped into Henry Bush, a long-time friend. The American took Bush to meet the girl who repeated how a servant kidnapped a boy as the Red Army overran the country. How for six years the father had paid the kidnappers monthly sums of money. She said the servant held the boy near an abandoned air-strip 350 miles North of Macau. Bush could barely conceal his scepticism but, like his companion, the girl's sincerity swayed him.

The following day she produced a detailed flight plan with maps and a comprehensive weather report. She accompanied the two men to Macau, took them to a Catalina bobbing off the Portuguese Enclave, and the men took-off at dawn.

The rest of the story is something of an anti-climax. Hugging the terrain they landed on the strip, took the boy aboard, and returned to Portuguese waters where a Chinese junk took the boy to Hong Kong. The girl, waiting in another junk, returned them to Macau where they all left with correct departure visas.

The Macau Government quickly denied that any plane had used Portuguese territory that day. MATCO, who operated Catalinas, through Captain Len Cosgrove, denied any involvement. The only other Catalina in the region belonged to the Netherlands-New Guinea Petroleum Company – a Shell associate. It was on jacks in the HAEC workshop! Captain Bush, to support his story, produced his passport that showed a Macau entry and exit visa for the period involved.

AIRPORT OF THE NINE DRAGONS, KAI TAK, KOWLOON

The SCMP's follow-up made other revelations. A Briton said he had accompanied Henry Bush. Mike Sullivan, a former British prize-fighter and prisoner-of-war of the Japanese, made his home in Thailand after the war. He married a Thai, and was an authority on ancient ruins in that part of the world. He was the then manager for Thai Airways sales.

Both men stated they refused the cash but accepted gold watches from a man they presumed was the boy's father – whose identity they never learned. Bush also stated he accepted a sapphire ring and some boxes and art objects. Bush refused the cash, the most negotiable of possessions, because he didn't want to get into any disputes with *Uncle Sam* and anyhow it was a *mission of mercy*. Yet, those other gifts would have attracted greater attention from the United States' authorities.

A story as bizarre as this has to be true!

CHAPTER 17

THE MIRACLE STRIP

*Those who follow the world must hurry
their footsteps. Wei Ying-Wu.*

The vibrancy of post-war Hong Kong attracted world attention. Its low flat-rate of income tax, an untapped source of cheap labour, and a lack of draconian regulations interested overseas companies.

The Western romanticism for things Eastern brought increased tourism. To live and breathe, even for a short time, the customs of an ancient land, and the closeness of the curtain of bamboo, caused exhilaration. Finally, the vast range of discounted, duty-free, name-brand products solved their holiday decision!

The problem was how to get the *time-strapped traveller* there. The ponderous ship travel of yesteryear did not fit the bustling era. The larger planes with increased passenger loading and the consequent reduction in fares solved the problem – but bigger planes needed bigger operational areas.

The existing Kai Tak Airport, surrounded by rugged terrain, prevented any worthwhile land expansions. Yet, only quick action would save Hong Kong from backwater obscurity. The Hong Kong Government had the courage to make far-sighted decisions.

* * *

The expansion limitations of Kai Tak Airport forced the RAF to seek a larger base for its four-engined planes. In September 1945, they selected a site in the Ping Shan Valley, New Territories. This site ultimately evolved into Sek Kong.

This RAF activity interested the Ministry of Civil Aviation, London. In February 1946, Ministry aerodrome surveyors checked the RAF site and found it did not meet civil requirements. A mountain-wave from the Colony's highest peak, Tai Mo Shan, affected the site.

The surveyors then proposed a civil site at Deep Bay between the villages of Lau Fau Shan and Mong Tseng Wai. Their survey showed a major airport conforming to international standards could be built there. Yet the development would be expensive, for it demolished some small coastal hills and reclaimed a section of shallow bay. The prime advantage was the unrestricted approaches. Other than the cost the prime disadvantage was the distance from the centre of population. Thirty miles of indifferent roads was a prime consideration.

The Hong Kong Government sought a site more centrally placed. Several prospects including Stanley Bay came into contention but were abandoned in favour of Stonecutter's Island in the western harbour. The approaches were clear and the location central. The Ministry's surveyors rejected this site because of development costs and that the existing installations would attract heavy compensation.

In late 1949 the United Kingdom Government offered a loan of HK$48 millions towards an airport construction that met ICAO standards. Their offer suggested further consideration for the Deep Bay site. The Hong Kong Government commissioned an engineering survey on Deep Bay that included some minor clearing. The reported costing proved beyond the means of the Government – they abandoned Deep Bay in 1950. With no other satisfactory site the Government decided to develop Kai Tak Airport.

In 1951, at the Government's invitation, the Ministry sent a technical mission to make proposals for upgrading Kai Tak to international standards. On June 14, 1951, the mission presented the then notable, but now mainly forgotten, *Broadbent Report*. In the broadest terms it proposed a new main runway bearing 145°/325° true, beginning roughly at the Runway 13 turning pad. It also recommended an extension towards the west for Runway 07/25. Mr R. Broadbent's report made no effort to minimise the restrictive nature of the proposals but it was the best compromise under the circumstances.

The Hong Kong Government and the Ministry of Civil Aviation accepted the Report in principle. In July 1952, the Government appointed Scott & Wilson, Kirkpatrick & Partners, consulting engineers of London. Their brief – to examine the proposed development and report on the construction problems involved.

In August they submitted findings that contained several minor modifications to the Broadbent Report. The Government and Ministry saw their reasoning and again accepted the presentation. The following month the Government instructed their consultant engineers to provide details of the work with an estimate of costs.

The consultants advised that any Kai Tak land the development freed had an equity far exceeding reclaimed land. Another minor cost reduction seemed possible when the plane builders and BOAC updated criterion for future jet transport operations. The Department realised they had over-estimated the runway length required. The Government, basking in these small gains, came down to earth with a thud. The consultants' investigative boring revealed extensive weakness in the runways. They found loosely compacted foundations – legacy of the POW builders. The consultants concluded that a new reclamation, properly compacted with selected fill, would not only be cheaper but stronger, than *repairing* existing facilities.

This resolved the Department to pursue a one-runway idea. They did this by swinging Broadbent's proposition to an orientation of 135°/315° sited entirely on reclaimed land in Kowloon Bay. The scheme allowed unfettered operation through Lei Yue Mun Pass and a curved flight technique from the opposite direction.

Approaching Runway 13 from the west a speed limit of 120 knots led into a 40° banked turn to the right. The turn had a radius of 5,090 feet followed by a straight run of 3,000 feet to the touchdown threshold. The Department had adopted the procedure from the ICAO visual approach funnel procedure for large aircraft. If airline operators would accept this curved idea, and minor diversions or delays for adverse cross-winds (20 knots), the idea seemed a reasonable compromise.

Meanwhile, the Deputy Operations Manager of BOAC visited the Colony to make an on-sight inspection. Back in England he prepared a mockup of the curved procedure at

THE MIRACLE STRIP

Blackbushe Airport and flew trials with Britannias and Comets. His favourable report brought a fillip to the stressed Director of Civil Aviation.

The initial proposals for the single-runway layout, that became *Phase 1 of Scheme D*, made provision for a 9,000-foot runway. The length suited the future jets flying long-hauls. The reclaimed promontory, 1,000 foot wide, included a parallel taxiway with a 500-foot clearance between the runway centre line and taxiway. The projected 307 reclaimed acres required 17 million cubic yards of dredging, at an average depth of 24 feet. The three million cubic yards of fill would come from hill excavation. To preserve the new runway's proposed curved operational gradient (1 in 40) some high ground and buildings faced demolition.

These were three blocks of flats owned by the Hongkong & Shanghai Bank. The ten-storey buildings, built to quarter its expanding staff, had ultra-modern facilities. There was a possibility of moving the buildings to another location but the Bank vetoed the idea. The Government agreed to demolish them and rebuild on a site of mutual agreement.

Several apartments, temporarily not required by the *Honkers and Shankers*, quartered Department of Civil Aviation staff. They found themselves evicted with the Bank's personnel – perhaps a little poetic justice!

The outcome had a different result – they removed the four top storeys of each block, preserving the flight gradient. This seemed a satisfactory compromise, but not to the occupants.

The noise generated by planes crossing Kowloon is an irritant to this day. In 1994, Peter Lok, the then Director of Civil Aviation, resolved to spend a night beneath the flight path. The next morning he appeared in his office with red sunken eyes. Had the noise pollution kept him awake? No! His lack of sleep resulted from a continuous stream of phone calls and door knocking from reporters. One with greater determination used a cherry-picker to check *he was at home*.

The runway, 17 feet higher than the mean high-water level, required 6,600 yards of sea wall to contain the fill. The estimates included a new terminal area, a RAF dispersal area, and ancillary works to support the new airport.

In June 1953 the consultants submitted their Report and a costing estimate of HK$140 million combined Civil and RAF requirements. The consultants determined the project would require five years to complete.

When the Government studied the Report they added additional items. This raised the capital expenditure to HK$149 million – or HK$136 million excluding RAF requirements. These amounts fell beyond the Government's financial capacity and it directed the Department to re-examine the scheme to cut costs.

The Government appointed an Inter-Departmental Committee, charging it to examine *Scheme D's* financial and economic implications. The Committee appraised the likely commercial benefits would exceed the capital expenditure and recurrent costs. They also realised any worthwhile cost reduction must come from reducing the area of reclamation. The Chairman instructed the consultants to prepare estimates for a modified scheme. The consultants suggested a 7,200-foot runway with a promontory width of 600 feet and a reduced terminal area – costed at HK$88 million. It would require four years to complete. Although the proposals for a regional airport resulted in a substantial cost reduction it left the Colony with two serious limitations. The shortened runway load-limited future jet transports – then called the *Lumbo*. The lost of a separate taxiway curtailed the number of operations.

In late September Mr Muspratt-Williams, the Director of Civil Aviation, flew to London. He discussed with the Ministry of Transport and Civil Aviation, Colonial Office, Air

AIRPORT OF THE NINE DRAGONS, KAI TAK, KOWLOON

Ministry, BOAC and aircraft manufacturers the suggested modifications. His presentation aroused polite enthusiasm, but he left London with less than unanimous support.

In October the Inter-Departmental Committee submitted its Report to the Government. It recommended the *modified Scheme D* for Kai Tak's development. It also recommended the Government accept the British interest-free loan of HK$48 million. Later discussions on the promontory width and RAF requirements raised the costing to HK$97 million.

On June 16, 1954, the Hong Kong Legislative Council met under the Presidency of His Excellency The Governor, Sir Alexander William George Herder Grantham, GCMG. The Official Report of Proceedings minuted the following resolution presented by The Honourable Mr Robert Brown Black, CMG, OBE, the Colonial Secretary:

> *That Council approve the scheme for the development of Kai Tak airport estimated to cost HK$96,750,000 and based on the construction of a single runway and overrun 7,500 feet long and 700 feet in width resting upon a reclamation of Kowloon Bay.*

Mr Black asked the hon. Members to make a textual amendment to the third-last word – of should read in. *We do not propose to reclaim the whole of Kowloon Bay.* Mr Black's attempt at whimsy had been prophetic. Kowloon Bay now has almost fallen to the reclaimer.

The Colonial Secretary then summarised the history of the project and the Colony's expectations from the capital outlay. The modified *Scheme D* had reduced the cost by nearly HK$40 million from that originally prepared by Scott & Wilson, Kirkpatrick & Partners. The saving came from reducing the promontory width and substituting two loops to replace the parallel taxiway. One loop was at the south-east end of the runway and the other at the half-way point. The loops allowed $9\frac{1}{2}$ movements an hour – an acceptable compromise for continuous day-night operation.

The Honourable Theodore Louis Bowring, OBE, Director of Public Works, seconded the Resolution. He went on to give some engineering aspects of the project.

The runway reclamation would contain 11 million cubic yards of fill stabilised by three miles of sea walls. To reach solid foundation dredges would remove two million cubic yards of silt – earmarked for the Kung Tong reclamation. The fill was a combination of sand and decomposed granite. The land excavations would provide this granite – also boulders, split into pitching blocks – for the sea walls. The distinction of boulder stone is its working reliability – it splits more evenly than bed-rock.

The sand would come from Hung Hom Bay where a tidal sweep of 10 knots prevents the accumulation of silt. The main source of material would come from the hills around Kowloon but the *Sacred Hill*, supporting a boulder weighing over 1,000 tons, would provide the remainder.

Mr. Bowring asked the hon. Members to imagine the material spread over the entire area of the Hong Kong Cricket Club ground forming a pile 300 feet higher than the Peak. While the 300,000 square yards of concrete or bituminous paving, stressed to 400,000lbs, equated to twice the area of the roadways around the New Territories.

The project received the unanimous support of the hon. Members and the necessary financial provisions made.

There would be periods, mid-morning and mid-afternoon, when arrivals and departures would be greater than the mean. Within these time frames overloading the system was a certainty. A separate taxiway would not be the whole remedy but helpful in minimising that overload. Also, the eastern sea wall was a waste of capital expenditure if the Government had a taxiway forced on it later.

After consideration the Legislative Council realised a separate taxiway was a necessity not a luxury. They approved this addition in February 1955. The Government called for tenders on June 30, 1955 – Scott & Wilson, Kirkpatrick & Partners prepared the contracts.

The modified promontory had a length of 8,340 feet and a width of 795 feet covering an area of 150 acres. It supported a 7,200-foot paved runway, with prepared over-runs – 300 feet at the southern end and 800 feet at the northern end. A 60-foot-wide taxiway parallelled the runway, with 365 feet between the centre lines of the runway and taxiway. The ICAO ideal was 500 feet! Throughout the work the existing airport would continue in full use.

The terminal area covered nine acres of reclamation. Maintenance and parking areas complemented the terminal building designed for 100 per cent on-going expansion without interrupting services. The initial flow control provided for 10 movements an hour for planes of 100 passenger capacity with catering for those in transit. The baggage, freight and mail received similar consideration.

The recoupment of some capital expenditure remained a priority. The terminal design and the RAF's improved land usage made substantial savings inside the old airport's perimeter. These 160 acres eventually sold to private enterprise with the yield returned to consolidated revenue.

The reduced length of the runway attracted criticism. At a regional meeting of ICAO in 1955 some airline operators took the Hong Kong delegation to task. The operators claimed they needed a minimum runway of 10,000 feet for their future aircraft. The delegates present contested these views. They reminded the operators that *each extra 1000 feet of runway cost an additional HK$10 million* – capital expenditure beyond their current resources. There could be no runway extension in the short term!

The delegates raised the proposition that modern planes generally require less length for landing than for take-off. They would support extending the landward end of the runway by 1,140 feet to a point 60 feet short of the first elevated lamp in the approach lighting. For other than landings from the north-west the extension would increase operational capability. Landings from the north-west followed a 1-in-40 gradient, with the threshold clearly marked.

At the seaward end the over-run increased from 200 to 300 feet. To increase safety over shipping and sea wall the touch-down threshold was 260 feet up the runway.

These changes provided the following lengths of paved runway:
Towards the south-east (Runway 13):
Take-off 8,340 ft
Landing 7,200 ft
Towards the north-west (Runway 31):
Take-off 8,340 ft
Landing 8,080 ft

The delegates conceded the operators faced restricted payloads for maximum-range operations. Yet the proposed revisions gave sufficient payload for the stage-lengths generally used by the then large jet airliners.

In August 1955, the Government awarded the contract to the Societe Francaise D'Enterprises De Draggage et de Travaux Publics. The French firm sub-contracted several major segments to Gammon (Malaya) Limited.

The contractors took six weeks to organise their equipment and personnel. This was a formidable achievement. They had two large bucket dredgers and a floating crane towed from France. From the United States came a grab-dredger and two small cutter-suction dredgers, also engines for the tugs and bucket dredgers. The excavators, bulldozers and other plant components came from Singapore. The United Kingdom supplied a fleet of tipping lorries – Hong Kong workmen fabricated their bodies. While others built nine tugs, 10 barges and four pontoons took shape in the Hong Kong dockyards. Finally, they purchased an additional floating crane and three flat-top barges in the Colony.

AIRPORT OF THE NINE DRAGONS, KAI TAK, KOWLOON

Gammon had the task of positioning the sea wall pitching blocks, the site drainage and runway construction. Its sub-contract involved excavating several sites and stabilising the rocky outcrop we now call the *Checker-Board*. Gammon also constructed a fenced-off access route from the excavation sites through bustling Kowloon City to the reclamation. This included two vehicular bridges to relieve the traffic congestion resulting from their *switch-back* road.

In January 1956, reclamation began at the south-west corner of the airport. In March, the bucket dredging sand in Hung Hom Bay and the other dredging silt in Kowloon Bay exceeded a combined output of 200,000 cubic yards each week. Gammon averaged 2,000 lorry-loads of decomposed granite fill per day. Their workmen reduced the Sung Stone to a slab bearing the original inscription.

The once *Sacred Hill* site, now flat and dusty, became the distribution point for the sea wall's 80,000 pitching blocks. Workmen quarrying the Kowloon Hills averaged 375 blocks each day. The larger two-ton blocks formed the promontory's western wall and the one-ton blocks the eastern. The sea wall grew about 80 feet a day.

Mr A. W. C. Villiers, the project's Chief Resident Engineer, controlled his 3,000 workers from an office near the reclamation. Scott & Wilson, Kirkpatrick & Partners stayed in close contact with Villiers through Wilson's son. Gordon was a keen cricketer – we met in the *middle* of the Kowloon Cricket Club. He always made the time to show me around the development. At the quarry face, one day, he arranged I *ride the switch-back* – it terrified me!

On March 13, 1957, Mr Villiers showed Governor Sir Alexander Grantham, GCMG, around the Kai Tak Airport Development Scheme. Sir Alexander's undisguised enthusiasm boosted the spirit of the people working on the scheme. Sadly, he would not do the opening ceremony expected about August 28, 1958, the contract's completion date. This honour would go to his successor – his erstwhile Colonial Secretary.

The most charitable word to describe the 1957 weather would be shrewish. The rainfall for May exceeded 35 inches, triple the month's average. *Dinger* Bell's Royal Observatory on Mount Elgin recorded the month had only eight days free of rain. The downpours, from the 17th to the 22nd, brought widespread flooding, landslides, and havoc to the runway reclamation. The rainfall recorded at Beacon Hill, one of Kowloon's *Nine Dragons*, showed the rain's irregularity. Beacon Hill, just four miles from the Observatory and a stone's throw from Kai Tak, received 28.21 inches on the 21st – five times that recorded at the Observatory on the same day. The men working the reclamation toiled manfully through these disagreeable times.

The fine weather over the following three months allowed a substantial increase in dredging. Typhoon *Gloria* shattered this tranquillity when, on September 22, she stormed out of the China Sea. For 14 hours the Observatory's equipment recorded gale-force winds. The passage of her *eye*, 30 miles to the south, brought hurricane winds that hammered the Colony for over an hour. The gust-peak of 101 knots tore ships from their moorings, driving them ashore.

The Airport Fire Service maintained patrols throughout that terrible night. They kept a fire check on several planes that slammed into others when their tie-down ropes had broken. The RAF fire-tenders helped them warily circle two multi-engined Service planes that were riding out the typhoon with engines running. The object – to keep the plane headed into the wind – but these gusts lacked any set direction. It was a dangerous operation.

The dawn showed nine planes badly damaged and the reclamation severely battered. Yet, the vital dredgers had survived *Gloria's* wrath.

In November 1957, Gordon Wilson phoned saying I should come to the site. I found him buzzing around an ancient cannon dredged from the mud of Kowloon Bay.

THE MIRACLE STRIP

At year's end the promontory runway, and its taxiway, had a sealing of asphalt. The shoulder areas had a good grass coverage from turf taken from the old airport.

Ancillary work had kept apace with the reclamation. The contractors had positioned the runway lights, the fire mains and installed the surface drainage.

The Airport Progress Committee and the Government approved other related components.

Eric Cumine and Company produced working drawings and specification for the Airport Fire Station and offered the tender in January 1958. The contract went to Yick Lee and Company. The Government chose the same company to construct the temporary control tower – both projects to be completed by August 1958.

A complicated work programme to divert the main nullah to an open-cut, and partially realign the Clear Water Bay Road, fell to the Union Construction Company. Their contract called for three bridges, one to take airport traffic to and from the main parking and aircraft areas, the second to provide passage, across the new open-cut nullah, from runway to HAEC maintenance, and the RAF station and the third to carry public traffic on the realigned Clear Water Bay Road. I remember, with no affection, the chaos that existed on that *stretch of confusion*.

The Department's heavy planning programme had affected several routine matters. This prompted the transfer of an Air Traffic Control Officer Grade II to Headquarters. His replacement was Mr W. V. Clarke, late of the DCA, East Africa High Commission. This was a welcome appointment but still left the Department one equivalent rank short. John Kingsley Saunders accepted this vacancy on January 9, 1958. John, born in 1923, had a Royal Air Force background. He went on to become Acting Deputy Director in 1974 and retired four years later.

This was the year Hong Kong recorded its first milestone towards aviation maturity. The one-and-a-half-mile miracle strip, won at great expense from the sea, was a reality. Careful planning had gone into its opening, but fate orchestrated the proceedings.

John Wallace, who I knew well, and Timothy Birch, who I knew slightly, of Radio Hong Kong, produced a splendid programme titled *Thirteen Thirty-one*. The title alluded to the compass bearing of the new Kai Tak runway. The programme included snippets from *Hammy* Hamilton, the Airport Manager, and from Captain Len Crosgrove, then flying the MATCO Catalina. Later we heard from John Henry and cricketing mate Gordon Wilson, both of Scott & Wilson, Kirkpatrick & Partners, the consultant engineers. Mr Gandy, speaking for the Chief Resident Engineer, concluded with a résumé of how they solved the reclamation's problems.

Major Harry Stanley, to become the father of the Hongkong Tourist Association, arrived in Hong Kong on 3 March. He found the Colony boasted but three worthwhile hotels, the *Gloucester, Peninsula* and *Miramar*. The Major operated from behind *two half-moon windows* on the mezzanine floor of the *Pen*. He retired in 1972 and returned to England.

Meanwhile, several minor events retained media interest in aviation matters. On April 7, 1958, a Taiwanese (Formosa) military plane force-landed at Kai Tak. The authorities quickly surrounded the sinister black Nationalist P4Y medium bomber and took the crew to the airport's VIP room as a protective measure. Later the commander told reporters his plane developed fuel problems while engaged on a routine patrol. His patrol extended from the southern tip of Taiwan to the Communist-held meteorology station on Pratas Island, in the South China Sea. He was at the turning point of his patrol when his problems occurred and with Kai Tak nearest he decided to land there. HAEC rectified the trouble and the plane and the 10 crew members returned to base.

On 26 May a former student of the Far East Flying Training School casually strolled out to a Stinson L-5. He calmly started VR-HFO's engine, obtained permission to taxi and off

AIRPORT OF THE NINE DRAGONS, KAI TAK, KOWLOON

he went *into the wild blue yonder*. After an exhilarating two-hour joy ride he returned to Kai Tak and into the arms of the waiting police. It seemed he forgot to get permission to fly!

The following month Captain Alex Wales brought Cathay Pacific's DC-6B on to Kai Tak with a perfect landing. Other members of the crew were Captain John Carrington, co-pilot, Chief Flight Engineer Bob Smith, Flight Engineer Leo Brennan, and one other. The delivery flight from Santa Monica had taken 54 flying hours, making stops at Honolulu, Wake Island, Guam and Manila. The arrival of this HK$6,736,860 piece of modern machinery was a heady event. I could hardly wait to get my hands on her! Yet, of greater interest to me was that other man. He was the Douglas Aircraft Company's renowned test pilot Bill Bridgeman. In 1951 he tested the *Skyrocket* and later became the *fastest man on earth* by shattering the speed and altitude records. He enjoyed telling of his test flight on the hush-hush *F-D-4*, a fighter that could climb to 50,000 feet in just over two minutes. And here was this famous pilot to teach me, and others, how to fly Cathay's latest asset. VR-HFG entered CX service June 22, 1958, becoming the property of Braathens on November 29, 1962.

On August 31, USAF C-54 (Skymaster) 0-72523, commanded by Captain J. A. Quillan, left Okinawa for Hong Kong. Approaching Kai Tak the skipper asked co-pilot Lieutenant J. A. Taylor to acknowledge his clearance to land on Runway 31. The C-54's right wheel struck the sea wall, the starboard undercarriage folded. The C-54 skidded 500 yards and shuttered to a stop at the intersection of the runways. The crew of five scrambled out seconds before the plane became an inferno. Later, a reporter asked Staff Sergeant James A. Austin if anyone had panicked. With a catching grin, the 24-year-old radio-operator replied – "Panic! Of course not. We are all United States Air Force men."

This accident forced the opening of the new runway 15 hours ahead of schedule. Although this upset the plans of the Department they were fortunate in having that choice. They had planned the last take-off on the old runway and the first landing on the new for Cathay's planes.

The first plane to land on the new runway was a US Navy Amphibian UF-1 Albatross. Lieutenant J. T. Burrell touched the pristine surface at 1420 hours. Peter Lok, the immediate past Director of Civil Aviation, remarks in his Foreword – *it loitered around for about four hours until everybody else holding had to divert*. The next to land was a civilian airliner commanded by Captain Manuel Conde. This Philippine Air Line plane, with 28 passengers from Manila, touched down at 1610 hours, almost two hours after the search-and-rescue amphibian.

Meanwhile, the race began for the honour of first take-off. Soon after the Albatross landed Cathay Pacific's DC-6 taxied out – a RAF *Venom* followed. As the airliner did its pre-flight checks Flight Lieutenant B. E. Forse got permission to take off and rolled at 1440 hours. The first civilian plane off was Cathay's DC-6 – five minutes after the *Venom*.

The morning of Friday, September 12 dawned with low clouds forming a waterfall effect over the *Nine Dragons*. Rain fell at frequent intervals and the wind gusted mischievously. Would the weather spoil the official opening of Hong Kong's aviation miracle? Fifty thousand spectators and 500 official guests decided it would not! Radio Hong Kong's John Wallace made a mistake by announcing the Governor's helicopter was in sight. This was the Government's other Widgeon making final checks of the runway. Then the Westland Widgeon carrying His Excellency Sir Robert Black, KCMG, OBE, Lady Black, Miss Barbara Black, and Captain J. Bunnell, the Governor's ADC, came into sight. Their pilot, struggling against 30-knot gusts, eased between two coloured poles. At 1730 hours the helicopter's nose severed a ribbon opening the runway, followed by the traditional salvo of firecrackers.

The Director of Civil Aviation, Mr Muspratt-Williams, and his daughter, Adine, greeted the Vice-Regal party. They escorted them to the dais in front of the Airport Fire Station. In his address, His Excellency praised those involved in the *imaginatively planned and construction processes* – he then opened the runway.

THE MIRACLE STRIP

Two green flares signalled Flight Lieutenant F. J. Barrett to lead No. 60 Squadron's Venoms into the air. Halfway into the take-off the rain pelted down. John Wallace's announcement of a passing shower stayed the crowd scrambling for shelter.

The FEFTS's Tiger Moth was to lead the civil contingent but the boisterous wind caused her scratching. This honour fell to a Cathay DC-3 that took off towards a gloomy Lei Yue Mun Pass, now framed by a glorious rainbow. The Cathay DC-6B followed, then a PanAm Boeing Stratocruiser. Two Super G Constellations, one from Air India and the other QANTAS, led a Hong Kong Airways Viscount 760. Following was a Canadian Pacific Air Lines' Britannia 314, the then quietest transport in service and called the *Whispering Giant*. The star of the show was a Comet 1V owned by BOAC, the first jet airliner to land at Kai Tak. With Group Captain John Cunningham, de Havilland's chief test pilot, in command the Vice-Regal party skimmed beneath the low overcast for a circuit of the Harbour.

The Comet 1V had come from England (Hatfield) with technical landings at Bombay and Bangkok – in one day – in daylight. G-APDA covered 7,925 miles in 18 hours 22 minutes with an actual flying time of 16 hours 16 minutes – 14 hours faster than the then scheduled service.

John *Cat's Eyes* Cunningham (a nick-name he loathed) finished World War II directing No. 11 Group, a night-fighter operation. Besides three DSOs and two DFCs he wore the American Silver Star.

The Band of the Hong Kong Police Force under the direction of Mr W. B. Foster, MBE, kept the guests entertained. That historic day closed when at 1945 hours they *Beat the Retreat*.

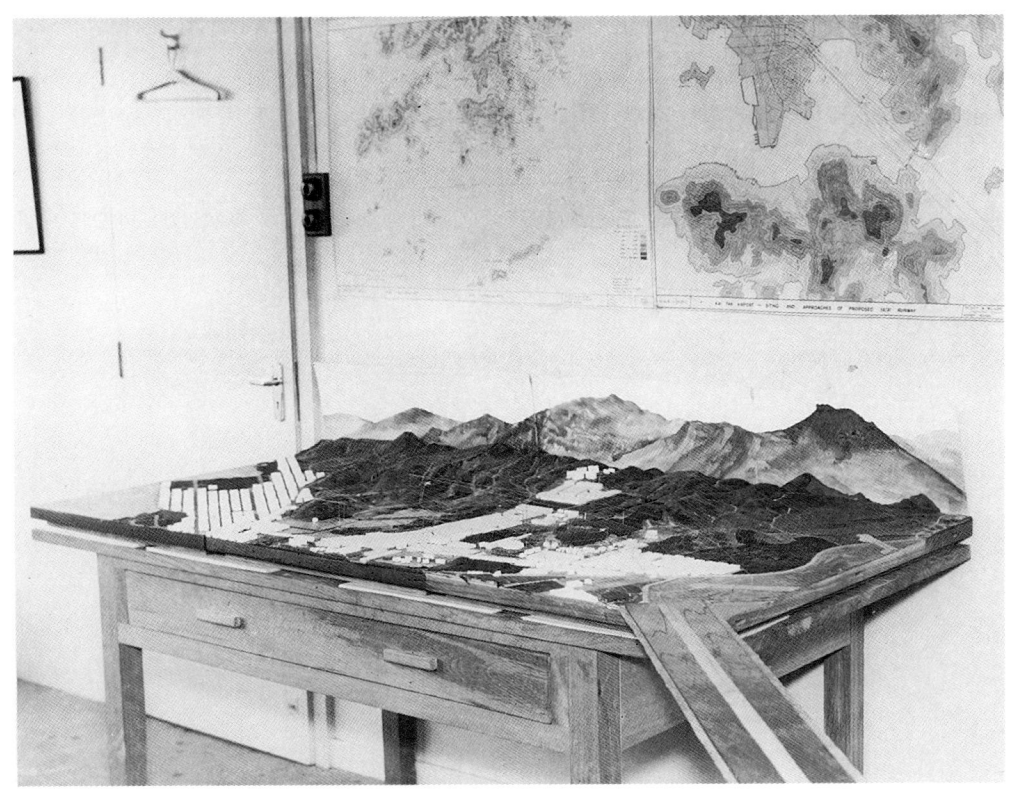

MOCK-UP OF PROPOSED RUNWAY 13/31
Model prepared by Scott & Wilson, Kirkpatrick & Partners, consulting engineers of London. View shows the north-west approach over Kowloon taken from south-east corner. Note the wall charts. (Photo: Henley Lo)

AIRPORT OF THE NINE DRAGONS, KAI TAK, KOWLOON

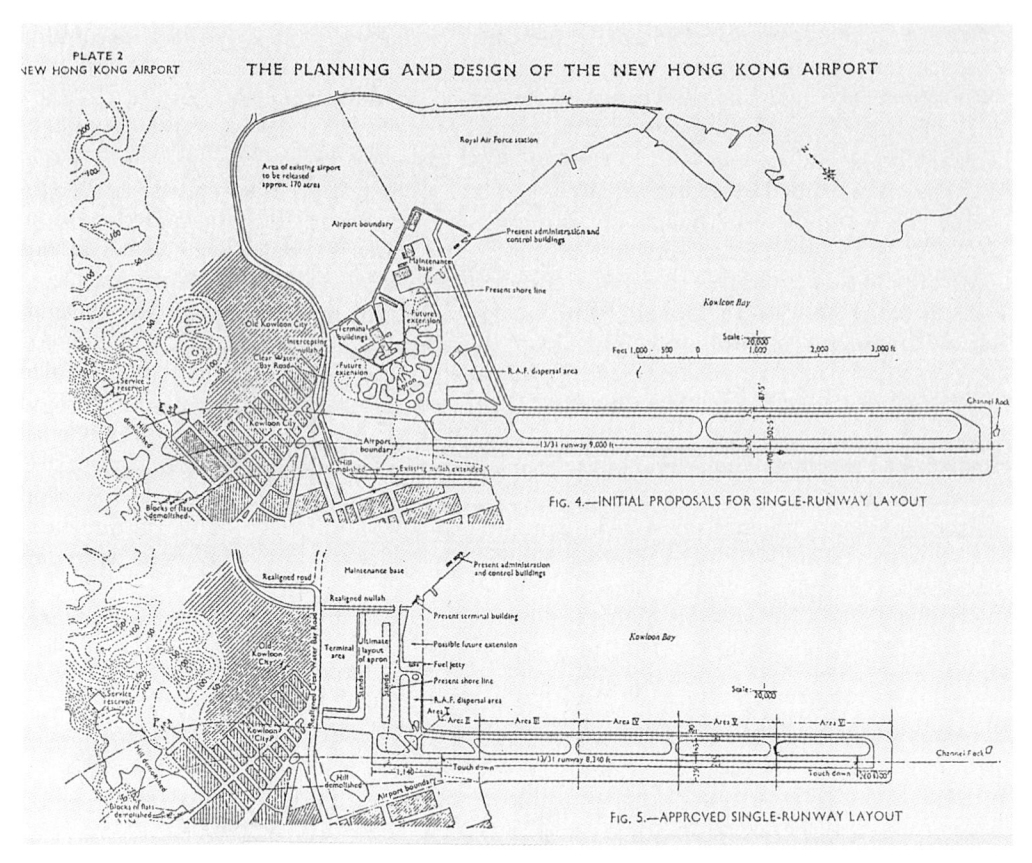

THE PLANNING & DESIGN OF THE NEW HONG KONG AIRPORT
The plates prepared by Scott & Wilson, Kirkpatrick & Partners, consulting engineers of London. The top plate shows the initial proposals for the single-runway layout. The bottom plate was the approved single-runway layout. (Drawings: Henley Lo)

KAI TAK AIRPORT DEVELOPMENT
This rare photograph shows the surveyor's notations of terrain and obstructions for demolition for a safe flight profile. This aspect, taken from water level in Kowloon Bay, views the proposed runway's centre line. (Photo: Henley Lo)

THE MIRACLE STRIP

KAI TAK AIRPORT DEVELOPMENT

View from the Kowloon Hills looking along the centre line of the proposed new runway. Photo was taken at an altitude of 300 feet and one mile from the proposed touch-down threshold. The inked addition shows the surveyor's overlay of the proposed reclamation. Note the remaining wall of the Kowloon Walled City, the centre line passing through the FEFTS, the Sacred Hill overlapping the right perimeter of the reclamation. Just off the left border is the Air Asia establishment. (Photo: Henley Lo)

PROGRESS OF THE RECLAMATION – 1 NOVEMBER, 1956

The Sacred Hill has almost disappeared. The small garden at the left middle border, containing the Sung Wong Toi stone, is being landscaped. (Photo: Noel Hitching, RAF)

AIRPORT OF THE NINE DRAGONS, KAI TAK, KOWLOON

THE SPECIAL ACCESS ROAD FROM KOWLOON HILLS – FEBRUARY 1956

Closed to all civilian traffic this road brought filling for the runway reclamation. The top photo looks west along Nga Tsin Wai Road with Kowloon City Market at right. The bump crossed Hau Wong Road. The bottom photo shows a truck tearing along the restricted road with a pedestrian overpass just ahead. A sharp right turn brought the truck into South Wall Road, another restricted road.

(Photos: Author)

THE MIRACLE STRIP

THE TERRACE OF THE SUNG DYNASTY EMPEROR
Workmen carefully drill the 1000-ton Sacred Stone. The characters are clearly discernible. The character portion was dressed and erected in a special garden near the airport. (Photo: Henley Lo)

THE SACRED HILL UNDER DEMOLITION – 1956
The area was used as a storage point for pitching blocks that formed the reclamation's sea wall perimeter. (Photo: Author)

AIRPORT OF THE NINE DRAGONS, KAI TAK, KOWLOON

PROGRESS – 27 DECEMBER. 1956

The reclamation is becoming more clearly defined.

(Photo: Noel Hitching, RAF)

PROGRESS – JUNE 1957

(Photo: Noel Hitching, RAF)

THE MIRACLE STRIP

PROGRESS – 7 SEPTEMBER 1957

(Photo: Noel Hitching, RAF)

PROGRESS OF THE NEW RUNWAY – MAY 1958

The new runway and parallel taxiway are curing before marking. The Airport Fire Station, the low flat group, right of the runway's threshold, is getting the finishing touches. The relocated FEFTS is further right of the Fire Station. The Fire Station and the FEFTS are on Sung Wong Toi Road.

(Photo: Fred Lillywhite, CAD)

AIRPORT OF THE NINE DRAGONS, KAI TAK, KOWLOON

THE ANCIENT CANNON
DREDGED FROM KOWLOON HARBOUR DURING BUILDING OF
THE KAI TAK RUNWAY – NOVEMBER 1957

The cannon was cast in the 4th Year of the Wing Lik Reign of the Ming Dynasty, 1649 A.D. A troubled time for the Emperor – the Manchu army had him in full retreat.

In 1975, the cannon had a permanent spot in the grounds of the Colonial Secretariat. It lay in the shadow of a huge gnarled tree that looked as old as its charge. The inscription:

Commissioned by Choi Governor of Waihoi and created Ting Hoi, General by Imperial Command – To, by Imperial Command appointed Governor General of Kwangtung and Kwangsi Provinces. Fan, General Officer Commanding Kwangtung and Guardian of the Imperial Heir. Colonel Siu Lei-Yan directed the casting for Ho Hing Cheung, Commander of the Ordinance Depot, Sixth Moon of the Fourth Year of Wing Lik. Weight 500 catties.   *Emperor.*

THE DREDGED CANNON – NOVEMBER 1975
The ancient cannon dredged from Kowloon Harbour during building of Kai Tak's runway.
(Photo: Henley Lo, Scott & Wilson, Kirkpatrick & Partners)

THE MIRACLE STRIP

THE FINISHED MIRACLE – 1958
(Photo: Fred Lillywhite)

FATE TAKES A HAND!

On August 31, 1958, USAF Skymaster 0-72523 wiped off the wheels on the sea wall of Runway 31. Sliding along the runway she stopped at the 07/25 intersection and burst into flames. There were no casualties but the Department was forced to open the new runway ahead of schedule.
(Photo: Fred Lillywhite, CAD)

AIRPORT OF THE NINE DRAGONS, KAI TAK, KOWLOON

THE OFFICIAL OPENING – 12 SEPTEMBER, 1958

The helicopter carrying His Excellency Sir Robert Black, KCMG, OBE, Lady Black and Miss Barbara Black eased into a gusty wind to sever a ribbon stretched between two barber poles. (Photo: Fred Lillywhite, CAD)

Sir Robert declaring the runway officially opened. The dais fronted the new Fire Station.

THE MIRACLE STRIP

AN HISTORIC MOMENT

A rain-spotted lens captures a vast crowd, ankle deep in water, cheering as Flight Lieutenant Barrett led three Venom planes into overcast skies. A line of commercial planes waited, on the sea wall, to take part in the ceremony. The FEFTS's Tiger Moth, scheduled to lead the fly-past, was grounded by the boisterous wind. That honour went to a Cathay Pacific Airways DC-3. Note the checked Tower at lower right corner – it was demolished when a permanent Tower was established atop the New Terminal Building in 1962.

(Photo: Carl Myatt, SCMP)

1959 – VIEW FROM 20,000 FEET

North of the Airport the Nine Dragons protect Kowloon.

(Photo: Fred Lillywhite)

CHAPTER 18

THOSE TRAUMATIC BUILDING YEARS – 1959-1962

From the day Government approved the runway they realised a large terminal building must complement it. In 1956, the Legislative Council directed the Civil Aviation Department to confer with Scott & Wilson, Kirkpatrick & Partners to this end. From these discussions they appointed the London architects Ramsey, Murray and Ward to design and cost a Terminal Building. The architects' submission received the support of the Kai Tak Progress Committee. They estimated the cost at HK$19 million.

Government retained Hong Kong's Eric Cumine and Company to prepare architectural and structural working drawings and manage the contract. Meanwhile the Civil Aviation Department formed an Airline Representatives' Committee. They consulted this body on every detail of planning.

The Freight Building was an easy decision. The contract went to Sang Hop Construction Company and site work began in February 1959. The structure could serve as a temporary terminal as work continued on the main building. Meanwhile, the *sea wall terminal* continued operations until September 21, 1959, when the *freight terminal* came into use.

1959

The official opening of the new runway ended an era. The Department closed the old strips with no fan-fare and fewer regrets. I had mixed thoughts – as one moves from youth to maturity the edge of adventure seems less keen. Did this happen with Kai Tak Airport?

The upcoming expansions did not overawe the Department. Senior staff took overseas leave and attended conferences as normal. *Hammy* Hamilton's title changed to Airport Commandant.

Mr M. A. Funk and Mr F. E. N. Wills accepted the two newly established Assistant Airport Manager posts. Airport Supervisor Michael Funk's promotion dated from July 1, 1958, whereas Frank Wills arrived from England on May 26, 1958. Frank had served in Malaya for several years receiving the *golden handshake*. He brought a wealth of experience to the post. Kau-kuen Wong, ex-CNAC *Hump* flight dispatch supervisor and erstwhile

THOSE TRAUMATIC BUILDING YEARS – 1959-1962

ERIC B. CUMINE
Eric Cumine & Company prepared architectural and structural working drawings and managed the Terminal Building contract. (Photo: Carl Myatt, SCMP)

Cathay Pacific radio officer, became Acting Marshalling Supervisor. *Hammy* installed *KK* in the abandoned sea wall Control Tower.

By March 31, 1959, the Department's establishment was 22 expatriates and 310 local officers.

In January the Far East Flying Training School resurrected their business. Their location was on the Sung Wong Toi Road near the Airport Fire Station. The new runway probably affected this business most – the centre line went through the School's main hangar.

On March 3, RAF Kai Tak was the venue for the parade marking the visit of the Duke of Edinburgh. The parade involved 3,500 men from the three Services. The Brigadier commanding the parade greeted Prince Philip with a ceremonial salute. The Prince backed off muttering: *God, the bloody man nearly stuck me!* With *live* microphones his remark came through loud and clear causing stern faces to show uncharacteristic signs of life. The march-past paraded 28 Squadron's standard to a Royal for the first time.

A few days later, the Governor, Sir Robert Black, accompanied the Duke on an aerial safari of the Colony. Royal Air Force Flight Lieutenant W. H. Johnson flew the HKAAF's Westland Widgeon helicopter with Pilot Officer H. N. Morison his co-pilot.

P/O Morison would join Cathay Pacific 10 days later. Neil, a good guy, would die on June 15, 1972, when a bomb tore his Cathay Convair 880M to pieces over Vietnam.

On March 31, Captains Dave Smith, Phil Blown and Pat Armstrong ferried Cathay's first Lockheed Electra from the States. Bob Smith and Len Weston handled the flight engineering duties the only way they knew – perfectly.

On April 24, VR-HFO entered CX service covering schedules to Manila, Bangkok and Singapore. The second Electra (VR-HFN) entered CX service on 9 July, extending coverage to Saigon, Kuala Lumpur, Tokyo and Taipei.

VR-HEN's proving flight to Sydney left Hong Kong on the 16th with Captain Dave Smith in command. Miss Jo Cheng, Cathay's senior air hostess, controlled the cabin. The Hong Kong media and travel agents had strong representation. The guests included Chinese film actress Ting Hung, *Jock* Sloan of HKTV, the Chamber of Commerce Chairman, the Hon. J. D. Clague, and his wife. Others were Ben Hewson, representing the Director of Civil Aviation, and Doctor and Mrs Herbert Kai-Chee Wong.

The Electra arrived at Manila Airport to a blaze of flash-bulbs. The sector to Darwin, commanded by Captain Pat Armstrong, took off after a short publicity delay. About 15 minutes into the cruise an electrical fault forced their return to Manila. Pat dumped fuel and landed. F/E Bob Smith soon rectified an essential electrical bus and they resumed the flight.

The remainder of the flight went smoothly with fiery *Herbie* Wong the exception. A real-life dental surgeon but secretly an unrequited thespian, now under Bacchanal power, decided this captive audience needed entertaining. Jo Cheng told Dave Smith *Herbie* kept

AIRPORT OF THE NINE DRAGONS, KAI TAK, KOWLOON

annoying those who wanted to sleep. He only settled down when Dave threatened to shove him in the brig.

Arriving in Sydney, *Herbie*, fully rested, bounded off the plane to head the line reserved for Australian passport holders. This annoyed a fussy New Australian immigration officer who ordered him to join the visitors' line. The diminutive *Herbie*, shoulders festooned with transistor radios and cameras, peered over glasses perched on the tip of his nose. In a voice audible in Martin Place, he stated he was a Melbourne-born Dinkum Aussie and, thrusting out an unshaven truculent chin, intended to stay where he was. The immigration officer slunk off licking his wounds!

The HK$2,800,000 airport lighting contract, going to British General Electric Company in November 1957, had experienced irritating delays. Finally the lighting complex only needed calibration. Several pilots of local airlines helped in this task – my licence became *night endorsed* in mid-July.

Although a PanAm Stratocruiser used the runway lights on June 29 for a special charter to Phnom Penh the official opening did not occur until the following month.

On 17 July, Cathay's DC-3 (VR-HDA) made the historic flight that officially opened Kai Tak to night flying. Now the airport operated 18 hours daily – from 0600 hours to midnight local time.

The same month BOAC started a same-day Hong Kong to London schedule with Comet 1Vs. This high-speed service cut the journey time to under 22 hours. The schedule called for stops at Rangoon, Karachi and Beirut.

During September, Canadian Pacific Air Lines introduced a Vancouver to Hong Kong service using a Britannia 314. Captain George Jarvos, flying CF-CZX the *Empress of Montreal*, commanded the first flight. It had taken nine months to introduce the service following a

NIGHT FLYING AT KAI TAK AIRPORT

Night operation officially commenced 17 July 1959. Note the lights that showed the circular approach profile.

(Photo: Fred Lillywhite, CAD)

THOSE TRAUMATIC BUILDING YEARS – 1959-1962

THE TEMPORARY PASSENGER TERMINAL

On 21 September 1959, the Sang Hop Construction Company completed the Freight building. The sea wall Terminal closed and the freight building became the temporary passenger terminal. (Photo: Fred Lillywhite, CAD)

heavy landing. On January 7, a 314 using Runway 13 burst the four types of the starboard undercarriage. There were no injuries to the 20 souls aboard.

On December 18, QANTAS inaugurated a Sydney, Port Moresby, Hong Kong service. They used a Lockheed Electra registered VH-ECB named *Pacific Explorer*.

1960

The airport's extended hours and additional movements required staff increases. Mr A. J. Pratt assumed the duties of Assistant Air Registration Board Surveyor on 2 February. Alan was on loan from the parent body in London. Mr B. D. Keep arrived as Telecommunications Officer on 2 April. Brian had a Royal Air Force background.

The Hsin Chong Company won the contract to construct the New Terminal Building. They began work on 18 February. The stipulated completion date was April 1962. The estimated final cost for the New Terminal, ancillary buildings and public area was HK$19 million.

In April, for a fleeting moment, Kai Tak returned to adventure. That day the *flying watchmaker* Peter Gluckmann arrived from Tokyo in a Beechcraft Bonanza. The San Franciscan arrived to attack the light aircraft record from Hong Kong to the United States through Japan. His sponsor was Bardahl International, an oil company.

As dawn broke over Kai Tak Airport on June 9 so did Typhoon *Mary* packing gusts of 103 knots. The S.S. *Malaya Fir*, losing her anchor and mooring chains, slammed on to the runway's lower sea wall. The crew abandoned her! An Airport Fire Service patrol found the exhausted men, many with injuries, on the runway perimeter. The survivors were not sure that all had escaped. Members of the patrol boarded the ship and searched without success. Later they found the missing men wandering along the grass verge. The *Malaya Fir* was a complete write-off.

The types of planes using Kai Tak Airport were as modern as its runway. PanAm *stole a march* on their competitors by scheduling Boeing 707s to the Hong Kong market. BOAC, QANTAS, Air India International, Air France and Lufthansa retaliated with the same type preserving the *status quo*. Japan Air Lines compensated with the DC-8C jet transport.

AIRPORT OF THE NINE DRAGONS, KAI TAK, KOWLOON

1961

This was another safe year for commercial planes operating at Kai Tak Airport. The Hong Kong Flight Information Region (FIR) enjoyed a civilian accident-free record exceeding eight years. Regrettably, military planes did not enjoy the same good fortune.

At 1807 hours on 19 April, in moderate rain, USAF C-47 No. 9014 rolled on Runway 13. During the take-off run the ILS/PAR operator identified her on monitor and advised the pilot. The Tower controller saw the wheels retract just as she entered cloud. The operator advised climb rate and heading steady towards Lei Yue Mun Pass. Without warning he saw the plane swing to the right then disappear from his scope.

Ng Yim-fair, 16-year-old Taikoo Dockyard apprentice heard a plane thundering above – then a dull boom. For two hours he, and other lads, scrambled up the muddy rock face. They arrived to a scene of carnage. The fuselage was in flames and lifeless bodies studded the area. A weak cry brought them to man covered in blood who they dragged to a safer spot – he was the only survivor of the 16. Tam Bing-kwan, 14 years of age, reported the crash to the Chaiwan Police Station and led them to the site. The C-47 had struck Mount Parker near Aldrich Village in the Shaukiwan area.

The USAF's investigation of C-47 No. 9014 allowed the Civil Aviation Department to hold a watching brief. The result apportioned no blame to the Department's personnel.

Bad weather returned to the Colony on 19 May. Typhoon *Alice*, with minimum pressure of 981 millibars, screamed in from the east-north-east with maximum wind gusts of 89 knots. She was a nuisance for six hours then moved south-west crossing the mainland near Macau. Her main legacy brought widespread landslides and the inevitable losses to unfortunates already living in poverty.

The same occurred, albeit on a milder scale, in September. The 986-millibar Severe Tropical Storm *Olga* arrived from the north-north-east with 64-knot wind gusts. She slipped away on the same track as her more ferocious sister.

WALL-TO-WALL HUMANITY – YET, THE JOB GOT DONE!

This scene, in the Freight Terminal, shows the chaos that was a regular occurrence. (Photo: Fred Lillywhite, CAD)

THOSE TRAUMATIC BUILDING YEARS – 1959-1962

An aviation bright spot happened in June. The Birthday Honours awarded the Air Force Cross to Flight Lieutenant B. J. Lemon. The citation highlighted his *levelheaded skill* in an incident of the previous December. His Venom shed a cowling that wrapped around the tail preventing proper control. With only minimum control he could have ejected, yet, he managed to bring his plane down to a safe landing.

On 8 September the Aviation Advisory Board assembled for its maiden meeting. They found the Department's estimates of passenger and freight increases were factually close. This prompted them to reconsider some New Terminal items deleted by the Kai Tak Progress Committee in 1958.

To strengthen their considerations the Board's Chairman, Mr Muspratt-Williams, Director of Civil Aviation, proposed appointing a Technical Sub-Committee. This received the approval of the members.

This Committee consisted of Mr Q. W. Lee, and Mr Don Bennett of BOAC, both Members of the Advisory Board. Others were Major H. F. Stanley of Hong Kong Tourist Association, Mr W. Shewan of Eric Cumine, the Terminal's Architect, and Mr Ben Hewson, Chief Operations Officer, Civil Aviation Department.

The Board assembled, for their second meeting, on 24 November. The Sub-Committee's report showed air traffic volume would increase dramatically. A 26 per cent increase in passenger and 15 per cent in freight per annum was a realistic estimate. With such figures the New Terminal would *burst at the seams* in the second year of operation – the extensions were vital.

The Board agreed and recommended to the Government to reinstate the North-West and Transit wings as a matter of urgency. Government immediately approved the recommendations.

In October Bill Dudman retired. For many years this dedicated man had brought not only enthusiasm but life to the Far East Flying Training School. Wing Commander P. O. Scales, of the Hong Kong Auxiliary Air Force, became his successor.

The year ends as it started with an aircraft accident. This time nobody suffered injury. On 17 November a RAF *Venom* had a total hydraulic failure. The pilot tried to lower the undercarriage by gravity but without success. He landed with it retracted. The crash crew had the runway cleared within a few minutes.

1962

Comet 4s, Boeing 707s, Douglas DC-8s and Convair 880 and 990s became commonplace in the Hong Kong Flight Information Region. With 550 mph speeds and heights to 40,000 feet they were a controller's delight – until mixed with propeller-driven planes. The slow climbs and descents of the older planes caused operational delays to the jets. Ultimately these problems sorted themselves out as fewer and fewer propeller-driven planes operated in the area.

On 6 February, Captain E B *Bernie* Smith of Cathay Pacific received taxi clearance. As he applied power the Tower ordered him to stop – and cut engines. Up the stairs bounded two Herculean policemen. Within seconds they emerged frog-marching a struggling man to a waiting paddy-wagon. They removed the stairs, closed the door, and the DC-6 continued to Seoul in a speculative atmosphere.

It seemed Jack Collins, a guest, left a sealed envelope for safe-keeping with the Hotel Astor's receptionist. It contained $3,400 in American notes. Shortly after a European asked the receptionist, Mr Joe Leong, for the envelope – he wished to add to the contents. The naive receptionist resealed the envelope and returned it to the safe.

AIRPORT OF THE NINE DRAGONS, KAI TAK, KOWLOON

AN ICON RETIRES

On 6 March 1962, Owen F. Hamilton, MBE, retired. Hammy is surrounded by his beloved staff. On his right is Fred Lillywhite and Michael Funk. On his left Clara Young, his secretary, and Frank Wills. (Photo: Fred Lillywhite, CAD)

When Mr Collins opened his envelope it contained newspaper cut to currency size. The enclosed note revealed a mischievous sense of humour – *"Jack, I've received it, John"*. I wonder if that brand of humour sustained him whilst he was a guest of Her Majesty?

Mr Owen F. Hamilton, MBE, Airport Commandant, left the Colony on 6 March for retirement leave. Mr F. R. J. *Fred* Lillywhite, Airport Manager, became Airport Commandant, and Mr F. E. N. *Frank* Wills, Assistant Airport Manager, the Airport Manager.

On April 2, Cathay Pacific's first Convair 880-22M touched down at Kai Tak with Captain Dave Smith, our Flight Superintendent, in control. Aboard the sleek beauty were seven captains, five co-pilots, and six flight-engineers. Others aboard were Bert Clifford, of the Hong Kong Air Registration Board, Don Delaney, Cathay's Assistant Chief Engineer, and two experts from the Convair plant. Captain U. S. *Sherm* Johnson was to monitor the pilots on the line while Flight Engineer C. J. *Chuck* Falkenthul attended to the engineers. The plane brought 2,600 lbs of woodwork machinery for the Hong Kong CARE self-help programme.

VR-HFS entered CX service on 8 April.

During May, Captain G. U. Allan, a Director of Malayan Airways, arrived in a Britannia 102. *Scotty* Allan was a well-known Australian pioneer aviator who had flown with the Royal Flying Corps in the first World War. He was Captain Charles Ulm's co-pilot on the first official airmail flight from Australia to New Guinea. They landed at Port Moresby July 27, 1934. He went on to pilot the tri-motor Fokker, the *Southern Cross*, with the legendary Sir Charles *Smithy* Kingsford Smith.

On 11 October, John *Pouch* James Williams, HAEC's Chief Maintenance Engineer, had a heart attack in the company's Kai Tak canteen. *Jackie* was 42 years of age – wife Vera and daughter Ann, aged five, surviving him.

THOSE TRAUMATIC BUILDING YEARS – 1959-1962

Pouch had an innocent involvement with gold smuggling. During a pre-flight check a DC-3 skipper *snagged* an irregular feathering sequence. When *Pouch* removed the propeller dome he found wafer-sized gold bars jamming the feathering gears. The Customs reward bought the Williams family a handsome Oldsmobile car.

An event that made the newspapers on 20 August brought relief to Grant Wolfkill's friends. This 38-year-old NBC cameraman had spent 15 months a captive of the Laos Communists. He shared a tiny dark cell with four other Americans. Other than some kicking around the first week their captors mainly ignored them. The Pathet Lao gave them one rice meal each day supplemented with grass, beetles and, occasionally, dog. Most Kai Tak habitues knew the Hong Kong-based 192-pounder yet few recognised the hollow-eyed bearded apparition that tottered off the plane.

In August, the China Sea spawned a weather pattern of 953.2 millibars, the lowest ever recorded in Hong Kong.

With Typhoon *Wanda* moving towards the Colony at 12 knots the Royal Observatory went through the range of weather signals. At 0415 hours on 1 September the Observatory hoisted the No. 9 storm signal showing an expected increase in gales. They replaced this with the No. 10 signal two hours later when the centre of *Wanda* was 50 miles away and moving towards the Colony. By 0900 hours nobody walked the streets, the rain was a continuous sheet, and murderous gusts played havoc.

People were dying under their collapsed homes and the sea claimed others. Entire fishing fleets ceased to exist. In the harbour a dozen large ships broke their moorings and piled ashore. At North Point an 8,000-ton freighter broached a cyanide store on the waterfront and lethal gas spewed into nearby streets. The tide in Tolo Harbour raised 10 feet above normal high-tide and at Tai Po Kau crests of wind-driven waves reached 23 feet above chart datum.

At 0950 hours *Wanda* passed 10 miles south of the Observatory, filling-in over the China mainland.

She left 138 dead, 34 missing presumed dead, 130 injured and thousands homeless. These were the official estimates – triple them for more realistic figures! *Wanda* brought the RAF's first typhoon casualties. Five airmen under training on Lan Tau Island took shelter in a stone hut. At the height of the typhoon it collapsed killing them.

Typhoon *Wanda* dumped 12 inches of rain and recorded a gust of 145 knots at the Observatory. The remote station at Tate's Cairn recorded a gust of 164 knots, and the RAF Radar Station on Tai Mo Shan took 200 knots of buffeting.

This was the most powerful typhoon since 1937 and one of the worst to strike the Colony. My recollections of her were of advertising signs, roofing, scaffolding, and massive trees blocking streets. I saw dozens of earth-slides, one with bare feet protruding from the mud. I saw hundreds of oil drums scattered the length of the runway and hundreds more bobbing in the harbour. The lost, haunted look in the eyes of the survivors remains a disturbing memory.

A confusing incident reached a conclusion on 11 October when Immigration Officials escorted a man to a Saigon-bound airliner. A few days earlier an American passport holder, Mr J. H. Hensing, an erstwhile Hong Kong resident, had his entry refused. Without fanfare the authorities put him on the first plane leaving the Colony. Within an hour the plane returned to Kai Tak with the deportee needing treatment for injuries – self-inflicted! An ambulance rushed Hensing to hospital where staff admitted him under police guard. The media now took an interest in the matter but immigration officials remained tightlipped.

The Director of Immigration heads a country's first line of protection with powers wide and multifold. They range from lacking a visa, to inadequate means of support, to the likelihood of promoting sedition. The Ordinance also covered contagious disease of the

AIRPORT OF THE NINE DRAGONS, KAI TAK, KOWLOON

loathsome or dangerous type. The Director, or his representative, need not give a reason for refusing entry – on that note the Hensing matter ended!

The following shows the expectancy that greeted every addition to the airport. The Government directed the Architectural office to produce drawings for a two-storey building suitable for letting to aviation interests. Their working drawings had a floor space of 9,000 square feet, with a design feature of two additional floors as needed. The number of interested tenants prompted them to build the four-storey building immediately, giving a floor area to 24,000 square feet. The contract's completion date was August – all space was let long before that.

The completion date for the New Terminal building, 20 April, had passed. Unexpected problems continued during site preparation with essential equipment delayed overseas.

On 2 November, Mr Muspratt-Williams, Director of Civil Aviation, led the Governor to the podium. His Excellency Sir Robert Black told the assembly the New Terminal would operate on a *two-level* system. The arriving passengers received processing on the ground floor and departing passengers mainly on the first floor. Immediately in front of the terminal the parking apron had space for 11 large planes. He then unveiled a bronze plaque to commemorate the event.

The public inspected the facilities for three days. The New Terminal became fully operational on November 12, 1962.

Hammy Hamilton did not receive an invitation! This saddened many people and led to a literary horse-whipping in a letter to the *South China Morning Post*. I support every word David Taylor wrote.

THE NEW TERMINAL BUILDING – PHASE 1

The Hsin Chong Company began construction on 18 February 1960. The contract stipulated completion in April 1962.

(Photo: Fred Lillywhite, CAD)

THOSE TRAUMATIC BUILDING YEARS – 1959-1962

THE GOVERNOR OPENS THE NEW FACILITY

On 2 November, 1962, His Excellency Sir Robert Black officially opened the Terminal. Cathay's DC-6B, VR-HFK, in background.
(Photo: Fred Lillywhite, CAD)

THE VICE-REGALS EXPLORE THE TERMINAL

Following the opening declaration Fred Lillywhite, Airport Commandant, conducted the Governor and Lady Black around the facility. L/R: Fred Lillywhite, Lady Black, Sir Robert. Director of Civil Aviation Muspratt-Williams stands at the extreme right.
(Photo: Fred Lillywhite, CAD)

CHAPTER 19

KAI TAK'S THICKENING WAISTLINE – 1963-1967

1963

The commissioning of the new Passenger Terminal concluded the major developments. There would be other impressive additions, but 1963 marked the beginning of consolidation with the airport operating on a 24-hour basis.

The Department continued to attract splendid staff with R. K. *Reg* Cooper, G. Whitehead, R. Cole bringing their expertise to Air Traffic Control. Peter Lok returned from a comprehensive course in England a fully qualified Air Traffic Control Officer and began his climb to the top.

Mr T. R. Thomson arrived in the Colony on 17 November to succeed Ralph Winship as Deputy Director of Civil Aviation. He assumed Ralph's duties on March 16, 1964.

The Aviation Advisory Board Operations Committee held its third meeting on 18 January. The new Airport Police Station officially opened on 23 January – it had quarters for 73 officers. A pier for the Air Sea Rescue Launch on the west side of the runway promontory came into service on 13 April.

The PWD returned the Temporary Terminal to its originally designed calling – the storage and handling of air freight. It was in full operation by 1 June.

The north-west wing of the Terminal became operational on 20 December. It provided a comfortable transit lounge and kitchen facilities.

HAEC's new hangar, completed and occupied on November 15, 1962, was a hive of activity. An army of workmen swarmed over the jets and older planes that crammed its 155,000 square feet of maintenance apron. HAEC shares were a good investment!

An event of some personal satisfaction occurred in August. It began in May when Captain Pat Armstrong set a commercial jet record from Singapore to Hong Kong. Flying a CX Convair 880-22M he claimed the honour by taking 2 hours and 54 minutes take-off to touchdown. Several other captains tried to wrest the record from Pat and on 14 August I succeeded. I *slashed* (the word used by the SCMP) the record by one minute.

KAI TAK'S THICKENING WAISTLINE – 1963-1967

CLEARWATER BAY ROAD & HAEC AREA – 1959

The Clearwater Bay Road realignment has not started. It would run through the old HAEC administration area and clip the northern corner of the old PAMAS (HAEC) hangar. This black-painted hanger was destined for the centre-piece of Run Run Shaw's Dream Factory. A Cathay Electra L188 faces Maintenance Hangar No. 3, with several Dakotas scattered around. Two Catalina PBYs stand in splendid isolation at mid-right. (Photo: Peter Onions, HAEC)

KAI TAK AIRPORT – 1962/3

A splendid view of the old and the new Runways 13/31. The picture highlights the rugged terrain and extensive development in the right foreground. (Photo: Ray Bull, RAF)

AIRPORT OF THE NINE DRAGONS, KAI TAK, KOWLOON

Pat treated it with magnanimity but could not resist reminding me my flight was Hong Kong to Singapore – the opposite direction! My eight crew and 92 raucous American tourists would have none of his hair-splitting. I wonder if that record still stands?

The year introduced two new jet types to the Hong Kong plane-watcher. Garuda Indonesian Airways introduced the Convair 990A and Thai Airways International the Caravelle.

Military plane accidents continued to occur. On 25 July, an Army Auster carrying two passengers crashed at the Tai Mo Shan Road and Route Twisk junction. The plane had left Sek Kong for Kai Tak. All aboard perished.

Kai Tak's tricky approaches kept commercial pilots on their metal. Their care helped the Department gain an accident-free reputation that had extended for $10\frac{1}{2}$ years.

That splendid record ended on 23 November when a Lufthansa plane made an emergency landing with the nose wheel retracted.

Captain Wilhelm Severens circled Hong Kong for an hour. He, and his crew, tried every combination of climbs and dives to dislodge the Boeing B720s gear without success. Meanwhile, word had spread of an airliner in trouble and crowds flocked to every vantage point. They watched as the Fire Brigade partly foamed the runway and the ambulances took strategic positions.

Finally, with fuel running low, the skipper made his approach. The plane crossed the threshold – the crowd's nervous chatter ceased – and as it screeched to a stop they rent the air with spontaneous applause.

The crew's professionalism had produced a copy-book emergency landing with not a scratch to the 73 people on board. The crash-removal squad continued this professionalism – they had the runway in operation within two hours.

1964

This was Hong Kong's *year of the typhoon*. It brought an unprecedented series of these climatic upheavals with local weather signals displayed for 570 hours.

On 1 April, Sir Robert Black retired from the governorship. Under his six years stewardship Kai Tak Airport had matured and thrived. The Chinese community presented Sir Robert with a eulogy in verse that said it all – *a character as pure as jade*. His replacement, Sir David Trench, brought the same characteristics.

On April 9, the Manila authorities detained a Cathay plane after checking manifested cargo. They found 50 cases, labelled *personnel effects*, contained cigarettes. The authorities considered this a smuggling offence and acting on a directive from President Macapagal seized the plane. They quickly clarified the problem but such publicity is never good for a company's image.

The *Hong Kong Government Gazette*, on 19 March, closed another personal chapter in Kai Tak's growth. Bert Clifford ceased to be an Air Registration Board Surveyor. His replacements were C. O. Turner and C. E. L. Wray. Cyril and I became close friends yet I hardly knew Colin Turner. The year brought several accidents that kept them busy.

July 6 found Lawrie King doing a route-check on me. These checks were a common occurrence and observed a pilot's emergency procedures and flying ability. The flight to Manila was without incident. The return segment had me flying the Convair 880M from the right-hand seat. As I intercepted the Kai Tak glide-path I asked for wheels down and a rumble indicated they were operating. A red light showed the nose wheel had not locked down. We went through the drill of raising and lowering again yet the red light still showed an unsafe condition.

We orbited Stonecutter's Island for the next 100 minutes while Don Brown, our flight engineer, tried to free the undercarriage from the *bell-hole*. This was a compartment containing electronic and other instrument equipment accessible from a trap-door on the flight deck.

By placing the landing gear level in neutral he could move the device that, in emergency, lowered the gear. While Don followed this procedure we pulled moderate G-force to help the extension, but without success. Don then attempted to release the up-lock through a small inspection window. He used a special bar to force the nose-gear strut to a down position, but with the nose strut retracted the up-latch was inaccessible. We followed other advice from Chief Engineer Don Delaney, with whom we were in contact by radio, but the up-latch remained jammed.

With the cabin prepared for an emergency landing we jettisoned fuel to 5,000 lbs in one and four tanks, giving us a landing weight of 110,000 lbs. Meanwhile the cabin crew moved passengers to the rear cabin to help keep the nose from contacting the runway too soon. The cabin crew had stowed all loose articles and fastened the emergency chutes at each door. A final briefing emphasised that the touchdown would be normal until the speed reduced and the nose hit the runway – then they could expect a moderate bump.

In the false light of early evening Captain King crossed the threshold of Runway 31 at 124 knots. The nose contacted the runway at 80 knots with hardly a bump, but the flurries of sparks temporarily obstruct forward vision. The cabin crew evacuated the 53 passengers without problem. The only injury was to a fireman whose head intercepted a high-heel shoe tossed from the top of the emergency chute. This left the poor fellow bemused and unamused!

Chairman W. C. G. *Bill* Knowles released a statement through Valentine Pope, our Public Relations Officer. The cause of the trouble to CX316 was *a metallic fracture of the hydraulic actuator's eye-bolt that operated the up-latch release. This jammed the undercarriage leg preventing use of the emergency release.*

HAEC had VR-HFS back on-the-line by 15 July.

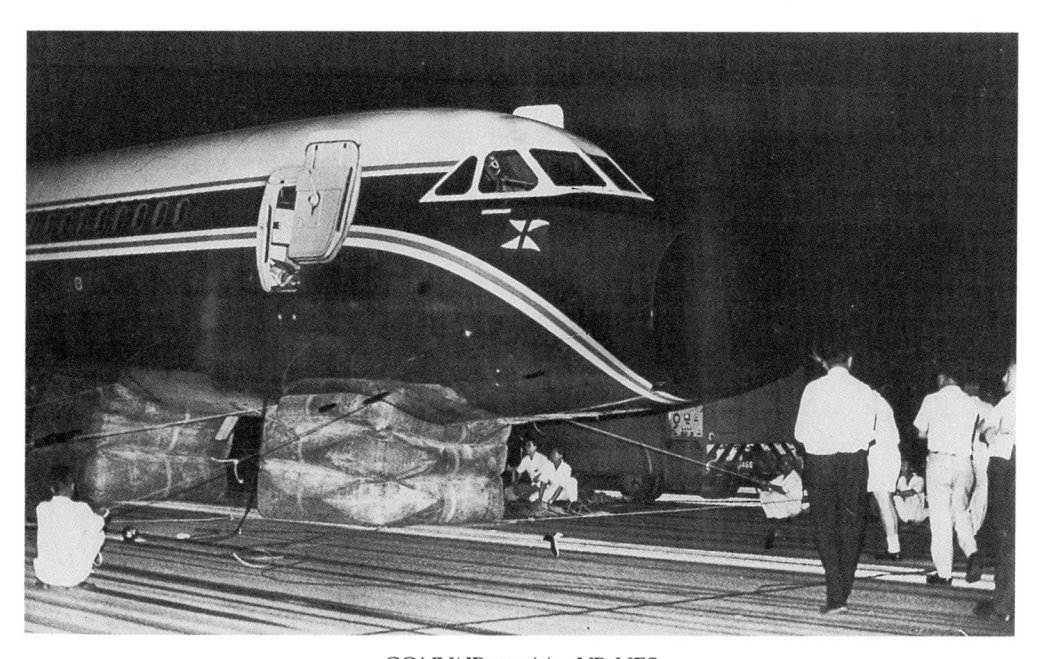

CONVAIR 880M – VR-HFS

On 6 July, 1964, we could not lower the nose-wheel. Fuel was dumped and a successful main wheels landing was made on Runway 31 – foamed. The HAEC engineers are lifting the nose with air-bags. (Photo: Don Delaney, Engineering Director CPA)

AIRPORT OF THE NINE DRAGONS, KAI TAK, KOWLOON

On August 17, a RAF Canberra aborted take-off on Runway 13. The pilot could not stop and the plane toppled into the sea. The four crew members escaped injury.

A wind gust from Typhoon *Tilda*, lurking in the China Sea, caused two planes to collide on 19 September. It blew a parked USAF C-54 number 72502 into a parked BOAC Comet. The C-54 took considerable damage to the nose section while G-ARDR escaped with a few dents to the wing's leading edge.

A landing accident to the Hong Kong Flying Club's Beechcraft Musketeer occurred on November 29. VR-HFU's ground-loop swung it off the runway to plunk on the sea wall ledge 10 feet below the grass verge. The plane received extensive damage but the chastened pilot crawled out uninjured.

In the evening of October 18 there occurred an event with the potential for calamity – I was a witness. The Tower controllers had a standing invitation for pilots to visit and discuss things of mutual interest. I was a frequent visitor, usually after a late flight. That evening I saw a Japan Air Lines DC-8, with 73 passengers, take-off for Tokyo. As it passed through Lei Yue Mun Pass we could see flames coming from a port-side engine. The Tower told the skipper who immediately returned for a landing. Confusion ruled the Kai Tak circuit for several minutes. In the excitement the Japanese crew could not follow the advice given by the Tower. In this chaotic atmosphere I left but saw the DC-8 make a hair-raising approach and landing. Later I learned the skipper had shut-down both port engines when they caught fire. Thankfully there were no injuries.

Cathay's purchase of a second Convair 880M was not an easy decision. The routes warranted additional equipment but the upheaval between BOAC and the Ministry caused misgivings.

In September 1963, Mr Julian Amery, the Minister of Civil Aviation, received the Corbett Report on BOAC's affairs. Mr Amery largely disregarded Mr Corbett's recommendations and dismissed the BOAC Board. He appointed Sir Giles Guthrie, Chairman and Chief Executive, replacing Sir Matthew Slattery and Sir Basil Smallpeice. Lord Rennell, whose agreement expired in 1964, refusing to be sacked in this manner and remained as BOAC representative on the Cathay Pacific Board.

Simultaneously, there was a complete reshuffle in the Ministry of Aviation. Michael Custance and Brightling moved on to other Departments and Alison Munro became principal of a girls' school.

In one swoop Cathay lost much of the support it had enjoyed from the BOAC Board. Only three men remained who had friendly leanings towards Cathay. These were Mr K. G. Granville, who respected Cathay's struggle but preferred Malaysian Airways, Basil Bampfylde, General Manager, Eastern Region, and John Linstead. Cathay's lone supporter in the Ministry was Ray Le Goy. When Captain S. G. Stan Giles, BOAC's Operations & Traffic Representative at Kai Tak retired in November Cathay felt almost friendless!

A record 5,648 passengers passed through the airport on 25 October, many of them returning from the Tokyo Olympic Games. The volume of air traffic continued to increase steadily during the year. Passengers increased 21 per cent and freight and mail 25 per cent and 8 per cent respectively over the preceding year.

1965

Air travel continued to gain popularity. The Hong Kong Airport's records show these dramatic increases, yet figures rarely give the true picture. The Terminal's *peak* period was an experience in wall-to-wall humanity. The Chinese, not known for their courteous demeanour, can turn themselves off to where they alone exist. With many hundreds embracing these formulae the departure area resembled Pamplona's running-the-bulls.

KAI TAK'S THICKENING WAISTLINE – 1963-1967

There was a dramatic 20,525 increase of international flights arriving and departing. This showed 1,308 or 6.8 per cent over the previous year. The total number of passengers arriving and departing was 930,851 – an increase of 120,853 or 15 per cent.

Cargo showed remarkable gains of 4,540 tons (42 per cent). Inboard cargo showed an increase of 991.1 tons (31.7 per cent) and outboard cargo an increase of 3,584.9 tons (46.5 per cent).

This virile atmosphere attracted John Trevor Thorpe. Born on June 28, 1932, *Trev* was a product of the RAF where he had qualified as a Briefing Officer. His initial appointment was Air Traffic Control Officer, Class II, effective 24 July. Trevor Thorpe progressed through the gambit of Departmental appointments until reaching the Directorship.

The demolition of the old Administrative Buildings and Terminal Building, by the sea wall, commenced on October 28, 1965. By December, photographs alone survived to record those important phases of Kai Tak's history.

Airports, planes and accidents go hand-in-glove. This is a gloomy outlook but an unfortunate truism. Kai Tak Airport, in 1965, reflected this observation.

On January 17, a HKAAF helicopter, VR-HFM, force-landed near Ho Chung Village, New Territories. The craft suffered substantial damage and the two crew members suffered minor injuries.

Another HKAAF plane, on March 7, ditched in the sea near Ma Wan Island. A fishing boat rescued the pilot and passenger. The Marine Police towed the Auster to a nearby beach.

On 8 June, a Canadair CL-44 plane landing on Runway 13 swung to port. The plane shuddered to a stop but not before the number four propeller had struck the runway. The extent of the damage was a roughening of the propeller blade. There were no casualties.

The *Kestrel*, an Agriculture and Fisheries trawler, on 18 August, made a strange catch. Entangled in her net was a plane's undercarriage. Departmental investigation determined they came from a Siamese Airways Dakota (HS-SAE) that ran out of petrol on April 9, 1951. This unexpected harvest solved a mystery of 14 years.

The Vietnam War brought an influx of U.S. troops on rest-and-recreation. Their main *stamping-ground* was the Wanchai area where their spending was a boon to the traders. They managed to irritate many others who preferred they were elsewhere yet nobody wanted what happened.

On 24 August a Marine Corps Hercules C-130 with 71 persons on board started its take-off on Runway 13. As the wheels left the runway there was a violent swing to port and the plane crashed into Yau Tong Bay in a ball of flame. When the spray settled 58 U.S. troops returning to *Nam* were dead. A team of divers, working in flames and razor-sharp metal, cut their way into the fuselage to release entombed men. The RAF Marine Craft Unit and fishermen pulled the lifeless and living on board. That frightful day recorded Kai Tak's worst aviation disaster.

In contrast, an accident on 15 September brought no casualties. A Douglas DC-8 jet made a heavy landing on Runway 31. All four tyres burst on the port undercarriage and the bogey caught fire. The Airport Fire Service soon had it extinguished. Of greater concern – the plane had stopped a short distance from the main Kowloon City shopping area!

1966

Although there were no notifiable plane accidents during 1966 the airport remained in a state of flux.

The Terminal building at Kai Tak continued a programme of rearrangement. On 17 January, work commenced on temporary office accommodation in the West Lounge. Two months later the 5,000 square feet had tenants clamouring for additional space!

AIRPORT OF THE NINE DRAGONS, KAI TAK, KOWLOON

Mervyn Jackson Muspratt-Williams, Director of Civil Aviation, began pre-retirement leave on 28 August. Thomas Russell Thomson OBE assumed the Directorship on that date.

The *Sun-Herald* issue of 16 October printed a letter from Owen Hamilton, the erstwhile Airport Commandant. He compared the smuggling of Xavier Cugat's chihuahua with a foiled attempt in the late fifties when he managed the airport. The band-leader had tried to sneak his tiny dog past the eagle eye of Colonel Rix, the Senior Veterinary Officer. The Colonel had refused entry – its papers were not in order! I recall the incident very clearly and *Hammy* was not as amused as this letter suggested. This most gentlemanly of men went into print and close to a fit over the matter.

In June an active trough of low pressure persisted along the South China Coast. For the first 11 days of the month it rained continuously.

Sunday, 12 June, brought the Hong Kong Police another emergency – dispensed by nature. The early risers awoke to a downpour the like few had seen. In one hour 6.18 inches of rain drenched the fishing port of Aberdeen.

In the 24 hours ending at noon that Sunday, 15.80 inches collected in the rain-gauge at the Royal Observatory. This was the highest ever recorded for a June day and equalled the normal rainfall for the whole month.

The resultant floods and landslides left 64 dead and more than 2,500 homeless. The slopes above Victoria City carried landslide scars for months to come. Surprisingly, Kai Tak records show only two diversions during that rain-soaked June.

On 25 November, an airport lavatory attendant prevented a Korean national from further stabbing himself. The attendant, hearing screams, found Chang Chang Hyun repeatedly thrusting a penknife into his neck.

CLEARWATER BAY ROAD & HAEC AREA – 1966
The Clearwater Bay Road is realigned. Concorde Road that services HAEC and Cathay's block, at far end, is well established. A Catalina is parked where the biggest hangar in the Far East would be built – foundation work began in 1969.

(Photo: Peter Onions, HAEC)

KAI TAK'S THICKENING WAISTLINE – 1963-1967

Chang had completed his contract with an American building construction company in Saigon and was returning to Seoul. His companions told the authorities that he had become depressed but did not know why!

1967

Kai Tak Airport was in the news with two plane accidents, both with fatalities.

On June 30, the Tower gave me taxi clearance to Runway 13. As I moved through the heavy rain, a legacy of Typhoon *Anita*, the Tower confirmed my departure would be radar monitored. At the holding-point we completed our checks and advised the Tower we were ready for take-off. The Tower controller ordered I return to the blocks – the runway had closed.

I changed frequency to learn that HS-TGI, a Thai International Airways Caravelle, had just hit the water. The impact point, near Channel Rock, was about 300 yards short of the runway. Seconds later helicopters and launches were bringing survivors to a field-hospital on the end of Runway 31. Of the 80 souls on board only 56 survived – Captain Vigor Thorsen and his crew among them.

Fate played a role in this frightful crash. As I taxied back to the blocks the weather front passed through and the sky became cloudless and blue. If Captain Thorsen had arrived a few minutes later or had made an overshoot his log-book would have recorded an uneventful flight. Fate is surely the hunter!

On 5 November the Cathay Convair 880M VR-HFX moved off the blocks at Kai Tak for Bangkok. Flight CX033 had 116 passengers and a crew of 11 headed by Captain Bob Howell DFC. Although it was a scheduled flight Bob was running a check on Captain Ron *Jacko* Jackson-Smith. The take-off proceeded normally until just before V1 (the abort decision speed) a retread tyre on the nose-wheel separated producing severe vibration. *Jacko* aborted the take-off but an uncontrollable swing to starboard caused the plane to run off the runway into Kowloon Bay.

The impact fractured the fuselage at two points ahead of the wing. A Vietnamese woman passenger, Mrs Tran Thi Tan, lost her life and 40 passengers suffered injuries. The cabin crew under Senior Purser *Johann* Chir Yung-Mur handled the evacuation splendidly. On October 31, 1968, he received the Airline Passengers Association's Safety Award from William A. Jennings, APA's Director.

Although the plane was an insurance write-off the nose section became our first 880 flight simulator.

CONVAIR 880M – VR-HFX

On 5 November 1967, an aborted take-off ended in Kowloon Bay. One passenger lost her life and 40 suffered injuries.

(Photo: Don Delaney, Engineering Director, CPA)

CHAPTER 20

THE DAYS OF ADVENTURE DECLINE – 1968-1973

*Another day, another day,
And yet another, glides away!*
The Bridal of Triermain
Sir Walter Scott.

1968

The Kai Tak aviation scene was more tranquil than the preceding year. The HK$5 departure tax was rumoured to increase by a contentious 100 per cent – it got the thumbs-down but happened anyway! The authorities also increased landing fees. To offset an uproar the Government advised that a scheme was under consideration to lengthen the runway, with users bearing the capital costs! The airlines accepted the landing-fee increase with little more than token resistance.

March was a good month for the private flying enthusiast. The Hong Kong Flying Club bought a single-engine Beechcraft Musketeer and the Aero Club of Hong Kong's new plane arrived. This was a Piper Cherokee-140 flown from Singapore through Borneo and the Philippines. Mike Gotfried and Brian Lewis, of Cathay Pacific, took turns at the controls.

On 31 August, a Bell 47G-5 helicopter owned by Dragonfly Helicopters Limited made its fourth trip of the day. Hired by Hong Kong Television Broadcasts Limited (HK-TVB) it brought the rest of the equipment for a relay station on Golden Hill. The helicopter, registered VR-HGD, hovering above the 1,300-foot site suddenly flipped and crashed on the verge of the hill.

The rotor splintered into a hundred razor-sharp fragments. A large piece decapitated Choi Tin, a labourer, and the construction foreman, Chung Chi-fat, had his leg badly gashed – doctors amputated it. A TVB cameraman, Henry K. Wong, filming the project for a newsreel, lost four fingers. The pilot, R. T. St John Fischer, escaped with slight injuries to his hands and face.

The Bell 47G-5 was a commercial helicopter that had cost HK$360,000. HAEC mechanics assembled the machine from the enclosed specifications. The pilot had 11 years

THE DAYS OF ADVENTURE DECLINE – 1968-1973

DRAGONFLY HELICOPTERS LTD's VR-HGD
On 31 August, 1968, a Bell 47G-5 helicopter crashed on Golden Hill. The rotor splintered – killing one and injuring others.

(Photo: DCA Archives)

experience of flying commercial helicopters overseas. The company's general manager was Mr R. S. Kilburn and a partner was Buji Dhabher, a cricketing mate.

An investigation found Mr Fischer had lost control because of abnormal turbulence around Golden Hill. The insurers withheld payment for several months. They claimed that the pilot had misrepresented his experience. They finally paid but the crash spelt the end of Buji's incursion into aviation. With better luck the partners would have established themselves and probably made a fortune – Dragonfly Helicopter Limited was the first to tap that market.

Yet, an accident that occurred six months earlier was the aviation highlight of the year. The world media covered it minutely because of the legal ramification to the professional pilot.

On 16 February, a Civil Air Transport (CAT) Boeing 727 left Kai Tak for Taipei with 52 passengers. In command of a crew of 11 was Captain Stuart E. Dew.

The pilot descended through thick cloud with frequent squally rain. About six minutes flying from Taipei, the plane sank below the flight path and crashed into a tea plantation. Twenty-one people perished including Gloria Hicks – the wife of Captain Hicks.

The SCMP of 5 February published the result of the investigation. Colonel Lai Hsun-yen, Director of the Civil Aviation Administration, determined that Mr Hicks did not efficiently control the altitude of the plane when it flew over Linkou, 12 miles northwest of Taipei. He stated that Hicks had ignored a red warning light when the plane was below 350 feet. His report further charged that Captain Dew had illegally handed over command to Captain Hicks. This was a report castigating the two men and found their actions the sole cause of the crash.

That day the Taipei District Court charged the pilots with manslaughter. Under the Taiwan Criminal Code a charge of manslaughter through negligence the penalty was imprisonment for not more than two years or a fine not exceeding Taiwan $6,000. On the charge of manslaughter through *occupational* negligence the penalty was imprisonment up to five years or a fine of Taiwan $9,000. Captain Hicks faced the former charge and Captain Dew the more serious one. On 25 March, Judge Huang Chao-hsi at the Taipei District Court heard the pilots plead not guilty.

A month later began a trial with the potential for sweeping changes. *No country in the world had ever brought a commercial pilot to trial following an accident.* Joseph K. Twan-muh, their Chinese counsel, argued that the case against Dew and Hicks lacked precedent and asked for acquittal. When the judges refused his submission he focused on the crew's qualifications. He established that Captain Hicks' name did appear on the crew manifest. He insisted that Captain Dew did not act irresponsibly by handing over command to his superior. Captain Hicks had an endorsement with recent flight experience on the type. He made his strongest point by charging that the instrument landing system (ILS) at Taipei Airport malfunctioned on the night in question.

On 21 May the trial ended. Judge Huang advised the Court he and his two colleagues would hand down their judgment on the 27th. Meanwhile Jan Bartelski, President of the International Airlines Pilots Association (IALPA), threatened to *boycott* Taipei if the Court convicted the men of manslaughter. The IALPA then petitioned Generalissimo Chiang Kai-shek to suspend the court proceedings and reopen investigation by civil aviation authorities.

The Court, convening on the 27th, heard a barely audible Judge Huang advise the packed courtroom – *We will reopen more hearings.* He then turned and slowly left his Court.

The trial of the two pilots reconvened in October with Judge Huang still presiding. A witness for the defence told the Court he believed the Taipei Airport's ILS system was not functioning properly on the night of the crash. Mr William Ruh was an authority on instrument landing systems from the Federal Electric Company of New Jersey. He delivered his testimony in the quiet voice that contrasts the expert from the quasi – his demeanour swayed the Court.

On January 21, 1969, this long-drawn-out trial ended in acquittal for Captains Dew and Hicks. This not only ended their torment but ended the passenger division of the colourful airline started by General Claire Chennault.

1969

During the year the Department of Civil Aviation lost some splendid advocates. On 30 June, Mervyn Jackson Muspratt-Williams died in Malta. He was 57. The once chief telecommunications officer Philip Wood died on 13 December.

Their deaths did little to curb the progress of the airport they had guided in its formative years.

The current facilities efficiently handled over 1,000 passengers each hour, but the *Jumbo* would double this by 1972. The ancillary work of nose-in parking baggage conveyor belts and more kerb space for cars would cost HK$15 million. The runway extension of 2,500 feet awaited a decision – it involved an estimated cost of HK$90 million.

On March 29, an associate company of the Hutchison International Group contracted for aircraft-to-terminal carriageways. The contract, worth HK$3 million, called for the supply and installation of six hydraulically-operated bridges. They could serve two floor levels with the same bridge – a system never used before. The contractor, Gordon, Woodroff and Company (Far East) Limited, completed the work in March 1970.

On March 27, foundation work began on the largest hangar in the Far East. HAEC's General Manager, *Tony* Wakeford, told the *Sunday Post-Herald* the structure measured 200 feet in depth and 48 feet from floor-to-ceiling girders. It had an unsupported internal span

RUNWAY EXTENSION TO 11,130 FEET

Work began on the extension of Runway 13/31 on 22 October, 1970. By the end of 1971 reclamation had swallowed Channel Rock. Then bad weather plagued the project. A revised completion date was estimated for late 1974.

(Photo: DCA Archives)

of 400 feet and a total ground area of 116,500 square feet. The hangar could house five Convair 880Ms or three DC8-63s, but not the 63 foot 6 inch tail of the *Jumbo*.

This was a massive structure when compared with the old PAMAS hangar they sold to the Shaw Brothers in 1962. To the best of my knowledge the studio is still making films in it on Clearwater Bay Road.

A pioneer Hong Kong aviator retired from BOAC on 24 May. Captain A. D. Bennett first landed at Kai Tak on March 24, 1929. He was a RAF pilot flying a Fleet Air Arm single-seater plane. Shortly after the end of World War II he returned to reopen BOAC's operations – becoming Manager, Orient. *Don* Bennett served on many committees associated with Kai Tak's formative years. This courteous man remained in the Colony as Far East Adviser for International Air Radio.

Aircraft accidents continued to attract media attention. A RAF Whirlwind *chopper*, on May 16, crashed into the sea.

On October 4, a Hong Kong Flying Club Musketeer, VR-HFU, suffered a nose-wheel failure while landing on Runway 31. The pilot, A. D. van der Sluis of HAEC, escaped injury. The plane suffered extensive damage to the nose-wheel unit and engine mount. *Alan* bore our boorish jokes with good humour – we figured he received a *spotter's* commission from HAEC. Airport Commandant Fred Lillywhite saw no humour at all – the accident closed his runway for a time at its busiest!

An incident on October 9 caught my imagination. That day RAF Kai Tak received a call for helicopter help in rescuing people from a 15-storey building in San Po Kong. A fire had started on the 11th floor of a plastics factory. The heat and smoke had choked the stairs to the street and driven three men on to the roof. Squadron Leader J. Canning, the Squadron's Commanding Officer, lowered the Whirlwind until one wheel rested on the roof's edge. His crew dragged the men on board just as licking flames swept the roof.

Later that month the RAF lost a Whirlwind and two crew members. On patrol near the border the *chopper* struck a power cable above a reservoir. It crashed and burned 3,000 metres east of Fanling.

1970

A yellow blip *painted* Roger Chan's long-range radar-scope. Roger beckoned to his senior controller Vic Clarke with the words *There she is!* Roger's radio transmission accepted the PanAm plane into Hong Kong airspace at *Yellowtail*. This is an imaginary point 175 miles east of Kai Tak where Taipei hands control over to Hong Kong. As the blip became a blob Roger Chan transferred *Clipper One* to the heavily bearded Approach Controller Vic Reynard.

Watched by a vast crowd the Boeing 747 appeared out of a light drizzle to a perfect landing. This historic date was 11 January. One wag remarked that *she resembles a flying warehouse with all the doors and windows open*. The era of the *Jumbo* jet had come to Kai Tak.

The next morning the *SCMP* published a delightful photograph. It showed the 48-year-old Captain William Saulsberry, a veteran of 22,000 hours, accepting a scroll from a diminutive Chinese lady. The 86-year-old *Sampan Annie* had befriended PanAm's Juan Trippe many years ago.

In February the Government decided to proceed with the long-delayed runway extension. The promontory extension of 2,525 feet would provide a paved surface of 11,130 feet. The costing amounted to HK$181 million and included additional taxiways, high-speed turn-offs, by-pass areas and a fire sub-station.

The contract called for a completion date of $2\frac{1}{2}$ years, with work beginning on 22 October. The Director closed Kai Tak Airport to all traffic from midnight to 0800 hours daily, effective from 21 October.

THE DAYS OF ADVENTURE DECLINE – 1968-1973

THE JUMBO ERA COMES TO HONG KONG

On 11 January, 1970, PanAm's Captain Saulsberry landed his Boeing 747 at Kai Tak Airport. (Photo: Norm Latham, CAD)

In November the Department took advantage of the closure hours by grooving selected portions of the runway. This gave improved friction and helped overcome aquaplaning in heavy rain.

The existing runway construction did not please everybody! Several pilots, through our association, questioned the distance between the runway and taxiway. We maintained that in strong cross-winds this was a border-line operation and compromised safety.

The pilots association produced evidence that Kai Tak's clearance fell short of the minimum safe distance recommended by the Federal Aviation Agency (FAA). This was by 50 feet for the Boeing 707 and considerably more for the Jumbo.

Acrimony began between pilots and the Department. Three airlines prohibited its pilots to backtrack when a plane landed in the opposite direction. The airlines had effectively told their pilots to disobey instructions from the operating authority. Later our wonderful *esprit de corps* returned when this became accepted practice in wet crosswind conditions.

On 23 July, Hong Kong Air International applied to the Department for a licence to operate non-scheduled commercial helicopter services. The Company proposed using two Alouette 111 helicopters.

This introduced a colourful character who sported a Jimmy Edwards RAF handle-bar moustache and a Van Dyke beard. These when combined with flashing eyes and a perpetual lear produced the most erogenous countenance I had ever seen. Captain Tony Clarke was the chief pilot of Hong Kong Air International. It seems this charismatic flyboy ran up against the staid Department's licensing authority.

AIRPORT OF THE NINE DRAGONS, KAI TAK, KOWLOON

The Company began services between the Airport and Harcourt Road heliport on 15 December. Captain Tony (*I'm always smiling, folks!*) Clarke was not part of the team.

1971

The Government gave financial approval for the next phase of the Airport Terminal's development. Called *Stage 1V*, it increased the passenger processing to 3,200 per hour.

This was a timely decision for the previous year 48,973 civil planes had operated through Kai Tak. The records showed 2,369,704 passengers had used the Terminal's facilities. The freight division handled 75,464 metric tons of cargo, an increase of 25.6 per cent.

Hong Kong Air International Limited carried 36,705 passengers. The Company's fleet had expanded to a 13-seat twin-engine Bell 212 and a Bell 47. These helicopters complemented the two six-seat Alouette 111s.

To compete with PanAm, Japan Airlines, Lufthansa and BOAC introduced the Boeing 747 to their schedules. China Airlines added the Caravelle to the B-727 and B-707 fleet. United Arab Airlines changed its stationery to Egyptair. The local airline, Cathay Pacific, who lacked a rich corporate brother, successfully competed with *hand-me-down* Boeing 707s.

On March 30, 45 people boarded a Philippine Airlines' plane at Manila. The BAC 1-11 left on schedule for Davao City on Mindanao Island. Reaching cruising level six hijackers ordered the captain to fly to Canton, China.

With almost empty tanks the Hong Kong authorities cleared the captain to land at Kai Tak. During refuelling officials negotiated the release of 19 adults and one child. The plane then left for Canton where the hijackers gained political asylum.

The following day the Chinese released the plane and the remaining passengers. The BAC 1-11 returned to Kai Tak – refuelled and left for Manila.

A joke circulated at the time. A man thrust himself on to a flight deck brandishing a pistol and screaming – *Take me to Havana*. The dazed pilot replied – *Sir! Our schedule is to land there*. This type of *black humour* amused few pilots whose association supported the death penalty for hijackers, or skyjackers, their original name.

On 4 June, Flying Officer R. Forsythe answered a routine casualty call from Lantau Island. He was to bring an epileptic suspect to Queen Elizabeth Hospital. They abandoned the epileptic diagnosis when the woman gave birth to a seven-pound daughter during the flight. Was this the first birth to take place on a helicopter? It was for RAF 28 Squadron! The hospital staff admitted its youngest miracle with her whole life ahead.

This contrasted starkly with an event on 18 July. Shum Ching-wing worked in the wheel-well of a Cathay Convair 880. In heavy rain a HAEC colleague coupled a tractor and towed the plane. The hapless Shum dropped out of the wheel-well and fell under the wheels. The Queen Elizabeth Hospital staff found the 30-year-old mechanic dead on arrival.

Meanwhile, the Department fenced off a portion of the northern end of Runway 13 for a road tunnel. The tunnel passed under the airport linking Kowloon City and Kwun Tong.

Progress on the runway extension fell behind schedule. Adverse weather and rough seas contributed to its slow progress. The contractors revised the operational date to late 1974.

Every improvement in the weather brought a work continuation with grim determination. By the end of the year the above-water reclamation had swallowed Channel Rock, some 1,450 feet from the old runway threshold. Many pilots had used the *Rock* to check position in reduced visibility. I did!

On 21 January, a Kai Tak icon proceeded on pre-retirement leave. *Fred* Lillywhite spent his early working life in the newspaper industry in England. He volunteered for the RAF at the outbreak of war and qualified in radio navigation. He left the Colony on 14 May, 1971, one day before his 55th birthday, having *logged* 23 years at the airport he loved. In retirement, with wife Mei, they established several shops in a hotel at London Airport.

Frederick Richard John Lillywhite died a wealthy man in September 1990.

1972

The Department lost another good friend with the death of W. J. Morgan. *Bill* had replaced Fred Lillywhite as Airport General Manager effective 15 February, 1971.

The Malaysia-Singapore Airlines dissolved their affiliation in September. Two separate companies arose from this erstwhile unworkable association. The Malaysian Airline System and the Singapore Airlines Limited commenced scheduled services to Hong Kong on 1 October.

At Kai Tak Airport the building of several projects came to a halt. Work had started on 26 September on a new link taxiway and in November on the airport tunnel road. These splendid additions connected a fast turn-off from Runway 31 to the apron with the tunnel giving rapid access to Kwun Tong.

Difficulties arose with subsoil conditions where the airport tunnel road crossed under the link taxiway. Was this a further legacy of the POW *builders?* The contractors amended the completion date to October 1973.

A precautionary landing to Chin Yew Keen's Campbell Cricket autogyro (VR-HGV) needed Cyril Wray's attention. The Cricket lost power on 7 April and landed on reclaimed ground beside the runway. The pilot escaped unscathed but the gyroplane suffered extensive damage.

This proved child's play for the likable surveyor, but the accident that followed taxed his skills to the limit.

On 15 June, Cathay Pacific lost a Convair 880M (VR-HFZ) near Pleiku in Vietnam. This was the result of the detonation of a high-explosive device in the cabin.

Captain Henry Neil Morison, Flight Captain of the Convair fleet, had left Bangkok with a crew of nine and 71 passengers. No one survived the blast and crash.

Mr R. J. *Remy* Cheong-Leen, the Acting Assistant Director of Civil Aviation (Operations), went to Saigon. He was to visit the crash site and report to the Director. He returned to Hong Kong on the 20th a chastened man.

On 2 September, the Thai authorities charged Lieutenant Somchai Chaiyasut with mass murder. The Court alleged he handed a package to his common-law wife, Somwang Promprin, just before the plane left for Hong Kong. The Lieutenant's eight-year-old daughter accompanied her. Somchai had insured their lives for HK$3 million.

A year elapsed before Lieutenant Somchai's trial began. Defended by his retired lawyer father Somchai pleaded not guilty. His defence was a heavily overloaded plane flying too fast and too high. Somchai's team proved more than a match for Foi Malikhao, who headed the prosecution.

Cyril Wray appeared as a witness for the Thai authorities. Throughout the 11-months trial Somchai showed his contempt by frequently falling asleep. On May 30, 1974, the three-judge panel retired to consider their verdict. Later that day they delivered a verdict of *not guilty* stating circumstantial evidence alone did not warrant convicting.

The prosecution immediately appealed. The Court upheld the not guilty verdict. The brilliant Foi Malikhao, who had never lost a trial, had met his match!

On December 22, 1976, Somchai won his final *victory*. The Court directed the insurance company to pay his claim. I know that my late Cathay colleagues and their passengers sleep with more composure than Lieutenant Somchai Chaiyasut!

AIRPORT OF THE NINE DRAGONS, KAI TAK, KOWLOON

CATHAY PACIFIC'S CONVAIR 880M – VR-HFZ

On 15 June, 1972 VR-HFZ was lost over Vietnam when a bomb exploded in the cabin. There were no survivors.

(Photo: Author & Cyril Wray, ARB)

1973

On 2 May, in the Year of the Ox, Roy Evans Downing became Director of Civil Aviation. His appointment coincided with the wettest year ever recorded in Hong Kong. The total rainfall of 3,100.4 mm. was 40 per cent above the annual average. The heavy downpours of July through September had *Dinger* Bell's meteorologists recording rainfall 70 per cent above average. Missed approaches and diversions reached worrying proportions.

They highlighted the weakness of the approach procedure. For a landing over the Kowloon peninsula the pilot depended entirely on maintaining visual reference for the last 12 miles. It was a difficult requirement and worst for pilots unfamiliar with the terrain.

This led to the introduction of an Instrument Guidance System for Runway 13. The IGS had a uniquely *curved* procedure that required exhaustive checks before being declared fully operational. Technically commissioned in August it became operational in January 1974. Backed by the Precision Approach Radar diversions and missed approaches became a rare occurrence.

Other matters had Cyril Wray, and his colleague, spending lengthy periods away, and the senior surveyor of West Malaysia filled-in.

On 29 June, a China Air Lines Boeing 707 overran the runway landing on Runway 13. The accident tore the starboard nose-wheel tyre to shreds. HAEC replaced the tyre – made several static retractions of the undercarriage – and soon had the plane back in service.

A HKAAF Musketeer, on 9 September, crashed into a densely wooded area. The location was 1½ miles north-east of Ting Kok (near Plover Cove). The sole occupant escaped uninjured.

Kai Tak was *host* to another Philippine Air Lines BAC 1-11 hijack on 11 October. The PAL plane had left Bacolod on Negros to continue its island-hopping milk-run. After take-off several hijackers took control, forcing it to divert to the capital. At Manila they exchanged the passengers for the Chairman of PAL and another hostage and took off across

THE DAYS OF ADVENTURE DECLINE – 1968-1973

the China Sea. At Kai Tak negotiators and hijackers agreed on terms! The hijackers surrendered their arms and they and the plane returned to Manila as guests of PAL. I have no further details of this bizarre episode.

Director Roy Downing's annual report disclosed some interesting statistics. The helicopter cross-harbour service had suffered a 10.56 per cent fall in revenue, the result of the cross-harbour tunnel opened by HRH Princess Alexandra the previous October.

Thirty airlines operated 992 scheduled services a week to and from Kai Tak. Their equipment linked Hong Kong to 65 major world cities – non-stop to 29 of these. The non-scheduled carriers operated an average of 80 services a week.

The worldwide air-transport industry operating in the depressed economy, resulting from the fuel crisis and consequent fare increases, showed a reduction in passenger travel. This trend seemed to have bypassed the Colony.

Kai Tak's passenger traffic maintained the high growth of the last two decades – doubling every fourth year. Air cargo traffic also attained a surprisingly high growth rate in the face of the cut-back on non-scheduled operations.

Roy Downing concluded with an astonishing forecast for 1974. The number of passengers expected through Kai Tak *would exceed Hong Kong's total population*.

AERIAL PICTURE OF KAI TAK AIRPORT – 1973

Shows progress on the airport tunnel under Runway 13/31 and the link taxiway. The tunnel would accelerate road traffic between Kowloon City and Kwun Tong. The link taxiway was to expedite plane movements by separating arriving and departing planes. Work began on the link taxiway in September 1972 and on the tunnel two months later.

(Photo: Norm Latham, CAD)

CHAPTER 21

KAI TAK TAKEN FOR GRANTED
1974-1975

1974

Mr H. M. Johnston accepted the position of Airport Management Advisor effective 28 February. He brought a wealth of experience from his former post – General Manager of Edinburgh Airport.

The runway extension became operational on 1 June. Coincident with this was the commissioning of a new Instrument Landing System (ILS) and a modified Visual Approach Slope Indicators (VASI) for Runway 31.

Two more nose-in parking bays were opened for operational use in September. These had the Burroughs Optical Lens Docking System – the *state-of-the-art*.

In March, after much soul searching, Cathay Pacific Airways ordered two Lockheed L-1011 Super TriStar planes costing HK$500 million. Their power came from British-built Rolls-Royce engines. Cathay had chosen the L1011 over the Douglas DC-10.

In 1972, Cathay had eliminated the A300B European Airbus – it lacked the range to operate Hong Kong to Tokyo. Japan provided 40 per cent of Cathay's traffic and was a petroleum-based economy. They also eliminated the 747 – it was too big at that stage.

Why did Cathay choose the L-1011? Was it because of its *quietest jet* reputation? Was it the British Rolls-Royce engines? Was it the recent DC-10 accident that claimed the lives of 346 people near Paris?

A Cathay spokesman shrugged off these possibilities. He did concede the Company's concern with the noise pollution within the Kai Tak flight-path. His fundamental reasoning was strictly financial – harnessed to the then fuel crisis. The TriStar obtained the same operation usage with just three engines. He went on: Cathay started its re-equipment exercise with fuel accounting for 14 per cent of its costs. At decision time it was 24 per cent – a dramatic increase.

Cathay's pre-crisis annual fuel bill was HK$48 million. Of the increased HK$72 million only a small proportion was retrieved. This was because the price of fuel rose 46 per cent on October 1, 1973, and there was no fare increase until the end of January 1974. And within a week of this fare increase, the price of fuel went up again by 50 per cent of the new price.

Cathay also had learned the value of a flight simulator – its training insurance had reduced dramatically. The preliminary proposal for a L-1011 simulator came from CAE Electronics Limited of Montreal, Canada, at a cost of HK$15 million. The Canadian simulator, unlike the *mockup* Convair one, had a visual system.

Cathay's next incursion into equipment *expansion* lacked fuel operating problems. On 15 November two Cathay crew members, Captain Geoff Green and Flight Engineer Ron Taaffe, flew Cathay's hot-air balloon at the Sek Kong Air Show. The 77,000-cubic-feet balloon, made in England for Cathay, registered G-BCNS, rose majestically resplendent in our distinctive livery.

Accidents, regrettably, were never far away. On 13 April, a Piper Cherokee of the Aero Club was involved in a minor mishap near the northern end of the runway. There were no casualties.

A second Kai Tak emergency within 30 hours occurred on 2 April. In failing light a Cathay Boeing 707 left for Manila. It carried 114 passengers and a crew of 12. Forty-five minutes into the flight the hydraulic system failed. The skipper dumped fuel in the designated area and landed without further trouble.

It was the emergency that occurred 30 hours earlier that concerned me. An Air India Boeing 707 landing on Runway 13 in heavy, squally rain began to aquaplane. The plane skidded on to the grass verge collapsing one leg of the undercarriage – thankfully all aboard escaped without a scratch. The CAD closed the runway.

Meanwhile, I commanded a Cathay Boeing 707 VR-HHD ferry flight that left Minneapolis on 29 March. Just after day-break on April Fool's Day we left Honolulu direct for Kai Tak. Our take-off weight was 316,000 pounds. Aboard were the Colony's first two Security Check Canopies.

About 100 miles out of Kai Tak I received instructions to divert to Taipei. We arrived in the Taipei circuit in heavy rain, low visibility, and the fuel needles bouncing on the red lines. After shut-down our fuel dip showed we had burned off 142,500 pounds of fuel. The flight time was 12 hours and 23 minutes. Navigator Ray Broadhead calculated we had flown non-stop for 5250 nautical miles – about a quarter of the distance round the earth. Now, that would scarcely raise an eyebrow – then it was a minor achievement.

In November, HAEC was back in the news. They had won an overhaul contract for three Viscount 843s owned by the China National Machinery Import and Export Corporation (Machimpex).

The bad weather continued into December and records show 87 planes diverted to alternate airports during the year. On 3 December the fury of Typhoon *Irma* drove thousands of seagulls to seek refuge on the puddled surface of Kai Tak's runway. A PanAm *Jumbo* from Guam landed in a flurry of feathers yet the plane suffered no damage – the invaders took heavy casualties. The CAD officials drove trucks among the *squatters* discharging shot-guns but it was over an hour before the runway could reopen.

We pilots know the seriousness of bird strikes. Many fatal plane accidents have resulted from encounters with our feathered friends. I was involved with many bird incidents, some causing expensive damage to the airframe. I also survived ingesting a large hawk, late in the take-off run, at Taipei in 1965. The size of the bird collapsed the number two engine of my Convair jet as one would crush tin-foil. Most of these incidents are beyond recall except one detail common to all – the appalling stench that pervaded the area of the strike.

The total number of civil international aircraft movements was 53,026 – a decrease of 2.1% compared with the preceding year. The Hong Kong Air International Limited suspended scheduled operation in May. This reduced to 5,140 civil helicopter movements

AIRPORT OF THE NINE DRAGONS, KAI TAK, KOWLOON

THE RUNWAY EXTENSION – 1974

The extension, started on 22 October, 1970, is getting its finishing touches. It was opened for traffic in June 1974.

(Photo: Peter Lok, DCA)

HONG KONG AIRCRAFT ENGINEERING COMPANY LIMITED – 1974

The extensive HAEC complex, that boasted the largest hangar in the Far East, is dwarfed by Lion Rock – the most distinctive of Kowloon's Nine Dragons.

(Photo: Peter Onions, HAEC)

1975

between the airport and the Harcourt Road Heliport. The increase in passenger traffic of 0.01% over the previous year saw by far the smallest increase in 23 years.

This was a year mainly of consolidation. The airport building programme continued with site clearance and piling for the eastern extension to the Terminal Building. Mr H. Worthington became Senior Divisional Commander (Air) on 25 February. He replaced Mr H. L. Elsworth, who returned to Fire Services Headquarters. Mr M. *Mike* Jenvey, Air Traffic Control Officer I, earned a promotion to Chief Operations Officer with effect from 1 March.

A few minutes of excitement occurred on 15 February when a Singapore Airlines Boeing 707 made an emergency landing. The front portion of its No. 3 engine had disintegrated. As the passengers evacuated the plane the fire service neutralised a potentially dangerous fuel leak from the ruined engine.

Probably the main event that caused interest was the death on 5 April of President Chiang Kai-shek. The *Gimo* had ruled Nationalist China for 50 years. And to a lesser degree was the arrival of Cathay's Super TriStar L-1011 on 2 September. Captain E. B. *Bernie* Smith the Director of Flight Operations, who commanded, called VR-HHK the most *intelligent* plane he had flown.

Unfortunately, I did not get my hands on the L-1011 or its simulator. My use-by date arrived on 2 August!

CATHAY PACIFIC'S SUPER TRISTAR L-1011 – VR-HHK
Cathay's first TriStar touched down 2 September, 1975 under the command of the Company's Director of Flight Operations, Captain E. B. Bernie Smith. The Gurkha band escort the graceful plane to the HAEC hangar. (Photo: Author)

AIRPORT OF THE NINE DRAGONS, KAI TAK, KOWLOON

A 1975 AERIAL VIEW OF RESTLESS KAI TAK

This picture shows the realigned Clearwater Bay Road. Skyscrapers stand on land once the threshold of Runway 13. Extensive reclamation continues at the right-lower side, the site of the Hong Kong Air Cargo Terminals Limited. The HACTL complex was commenced in February 1974 and was officially opened on 12 May, 1976. The Fuel Farm (lower left border), where once stood the RAF Airmen's 1927 Mess, is a hive of activity. Several of Cathay's superseded Convairs are podded, waiting for a buyer.

(Photo: Reg Thatcher, CPA)

KAI TAK TAKEN FOR GRANTED – 1974-1975

1992 VIEW FROM 15,000 FEET LOOKING NORTH-EAST

The Miracle Strip points to Lei Yue Mun Pass. Does the Pass look friendlier? Perhaps it is my imagination!

(Photo: Peter Lok, DCA)

1993

Colonial Secretary Black's 1954 unintended prophecy is approaching fulfilment – Eastern Kowloon Bay is virtually reclaimed. This photograph captures an arriving jet on the link taxiway. The exit of the airport tunnel is clearly visible. Even from 12,000 feet one can feel the vibrancy of the area.

(Photo: Peter Lok, DCA)

CHAPTER 22

EPILOGUE – TWILIGHT OF THE NINE DRAGONS MIDNIGHT 30 JUNE 1997

> Soon to die
> Yet noisier than ever:
> The autumn cicada.
> Shiki Masaoka (1867-1902)

How do I finish this story – this my story of Kai Tak Airport – *Airport of the Nine Dragons?* I could continue recording seemingly trivial details of plane accidents, of promotions and changes in the Civil Aviation Department. Of the comings and goings of flight and ground crews and the people who brought life to the lifeless concrete of the runway and buildings that are the Kai Tak complex. The current role of the RAF's Wessex helicopters based at Sek Kong. Of the Royal Hong Kong Auxiliary Air Force (RHKAAF) that became the Government Flying Service (GFS) in May 1993. Of the planes that used and will use Kai Tak until replaced by Chek Lap Kok. Of Chek Lap Kok's mines that produced the marble for the old Hong Kong & Shanghai Bank. Without hesitation I concede these are essential to the future historian. Yet, unashamedly, I record that my days of flying excitement and exhilaration ended with the closure of the old runways at Kai Tak.

I picture myself inching through Lei Yue Mun Pass in rain so heavy the wipers lacked effect. Then throwing open the storm window and rain needles boring into my straining eyes – my uniform shirt thoroughly soaked. Of crabbing *Betsy* to see ahead and dodging flag-masted junks.

I picture myself screeching around a circuit – a circuit existing mainly in my memory – of ghostly buildings that somehow avoided my banked wings. Then a hill-top cemetery flashing by and of smiling in the knowledge that *final* resting place put me on *final* approach. Of touching down on a water-saturated runway and hitting the brakes, hoping that slight reduction in speed was not just imagination. Then taxiing to the Terminal's tarmac, that

EPILOGUE – TWILIGHT OF THE NINE DRAGONS – MIDNIGHT 30 JUNE 1997

tarmac an unbroken sheet of water, exhilarated at again outwitting the most dangerous and exacting airport in the world.

These are not alone my memories – most pilots of the day tell the same stories – doubtless better than have I.

With such memories it is anticlimactic to go on so I close with my thoughts for Hong Kong's future – of the Colony I love – and where I found my true love.

* * *

*Study the past,
as Confucius once said,
if you would divine the future.*

In the era under British control Hong Kong has had many splendid governors. Though they primarily forwarded the interests of the great Hongs they never forgot the small person. As the *sands-run-out* for this hustling Colony we see Britain reverting to a bellicose style of government – a feature of its birth.

In recent years we have witnessed anomalous mistakes made by experienced persons of State. In 1982, British Prime Minister Margaret Thatcher, buoyant from her Falkland Island triumphs, visited the Chinese leader Deng Xiaoping. Her forceful assertions of British Hong Kong's rights, based on the treaties, annoyed Deng to where he went into a rage. The *Iron Lady's* trip to Beijing was a disaster!

A decade later the appointment of the untitled Governor Christopher Patten did nothing to placate Beijing. His forthright attitude seems *patterned* on the Thatcher style. Governor Patten's qualifications lacked diplomatic experience. He was Party Chairman of the ruling Tories then lost his seat in Parliament. There is a name for this type of appointment – *jobs for the boys*.

The pending hand-over brings many questions to mind! Does the hand-over include records held by Immigration, Customs, Internal Revenue, Police, Judiciary, and Corporate Affairs? Many of these will be of a sensitive nature. Will we witness frantic shredding and *Providential* computer power spikes – the methods of *mislaying* such information?

Without doubt, Beijing will continue welcoming foreign business, but the stability of a British-governed Hong Kong as a spring-board will be lost. The attraction for investment and expatriates is Hong Kong's miniscule flat-rate of income tax. Surely, it is unrealistic to think this will continue? Will Hong Kong's extravagant self-serving life style, where money is the yard-stick of the successful, change? Almost a certainty!

China's investments in Hong Kong are immense. Taiwan also holds vast investments on the mainland and in Hong Kong. Whereas Taiwan's investments are for a quick profit, China's investments seem more a calming prelude to the main-event. Surely, the pending hand-over already makes them the titular owner of Hong Kong and all it surveys. This, therefore, seems to suggest that Beijing wants to avoid inheriting another Shanghai-style *ghost city*.

It is true that many locals now direct top tiers of government. Chinese they are, yet has there been serious consultation with Beijing of their future acceptability? The recent democratic elections show an inability to read the mood of the Central Government and thus an exercise in futility. It is not difficult to forecast the fate of those autonomous electees.

Yet, my concern is with the person-in-the-street. The rich local, whose stated aim is to stay in the Colony when it reverts to China, is piss and wind. Most of them have *bolt-holes* and property holdings in foreign countries. With their monetary resources any hint of trouble will see them disappear like *will-of-the-wisps*. The small person spoiled by a capitalistic outlook will be left holding the bag. It will be a bag brimming with heartburn and pain. Still, the hardworking Chinese adjust and time will see their survival.

I believe Hong Kong's reversion to China will mark the end of a standard of living that rivals and, often, surpasses the great democracies. If Beijing allows democracy to return it will be of Chinese style – not Western. We saw this happen when they chose the socialist path and developed their style of Communism. The Communism of China retained few similarities to the Communism of the Russians.

Finally, one must not overlook the strong Nationalist presence in Hong Kong. I speculate as that 1997 date nears they will begin to cause disruptions. Then world opinion may excuse China's occupational military *over-kill* – for that, I expect, will happen!

The BEGINNING of troubled times.

APPENDICES

APPENDIX 1

CIVIL AVIATION DEPARTMENT – HONG KONG. PERSONNEL

DIRECTORS OF AIR SERVICES

Period:
c1929-40	Comdr George Francis HOLE, RN(Rtd) – Harbour Master
1940-45	James JOLLY, CBE, RD(CMG) – Harbour Master
1946-48	Albert James Robert MOSS

DIRECTORS OF CIVIL AVIATION

Period:
1948	Albert James Robert MOSS
1952-66	Mervyn Jackson MUSPRATT-WILLIAMS
1966-72	Thomas Russell THOMSON
1972-78	Roy Evans DOWNING
1978-83	Brian D. KEEP
1983-88	John Trevor THORPE
1988-95	Peter K. N. LOK
1996-	Richard A. SIEGEL

* * *

CAD – CONTROLLERS OF KAI TAK AIRPORT

Period:
1953-57	Airport Manager	Owen F. HAMILTON
1958-62	Airport Commandant	Owen F. HAMILTON
1963-71	Airport Commandant	Fred R. J. LILLYWHITE
1972	Airport General Manager	W. J. MORGAN
1973	Airport Management Advisor	K. R. SMITH
1974	Airport Management Advisor	H. M. JOHNSTON
1975-79	Airport Management Advisor	K. R. SMITH
1980-90	Airport General Manager	Richard A. SIEGEL
1991-93	Airport General Manager	W. C. HUTCHINGS
1994-95	Airport General Manager	Albert K. Y. LAM
1996	Airport General Manager	A. B. NORMAN

(Statistician – David Chan, CAD, 26 January 1996)

APPENDIX 2

AIRCRAFT ON HONG KONG REGISTER

REG MARK	FIRST REGISTERED OWNER	ACFT TYPE	DATE FIRST REGD	DATE DEREGD	REASON
VR-					
HAA	HONG KONG FLYING CLUB	AVRO AVIAN 594 MK IV/M	10/03/30	11/09/30	Withdrawn from Use
HAB	HONG KONG FLYING CLUB	AVRO AVIAN 594 MK IV/M	19/08/30	10/12/31	Withdrawn from Use
HAC	WESTLAND AIRCRAFT WORKS	WESTLAND WAPITI	23/03/31	25/01/35	Sold
HAD	FAR EAST AVIATION CO LTD	AVRO AVIAN 594	25/09/30	30/12/31	Sold
HAE	HONG KONG FLYING CLUB	AVRO AVIAN 594 MK IV/M	27/12/30	30/05/39	Withdrawn from Use
HAF	FAR EAST AVIATION CO LTD	AVRO AVIAN MK IV/M	17/07/31	04/08/31	Sold
HAG	FAR EAST AVIATION CO LTD	AVRO AVIAN MK IV/M	17/07/31	04/08/31	Sold
HAH	FAR EAST AVIATION CO LTD	AVRO AVIAN MK IV/M	17/07/31	04/08/31	Sold
HAI	FAR EAST AVIATION CO LTD	AVRO AVIAN 594 MK IV/M	05/01/32	13/01/32	Sold
HAJ	FAR EAST AVIATION CO LTD	AVRO AVIAN MK 594 IV/M	05/01/32	13/01/32	Sold
HAK	FAR EAST AVIATION CO LTD	AVRO AVIAN 594 MK IV/M	05/01/32	22/02/32	Sold
HAL	FAR EAST AVIATION CO LTD	AVRO AVIAN 594 MK IV/M	05/01/32	22/02/32	Sold
HAM	FAR EAST AVIATION CO LTD	AVRO AVIAN MK IV/M	26/02/32	07/03/32	Sold
HAN	FAR EAST AVIATION CO LTD	AVRO AVIAN MK IV/M	26/02/32	25/07/32	Unknown
HAO	FAR EAST AVIATION CO LTD	AVRO AVIAN MK IV/M	29/03/32	08/04/32	Sold

AIRPORT OF THE NINE DRAGONS, KAI TAK, KOWLOON

REG MARK	FIRST REGISTERED OWNER	ACFT TYPE	DATE FIRST REGD	DATE DEREGD	REASON
VR-					
HAP	FAR EAST AVIATION CO LTD	AVRO AVIAN	29/03/32	08/04/32	Sold
HAQ	FAR EAST AVIATION CO LTD	AVRO MONOPLANE SERIES V1	30/03/32	25/01/35	Sold
HAR	ARNHOLD & CO LTD	DH TIGER MOTH	11/04/32	11/02/35	Sold
HAS	FAR EAST AVIATION CO LTD	AVRO AVIAN	26/04/32	25/01/35	Sold
HAT	FAR EAST AVIATION CO LTD	AVRO AVIAN	26/04/32	05/05/32	Sold
HAU	FAR EAST AVIATION CO LTD	AVRO TRAINER	19/05/32	17/06/32	Unknown
HAV	SIR W. G. ARMSTRONG WHITWORTH AIRCRAFT LTD	ATLAS MK 11	30/05/32	17/06/32	Unknown
HAW	FAR EAST AVIATION CO LTD	AVRO TRAINER 626	30/05/32	15/07/32	Unknown
HAX	SIR W. G. ARMSTRONG WHITWORTH AIRCRAFT LTD	ATLAS MK 11	31/05/32	13/06/32	Unknown
HAY	FAR EAST AVIATION CO LTD	SARO "CUTTY SARK"	02/06/32	25/01/35	Sold
HAZ	SIR W. G. ARMSTRONG WHITWORTH AIRCRAFT LTD	A W 16	02/06/32	26/10/32	Unknown
HBA	SIR W. G. ARMSTRONG WHITWORTH AIRCRAFT LTD	ATLAS MK 11	13/06/32	22/08/32	Unknown
HBB	FAR EAST AVIATION CO LTD	AVRO AVIAN	25/06/32	25/01/35	Sold
HBC	FAR EAST AVIATION CO LTD	AVRO AVIAN	25/06/32	06/07/32	Unknown
HBD	SIR W. G. ARMSTRONG WHITWORTH AIRCRAFT LTD	ATLAS MK 11	30/06/32	07/07/32	Unknown
HBE	SIR W. G. ARMSTRONG WHITWORTH AIRCRAFT LTD	ATLAS MK 11	06/07/32	15/07/32	Unknown
HBF	FAR EAST AVIATION CO LTD	AVRO V1 MONOPLANE	13/07/32	23/07/32	Unknown
HBG	SIR W. G. ARMSTRONG WHITWORTH AIRCRAFT LTD	ATLAS MK 11	16/07/32	29/07/32	Unknown
HBH	SIR W. G. ARMSTRONG WHITWORTH AIRCRAFT LTD	A W 16	19/07/32	19/11/32	Unknown
HBI	FAR EAST AVIATION CO LTD	AVRO AVIAN	04/08/32	25/01/35	Sold
HBJ	FAR EAST AVIATION CO LTD	AVRO AVIAN	04/08/32	14/09/32	Unknown
HBK	SIR W. G. ARMSTRONG WHITWORTH AIRCRAFT LTD	A W 16	09/08/32	26/10/32	Unknown
HBL	FAR EAST AVIATION CO LTD	AVRO AVIAN	31/08/32	25/01/35	Sold
HBM	FAR EAST AVIATION CO LTD	AVRO AVIAN	02/09/32	06/01/33	Unknown
HBN	SIR W. G. ARMSTRONG WHITWORTH AIRCRAFT LTD	A W 16	21/10/32	21/11/32	Unknown
HBO	FAR EAST AVIATION CO LTD	AVRO AVIAN	21/11/32	06/01/33	Unknown
HBP	FAR EAST AVIATION CO LTD	AVRO AVIAN	21/11/32	06/01/33	Unknown
HBQ	SIR W. G. ARMSTRONG WHITWORTH AIRCRAFT LTD	A W 16	22/11/32	13/12/32	Unknown
HBR	MR A. V. HARVEY	AVRO AVIAN	21/12/32	19/08/35	Crashed in 1934
HBS	FAR EAST AVIATION CO LTD	AVRO AVIAN	14/02/33	19/10/33	Unknown
HBT	FAR EAST AVIATION CO LTD	AVRO AVIAN	14/02/33	19/10/33	Unknown
HBU	FAR EAST AVIATION CO LTD	AVRO AVIAN	14/02/33	19/10/33	Unknown
HBV	FAR EAST AVIATION CO LTD	AVRO AVIAN 594 MK IV/M	22/02/33	19/10/33	Unknown
HBW	FAR EAST AVIATION CO LTD	AVRO AVIAN 594 MK IV/M	22/02/33	19/10/33	Unknown

APPENDIX 2

REG MARK	FIRST REGISTERED OWNER	ACFT TYPE	DATE FIRST REGD	DATE DEREGD	REASON
VR-					
HBX	FAR EAST AVIATION CO LTD	AVRO TRAINER	06/03/33	19/10/33	Unknown
HBY	FAR EAST AVIATION CO LTD	AVRO AVIAN 594 MK IV/M	09/03/33	19/10/33	Unknown
HBZ	FAR EAST AVIATION CO LTD	AVRO TRAINER	08/05/33	19/10/33	Unknown
HCA	FAR EAST AVIATION CO LTD	AVRO TRAINER	08/05/33	19/10/33	Unknown
HCB	FAR EAST AVIATION CO LTD	AVRO AVIAN 594	06/06/33	19/10/33	Unknown
HCC	FAR EAST AVIATION CO LTD	AVRO AVIAN 594	06/06/33	19/10/33	Unknown
HCD	FAR EAST AVIATION CO LTD	ATLAS MK 11	22/06/33	19/10/33	Unknown
HCE	FAR EAST AVIATION CO LTD	AVRO 637	15/07/33	19/10/33	Unknown
HCF	FAR EAST AVIATION CO LTD	AVRO AVIAN 594	20/07/33	19/10/33	Unknown
HCG	FAR EAST AVIATION CO LTD	AVRO AVIAN 594	20/07/33	19/10/33	Unknown
HCH	FAR EAST AVIATION CO LTD	AVRO 637	02/08/33	19/10/33	Unknown
HCI	FAR EAST AVIATION CO LTD	AVRO 637	11/08/33	19/10/33	Unknown
HCJ	FAR EAST AVIATION CO LTD	AVRO AVIAN	28/10/33	14/11/33	Unknown
HCK	FAR EAST AVIATION CO LTD	AVRO AVIAN	28/10/33	16/11/33	Unknown
HCL	FAR EAST AVIATION CO LTD	AVRO CADET 631	19/02/34	30/07/34	Unknown
HCM	FAR EAST FLYING TRAINING SCHOOL LTD	AVRO CADET 631	19/02/34	12/11/42	Unknown
HCN	FAR EAST FLYING TRAINING SCHOOL LTD	AVRO CADET 631	19/02/34	25/05/42	Unknown
HCO	FAR EAST FLYING TRAINING SCHOOL LTD	AVRO TRAINER 626	19/02/34	28/11/34	Unknown
HCP	FAR EAST AVIATION CO LTD	AVRO 637	07/03/34	28/11/34	Unknown
HCQ	SIR W. G. ARMSTRONG WHITWORTH AIRCRAFT LTD	ATLAS MK 11	21/06/34	05/07/34	Unknown
HCR	SIR W. G. ARMSTRONG WHITWORTH AIRCRAFT LTD	ATLAS MK 11	21/06/34	05/07/34	Unknown
HCS	FAR EAST FLYING TRAINING SCHOOL LTD	AVRO 631	18/08/34	07/02/36	Lost at Sea 1936
HCT	FAR EAST FLYING TRAINING SCHOOL LTD	AUTOGIRO C30A	27/12/34	19/11/36	Unknown
HCU	FAR EAST FLYING TRAINING SCHOOL LTD	DH MOTH MAJOR	26/04/35	30/04/38	Unknown
HCV	FAR EAST AVIATION CO LTD	MILES FALCON M3A	27/05/35	30/05/39	Sold
HCW	FAR EAST FLYING TRAINING SCHOOL LTD	DH HORNET MOTH	23/08/37	16/01/42	Unknown
HCX	FAR EAST FLYING TRAINING SCHOOL LTD	DH HORNET MOTH	17/12/37	30/09/39	Unknown
HCY	LEWIS ARCHIBALD	PORTERFIELD 70	26/07/38	22/10/41	Sold
POST WAR:					
HDA	CATHAY PACIFIC AIRWAYS LTD	DOUGLAS DAKOTA C47	03/10/46	25/07/61	Sold AL 24/07/61
HDB	CATHAY PACIFIC AIRWAYS LTD	DOUGLAS DAKOTA C47	03/10/46	06/08/55	Sold MA 06/08/55
HDC	LEE KIM BUN	HARVARD 11 F MONOPLANE	28/10/46	23/04/48	Unknown
HDD	FAR EAST FLYING TRAINING SCHOOL LTD	STINSON L5	22/11/46	10/03/50	Withdrawn From Use
HDE	FAR EAST FLYING TRAINING SCHOOL LTD	STINSON L5	22/11/46	13/01/49	Written Off in 1948
HDF	FAR EAST FLYING TRAINING SCHOOL LTD	STINSON L5	22/11/46	22/06/51	Sold

AIRPORT OF THE NINE DRAGONS, KAI TAK, KOWLOON

REG MARK	FIRST REGISTERED OWNER	ACFT TYPE	DATE FIRST REGD	DATE DEREGD	REASON
VR-					
HDG	CATHAY PACIFIC AIRWAYS LTD	DOUGLAS DAKOTA C47	23/11/46	18/03/49	Crashed HKG 24/02/49
HDH	CATHAY PACIFIC AIRWAYS LTD	PBY-5A CATALINA	21/02/48	16/07/62	Sold MATCO 01/07/48
HDI	CATHAY PACIFIC AIRWAYS LTD	DOUGLAS DAKOTA C47	11/03/48	07/04/50	Sold ANA 07/07/51
HDJ	CATHAY PACIFIC AIRWAYS LTD	DOUGLAS DAKOTA C47	30/11/46	06/04/51	Sold MAL 06/04/51
HDK	FAR EAST FLYING TRAINING SCHOOL LTD	RYAN ST-M	01/10/47	14/03/51	Sold
HDL	FAR EAST FLYING TRAINING SCHOOL LTD	RYAN ST-M	01/10/47	05/04/52	Sold
HDM	FAR EAST FLYING TRAINING SCHOOL LTD	RYAN ST-M	01/10/47	02/05/51	Dismantled
HDN	HONG KONG AIRWAYS LTD	DOUGLAS DAKOTA C47	09/10/47	28/10/50	Sold
HDO	HONG KONG AIRWAYS LTD	DOUGLAS DAKOTA C47	10/12/47	09/08/50	Sold
HDP	HONG KONG AIRWAYS LTD	DOUGLAS DAKOTA C47	09/10/47	08/01/51	Sold
HDQ	HONG KONG AIRWAYS LTD	DOUGLAS DAKOTA C47	12/02/48	11/07/49	Crashed in 1949
HDR	NO RECORDS				
HDS	CATHAY PACIFIC AIRWAYS LTD	PBY-5A CATALINA	30/07/47	14/08/51	Sold MATCO 01/07/48
HDT	CATHAY PACIFIC AIRWAYS LTD	PBY-5A CATALINA	05/12/47	31/01/48	Pirated near Macau 16/07/48
HDU	CATHAY PACIFIC AIRWAYS LTD	AVRO ANSON	05/01/48	01/01/68	Sold Cannon Nov. '50
HDV	LEE KIM BUN	SEE-BEE AMPHIBIAN	27/01/48	18/01/49	Sold
HDW	CATHAY PACIFIC AIRWAYS LTD	DOUGLAS DAKOTA C47	19/01/48	08/05/50	Destroyed Burma 13/09/49
HDX	CATHAY PACIFIC AIRWAYS LTD	AVRO ANSON	21/01/48	01/01/68	Written off Burma 09/02/48
HDY	FAR EAST FLYING TRAINING SCHOOL LTD	PIPER L4J	06/07/48	05/07/49	Unknown
HDZ	HONG KONG FLYING CLUB LTD	PIPER SUPER CRUISER CUB	15/09/48	16/06/49	Unknown
HEA	FAR EAST FLYING TRAINING SCHOOL LTD	SEA OTTER MK1	20/09/48	31/07/49	Unknown
HEB	L. C. MCCLELLAN	BEECHCRAFT	22/09/48	24/06/49	Sold
HEC	LADNOR MANRISE MOORE	DOUGLAS DAKOTA C47	14/10/48	18/10/49	Unknown
HED	K. M. HAMPSHIRE	BEECHCRAFT C45F	14/10/48	12/10/49	Sold
HEE	LEE KIM BUN	BEECHCRAFT VC43HB	15/11/48	17/02/51	Sold
HEF	FAR EAST FLYING TRAINING SCHOOL LTD	PIPER CUB L-4	15/11/48	17/12/50	Unknown
HEG	A. W. HOE	CATALINA PBY-5A	16/11/48	22/06/49	Sold
HEH	HAROLD ROBERT MADSEN	NAVIAN NORTH AMERICAN	19/01/49	01/01/69	Unknown
HEI	OEI TJONG IE	CESSNA 170	26/01/49	25/01/50	Sold

APPENDIX 2

REG MARK	FIRST REGISTERED OWNER	ACFT TYPE	DATE FIRST REGD	DATE DEREGD	REASON
VR-					
HEJ	FAR EAST FLYING TRAINING SCHOOL LTD	PIPER CUB L-4	21/10/49	05/03/51	Unknown
HEK	NO RECORDS				
HEL	HONG KONG FLYING CLUB LTD	TIGER MOTH TRAINER DH82A	22/04/49	28/08/50	Withdrawn From Use
HEM	HONG KONG FLYING CLUB LTD	TIGER MOTH TRAINER DH82A	22/04/49	12/06/50	Withdrawn From Use
HEN	CATHAY PACIFIC AIRWAYS LTD	DOUGLAS C47A	30/04/49	05/12/50	Sold 05/12/50 Hanoi
HEO	VINCENT WONG	STINSON L-5B	23/07/49	31/12/53	Sold
HEP	A. W. HOE	DOUGLAS C47B	14/07/49	01/10/51	Crashed 1951
HEQ	VINCENT WONG	STINSON L-5B	29/07/49	11/12/56	Sold
HER	FAR EAST FLYING TRAINING SCHOOL LTD	CESSNA 140	24/08/50	23/08/51	Unknown
HES	AIR CARRIERS LTD	DOUGLAS DAKOTA C47	29/08/49	12/11/51	Sold
HET	AIR CARRIERS LTD	DOUGLAS DAKOTA C47	21/10/49	09/04/54	Sold
HEU	CATHAY PACIFIC AIRWAYS LTD	DOUGLAS DC54 SKYMASTER	03/09/49	23/07/54	Shot Down nr. Hainan Isl. 23/07/54
HEV	MACAU AIR TRANSPORT (HK) LTD	CATALINA PBY-5A	07/12/49	07/12/50	Captured at Sea 15/12/50
HEW	CYRIL OSWALD CHAMBERS	STINSON L-5C	09/08/50	09/12/50	Dismantled
HEX	INTERNATIONAL AIR TRANSPORT LTD	DOUGLAS DAKOTA C47	03/05/50	18/11/50	Acft Sold
HEY	JAMES WYBERT MANSEL-SMITH	CESSNA 120	24/03/50	07/05/51	Unknown
HEZ	EASTERN AIR ASSOCIATES LTD	AERO 45	31/08/50	01/11/58	Unknown
HFA	EASTERN AIR ASSOCIATES LTD	COMMANDO C46F	15/08/50	01/01/70	Unknown
HFB	FAR EAST FLYING TRAINING SCHOOL LTD	AUSTER MKV	15/02/51	15/02/67	Unknown
HFC	FAR EAST FLYING TRAINING SCHOOL LTD	AIRSPEED AS40 OXFORD	18/12/51	17/02/58	Dismantled
HFD	FAR EAST FLYING TRAINING SCHOOL LTD	STINSON L5A	06/11/51	18/07/67	Sold
HFE	AIR ASIA LTD	DOUGLAS C47B DAKOTA	25/07/52	21/05/53	Sold
HFF	CATHAY PACIFIC AIRWAYS LTD	DOUGLAS DC4 SKYMASTER	11/08/54	19/01/63	Sold Starways 18/01/63
HFG	CATHAY PACIFIC AIRWAYS LTD	DOUGLAS DC6	07/02/55	23/12/62	Sold Saigon 20/12/62
HFH	FAR EAST FLYING TRAINING SCHOOL LTD	TIGER MOTH DH82A	28/03/55	29/12/62	Withdrawn From Use
HFI	HONG KONG AIRWAYS LTD	VISCOUNT 760D	15/06/55	01/08/59	Sold
HFJ	HONG KONG AIRWAYS LTD	VISCOUNT 700D	15/06/55	01/08/59	Sold
HFK	CATHAY PACIFIC AIRWAYS LTD	DOUGLAS DC6B	25/02/58	22/11/62	Sold Norway 29/11/62
HFL	HONG KONG GOVERNMENT	WESTLAND S.51	30/06/58	09/12/65	Sold
HFM	HONG KONG GOVERNMENT	WESTLAND S.51	30/06/58	17/01/65	Crashed 1965
HFN	CATHAY PACIFIC AIRWAYS LTD	LOCKHEED ELECTRA 188A	14/06/58	23/03/67	Sold Miami 22/03/67
HFO	CATHAY PACIFIC AIRWAYS LTD	LOCKHEED 188 ELECTRA	14/06/58	01/06/65	Sold Convair 01/06/65
HFP	MACAU AIR TRANSPORT CO (HK) LTD	PIAGGIO P-136-12	28/11/60	21/10/67	Sold
HFQ	FAR EAST FLYING TRAINING SCHOOL LTD	DH CHIPMUNK T21	20/10/60	15/02/67	Unknown

AIRPORT OF THE NINE DRAGONS, KAI TAK, KOWLOON

REG MARK	FIRST REGISTERED OWNER	ACFT TYPE	DATE FIRST REGD	DATE DEREGD	REASON
VR-					
HFR	BERTRAM Y. M. TO	DOUGLAS C47D DAKOTA	13/05/61	01/10/63	Unknown
HFS	CATHAY PACIFIC AIRWAYS LTD	CONVAIR 880-22M	31/10/61	28/04/75	Withdrawn From CX Service 09/11/73
HFT	CATHAY PACIFIC AIRWAYS LTD	CONVAIR 880-22M	14/03/64	28/04/75	Withdrawn From CX Service 25/03/73
HFU	HONG KONG FLYING CLUB	BEECHCRAFT MUSKETEER	30/07/64	17/11/80	Withdrawn From Use
HFV	AERO CLUB OF HONG KONG	AUSTER AIGLET 5J1B	09/09/64	18/07/67	Sold
HFW	AERO CLUB OF HONG KONG	CESSNA 172E SKYHAWK	19/01/65	22/06/77	Sold
HFX	CATHAY PACIFIC AIRWAYS LTD	CONVAIR 880-22M	21/09/65	05/11/67	Crashed HKG 05/11/67
HFY	CATHAY PACIFIC AIRWAYS LTD	CONVAIR 880M	03/11/66	28/04/75	Withdrawn From CX Service 05/02/74
HFZ	CATHAY PACIFIC AIRWAYS LTD	CONVAIR 880M	30/06/67	15/06/72	Destroyed by Bomb – Vietnam 15/06/72
HGA	CATHAY PACIFIC AIRWAYS LTD	CONVAIR 880M	22/01/68	28/04/75	Withdrawn From CX Service 10/04/74
HGB	ORIENTAL AIR TOURS LTD	PIPER PA-28-140	05/03/68	25/02/78	Sold
HGC	CATHAY PACIFIC AIRWAYS LTD	CONVAIR 880-22M	23/11/68	28/04/75	Withdrawn From CX Service 15/06/74
HGD	DRAGONFLY HELICOPTERS LTD	BELL 47G-5	18/06/68	30/08/68	Crashed 31/08/68
HGE	HONG KONG FLYING CLUB	CHIPMUNK DHC T-22	15/03/69	24/10/71	Crashed 1971
HGF	CATHAY PACIFIC AIRWAYS LTD	CONVAIR 880-22M	07/01/70	19/09/75	Withdrawn From CX Service 15/09/75
HGG	CATHAY PACIFIC AIRWAYS LTD	CONVAIR 880-22M	26/06/70	19/09/75	Withdrawn From CX Service 15/09/75
HGH	CATHAY PACIFIC AIRWAYS LTD	B707-351B	29/06/71	28/08/77	Sold
HGI	CATHAY PACIFIC AIRWAYS LTD	B707-351B	29/12/71	02/12/77	Sold Laker 01/12/77
HGJ	HONG KONG AIR INTER-NATIONAL LTD	AEROSPATIAL E SE3160 ALOUETTE	09/07/70	16/01/74	Sold
HGK	HONG KONG AIR INTER-NATIONAL LTD	AEROSPATIAL E SE3160 ALOUETTE	11/08/70	12/11/73	Sold
HGL	HONG KONG AIR INTER-NATIONAL LTD	BELL 212	15/06/71	26/03/74	Sold
HGM	HONG KONG AIR INTER-NATIONAL LTD	BELL 47J2A	15/06/71	30/06/74	Sold
HGN	CATHAY PACIFIC AIRWAYS LTD	B707-351B	28/04/72	02/05/78	Sold Laker 02/04/78
HGO	CATHAY PACIFIC AIRWAYS LTD	B707-351B	25/08/72	26/10/78	Sold to Euro 10/09/78
HGP	CATHAY PACIFIC AIRWAYS LTD	B707-351C	15/11/72	03/11/80	Sold
HGQ	CATHAY PACIFIC AIRWAYS LTD	B707-351C	23/05/73	01/06/82	Sold
HGR	CATHAY PACIFIC AIRWAYS LTD	B707-320C	06/08/73	20/09/80	Sold
HGS	AERO CLUB OF HONG KONG	FUJI FA 200-180	19/07/73		
HGT	CHIN IO CHONG	BEAGLE PUP 121-1	04/10/74	15/05/95	Change of Ownership
HGU	CATHAY PACIFIC AIRWAYS LTD	B707-320C	05/11/73	12/11/82	Change of Ownership
HGV	CHIN YEW KEEN	CAMPBELL GYRO-PLANE CRICKET	20/03/72	19/12/75	Withdrawn From Use
HGW	ORIENTAL PEARL AIRWAYS LTD	DOUGLAS DC-6BF	12/10/72	02/11/73	Sold
HGX	HONG KONG AIR INTER-NATIONAL LTD	AEROSPATIAL E SE318C ALOUETTE	21/03/74	09/06/76	Sold

APPENDIX 2

REG MARK	FIRST REGISTERED OWNER	ACFT TYPE	DATE FIRST REGD	DATE DEREGD	REASON
VR-					
HGY	HONG KONG AIR INTERNATIONAL LTD	AEROSPATIALE SE318C ALOUETTE	21/03/74	09/06/76	Sold
HGZ	HONG KONG FLYING CLUB	BEAGLE PUP 150-2	28/01/75	27/09/78	Crashed 1978
HHA	PAN ASIA ENGINEERING CONSULTANTS LTD	CESSNA 340	30/12/74	20/03/84	Sold
HHB	CATHAY PACIFIC AIRWAYS LTD	B707-351C	18/01/74	25/04/80	Sold
HHC	TRANSMERIDIAN AIR CARGO (HONG KONG) LTD	CANADAIR CL44-D4-2	27/11/75	08/11/79	Sold
HHD	CATHAY PACIFIC AIRWAYS LTD	B707-351C	29/03/74	11/09/79	Sold
HHE	CATHAY PACIFIC AIRWAYS LTD	B707-351C	01/08/74	30/04/83	Sold
HHF	AERO CLUB OF HONG KONG	CESSNA 182P	16/01/76		
HHG	CATHAY PACIFIC AIRWAYS LTD	L1011-385-1-00	01/12/76	19/09/80	Sold
HHH	SIM AIR LTD	BELL 206B JETRANGER	29/09/76	20/07/77	Change of Ownership
HHJ	CATHAY PACIFIC AIRWAYS LTD	B707-351C	31/05/74	30/03/83	Sold
HHK	CATHAY PACIFIC AIRWAYS LTD	L1011-385-1-15	08/08/75		
HHL	CATHAY PACIFIC AIRWAYS LTD	L1011-385-1-15	30/09/75	18/07/95	Lease Completed
HHM	ROTAIR LTD	HUGHES 500D (S/N 711019D)	20/10/82		
HHN	AERO CLUB OF HONG KONG	CESSNA 15211	22/06/77		
HHO	CATHAY PACIFIC AIRWAYS LTD	CAMERON BALLOON	04/01/77	14/08/89	Acft Destroyed
HHP	AERO CLUB OF HONG KONG	CESSNA 152 AEROBAT	08/11/77		
HHQ	A. W. ROONEY	LUSCOMBE SILVAIRE 8A	24/04/79	17/01/85	Sold
HHR	HONG KONG FLYING CLUB	BEECHCRAFT MUSKETEER B19	22/06/79	11/12/86	Sold
HHS	HELISERVICES (HK) LTD	AEROSPATIALE SA315B LAMA	16/02/79	27/06/80	Crashed in 1980
HHT	EASTERN ENTERPRISES LTD	HUGHES 500D (S/N 300689D)	13/09/82	03/10/89	Sold
HHU	HELISERVICES (HK) LTD	AEROSPATIALE SA315B LAMA	16/02/79	21/03/79	Crashed in 1979
HHV	CATHAY PACIFIC AIRWAYS LTD	L1011-385-1	25/03/77		
HHW	CATHAY PACIFIC AIRWAYS LTD	L1011-385-1	14/10/77	27/09/95	Lease Completed
HHX	CATHAY PACIFIC AIRWAYS LTD	L1011-385-1	11/05/77		
HHY	CATHAY PACIFIC AIRWAYS LTD	L1011-385-1	17/07/78		
HHZ	HELISERVICES (HK) LTD	AEROSPATIALE SA315B LAMA	29/03/79	19/04/85	Sold
HIA	CATHAY PACIFIC AIRWAYS LTD	B747-267B	24/04/80		
HIB	CATHAY PACIFIC AIRWAYS LTD	B747-267B	16/07/80		
HIC	CATHAY PACIFIC AIRWAYS LTD	B747-267B	19/12/80		
HID	CATHAY PACIFIC AIRWAYS LTD	B747-267B	25/06/81		
HIE	CATHAY PACIFIC AIRWAYS LTD	B747-267B	23/07/82		
HIF	CATHAY PACIFIC AIRWAYS LTD	B747-267B	23/05/83		
HIG	DELTA AVIATION LTD	CESSNA 172N	23/12/85		
HIH	CATHAY PACIFIC AIRWAYS LTD	B747-267B	27/04/84		
HII	CATHAY PACIFIC AIRWAYS LTD	B747-367	13/06/85		
HIJ	CATHAY PACIFIC AIRWAYS LTD	B747-367	14/02/86		
HIK	CATHAY PACIFIC AIRWAYS LTD	B747-367	10/10/86		
HIL	HELISERVICES (HK) LTD	AEROSPATIALE SA315B LAMA	30/03/79	04/01/86	Sold

AIRPORT OF THE NINE DRAGONS, KAI TAK, KOWLOON

REG MARK	FIRST REGISTERED OWNER	ACFT TYPE	DATE FIRST REGD	DATE DEREGD	REASON
VR-					
HIM	MCALPINE AVIATION ASIA LTD	HS 125-700B	25/09/79	16/01/81	Sold
HIN	MCALPINE AVIATION ASIA LTD	HS 125-700B	22/10/79	03/01/81	Sold
HIO	D. A. RUSSELL	TAYLOR MONOPLANE	22/06/79	17/08/92	Withdrawn From Use
HIP	HELISERVICES (HK) LTD	AEROSPATIALE SA315B LAMA	18/07/79		
HIQ	HELISERVICES (HK) LTD	AEROSPATIALE SA315B LAMA	18/07/80	10/01/83	Sold
HIR	HELISERVICES (HK) LTD	AEROSPATIALE SA3160 ALOUETTE	30/09/80	27/01/81	Crashed in 1981
HIS	B. A. BOWER	SONERAI 11	06/06/80	24/03/87	Sold
HIT	T. R. W. MATHEWS	PIPER CUB J3C	08/10/79	18/01/82	Sold
HIU	BAKERS, BROSTER, HANNA, PERRET, ROSE	CAC CA-18 MK22 MUSTANG	28/07/81	01/05/85	Sold
HIV	H. R. MULLER	HOMEBUILT WING B10 MITCHELL	16/02/81	02/06/82	Withdrawn From Use
HIW	HELISERVICES (HK) LTD	AEROSPATIALE AS350B ECUREUIL	30/03/81	10/10/81	Withdrawn From Use
HIX	HONG KONG FLYING CLUB	BEECH C23 SUNDOWNER	02/09/80	15/07/86	Change of Ownership
HIY	H. F. MARCHINI	HIWAY HANG-GLIDER	14/07/82	10/04/85	Unknown
HIZ	BARLOW, MCKAY, TODKILL, VAN DE KLEE	PITTS S2-A	10/03/81	29/12/84	Change of Ownership
HJA	C. H. HARVEY & M. GOTFRIED	ROTOWAY EXECUTIVE	15/02/85	29/09/87	Sold
HJB	I. M. BARTLETT	SCORPION 145	18/02/81	28/10/85	Sold
HJC	HELISERVICES (HK) LTD	BELL 206B JETRANGER 11	04/11/83	18/02/86	Sold
HJD	HELISERVICES (HK) LTD	AEROSPATIALE AS350B ECUREUIL	21/01/86	28/07/92	Sold
HJE	HELISERVICES (HK) LTD	SA315B	29/04/88	21/05/92	Crashed 1992
HJF	HELISERVICES (HK) LTD	AS350BA	19/06/92	08/02/95	Sold
HJG	HELISERVICES (HK) LTD	SA315B	06/06/91		
HJH	HELISERVICES (HK) LTD	SA315B	25/09/92		
HJI	CORDERMAN INVESTMENTS LTD	MD500E-369E	24/04/92		
HJK	HELISERVICES (HK) LTD	AS355N	18/11/94		
HJL	HELISERVICES (HK) LTD	SA315B LAMA	01/08/95		Formerly Rego VR-HJE
HJM	HELISERVICES (HK) LTD	SA315B LAMA	27/07/95		
HJT	EASTERN ENTERPRISES LTD	MD500E-369E	09/08/89		
HKA	HONG KONG AVIATION CLUB	CESSNA-RHEI MS F172-P	26/02/86		
HKB	AHK AIR HONG KONG LTD	B747-121	12/11/92	21/05/93	Termination of Charter
HKC	AHK AIR HONG KONG LTD	747-132SF	04/05/93	10/03/94	Termination of Charter
HKG	CATHAY PACIFIC AIRWAYS LTD	B747-267B	20/07/79		
HKI	JOHN MARTIN STOCKWELL	GLIDER "WOODSTOCK"	27/10/95		
HKK	AHK AIR HONG KONG LTD	B707-336C	09/11/87	09/10/92	Sold
HKL	AHK AIR HONG KONG LTD	B707-321C	25/05/89	14/10/92	Sold
HKM	AHK AIR HONG KONG LTD	B747-132SF	13/08/91		Sold
HKN	AHK AIR HONG KONG LTD	B747-132SF	10/07/91		
HKP	HONG KONG DRAGON AIRLINES LTD	B737-2L9	21/06/85		
HKQ	CATHAY PACIFIC AIRWAYS LTD	DUCHESS BE76	21/02/95	08/09/95	Sold

APPENDIX 2

REG MARK	FIRST REGISTERED OWNER	ACFT TYPE	DATE FIRST REGD	DATE DEREGD	REASON
VR-					
HKR	CATHAY PACIFIC AIRWAYS LTD	BEECHCRAFT DUCHESS 76	11/09/95		
HKW	K. P. WORDSWORTH	HOMEBUILT AMPHIBIAN	13/05/80	25/02/91	Withdrawn From Use
HLA	CATHAY PACIFIC AIRWAYS LTD	A330-342	24/03/95		
HLB	CATHAY PACIFIC AIRWAYS LTD	A330-342	24/02/95		
HLC	CATHAY PACIFIC AIRWAYS LTD	A330-342	31/03/95		
HLE	CATHAY PACIFIC AIRWAYS LTD	A330-342	18/08/95		
HLF	CATHAY PACIFIC AIRWAYS LTD	A330-342	24/11/95		
HLG	CATHAY PACIFIC AIRWAYS LTD	A330-342	15/12/95		
HLH	CATHAY PACIFIC AIRWAYS LTD	A330-342	19/01/96		
HMC	TOPJET DEVELOPMENT LTD	R22BETA	27/02/92		
HMR	CATHAY PACIFIC AIRWAYS LTD	A340-211	26/10/94		
HMS	CATHAY PACIFIC AIRWAYS LTD	A340-211	28/11/94		
HMT	CATHAY PACIFIC AIRWAYS LTD	A340-211	06/02/95		
HMU	CATHAY PACIFIC AIRWAYS LTD	A340-211	04/04/95		
HMV	CATHAY PACIFIC AIRWAYS LTD	L1011-385-1	29/05/90		
HMW	CATHAY PACIFIC AIRWAYS LTD	L1011-385-1	09/03/93	09/10/95	Lease Completed
HOA	CATHAY PACIFIC AIRWAYS LTD	L1011-385-1	01/07/87	01/12/95	Lease Completed
HOB	CATHAY PACIFIC AIRWAYS LTD	L1011-385-1	01/07/87		
HOC	CATHAY PACIFIC AIRWAYS LTD	L1011-385-1	28/05/87		
HOD	CATHAY PACIFIC AIRWAYS LTD	L1011-385-1	01/07/87		
HOE	CATHAY PACIFIC AIRWAYS LTD	L1011-385-1	19/04/88		
HOF	CATHAY PACIFIC AIRWAYS LTD	L1011-385-1	24/03/88	16/11/94	Sold
HOG	CATHAY PACIFIC AIRWAYS LTD	L1011-385-1	09/12/88	20/04/95	Sold
HOH	CATHAY PACIFIC AIRWAYS LTD	L1011-385-1	17/08/88	02/03/95	Sold
HOI	CATHAY PACIFIC AIRWAYS LTD	L1011-385-1	13/05/89	02/08/95	Lease Completed
HOJ	CATHAY PACIFIC AIRWAYS LTD	L1011-385-1	15/05/89	20/04/95	Sold
HOK	CATHAY PACIFIC AIRWAYS LTD	L1011-385-1	09/08/89		
HOL	CATHAY PACIFIC AIRWAYS LTD	B747-367	12/02/87		
HOM	CATHAY PACIFIC AIRWAYS LTD	B747-367	18/11/87		
HON	CATHAY PACIFIC AIRWAYS LTD	B747-367	20/07/88		
HOO	CATHAY PACIFIC AIRWAYS LTD	B747-467	08/06/89		
HOP	CATHAY PACIFIC AIRWAYS LTD	B747-467	08/06/89		
HOR	CATHAY PACIFIC AIRWAYS LTD	B747-467	09/02/90		
HOS	CATHAY PACIFIC AIRWAYS LTD	B747-467	11/05/90		
HOT	CATHAY PACIFIC AIRWAYS LTD	B747-467	28/09/90		
HOU	CATHAY PACIFIC AIRWAYS LTD	B747-467	18/01/91		
HOV	CATHAY PACIFIC AIRWAYS LTD	B747-467	24/04/91		
HOW	CATHAY PACIFIC AIRWAYS LTD	B747-467	20/08/91		
HOX	CATHAY PACIFIC AIRWAYS LTD	B747-467	25/09/91		
HOY	CATHAY PACIFIC AIRWAYS LTD	B747-467	22/11/91		
HOZ	CATHAY PACIFIC AIRWAYS LTD	B747-467	22/06/92		
HPC	CORDERMAN INVESTMENTS LTD	HUGHES 500D-3690	28/09/82	24/05/90	Sold
HPM	TOPRICH PROPERTIES LTD	MD500E-369E	19/03/93		
HRG	H. C. JOSEY & G. TODKILL	CESSNA CE172 CUTLASS RG 11	10/03/82	03/02/89	Sold
HRH	HONG KONG AVIATION CLUB	CESSNA 172P	04/07/95		
HSB	HONG KONG AVIATION CLUB	T67M-MK11	28/10/91		
HTC	TRANSCORP AIRWAYS (HONG KONG) LTD	B707-330C	20/12/85	27/10/88	Sold
HTS	DAVID MAN-CHAN TONG	T337H	17/07/92	07/12/93	Owner's Request
HUA	CATHAY PACIFIC AIRWAYS LTD	B747-467	30/07/92		

AIRPORT OF THE NINE DRAGONS, KAI TAK, KOWLOON

REG MARK	FIRST REGISTERED OWNER	ACFT TYPE	DATE FIRST REGD	DATE DEREGD	REASON
VR-					
HUB	CATHAY PACIFIC AIRWAYS LTD	B747-467	09/10/92		
HUC	CLEVERDRAGON LTD	CAARP CAP 10B	09/06/86		
HUD	CATHAY PACIFIC AIRWAYS LTD	B747-467	10/12/92		
HUE	CATHAY PACIFIC AIRWAYS LTD	B747-467	07/05/93		
HUF	CATHAY PACIFIC AIRWAYS LTD	B747-467	20/08/93		
HUG	CATHAY PACIFIC AIRWAYS LTD	B747-467	10/12/93		
HUH	CATHAY PACIFIC AIRWAYS LTD	B747-467F	01/01/94		
HUI	CATHAY PACIFIC AIRWAYS LTD	B747-467	10/06/94		
HUJ	CATHAY PACIFIC AIRWAYS LTD	B747-467	23/05/95		
HUK	CATHAY PACIFIC AIRWAYS LTD	B747-467F	12/07/95		
HVX	CATHAY PACIFIC AIRWAYS LTD	B747-267F	28/02/90		
HVY	CATHAY PACIFIC AIRWAYS LTD	B747-236F	22/03/82		
HVZ	CATHAY PACIFIC AIRWAYS LTD	B747-236F	22/09/87		
HWC	ALTOSTRATUS AVIATION LTD	PA32R-301T	06/04/89	22/07/93	Sold
HYA	HONG KONG DRAGON AIRLINES LTD	A330-342	22/05/95		
HYB	HONG KONG DRAGON AIRLINES LTD	A330-342	27/07/95		
HYC	HONG KONG DRAGON AIRLINES LTD	A330-342	28/09/95		
HYK	HONG KONG DRAGON AIRLINES LTD	B737-2S3	08/11/86	01/06/93	Charter Terminated
HYL	HONG KONG DRAGON AIRLINES LTD	B737-2L9	02/04/87	01/07/93	Charter Terminated
HYM	HONG KONG DRAGON AIRLINES LTD	B737-2L9	27/04/89	02/07/93	Charter Terminated
HYN	HONG KONG DRAGON AIRLINES LTD	B737-2L9	05/07/90	13/09/93	Charter Terminated
HYO	HONG KONG DRAGON AIRLINES LTD	A320-231	26/02/93		
HYP	HONG KONG DRAGON AIRLINES LTD	A320-231	16/03/93		
HYR	HONG KONG DRAGON AIRLINES LTD	A320-231	18/05/93		
HYS	HONG KONG DRAGON AIRLINES LTD	A320-231	27/07/93		
HYZ	HONG KONG DRAGON AIRLINES LTD	B737-2Q8	16/11/89	11/04/90	Owner's Request
HZA	HONG KONG GOVERNMENT	S76A+	10/12/92		
HZB	HONG KONG GOVERNMENT	S76A+	01/04/93	14/12/95	Sold
HZC	HONG KONG GOVERNMENT	S76A+	01/04/93	14/12/95	Sold
HZD	HONG KONG GOVERNMENT	S76A+	01/04/93		
HZE	HONG KONG GOVERNMENT	S76A+	01/04/93		
HZF	HONG KONG GOVERNMENT	S76A+	01/04/93		
HZG	HONG KONG GOVERNMENT	S76C	01/04/93		
HZH	HONG KONG GOVERNMENT	S76C	01/04/93		
HZI	HONG KONG GOVERNMENT	S70A	29/03/93		
HZJ	HONG KONG GOVERNMENT	S70A	01/04/93		
HZK	GOVERNMENT FLYING SERVICE	SIKORSKY S70A	15/12/95		
HZM	HONG KONG GOVERNMENT	B200C	15/12/92		
HZN	HONG KONG GOVERNMENT	B200C	03/02/93		
HZP	HONG KONG GOVERNMENT	T67M200	01/04/93	24/03/94	Sold
HZQ	HONG KONG GOVERNMENT	T67M200	01/04/93		
HZR	HONG KONG GOVERNMENT	T67M200	01/04/93	24/03/94	Sold

APPENDIX 2

REG MARK	FIRST REGISTERED OWNER	ACFT TYPE	DATE FIRST REGD	DATE DEREGD	REASON
VR-HZS	HONG KONG GOVERNMENT	T67M200	01/04/93		
VR1HHM	ROTAIR LTD	HUGHES 300C (S/N 440299)	16/08/74	26/05/78	Change of Ownership
VR1HHT	EASTERN ENTERPRISES LTD	HUGHES 300C (S/N 440299)	27/05/78	23/08/82	Registered as VR1HHM Before
VR2HHM	ROTAIR LTD	HUGHES 500D (S/N 970188D)	30/05/78	27/09/82	Registered as VR-HPC Later

Statisticians: Mr W. C. H. *Bill* Darragh 08/08/95
Mr David Chan CAD 24/01/96

NOTES

APPENDIX 3

KAI TAK AIRPORT – CONTROL TOWERS, TERMINALS & DCA LOCATIONS

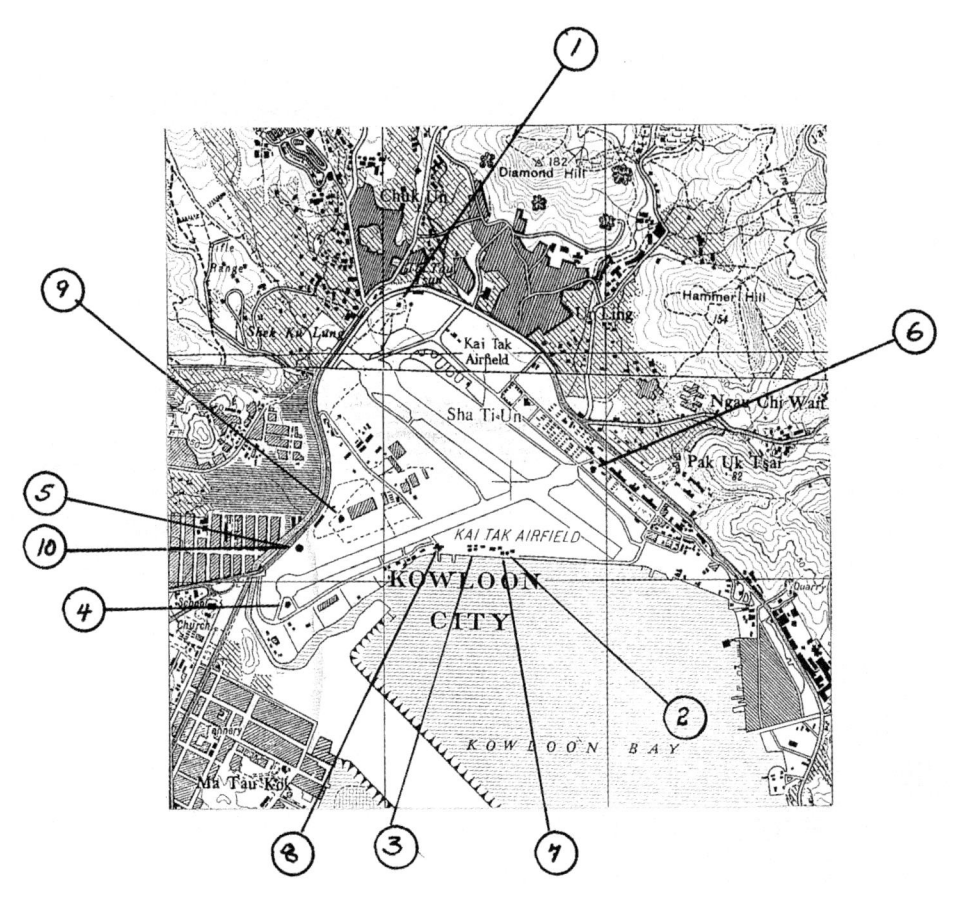

(Information courtesy of Roy Downing, DCA)

APPENDIX 3

CONTROL TOWER LOCATIONS

[1] JAPANESE CONTROL TOWER . . . 1941-1945
[2] RAF/CIVIL POST WAR CONTROL TOWER . . . 1945-1948
[3] TOWER ON ROOF OF JARDINE'S BUILDING . . . 1948-1958
[4] NEW RUNWAY TEMPORARY CONTROL TOWER . . . 1958-1962
[5] TERMINAL BUILDING CONTROL TOWER . . . 1962-to date

PASSENGER TERMINAL LOCATIONS:

[6] RAF TRANSPORT COMMAND/CIVIL TERMINAL . . . 1945-1946
[7] TENT CITY TERMINAL . . . 1946-1947
[8] SEA-WALL TERMINAL . . . 1947-1959
[9] FREIGHT/CARGO TERMINAL . . . 1959-1962
[10] MAIN AIRPORT TERMINAL . . . 1962-to date

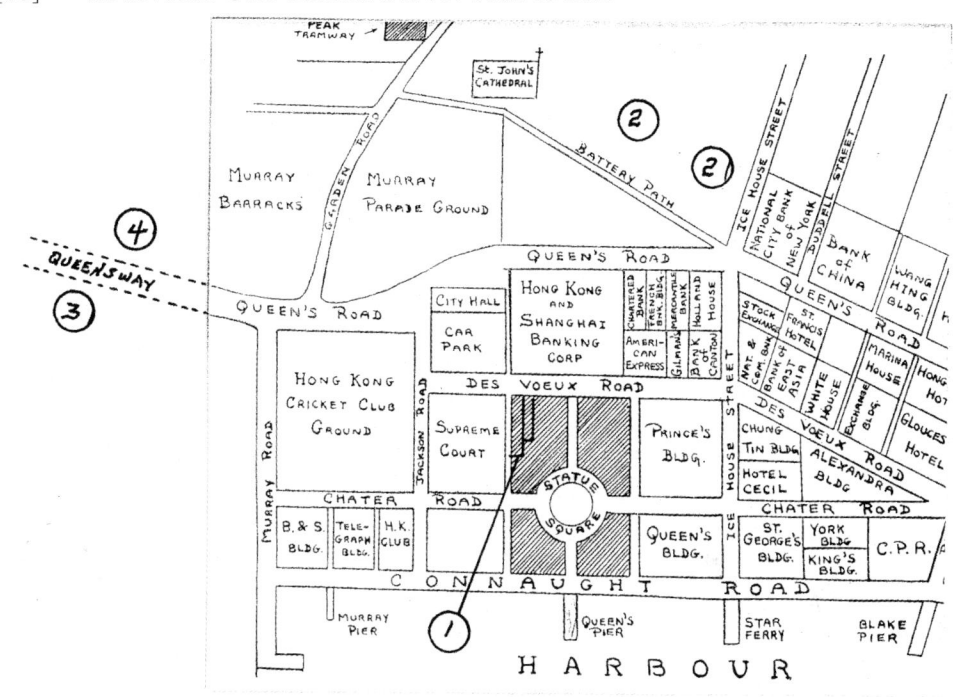

THE DEPARTMENT OF CIVIL AVIATION LOCATIONS

[1] STATUE SQUARE 1947-1954
Accommodated in wooden huts that paralleled the Supreme Court.
[2] CENTRAL GOVERNMENT OFFICES (CGO) – 1954-1972
Occupied several sites within the CGO as the Department expanded.
The initial move was to the East Block, 5th Floor, Lower Albert Road, Hong Kong.
Then to more spacious accommodation on the 3rd Floor.
The next move was to the West Block, 5th Floor, Ice House Street.
[3] NEW RODNEY BLOCK – 1972-1987
East Wing, 99 Queensway, Hong Kong.
In 1972, occupied half of the 1st Floor.
In 1974, occupied the entire 2nd Floor.
[4] QUEENSWAY GOVERNMENT OFFICES – 1987-to date.
46/F, Queensway Government Offices, 66 Queensway.

APPENDIX 4

HONG KONG AVIATION CORPORATIONS – BRIEF NOTES

AIR ASIA LIMITED

Was incorporated in Hong Kong under the Companies Ordinance on 11 April 1951.

Original Subscribers: Daniel Beard, 308 Prince Edward Road, Kowloon (Airline Pilot) Number of Shares: One.

John Patrick Reid, 308 Prince Edward Road, Kowloon (Airline Executive) Number of Shares: One.

First Directors:
John Patrick Reid
Daniel Beard (Chairman of Directors)
Eric William Aylward (Aircraft Engineer)

* * *

AMPHIBIAN AIRWAYS, INCORPORATED

Amphibian Airways, Inc, filed Articles of Incorporation in Manila on 2 May, 1947. Amphibian Airways seemed to me a shadowy company! Roy Farrell's name does not appear on the documentation as either a director or subscriber. Although a Philippine incorporated company it occasionally supplied crews to Cathay Pacific. On one of these occasions Captain Don Teeters did my command training on the Catalina type on January 1, 1949. His certification is on Amphibian Airway's stationery when he was its Operations Manager and concurrently flying Cathay's Catalinas on the *gold-run*!

Farrell brought several of Amphibian Airways' Catalinas to Burma during the Karen Insurgency. In his haste to get into that lucrative charter market he overlooked the correct paper-work. When the Insurgency ended he had to abandon several of his Catalinas that rotted away at Mingaladon, Rangoon.

Born in 1911, Captain Roy Clinton Farrell died on 3 January 1996.

* * *

APPENDIX 4

CATHAY PACIFIC AIRWAYS LIMITED

Was incorporated in Hong Kong under the Companies Ordinance on 24 September, 1946.
Original Subscribers: Roy Clinton Farrell, Peninsula Hotel, Kowloon (Merchant) Number of Shares: One.
Sydney Hugh deKantzow, Peninsula Hotel, Kowloon (Merchant) Number of Shares: One.
First Directors: Roy Clinton Farrell, Sydney Hugh deKantzow, Neil Buchanan.
Extraordinary General Meeting: Saturday, 3 April, 1948. Present: Sydney Hugh deKantzow (Chairman), H. Angela deKantzow, Roy Clinton Farrell, Robert S. Russell.
The company was sold to the Butterfield & Swire interests that incorporate the present Cathay Pacific Airways on 18 October, 1948. During the take-over the original Cathay became Cathay Pacific Holdings Limited.

* * *

CATHAY PACIFIC HOLDINGS LIMITED

The Company filed for registration on 5 May, 1948 with a nominal value of HK$10,000,000.
The shareholdings were CNC and ANA each with 35 per cent. John Swire & Sons Limited, Sydney H. deKantzow, and the American share-holders each retained a 10 per cent interest.
The initial issue of shares were made in accordance with the *Basis of Agreement* between China Navigation Company Limited (CNC), Australian National Airways Pty. Limited. (ANA) and John Swire & Sons Limited of the one part and the Company then known as *Cathay Pacific Airways Limited* but now known as *Cathay Pacific Holdings Limited* of the other part which said Basis of Agreement was signed in Hong Kong on 5 May, 1948, and was subsequently amended and ratified in Melbourne on 1 June, 1948, and was again amended by a letter of 15 September, 1948 from Mr John Kidston Swire to Captain I. N. Holyman and Captain Sydney H. deKantzow.

* * *

CATHAY PACIFIC AIRWAYS (1948) LIMITED

The interested parties were the China Navigation Company (CNC), Butterfield & Swire (B&S), Australian National Airways Pty. Limited (ANA), Cathay Pacific Airways (CPA), Skyways and Far East Aviation Company Limited. Later, Skyways and Far East Aviation Company Limited refused to ratify and dropped out.
The parties confirmed the Agreement on 1 June, 1948. Although operations started on 1 July, they did not register the company until 18 October. They dropped the *1948* portion and continued to use the original name with C.C. Roberts as Chairman and Mount Stephen Cumming Managing Director. The other directors were John Kidston Swire, Captain Ivan Neil Holyman, Ian Herman Grabowsky and Captain Sydney Hugh deKantzow, as Manager. The new Cathay's registered office was 1 Connaught Road, Central – the old Butterfield & Swire building.

* * *

CATHAY HOLDINGS LIMITED

Was incorporated in Hong Kong under the Companies Ordinance on 8 June, 1959.
Registered office: 1 Connaught Road, Central, Hong Kong.
Original Subscribers: William Charles Goddard Knowles, and William Bruce Rae-Smith.

Directors: W. C. G. Knowles (Manager B&S); Reginald Myles Ansett (Managing Director, Ansett Transport Industries Limited); James Worswick Cairns (Chief Accountant, B&S); John Trefillian Gething (Chief Engineer, CPA); William Charles Rae-Smith (Sub-Manager, B&S); John Kidston Swire (Director, John Swire & Sons, London); George Thomas Tagg (Managing Director, Mackinnon, Mackenzie & Co. Ltd.); Richard Daniel Collins (Assistant Managing Director, Ansett Transport Industries Limited).

Changed Registered Office 13 June, 1960, to Union House, 9 Connaught Road, Central, Hong Kong.

* * *

THE FAR EAST AVIATION COMPANY LIMITED

Was established by Mr R. Vaughan Fowler and Mr F. C. Smith c1929/30.

In 1934, Mr Vaughan Fowler resigned from the Company and the business management developed upon Mr Vere Harvey. Mr Harvey first went out to the East as demonstration pilot for the firm. He had recently returned from demonstrating the Fairey Fox 1V (Rolls-Royce *Kestrel*) in South China. Meanwhile, *Fairey's* Chief Pilot Bennett was presenting the type to the Central Government of China, at Shanghai.

* * *

THE FAR EAST FLYING TRAINING SCHOOL, LIMITED

Was incorporated in Hong Kong under the Companies Ordinance on 7 November, 1933.

Original Subscribers: George G. N. Tinson (Solicitor), A. Ritchie (Chartered Accountant), and D. S. Scott (Merchant).

Mr W. F. Murray was the Commandant of the School, and Lord Malcolm Douglas-Hamilton the Chief Instructor. The staff consisted of Mr E. Waldron, as Chief Engineer, Mr W. Wilcocks, as Ground Instructor, and Mr D. H. Blake in charge of accounts. Mr Hung Tsi Ming was liaison officer for the Chinese pupils.

Records – Post War:

The Directors at 28 May, 1947 were: John Robinson (Managing Director, Reiss, Bradley & Co. Limited), Maurice Murray Watson (Principle of Johnson, Stokes & Master).

Shares: The Far East Aviation Co. Ltd.	11,508 shares
Archibald Ritchie (Chartered Accountant)	1 "
George Gwinnett (Deceased)	1 "
Kenneth Sinclair Morrison (Deceased)	1 "

3 June, 1947 – Extraordinary General Meeting, capital increased to HK$1,000,000 – by the creation of 50,000 new shares at HK$10 each.

13 April, 1948 – Directors:

John Robinson (Merchant, Mng. Dir. Reiss, Bradley & Company)

William Forrest Dudman (Aeronautical Engineer, Director Far East Aviation Company Limited),

Donald Brittan Evans (Alternative Director to Hon. M. M. Watson),

Hon. Maurice Murray Watson (Solicitor, Partner, Johnson, Stokes & Master).

The passing years show many changes in the listing of directors. The schedule dated 20 December, 1967, records the names John Louis Marden, John Douglas Clague, Peter Oswald Scales, William John Lees, Hon-Wah Leung, and the splendid Hew Kui Watt (Vice-Principal of the School).

APPENDIX 4

FAR EAST FLYING & TECHNICAL SCHOOL LIMITED

By special resolution of the Company and with the approval of His Excellency the Governor it changed its name to FAR EAST FLYING AND TECHNICAL SCHOOL LIMITED on February 3, 1971.

* * *

THE HONG KONG AIRCRAFT ENGINEERING COMPANY (HAEC)

Was incorporated in Hong Kong under the Companies Ordinance on 23 November, 1950, with Registered Office at Kai Tak Airport, Kowloon. Capital: HK$20,000,000 – divided into 10,000,000 shares of HK$2 each.

Original Subscribers: David Fortune Landale, and Charles Collingwood Roberts.
21 November, 1950 – Directors:
Hon. David Fortune Landale (Merchant – 100 shares),
Eric Francis Watts (Merchant – no record),
George Ernest Marden (Merchant – 100 shares),
Michael William Turner (Banker – 100 shares),
Charles Collingwood Roberts (Mng. B&S – 100 shares),
William Charles Goddard Knowles (Sub-Manager B&S – 100 shares),
John Finnie (Dir. Taikoo Dockyard & Eng. Co. of HK – 100 shares), and Sydney Hugh deKantzow (Dir. Roy Farrell Export-Import Company 100 shares).

This Board set the standard for those that followed, men with the business acumen of Duncan Bluck, John Bremridge, John Browne, James Cassels, John Marden, David McLeod, David Newbiggen, Richard Sheldon, and many others. Their direction, combined with a dedicated work-force, raised the Hong Kong Aircraft Engineering Company Limited to the pinnacle of aircraft maintenance.

* * *

HONG KONG AIRWAYS LIMITED

Was incorporated in Hong Kong under the Companies Ordinance on 4 March, 1947.
Original Subscribers: Arthur Donald Bennett (Manager Far East Area – BOAC), and Donald Brittan Evans (Solicitor).
Registered Office: 18 Pedder Street, Hong Kong.
Capital: HK$ 1,200,000 divided into 1,200,000 shares at HK$ 1 each.
Shareholdings 24 October 1947:

BOAC	249,998 ordinary shares
The Hon. D. F. Landale	10,000 "
A. D. Bennett	10,000 "
Lee Hsiao-Wo	10,000 "
N. O. G. Marsh	10,000 "
J. A. D. Morrison	10,000 "
HK & S Banking Corporation	10,000 "

Directors 1 November, 1947:
Arthur Donald Bennett
David Fortune Landale (Merchant)
Norman Oswald Cyril Marsh (Mackinnon Mackenzie & Co)
Lee Hsiao-Wo (Banker)
John Alexander Duke Morrison (Banker)

Change of Address: 29 January, 1959, from Jardine House to Butterfield and Swire, 1 Connaught Road, Central.
Directors – 16 July, 1959:
Hugh David MacEwen Barton (Merchant)
Sir Wilfrid Charles George Cribbett, KBE, CMG (BOAC)
Lord Rennell of Rodd, KBE, CB
Arthur Donald Bennett (BOAC)
William Charles Goddard Knowles (Manager B&S)
John Kidston Swire (Director, B&S)
James Worswick Cairns (Chief Accountant, B&S)
Reginald Myles Ansett (Mng. Dir. Ansett Transport Industries)
William Bruce Rae-Smith (Sub-Mng. B&S)
George Thomas Tagg (Mng. Dir. Mackinnon, Mackenzie)
John Trefillian Gething (Chief Engineer, CPA)
Change of Address: 13 June, 1960, 9 Connaught Road, Union House, Central.

* * *

JARDINE AIRCRAFT MAINTENANCE COMPANY LIMITED (JAMCo)

Was incorporated in Hong Kong under the Companies Ordinance on 3 October, 1947, with Registered Office 18 Pedder Street, Hong Kong. Capital: HK$10,000,000 divided into 500,000 shares of HK$20 each.
Directors: David Fortune Landale (Merchant) and Robert Gordon (Merchant).
Directors 28 July 1948:
David Fortune Landale (Merchant), Erik Francis Watts (Merchant),
Ellie Joseph Hayim (Broker), Frank Garside Harrison (Broker),
Donald Cater Davis (Banker), George Ernest Marden (Merchant),
Frederick John Horman-Fisher (Merchant),
Whiting Willauer (Merchant, Shanghai), Hsu Ke Mo (Banker).
JAMCo merged with Pacific Air Maintenance & Supply Company Limited on 1 November, 1950 to form Hong Kong Aircraft Engineering Company Limited (HAEC).
JAMCo was voluntarily liquidated on 4 October, 1956.

* * *

MACAU AIR TRANSPORT COMPANY (HONG KONG) LIMITED (MATCO)

Was incorporated in Hong Kong under the Companies Ordinance on 8 July, 1948. MATCO (Compania Transportes Aerios dos Macau Limitada) had its registered office in the Prince's Building at 4A Chater Road, Victoria, Hong Kong.
Original Subscribers: Sydney Hugh deKantzow, Reginald William *Hokum* Harris, Stanley Ho, Rogerio Hyndman Lobo, each holding one (1) share.
Cathay Pacific's two unwanted Catalinas, VR-HDS and VR-HDH, had become MATCO assets on 1 July, 1948.
An early MATCO pilot came from the Sunderlands of RAF 88 Squadron. Cathay Pacific offered Len *Cos* Cosgrove a job in July 1948 but he could not get his service release until 1 November. Then deKantzow transferred *Cos* to MATCO because of his flying-boat experience. Later that month Captain James *Jimmy* Ennis became MATCO's chief pilot.

APPENDIX 4

MATCO employed some interesting personalities during the 20 years of existence. When it filed for voluntary liquidation on November 12, 1968, its planes had transported over ten-million fine ounces of gold into or out of Macau. It never lost a single ounce!

* * *

PACIFIC AIR MAINTENANCE & SUPPLY CO. LTD. (PAMAS)

Was incorporated in Hong Kong under the Companies Ordinance on 4 November, 1948.

The Registered Office was 1 Connaught Road, Central, Hong Kong.
Capital: HK$5,000,000.

Number of Shares allotted payable in cash	...	25,000 shares
Nominal amount of the Shares so allotted	...	HK$2,500,000
Amount paid and due or payable on each share	...	HK$100 per share

The Share Allotments:

	Shares
Edward McLaren (Manager, B&S)	1
Ian Herman Grabowsky (Sub-Manager, A.N.A.)	1
Sydney Hugh deKantzow (Director, Roy Farrell Export-Import)	2,000
Australian National Airways Pty. Ltd. (ANA)	6,999
The China Navigation Company Limited (CNC)	7,000
The Taikoo Dockyard & Engineering Co. of H.K. Limited	5,000
Cathay Pacific Holdings Limited	2,000
John Swire & Sons Limited	1,999
	25,000

23 November, 1948 – The directors were Sir John Robertson Masson, Mount Stephen Cumming, Capt. Ivan Neil Holyman, Ian Herman Grabowsky, Edward McLaren, John Finnie and Sydney Hugh deKantzow.

PAMAS merged with Jardine Aircraft Maintenance Company Limited on 1 November, 1950, to form The Hong Kong Aircraft Engineering Company (HAEC).

PAMAS voluntarily liquidated on 22 July, 1972.

* * *

APPENDIX 5

PIONEER FLIGHTS TO THE FAR EAST

LIEUTENANT GEORGES PELLETIER d'OISY (DOISY)
FLIGHT: PARIS TO TOKYO – 24 APRIL TO 9 JUNE, 1924

Frenchman Lieutenant d'Oisy left Paris (Villacoublay) on 24 April, 1924. His mechanic was l'Adjudant Bernard Vesin (Besin) and their plane was an Avion Breguet XIX powered by a Lorraine 450 CV(hp) motor.

Their journey of seven weeks was a saga of adventures with an engine change at Hanoi. d'Oisy's landing was *hot* at Shanghai where he *wrote-off* his plane in a ditch. Without hesitation the Chinese loaned him another Breguet to finish his flight to Tokyo.

Their flight continued uneventfully from Shanghai through Peking, and Mukden to Pingyang (Pyong-Yang), the old capital of Korea. On 4 June, they left Pingyang at dawn and after flying about 300 miles arrived at Tai-ku (near Fu-san) in South Korea four hours later.

The next morning they started across the Korea Strait to Japan, but thick fog forced their return to Tai-ku. Sunday (8 June) they tried again, and crossed the 120 watery miles, landing at Hiroshima on the S.W. coast of Japan. Refuelling delayed them for less than an hour and they reached Osaka by 1400 hours.

They completed the final 300 miles to Tokyo the next morning. Their time from Osaka to Tokorosawa aerodrome took three hours.

Although the mishap at Shanghai deprived them of their original machine their flight was no less meritorious. They completed the final, difficult 2,300 miles to Tokyo in an older and slower machine. This they handled with the same degree of hustle that marked the earlier stages of their flight.

Lieutenant d'Oisy and Bernard Vesin had flown 11,500 miles in 46 days. Here is the log of their splendid 1924 achievement.

		Miles
1924:		
April 24	Paris – Bucharest	1,240
25	Bucharest – Aleppo	930

1924:		Miles
26	Aleppo – Baghdad	460
27	Baghdad – Bushire	500
28	Bushire – Bandar Abbas	340
29	Bandar Abbas – Karachi	700
May 3	Karachi – Agra	700
5	Agra – Calcutta	750
9	Calcutta – Rangoon	650
10	Rangoon – Bangkok	350
11	Bangkok – Saigon	480
13	Saigon – Hanoi	750
18	Hanoi – Canton	500
20	Canton – Shanghai	800
29	Shanghai – Peking	700
June 2	Peking – Mukden	400
3	Mukden – Pingyang (Korea)	230
4	Pingyang – Tai-ku (Korea)	300
8	Tai-ku – Osaka (Japan) via Hiroshima	425
9	Osaka – Tokorosawa (Tokyo)	295
	TOTAL	11,500

*

China, in 1923, bought 70 aeroplanes designated Breguet 14/400 and powered by the 400hp 12Da Lorraine-Dietrich. The type played a part in many internal wars in China in the inter-war years.

In 1926, Capitaine d'Oisy made another flight to the Far East. On 11 June, again flying an Avion Breguet XIX, he left Paris. Just seven days later, on 18 June, he arrived in Peking. He had covered 6,306 miles in 63 hours 30 minutes flying time! An extraordinary achievement!

*

In the following years France's aerial hero was rarely out of the news. Born on March 9, 1892, Gunural de Brigade, Commaneur de la Lugion d'Honneur, Georges Pelletier d'Oisy died on May 15, 1953.

* * *

THE AMERICAN ROUND-THE-WORLD FLIERS – 1924.

On March 17, 1924, four Douglas World Cruisers flew out of Santa Monica, California. They were on the first stage of their attempt on the round-the-world record and under the leadership of Major Frederick L. Martin. Their successful trip took 175 days and covered 27,534 miles (44,312km). It included 15 days, 11 hours and 7 minutes of flying time. Just two of the original planes arrived back in Seattle. The date was September 28 and the US Army Air Service had completed the first circumnavigation of the world.

The Douglas World Cruiser was a specially designed, two-seater, dual-controlled biplane to operate from both land and water. A single 400hp, 12-cylinder Liberty engine produced a top speed of 103mph (166km/h). Range of the DWC (the service designation) was 2,200 miles (3,550km) as a land plane and 1,650 miles (2,660km) when fitted with floats. Donald Wills Douglas built five DWCs, four for the flight and one as the back-up aircraft.

AIRPORT OF THE NINE DRAGONS, KAI TAK, KOWLOON

Major Martin and his mechanic, Staff Sergeant Alva Harvey, crewed *Seattle*, the number one aircraft. Lieutenant Lowell H. Smith and Sergeant Arthur Turner drew *Chicago*, with *Boston* going to Lieutenant Leigh Wade and Sergeant Henry Ogden and Lieutenants Erik H. Nelson and John Harding getting *New Orleans*. Lieutenants Leslie P. Arnold and LeClaire Schultze were the reserve pilots. When Sergeant Turner reported sick Lieutenant Arnold replaced him.

Their route was Seattle-Japan-India-Europe-Iceland-Greenland-Seattle. From a comfortable chair that looked less than formidable. Yet with most paper plans it was to prove an illusion. Ahead were 57 *hops* with the expectation of foul weather, crashes, and high drama.

The trip got off to a good start but trouble was just ahead. At Prince Rupert, British Columbia, Major Martin landed the Seattle in shallow water and damaged a float. Repairs would take time so Martin ordered the other three crews to continue to the next scheduled stop. With repairs completed bad weather prevented his departure until 25 April. While en-route to Dutch Harbour, Martin encountered heavy fog and flew into a mountain top. The crash demolished the *Seattle* but the men survived. Meanwhile, at Dutch Harbour the weather prevented the others from mounting a search. Ten days later Martin and Harvey trudged out of the wilderness to civilisation.

Major Martin then made a hard decision. He could have waited for the spare DWC but figured that the delay might give another nation the chance to become first round-the-world. Martin ordered the flight to proceed and appointed Lieutenant Smith to assume command.

The flight did continue, across two oceans, jungles and deserts. The remaining DWCs battled fog and drifting icebergs. The planes' small glass windshields were about six inches high and 18 inches in width and gave little protection from the slipstream and freezing rain. They screeched through passes of unmarked mountain peaks. Malaria-carrying mosquitoes spoiled their rest. There were no weather forecasts and mechanical problems were never far away.

By June 2 they had reached Kagoshima, Japan, where 50,000 flag-waving Japanese gave them an enthusiastic welcome. Just after midday, on June 8, they flew through Lei Yue Mun Pass and touched down in Kowloon Harbour, Hong Kong.

Leslie Arnold tells a humorous story when his engine overheated. "We landed in a river in Indochina, the other boys landed alongside. A cracked cylinder meant we had to get a new engine, so the others took off for Tourane, our closest spares pool. Lowell Smith and I stayed in the airplane sleeping on the wings. Days passed, until one night the Swedish accent of Erik Nelson wafted down the river. He arrived with a fleet of sampans that took us in tow. With the rising sun I could see the headman sitting beneath a parasol, surrounded by cushions, being fanned by his favourite wives. This gave me much to think about! Was I living in the wrong country? Several days later we arrived at the Standard Oil wharf in the capital of the French Province of Annam."

On the homeward-bound leg *Boston's* engine seized. Wade and Ogden successfully ditched in the Atlantic. They were picked up and taken to join the other two DWCs waiting at Newfoundland. The back-up plane at Seattle became *Boston II* and flown to Newfoundland for Wade and Ogden to complete the flight.

They returned to a heroes' welcome. President Calvin Coolidge praised their achievement and all America revelled in the glory of being the first around the world.

Here is a summary of the great flight. Total elapsed time 175 days; mileage 27,534; days actually in the air 66; actual flying time 351 hours 11 minutes; average speed 76.26 mph.

Today *Chicago* is in the National Air and Space Museum, Washington, and *New Orleans* in the USAF Museum, Ohio. But Major Frederick Martin's role in that great adventure has slipped from memory.

APPENDIX 5

Major Martin rose to the rank of major-general but was fated to end his career under a less than silver-lined cloud. He commanded Hickham Field, Hawaii on that fateful Sunday morning of December 7, 1941. General Martin was criticised for not dispersing his aircraft to minimise the damage of that sneak attack. Frederick Martin again faded into obscurity and died in 1954 at the age of 72.

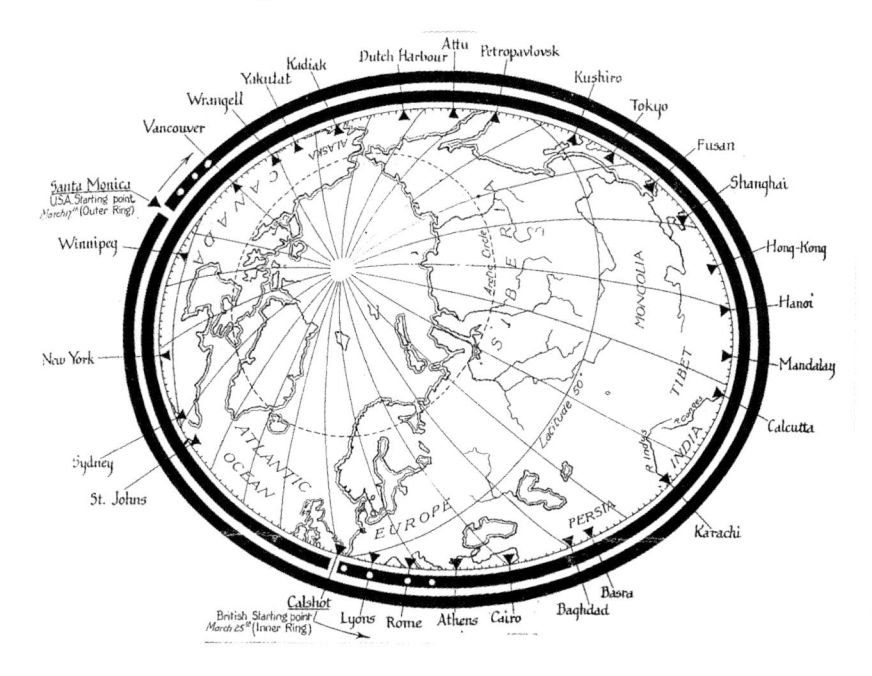

The above chart, published in *Flight* magazine of April 3, 1924, permitted the reader to plot the weekly progress of the American and British round-the-world flights. The Americans flew clockwise (i.e. east to west), and the Vickers *Vulture* anti-clockwise.

THE AMERICAN ROUND-THE-WORLD FLIGHT – 1924
MARCH 17 – SEPTEMBER 28

Major Frederick L. Martin, leader of the flight.

(Photo: US Air Force Central Museum, Ohio)

Lieutenant Leslie P. Arnold during the world flight.

(Photo: US Air Force Central Museum, Ohio)

AIRPORT OF THE NINE DRAGONS, KAI TAK, KOWLOON

The Douglas World Cruisers prepare for the Atlantic Ocean crossing. In the foreground is New Orleans, *piloted by Lts Harding and Nelson. It is preserved at the US Air Force Central Museum, Ohio.* (Photo: US Air Force Central Museum, Ohio)

* * *

THE BRITISH WORLD FLIGHT ATTEMPT – 1924

With little fanfare three British aviators left Calshot, Tuesday, March 25. The Vickers-Napier Vulture amphibian biplane slid down the slipway, headed towards Southampton while taking off, circled back over Calshot, and quickly disappeared in the distance. The British round-the-world flight had opened – it was just after noon.

"We have failed, but we did our best.

We were beaten in the end by fog."

With these words Squadron Leader Archibald Stuart Charles S. MacLaren, OBE, MC, DFC, AFC, concluded his narrative of the British failure to fly around the world.

Squadron Leader MacLaren had begun with congratulations to the successful American airmen. Then a tribute to gallant Flying Officer William Noble Plenderleith, who piloted the plane, and Flight Sergeant R. Andrews, his engineer. The distinguished audience at the Hotel Cecil heard this exciting account of the flight.

"Soon after leaving the English coast we found fog waiting for us in the Channel. It forced us lower and lower. By a hair's breadth we avoided colliding with the French cliffs near Havre. This was a bad start but the weather worsened across France and Italy. While crossing the Apennines in dense rain-laden clouds and failing light a small gap appeared in the clouds below us. We found ourselves in a small valley with a railway line that we followed to Brindisi. I still ponder what would have happened if a tunnel . . .

"Our next incident occurred en route to Corfu. We had just completed the sea crossing from Italy, when our engine gave a tremendous backfire, severely vibrated, and then seized. Plenderleith lowered the nose and as we broke through cloud we found ourselves over a large lake – the only possible landing place for miles. The Greek Navy hauled our machine out of the lake, got us into the sea then towed us to Corfu. The ratings from the British battleship the *Emperor of India* installed a spare Napier engine and we arrived at Cairo by moonlight.

APPENDIX 5

"We made good time to Baghdad, albeit losing sight of the desert track for an anxious half-hour. All went well from Baghdad to Karachi, then our tribulations returned. Another seized engine forced our landing in the scorching Sind desert near the village of Parlu. The Royal Air Force dispatched another engine from Baghdad.

"Little happened until we reached Akyab, but the 17 days lost in the Sind meant we hit a furious monsoon. For three days our plane was soaked by torrential rain. Our plane was sluggish on take-off, we just cleared the boundary trees, but Plenderleith could not keep us airborne – we struck the water. This severely damaged our hull and we started to sink. A boat towed us to a beach.

"The damage proved beyond repair. Shrugging off our disappointment we cabled home for our spare plane waiting at Tokyo. The American Navy wasted little time in bringing our replacement Vulture.

"The delay at Akyab had not improved the weather across the Arakan Yoma (mountains) to Rangoon. After leaving Rangoon for Bangkok impenetrable, towering cumuli clouds prevented us crossing that vast range of mountains. We were finally forced to abandon our attempt and land at Tavoy on the southern Burma coast. The next day we managed to make a nervous crossing to land in the Bangkok River.

"The mountain range between Siam and Indo-China provided more anxiety. As we approached the mass of sinister black clouds blanketing the range Plenderleith couldn't out climb them. By this time, we had all got the wind up, and backtracked to find some opening in the clouds. We found a hole and sighted a clearing in the middle of the jungle. We decided to land and wait for an improvement in the weather. As we approached we disturbed a herd of elephants that rushed trumpeting into the trees. The lower we came the longer grew the grass until in horror we realised our clearing was a vast swamp. With no alternative Plenderleith climbed back into the clouds until blue sky appeared above. After an hour we saw the distant sea. The three of us solemnly shook hands on that splendid sight.

"Our flight to Hong Kong, Shanghai, across the China Sea, to Tokyo was a pleasant experience. The Japanese people treated us as royalty. We left Tokyo with a passenger, Colonel Broome, and almost immediately our nemesis had returned – fog! We made three forced landings during that first day's flight yet we reached Yetorup, the first of the Kurile Islands, landing safely in a large lake.

"Dense fog delayed us a day, and when we finally got off we met more fog and storms. We had to turn back and land in a small open bay on Tokotan, another of the Kurile Islands. Our anchors didn't hold, and it was with the utmost difficulty that we prevented the machine from being dashed on the beach. Plenderleith nursed the machine out to sea, got her airborne and landed in a small lake just inland. The machine weathered a most unpleasant night, but it was nothing to the dense fog, rain, and gales of the next two days. On the third day a Japanese destroyer found us and radioed the world of our safety. We resumed our journey seven days after landing at Tokotan.

"The passage along the Kuriles was an anxious one. Plenderleith battled dense fog all the way to Petropavlovsk in Kamchatka. There our gallant little supply ship *Thiepval* waited patiently for us.

"Now I come to the last day of our flight, 2 August. We left Oest Kamchatka facing 130 miles of angry sea. Within minutes thick fog forced us to within 50 feet of the ocean. As we neared the coast the fog forced us even lower until we flew between the ocean swells. Without warning black cliffs of a small inlet loomed ahead – Plenderleith swerved just in time. We were now in a state of nervous prostration and decided to land in the open sea. Plenderleith made a perfect landing in that murderous sea but while taxiing a huge wave smashed our port float to kindling and buried the wing's tip in the water. The machine swung suddenly dipping the starboard wing that tore off that float and part of the wing-tip. We were now hopelessly lost but Plenderleith kept us moving on a northerly bearing towards Bering Island. Meanwhile Broome and I ran up and down the wing trying to balance the machine. After three hours of this the fog suddenly lifted and we saw the coastline about half a mile ahead. With the machine breaking-up we anchored just off the surf line, jumped into the icy water, and struggled to the beach. We were only a mile or two from Nikolski. The *Thiepval* salved the remains of our machine the next morning."

A bitterly disappointed Squadron Leader MacLaren retained a semblance of humour – never again would he criticise the London *pea-soupers* – they were child's play!

* * *

MAJOR PEDRO ZANNI – 1924

The Argentine Air Service chose Major Zanni, Lieutenant Page Nelson and Chief Engineer F. Beltrame, for its aerial round-the-world dash. The only difference to the route followed by Squadron-Leader MacLaren's British team was the starting and finishing points – Amsterdam.

Under the guidance of Mijnheer Anthony Fokker, the famous aeroplane designer, they settled on Fokker C.1V machines powered by British Napier Lion engines. They would use a land type for the first stage to Tokyo, a float type for the Pacific crossing, and a specially constructed Fokker-Napier mono-seaplane for the Atlantic hop.

The morning of July 26, 1924, Lieutenant Page Nelson (navigator) became seriously ill. Major Zanni decided to proceed without him, and by 0630 hours Zanni and Beltrame had set course over Amsterdam. They arrived at Le Bourget at 1500 hours following a technical landing at Le Cateau.

They departed from Paris at 1056 hours the following morning, arriving at Lyons at 1345 hours. Monday, 28 July, found them *en route* to Rome.

On July 30, they landed in Constantinople, and after an hour's stop flew on to Aleppo. They were in Baghdad early the next day, and continued on to Basra. By August 1, they had reached Bandar Abbas, and by the fifth had reached Naserabad after landing at Karachi. With buoyant spirits they realised they had covered 5,500 miles in 11 days.

Allahabad was their next stop arriving in the early afternoon of 6 August. At Allahabad their luck deserted them! During the night torrential rain made the airfield a quagmire. The following morning's take-off ended when the wheels sank into the mud smashing the propeller. They found a replacement propeller but the delay prevented them leaving for Calcutta until late in the morning.

A crowd of officials and spectators awaited their arrival at Dumdum Aerodrome. They waited in vain! Neither men, machine, nor news of their whereabouts reached the aerodrome

APPENDIX 5

and the well-wishers dispersed. On the following morning (August 8), the Fokker turned up at Calcutta. Zanni stated he made a forced landing near Isri (Bikar), 200 miles or so from Calcutta. Thick fog was the culprit. He saw little future in dodging trees and water-buffaloes just above the ground and landed in an open space. They tried to sleep in their machine but a large crowd of Indians touching and shaking their Fokker kept them awake.

At Calcutta they fitted a new propeller. Beltrame also made a thorough check of the engine – it showed signs of rough running. This was the probable result of the propeller striking the ground at Allahabad. Not until Thursday, August 14, did they get out of Calcutta, flying direct to Akyab and then to Rangoon where they landed in late afternoon. Zanni reported the flight from Akyab was a nightmare of heavy rain and severe turbulence.

More trouble came to the Argentine airmen on take-off from Hanoi. With rain saturating the field their Fokker overturned and suffered extensive damage. The men escaped injury.

Major Zanni cabled Hong Kong for their replacement Fokker float-plane. The S.S. *President Madison* had positioned it some weeks beforehand. The Japanese steamer *Chukwa Maru* brought it to Haiphong.

They left Hanoi August 22, landing in Kowloon Harbour the next day. The Chinese authorities withheld ongoing clearance as the country was in the grip of internal strife. Their permission to fly to Shanghai came on 27 September. At Foochow, adverse weather grounded them for several days, until, on October 1, they landed in Shanghai. They had covered the 500 miles from Foochow in five hours.

Zanni and Beltrame left Shanghai on October 9 for the Japanese city of Kagoshima. The following day they flew the 300 miles to Kushimoto in good time. On the 10th they landed at the Kasumigaura naval air station, near Tokyo. There, Major Zanni ended the flight because of the lateness of the season.

Major Zanni and Chief Engineer Beltrame had taken 19 flying days for their Amsterdam-Tokyo flight – one day less than Pelletier d'Oisy's Paris-Tokyo flight. They flew the first 7,500 miles (Amsterdam-Hanoi) in 17 flying days, with one Napier Lion engine.

HAIPHONG – 21 AUGUST, 1924
Major Zanni's Fokker C.1V being refuelled by Shell-Mex. This was the standby plane (float version) brought by the Japanese steamer Chukwa Maru *from Hong Kong.* (Photo: Courtesy Royal Air Force Museum)

AIRPORT OF THE NINE DRAGONS, KAI TAK, KOWLOON

THE SPANISH RAID – MADRID TO MANILA – 1926

PILOTS: Captains;
RAFAEL MARTINEZ ESTEVE
EDUARDO GONZALEZ GALLARZA (1899-1986)
JOAQUIN LORINGA (TABOADA) (1895-1927)

MECHANICS:
JOAQUIN AROZAMEN
PEDRO MARIANO CALVO
EUGENIO PEREZ

The great Spanish *raid* from Madrid to Manila germinated in the minds of Jose Carillo, Eduardo Gallarza and Joaquin Loringa in June 1924. This followed a successful delivery flight from Paris to Madrid in a *Potez XV* plane. The dream ended for Jose *Pepe* Carillo when, in October, he died fighting Moroccan rebels.

The motives for the flight paralleled those of other aerial-minded nations – prestige, emotion and sentiment. The loss of the Philippines, then under American control, had ended Spain's Colonial Empire. This flight would rejoin the two like-speaking countries and show the advances made by Spanish fliers. The 94,000 pesetas cost of the flight was an investment in a future passenger service.

The planned flight was 20 stages over 30 calendar days. The Spanish Air Force meteorologists set a starting frame before 25 March and not later than 15 April, the desert heat and the typhoons that spawned in the China Sea the deciding factors.

The plane chosen was the Breguet X1X A2 powered by the double V 12-cylinder Elizade A4 Lorraine Dietrich that developed 450 hp. The longest stage was between Cairo and Baghdad. They increased the Breguet's fuel capacity for this 1400 km sector.

At 0815 hours on 5 April, 1926, three Breguet X1Xs of the Elcano Squadron took off in perfect formation from Madrid. At an altitude of 1500m they passed between Alicante and Cartagena. They arrived at Argel (Maison Blanche) just under five hours and 900 km later.

On the second day low cloud and unexpected headwinds separated the formation. Martinez Esteve followed the coastline at a minimum height dodging trees and rugged outcrops. A check on his fuel showed he could not make Tripoli so he diverted to Tunis. Then a rough running engine forced him to land at Garros. The problem taxed Calvo's ability and he took hours to rectify the fault.

Esteve made every effort to catch up but when Gallarza and Loriga landed in Cairo on April 8, Esteve trailed them by a day. They extended their stay in Cairo to allow Esteve and Calvo to rest and check their plane.

The sector from El Cairo to Baghdad was the most difficult. On the 11th the three Breguets climbed to 3,000m and logged abeam of Port Said. Mount Sinai, protruding from a sea of blue haze, floated by to starboard. Gaza slipped by and they crossed into Palestine passing the spires of sacred Jerusalem with the Dead Sea off their starboard beam. Ahead was the Trans-Jordan city of Amman and beyond – the forbidding Syrian Desert.

Gallarza's engine then lost power and he fell behind and forced landed 60 km from Amman. The dust-laden air then caused Esteve's engine to over-heat and he landed at a British emergency field. Loriga circled as Esteve lost altitude and safely landed. He then continued on to Baghdad, only relaxing when the Euphrates River appeared out of the haze. There was no news of Gallarza or Esteve. Some hours later Gallarza's plane screamed out of the fading light and parked beside Loriga's plane.

Esteve and Calvo's *raid* on Manila ended in the sands of the desert. Esteve later wrote *Una Aventura En el Desierto – An Adventure In the Desert* – it enjoyed instant success. He told of Calvo finding the cause of the failure within minutes of landing. Sand particles had blocked the fuel line. This proved easy to fix, but a check of the carburettor found a collapsed float.

They built a smoke fire but could not attract several planes that flew overhead. Esteve decided they should walk towards a Bedouin caravan he had seen snaking its way through the dunes just before he landed. They could not find it! Within two hours of leaving an RAF patrol found their abandoned plane.

By the 14th they were ravenously hungry with little water. When Calvo, now weak and delirious, dropped off to sleep Esteve went exploring and got lost. The next afternoon a British patrol passed less than 50 yards away yet Esteve was too weak to attract their attention.

The RAF 47th Squadron found Calvo on the 17th and shortly thereafter Esteve. They had survived in the desert with little food and water for seven days.

Then Madrid instructed Esteve to abandon their flight. Their delay had brought them into the China Sea typhoon season. With the others already in Calcutta this was a wise decision.

Gallarza and Loriga left Calcutta on 18 April, staging through Rangoon, Bangkok and Saigon. They made a refuel stop at Vink and landed at Hanoi late on the 26th.

On May 1, they left Hanoi for Macau. Loriga landed at Macau on a tree-enclosed football field with a seized engine. Gallarza, following him, landed too fast and finished in the branches of a tree. The Macanese gave the Spanish airmen unfettered use of their workshops but their engineers lacked aeronautical experience. Two British aircraft fitters, sent from Hong Kong, winched Gallarza's plane from the tree and repaired the bent airframe. They could do little with Loriga's useless engine.

A single Breguet X1X commanded by Gallarza, with Loriga his observer, left Macau on 11 May. They landed in Manila two days later.

* * *

FLIGHT LOG: MADRID – MANILA 1926

1926	TRIP	Distance (km)	Flying hr min	Average Speed (km/h)
5 March	Cuatro Vientos – Argel	900	4 40	192.9
6	Argel – Tripoli	1300	7 00	185.7
7	Tripoli – Bengasi	950	6 00	158.3
8	Bengasi – El Cairo	1150	7 40	150.0
	Sub-Total 1	4300	25 20	169.7
11	El Cairo – Bagdad	1400	8 10	171.4
13	Bagdad – Bushire	900	4 30	200.0
13	Bushire – Bander Abbas	600	3 00	200.0
14	Bander Abbas – Karachi	1250	7 30	166.7
	Sub-Total 2	8450	48 30	174.2
16	Karachi – Agra	1250	6 50	182.9
18	Agra – Calcutta	1300	7 00	185.7
21	Calcutta – Rangoon	1200	7 30	160.0
22	Rangoon – Bangkok	700	4 00	175.0
22	Bangkok – Saigon	750	5 00	150.0
	Sub-Total 3	13650	78 50	173.1
26	Saigon – Vink	1000		
26	Vink – Hanoi	300	10 35	122.8
1 May	Hanoi – Macau	850	6 55	122.9
11	Macau – Aparri	900	6 55	130.1
13	Aparri – Manila	400	3 00	133.3
	Grand Total	17100	106 15	161.1

THE PRIDE OF DETROIT – SCHLEE & BROCK – 1927.

It was in 1926 that Eddie Stinson's company built the SB-1 Detroiter. In April 1927 the new SM-1 emerged. Like the original version it was a large high-wing monoplane offering 400lb (188kg) more payload than its predecessor. Stinson retained the 220hp Wright Whirlwind J-5 engine. The Wayco Air Service, owned by Schlee, bought the first aircraft and named it *Pride of Detroit*.

Edward *Ed* Schlee was also the President of the Wayco Oil Corporation, and could fly a plane. His pilot was William *Billy* Brock, who learned to fly at the age of 16 years. Brock had honed his skills flying the U.S. air mail and was held in high regard by his peers.

On August 22, 1927, the *Pride of Detroit* set course from Detroit's Ford Airport on a planned 15-day round-the-world flight. The two Americans crossed the Atlantic from Harbour Grace, Newfoundland, to London in 23 hours 19 minutes arriving at 1033 hours Sunday, August 28, having covered 2,850 miles. A Plymouth observer sighted a yellow monoplane overhead about 0700 hours, but the airmen didn't know of this. They did see land but thought it was Ireland. Their maps were crude and this placed them at a disadvantage identifying the terrain of a strange country. They circled for a long time and then flew along the Devon coast to Seaton, where they dropped messages asking for the name of the town and country. A large Union Jack spread out on the ground answered for the country, but they couldn't read the scrawled name. They carried on and finally recognised landmarks that brought them to Croydon. With no news since their Plymouth sighting the authorities thought they had continued on to the Continent. A mere 50 people applauded their splendid deed.

At Croydon they told an exciting story of their crossing. In mid-Atlantic a storm had raged that Billy Brock described as appalling. At times they operated between 200 and 10,000 feet until the freezing cold forced them down to be again battered by turbulence. As the sun set they ran into a sinister line of thick cloud and when dawn broke they were still in it. They sighted two ships during the crossing, and during a brief thinning of the cloud they thought they glimpsed the Fastnet Rock Light.

Not discouraged they left Croydon for Munich the next morning and landed there at 1559 hours the same day. They reached Belgrade at noon on August 30. Their flight continued across the sub-continent of India until they landed at Kai Tak, Hong Kong.

Schlee and Brock eventually arrived in Tokyo 18 days after leaving Newfoundland. They shipped their plane from Yokohama to the States. Again taking to the skies over San Francisco the *Pride of Detroit* touched down at Detroit's Ford Airfield after six weeks of high adventure.

THE PRIDE OF DETROIT

The Stinson SB-1 Detroiter at Hong Kong on September 9, 1927. (Photo: Fred Lillywhite)

APPENDIX 5

THE RAF's FAR EAST FLIGHT – 1927-1928

A year before this great saga began two flying boats skipped off the waters of Plymouth. They were Supermarine Mk 1 Southamptons commanded by Squadron Leader *Gerry* E Livock, DFC, AFC. His mission was to fly to Aboukir, Egypt and Cyprus and return to England within 29 days, a distance of 11,265km (7,000 miles). This, the RAF's first true long-range flight into foreign waters, was successful and paved the way for the more ambitious project soon to be.

The Mk I had a hull constructed of wood. Its disadvantage was that it could soak up 180kg (400lb) of sea water, which created problems in handling. The Mk II, fitted with a corrosion-resistant duralumin hull, offered a structure 245kg (540lb) lighter than its predecessor, and no soakage penalties. With twin 502hp Napier Lion V engines providing the power the Southampton had a maximum range of 1,500km (930 miles). The type made many notable long-distance flights; the most famous was the one that follows.

On October 14, 1927, four Southampton 11's left Felixstowe to fly to Plymouth. Named the *Far East Flight*, its commander was Group Captain H. M. Cave-Brown-Cave, DSO, DFC. His co-pilot was Flying Officer S. D. Scott. The Group Captain's second-in-command was Squadron Leader Gerry Livock, DFC, AFC, whose assistant was Flight Lieutenant H. G. Sawyer. The two other boat captains were Flight Lieutenant Andrew Carnegie, AFC, helped by Flight Lieutenant P. E. Maitland, and Flight Lieutenant C. C. Wigglesworth supported by Flying Officer G. E. Nicholetts.

Cave-Brown-Cave's mandate was to open an air route to Australia and the Far East. They were to assess routes and select landing sites for flying-boat operation, independent of established bases, and record the Southampton's performances under different climatic conditions. Then the opportunity of *showing the Union Jack* in countries previously unvisited or unexplored was too good to ignore. The preparations for such an extended cruise took almost a year.

Three days later all four took-off from Plymouth Sound and, in formation, smoothly rolled on to the first leg of their cruise to Singapore. This was the first time a RAF flying-boat had attempted such a lengthy flight. A flight that covered vast stretches of sea and land unfamiliar to the men. With their splashdown at Singapore's Seletar, on 28 February 1928, each plane had behaved splendidly.

On 21 May they commenced a tour of Australia, returning to Singapore on 13 September. On 1 November, with a substitute Southampton, the Far East Flight crowned their success with a tour of South-East Asia. They landed at Kuching, Labuan, Puerto Princesa and Manila. From Salamague, near the northern tip of Luzon, they set a westerly course across the restless China Sea, and buoyed in Kowloon Bay on November 18, 1928. After a week's rest they returned to the Lion City through Tourane, Coconut Bay, Bangkok, Victoria Point and Penang. When their great adventure concluded at Singapore on December 11, 1928, they had completed 5,340 miles in 41 days.

The *Daily News* applauded it *the greatest flight in history* – a fitting description of an outstanding feat of navigation and endurance that remains the Southampton's most celebrated triumph. At Seletar the Southamptons become the initial equipment of the reformed No. 205 Squadron. On January 8, 1929, Squadron Leader G. E. *Gerry* Livock, DFC, AFC, became the unit's first commander.

AIRPORT OF THE NINE DRAGONS, KAI TAK, KOWLOON

SUPERMARINE Mk II SOUTHAMPTON FLYING BOAT

Arrived in Hong Kong November 18, 1928. At RAF Station Seletar, Singapore, receiving the final overhaul for the Australian segment of the Far East Flight. Departure date May 21, 1928. (Photo: Royal Air Force Museum)

* * *

MARGA von ETZDORF

The stately Fraulein Marga von Etzdorf was the tragedienne of German aviation. Marga was born into a famous Berlin Army family on August 1, 1907. She was among the greatest sports flyers that Germany produced in the late twenties and early thirties. In the smallest planes she *raided* the world's distant skies. Blessed with exceptional courage her career was a spate of accidents.

On August 29, 1931, she flew her Junkers Junior, affectionately called *Kiek in die Welt* (Jump into the World), equipped with a 80 hp Genet-Motor, from Berlin to Tokyo (Haneda). Her track took her to Constantinople, the Canary Islands and to Tokyo. Against advice she took off into the teeth of a threatening storm that worsened as she crossed the Mediterranean from the African Coast to Sicily. At Sicily she hit a wall on the aerodrome and badly damaged her plane.

In April 1932, she landed at Kai Tak en route Japan to Surabaya. At an intermediate landing she suffered extensive injury. Her beloved Junior was a write-off.

Fraulein Marga von Etzdorf – 1931.
(Photo: Courtesy Deutsches Museum, Munich)

APPENDIX 5

On 27 May, 1933, she left Berlin in a Klemm KL32 plane bound for Australia. She seriously damaged her plane on landing near Aleppo in Syria.

This, her third major accident, preyed on her mind. She told friends that her head was a mass of pain and decided to make an early night. Turning on the stairs she said it would be a relief if she would not wake again! That night she ended her life.

Fraulein Marga von Etzdorf's writing leaves a splendid picture. She describes the wonderful art of flying and her opinion of the planes she handled.

She was awarded the Golden Service Medal of the Kaiser Japanese Aero Clubs. An honour given to few!

Her name is inscribed on the Aero Club of Deutschland's Golden Roll of Honour. She is in splendid company – Elly Beinhorn, Kohl von Hunefeld, Eckener and von Koenig-Warthausen – other famous flyers.

* * *

THE FLYING HONEYMOONERS – Mr & Mrs C. H. DAY

The round-the-world honeymooners came from Ridgewood, New Jersey, USA. In a biplane, designed by the groom, they left Heston on 30 May, 1931. They planned to visit Paris, Brussels, Berlin, Constantinople, Palestine, Iraq, India and China. From Shanghai they intended to ship their plane home across the Pacific. In early October they arrived in Hong Kong and left on the 9th – next stop Amoy.

* * *

CAPTAIN FERNANDO REIN LORING
Spanish Pioneer Aviator
Birth: September 9, 1902.
Death: June 24, 1978. (76 years).

First *Raid* (flight) Madrid-Manila –
April – July 1932

For his first *raid* – Madrid to Manila – Fernando Rein Loring chose a plane built by his Uncle Jorge. This was a Loring E-II designed by the Spanish engineer Eduardo Barron. A Kinner K5 of 100 CV (hp) with five cylinders powered the tiny craft. Carrying the registration EC-ASA and the nickname *la Pepa*, he left his uncle's aerodrome, Cuatro Vientos, at 0600 hours on 25 April, 1932.

The flight experienced few untoward problems until he arrived in Hong Kong on 31 May. Throughout June a strong southerly wind swept the South China Sea, preventing Loring from completing the final segment of his flight.

The meteorologists' forecasts were not encouraging and he sought permission from the Japanese authorities on Formosa for permission to make an intermediate stop there.

Several weeks elapsed before the Japanese granted their permission. Almost simultaneously the southerly winds abated.

In early July he left Hong Kong on the final segment of his flight. The trip lacked problems and he landed in Manila after a refuelling stop at Aparri, on the northern point of Luzon Island.

The flight's log

Route:	Kilometres
Madrid – Malaga	420
Malaga – Argel (Algiers), 750km and Argel – Tunez (Tunis), 650km	1400
Tunis – Tripoli, 650km and Tripoli-Benghazi 850km	1500

Benghazi – Cairo, 1120km, and Cairo-Gaza, 350km 1470
Gaza – Baghdad 960
Baghdad – Bushire (Bushehr), 800km and
Bushire – Lingeh (Bandar-e Lengeh), 500km 1300
Lingeh – Jask, 380km and Jask – Karachi 960km 1340
Karachi – Jodhpur, 620km and Jodhpur – Allahabad, 880km 1500
Allahabad – Calcutta, 740km and Calcutta – Akyab, 650km 1390
Akyab – Rangoon, 520km and Rangoon – Bangkok, 640km 1160
Bangkok – Hanoi 975
Hanoi – Hong Kong 900
Hong Kong – Aparri 900km, and Aparri – Manila, 400km 1300

Total Distance 15,615

* * *

Second Raid (flight) Madrid-Manila – 18 March-10 April, 1933

Loring continued his preference for small single-seater planes. This time he settled on a British Swift built by Nick Comper and powered by a Pobjoy 90hp engine. He baptised his Swift *Ciudad de Manila*. The *City of Manila* carried the Spanish registration EC-AAT.

For twelve days of flying he pressed his tiny plane and his *City of Manila* responded. The 90hp Pobjoy didn't miss a beat. The following log shows her reliability.

Date 1933	Route km	Distance km	Time hr min
18 March	Madrid-Tunis	1,460	7.30
19	Tunis-Benghazi	1,510	8.15
20	Benghazi-Cairo	1,100	5.15
21	Cairo-Baghdad	1,250	7.15
22	Baghdad-Bushire	800	4.00
24	Bushire-Jask-Jodhpur	2,400	12.00
25	Jodhpur-Calcutta	1,620	8.30
26	Calcutta-Rangoon	1,170	6.00
27	Rangoon-Lhankon (Thekek)	1,250	10.00
7 April	Lhankon-Hanoi	450	2.30
8	Hanoi-Hong Kong	850	5.00
10	Hong Kong-Manila	1,140	6.25
	Total	15,000km	82.40

Comparison of his two planes:

Dimension	Loring E-II	Comper Swift
Wing	12.50 m	7.32 m
Length	8.10 m	5.39 m
Height	2.80 m	-
Empty Weight	500 kg	280 kg
AUW	910 kg	531 kg
Engine	Kinner K.5 5 cylinder 100 hp	Pobjoy R Radial 7 cylinder 90 hp.
Maximum Speed	185 km/h	210 km/h
Cruise Speed	150 km/h	193 km/h
Radio Range	1,300 km	1,600 km

APPENDIX 5

CAPTAIN FERNANDO REIN LORING:

2nd Raid *(flight)* Madrid-Manila – 18 March-10 April, 1933. Posing with the British Comper Swift – *the* City of Manila – EC-AAT.

(Photo: Felipe E. Ezquerro)

WOLFGANG von GRONAU

In an aviation career of outstanding achievements von Gronau's greatest adventure occurred in 1932. In four months, beginning on 22 July, his world flight covered 44,000km. He tracked to Iceland, Greenland, Canada, USA, Alaska, Aleutians, Japan and Shanghai. On 27 September he arrived in Hong Kong just before noon. He returned to List auf Silt on 9 November having visited Indonesia, Rangoon, Ceylon, Karachi, Baghdad, Athens, and Rome.

The plane that gave him the victory was the one that Roald Amundsen flew to the North Pole. The Dornier – Gronland -*Wal* (Whale) carried the registration D-1422. Von Gronau had a splendid crew; Funker Albrecht (radio), Flugzeugfuhrer Zimmer (co-pilot) and Bordmonteur Hack (mechanic).

Wolfgang was born in Berlin on 25 February, 1893. He grew up in East Prussia, Insterburg and Konigsberg. His father was General of Artillery and Governor of Thorn.

In 1911, he became a sea-cadet in the Kaiserliche Marine. Appointed a Naval Lieutenant (second class) in 1915 he took command of the sea-flying station at Norderney. He kept this secret from his family – his older brother lost his life flying patrol. Wolfgang told his parents he had joined the zeppelin service as many considered it safer than flying aeroplanes because of unreliable motors. He was a *secret* flyer!

On May 1, 1915, a propaganda release exposed his secret when his family learned that he commanded the Seefliegerabzeichen. This was the future Naval Air Arm. His group gathered information deep into the North Sea operating from the Isle of Borkum. In November 1915, he commanded flight operations from the mother ship *Answald* that operated out of Kurland. In December while on patrol, a Russian warship shot him down but he managed to crash in the shallow surf. A German cavalry unit found him wandering along a beach near Kurlands.

In February 1916, he took command of a special commando group at the Heinkel works at Warnemunde. The Heinkel torpedo planes operated from there.

He finished the war an admiralty staff officer, attached to flight command of High Sea Fleet. After the war he became a country landowner when he inherited the family estate of *Schonwaldchen* (lovely wood).

The surrender terms forbad Germany building power-operated planes. To avoid this Dornier built a factory in Marina di Pisa in Italy. There the company developed the Wal (Whale), a seaplane of world class. Later, Dornier relocated at Friedrichshafen and continued building planes as the Manzell-Dornier-Metallbauten Company.

In 1927, von Gronau was the principal of seaplane flight training at the German Traffic Flying School. He had established his school without the permission of the Transport Ministry.

In secrecy he had started with a reconstructed Dornier – *Wal* flying boat – Roald Amundsen's trustworthy plane. In 1931, von Gronau flew his Whale over Greenland to Chicago. This was the first crossing of the inhospitable icy terrain of Greenland in a plane. In so doing he discovered a mountain range on the east coast. Later, the Danish Government honoured him by naming the range *Gronau-Nunatacker*. After a forced landing because of contaminated petrol, he was back in the air transiting Hudson Bay to Chicago. He had pioneered the Polar route.

On his return, the Ministerial Director of Brandenburg presented him the Kleist *Prince of Homburg* for his triumphs – albeit done without permission!

Italian General Italo Balbo invited him to accompany his mass formation long-distance propaganda flight across the Atlantic to North America. Twenty-four Savoia-Marchetti S.55X monoplane flying boats left Orbetello, Rome, on July 1, 1933. On 12 August, 23 planes arrived back over Rome. Mussolini promoted Balbo Italy's first Air Marshal. Balbo died in an Allied air-raid on Tripoli in 1941.

In 1934, von Gronau became vice-president of the Aero Club of Deutschland and then six months later the Club's president. In 1938, his wife Hertha accompanied him in a Messerschmitt Taifun (Typhoon) in a Cairo competition.

The death-bed words of this exceptional airman show his clarity of purpose:

"Throughout my flying career I did nothing lightheartedly but to pioneer airline routes for the future."

* * *

THE AMERICAN FLYING HEIRESS – Miss BESSIE OWEN – 1937

Her adventure started with her take-off from California. She landed at New York and loaded her single-engined plane onto an Antwerp bound ship. By small stages she flew her red *Waco* around Europe. In Switzerland a mechanic, Henri Magnenat, joined her for the flight through the Balkans to Turkey. They continued across the Persian Gulf to India, Burma, Siam, Indo-China, Nanning landing in Hong Kong on 16 January 1937.

Her fame spread to the Philippines where an enthusiast wanted her plane. Loading her *Waco* aboard the S.S. *Haitan* she crossed a stormy China Sea and closed the deal. Bessie returned to her California home, a passenger, aboard the PanAm Clipper service.

* * *

APPENDIX 5

MAURICE NOGUES (1889-1934)

Officier de la Legion d'Honneur
Medaille Militaire
Croix De Guerre 1914-1918 avec 5 citations a l'Ordre de l'Armee
Grande Plaque de la Ligue Aeronautique de France (1915)
Grande Medaille De Vermeil de l'Aero-Club de France (3 March 1928)
Grande Medaille D'Or de l'Aero-Club de France (1930)
Grande Medaille De Vermeil de la Societe d'Encouragement au Progres (9 March 1924)
Cite a l'Ordre de la Nation (1934)

* * *

Maurice Nogues began flying in 1909 at Issy Les Moulineaux in an Avion (Voisin). That year he participated in a meeting at the Crau. He received International Pilot Licence No. 114 on 20 June, 1910 and celebrated by competing in the *Aviation Week* held at Lyon and Reims. In 1912 he participated in a flying competition at Nancy.

On 22 August, 1914, he volunteered for air service at Mairie, Versailles. He became military pilot No. 682 and served in Squadrons F29, N515, VB107 and N73 – the famous Cigogne (*Stork*) Escadrille. This Corps d'Elite did not wear traditional wings – these they replaced with a small stork emblem. Later he became a formidable night-bombing pilot. Captain Nogues was twice wounded and, at war's end, wore the decorations of the Legion d'Honneur, Medaille Militaire and the Croix De Guerre.

In 1922, he became a pilot with the Franco-Roumaine Company. One year later he commanded his first flight Paris to Bucharest with intermediate landings at Strasbourg and Belgrade.

In 1924, Nogues became Chief Pilot and assessed the following Franco-Roumaine routes; Constantinople to Angora, Zurich to Vienna through Innsbruck, Paris to Moscow, and the next year the route Paris to Teheran.

In 1926, he resigned from the Franco-Roumaine and joined the Trans Aviation Company as Director of Development. In 1927, he carried out safety checks on the route Marseille to Beirut with landings at Naples, Corfu, Athens, and Castelloriz. He piloted the first regular passenger flight Marseille to Beirut, in 1928, and followed with an assessment of the route to Baghdad.

During 1930, Trans Aviation expanded its activities to the Far East. In a Farman monoplane, with Captain Marsot at the controls, he surveyed the route from Paris to Saigon. In the following year he accompanied the first regular passenger service to Saigon with Captain Andre Launay at the controls.

In late 1932, Nogues was the non-flying commander that evaluated the Orient air-mail link from Saigon to Hanoi, Hong Kong, Canton and Shanghai. The plane was an Avion Fokker V11 b-3m, registered F-ALSB *La Zelle*. The operating crew were Captain Andre Launay, Mechanic Schwayer and Radio Officer Queyrel. Aboard the plane the French Postal Service had dispatched several bags of mail for Hong Kong, Canton and Shanghai.

La Zelle left Saigon at 0600 hours on 30 October, 1932 for Hanoi with observers Glaize and Commandant Robert Gannay.

They departed the next day for Fort Bayard (Kouang-Tcheou) landing at 1530 hours. They continued their trip to Canton arriving late in the evening. Their flight to Hong Kong on 1 November took slightly less than 2½ hours.

Returning from Shanghai they began their return flight from Hong Kong on 4 November. They arrived in Saigon on 8 November.

Their *postal* flight was a signal success. In Paris they off-loaded air mail franked Shanghai, Canton and Hong Kong. They had brought and carried the first air-mail between the Orient and France.

In 1933, Maurice Nogues (now Colonel) became the Assistant General Manager of Air France. That year he inspected the Company's route from Paris to South America. Returning from checking the Paris, Saigon, Paris route his plane, an Emeraude (Emerald), crashed near Corbigny on 15 January 1934. A grateful Government held a national memorial service for him and his companions.

* * *

MARIE-ANTOINETTE MARYSE HILSZ: (1901-1946)

Capitaine des Forces Feminines de l'Air.
La Legion d'Honneur – Chevalier 1933 – Officier 1937.
International League of Aviators – Honoured 1931 & 1934.
Plaque of the Aero Club of France – Presented 1937.

* * *

Maryse Hilsz was born 9 March, 1901, at Levallois-Perret (Seine). Her family originally hailed from the d'Alsace district.

In 1922, she found employment in a ladies fashion salon. That year she made her first exhibition parachute jump with the Mamet *Squadron* – for flying tuition. Soon she became a specialist *jumper* with the Maurice Finat dare-devils. By 1929 she had made 122 parachute descends.

Maryse's flight instructor considered her a pilot of exceptional talent. On 24 June, 1929, she flew a Morane-Saulnier plane from Le Bourget to London and back. Her plane, powered by a Clerget 130 hp engine, took a flight time of 5h 45m.

Three days later, in the same plane, she attempted a flight to Amsterdam. With the Dutch border in sight a broken oil line forced her down 500m short of the air-field at Hasselt (Belgium). Maryse's plane was a write-off.

On 21 April, 1930, she received Commercial Pilot Licence No. 1293. In November she celebrated this milestone with a flight to Saigon. Her plane was a biplane Morane-Saulnier Moth powered by a Gipsy 100 hp engine. Her flight log shows she reached Calcutta on 24 November. By 5 December she had reached Saigon after 92 hours flying time. Considering an enforced stop in Rangoon waiting for a replacement fuel tank this was a splendid achievement. She left Saigon on 11 December and with Le Bourget almost in sight a broken fuel line forced her to land – the date was 18 December.

In 1931, the Orient beckoned again! On 10 January she left France bound for Indo-China. By 7 February she was back at Le Bourget, despite a force-landing 60k from Athens in heavy fog and several mechanical problems. She had covered an astonishing 27,000 km and, even more meritorious, she did the flight solo.

January 31, 1932, she flew a Farman 190, *Joe II*, with a Gnome 300 hp, Le Bourget to Madagascar, with Mechanic Dronne. Her flight log shows they landed at Niamey (French West Africa) on 3 February. On the 5th they left for Zinder and Fort-Lamy but a broken oil pipe forced her to land at Berni 80 km after leaving Naimey. The splendid aviator Vicomte de Sibour flew her replacement parts from Paris.

They were delayed at Berni until 15 March and arrived in Bangui (Central African Republic) three days later. On the 31st she had reached her goal, landing at Tananarive (Madagascar) after a flight of 10,000 km. They were back at Le Bourget by 7 May – the first woman to fly from Brazzaville to Paris.

APPENDIX 5

At Villacoublay, on 20 August, she captured the female altitude record. In a Morane-Saulnier 222, powered by a Gnome-Rhone Jupiter 450 hp, she reached 10,200 m.

Her restless nature saw her airborne from Le Bourget, on 1 April 1933, with her sights set on Tokyo. This time Lemaire looked after the mechanism of her beloved *Joe II*. Twelve thousand kilometres later they were in Hanoi having staged through Brindisi, Athens, Alep, Karachi, Calcutta and Vientiane. At Hanoi, Lamaire gave *Joe II* a thorough check before continuing their flight on 13 April. The following day they were in Hong Kong and reached Tokyo two days later.

January 26, 1934, she left Villacoublay for Tokyo. Her mechanic was Prax and their plane was a Breguet 330 powered by a Hispano 650 hp engine. Arriving in Tokyo on 6 February they were back in the air on 20 March and at Le Bourget on 28 April after a casual trip.

In 1935, she attacked her 1932 altitude record in a Morane-Saulnie. That June 17, the powerful 600 hp Gnome-Rhone Mistral K-9 carried her to 11,289 m above Villacoublay.

September 1 found her capturing the late Helene Boucher's record between Buc and Cannes. Ten days later over Villacoublay she reached an altitude of 6,500 m. Her plane was a tiny Mauboussin, with an 80 hp Salmson engine.

On 24 September she gained the female altitude record for planes of the second category. This was for monoplanes up to 450 kg – she reached 7,338 m.

June 23, 1936, flying a Portez 50 with a Gnome-Rhone 14 *Krsd* engine, she regained the female altitude record. In just 36 minutes, above Villacoublay, she reached 14,309m.

In August she bought the late Helene Boucher's Caudron Super-Rafale 680-5 for 25,000Fr. On the 29th the reliable 220 hp Renault engine screamed around the 760 km Bruc-Cannes course in 1 hour 52 minutes 43 seconds.

On 19 December she escaped death by a thread while assaulting the women's air speed record. She was flying the Caudron monoplane in which M. Michel Detroyat scored his triumphs at the National Air Races in America that summer.

Mlle. Hilsz left the Istres aerodrome and turned while climbing towards the south. During a full-speed run she felt the controls go mushy and throttled back. The same happened on her second run, but before she could reduce power she was thrown out of the plane. Her parachute saved her life but in opening broke two of her ribs.

The parachute, an automatic-opening type, did not have the built-in safety feature that delays opening until an object's velocity decreases. The natural terminal velocity of an un-streamlined human form is about 110 mph – the plane's then speed exceeded 280 mph!

Mlle. Hilsz fell into L'Estorac Lake, but the parachute dragged her across its surface faster than would-be rescuers could row. The wind tossed her on a beach from where she was rushed to a Marseille hospital.

The then women's air speed record was 276 mph. The late Helene Boucher retained her splendid 1934 achievement.

In the years preceding World War II her name was rarely out of the news. She continued to make inroads into long-distance flying, altitude and speed records. She held her own against the men.

In September 1939, she flew beside her male counterparts against the German invader. She was a highly regarded aerial photographer. That day in June 1940 when France capitulated she refused to leave her homeland. *Maryse* ignored German directives to organise aviation in Provence, and returned to her first job of modelling women's apparel.

After the Liberation, she returned to the Feminine Forces of the Air. She accepted an appointment with the Liaison Airport Ministry Group (GLAM). On 30 January 1946, she left Villacoublay for Marigname in a Siebel 204. An engineer and radio operator accompanied her. The Siebel 204 encountered severe turbulence and disintegrated – crashing near Bourg-en-Bresse.

Mlle. Marie-Antoinette *Maryse* Hilsz's memory is perpetuated at Levallois-Perret. A simple monument salutes the deeds of this exceptional aviatrix.

* * *

VICOMTE DE SIBOUR

A lesser-known aviator to visit the Orient was the French nobleman Vicomte de Sibour.

The aviation world saluted him when, on 16 June 1931, he left Paris for Peking in his Avion Farman 190. Mechanic Damet was in charge of the Gnome Rhone Titan Major 300hp engine. Comptesse de Sibour and Mme Wilden were his passengers.

This flight log records the segments of his flight. Unfortunately, sector times are not available.

Date	Segment	Distance
16 June	Paris – Koenigsberg	1,400 km
18	Koenigsberg – Moscow	1,150
19	Moscow – Omak	2,250
21	Omsk – Irkutsk	2,050
23	Irkutsk – Tchita	650
24	Tchita – Kharbine – Moukden	1,700
26	Moukden – Peking	650

Return Flight

Date	Segment	Distance
25 August	Peking – Tchita	1,400 km
26	Tchita – Irkutsk	650
27	Irkutsk – Novo Sibirsk	1,450
28	Novo Sibirsk – Sverdlovsk	1,040
29	Sverdlovsk – Kazan	1,120
30	Kazan – Weliki Louki – Koenigsberg	1,800
31	Koenigsberg – Berlin – Shaffen	1,170
1 September	Shaffen – Le Bourget, Paris	270

* * *

On 23 September 1933, he left Cannes, France, in a twin-engined (Gipsy designation) de Havilland DH84. Aboard the Dragon were his Comtesse, their sons, and mechanic Damet. A month later they arrived at Saigon and on 12 November – Hanoi. In early December they landed at Kai Tak, Hong Kong.

Their return to France was as casual as their outward flight. They returned to Paris (Le Bourget) on 20 February 1934.

*

Other than a desert incursion to bring spare parts to *Maryse* Hilsz, in February 1932, few records are available of this splendid French pioneer.

APPENDIX 6

TRIPPE'S PAN AMERICAN AIRWAYS SYSTEM

Juan Terry Trippe was born in Sea Bright, New Jersey, U.S.A., in 1899. He graduated from Yale in 1923. After working for a year in banking, he organised Long Island Airways with surplus aeroplanes (seven) from World War I. In October 1925, he won a Post Office contract between Key West and Cuba for his newly formed Colonial Air Transport.

He founded, in July 1927, Pan American Airways System. Within three years this aggressive and far-sighted man had thrown an aerial loop around South America.

His dream expanded to put PanAm around the world using a trans-Pacific route. Trippe used islands controlled by the United States as *stepping-stones*. His routing after Honolulu was Midway, Wake Island, Guam and then the Philippines.

For this vast distance his airline needed bigger aeroplanes. He consulted Colonel Charles A. Lindbergh and Andre A. Priester. Then Lindbergh was PanAm's technical director and Priester was chief engineer. Lindbergh, without hesitation, proposed flying-boats – the landing fields of his *stepping-stone* islands were inadequate. Trippe accepted Lindbergh's reasoning and sent his required flying-boat specifications to the premier aircraft builders of the day.

Igor Ivanovich Sikorsky (1889-1972) won the contract and in December 1929 production began on his *Winged-S*. Sikorsky's pilot Boris Sergievsky had command of testing. In April 1931, pushing the throttles to 1,950 rpm the $125,000 giant four-engined flying-boat skipped off the water. Sikorsky's *Winged-S*, designated S-40, received Department of Commerce approval and was licensed NC80V.

The Sikorsky S-40 had four 575hp Hornet engines mounted on struts (*pod-and-boom*) beneath the 35m (114ft) span wing. Three of these 44-passenger amphibians came to PanAm – *American Clipper, Caribbean Clipper* and *Samoan Clipper*.

Juan Terry Trippe (Photo: Courtesy PanAm.)

AIRPORT OF THE NINE DRAGONS, KAI TAK, KOWLOON

These were the first machines to bear the famous *Clipper* name. An inaugural flight left Miami bound for Cristobal on 19 November, 1931, with Lindbergh in command.

PanAm took delivery of an improved S-42 Sikorsky on June 5, 1934. The S-42 carried out most of PanAm's trans-Pacific pioneering. These were the Alameda-Honolulu and Alameda-Honolulu-Wake Island flights of April and June 1935 that extended to Guam in October.

Late in 1935 saw the first of Glenn Martin's beautiful M-130 four-engined long-range civilian flying-boats take to the air. This, the *China Clipper*, had a wing span of 40m (130ft), length 28m (91ft), maximum take-off weight 23,600kg (52,000lb) and speed 210km/h (130mph).

Martin built two more M-130s for PanAm's trans-Pacific service – they became the *Philippine Clipper* and the *Hawaiian Clipper*. On November 22, 1935, the *China Clipper* inaugurated the first schedule airmail flight to Manila.

The M-130 could carry 24 passengers on short stages, but the longer sectors meant a reduced payload. The M-130 became an accounting nightmare incapable of earning her keep. This problem brought the Sikorsky S-42s back into contention. The S-42s became the prime link between Hong Kong, on the Asiatic mainland, and the United States more than 8,500 miles away.

January 11, 1938, was a sad day for many Hong Kong residents. On that day Captain Edward Musick and his crew died, while refuelling at Pago Pago, Samoa. Without warning his plane exploded to become a flaming inferno.

Ed Musick had become a popular local figure when he inaugurated the first scheduled airmail flight across the Pacific. As a mark of respect Trippe suspended (temporarily) PanAm's South Pacific Service.

In Hong Kong, Monday 8 December, 1941, Captain Fred S. Ralph's launch headed towards his moored Sikorsky S-42B. A Japanese squadron screaming overhead strafed his beautiful *Hong Kong Clipper*. He watched her fire-contorted frame settle in the foul mud of Kowloon Bay.

SIKORSKY S-43 AMPHIBIAN AT KAI TAK – 1936

Kai Tak had no terminal facilities, passengers drove out to the amphibian to embark. A launch brought her crew. The loaded plane waddled down the slipway and took off on Kowloon Bay. Sikorsky's first American-built aeroplane, the S-29, crashed while making the 1930 motion picture Hell's Angels.

(Photo: Courtesy Hong Kong Government Information Service)

APPENDIX 6

PanAm seemed to lose direction when Trippe retired as chairman and chief executive in 1968.

Then PanAm lost Flight 103 over Lockerbie, Scotland, on December 21, 1988. That day 270 people rode the *Maid of the Seas*, a Boeing 747, to their death.

The United States Federal Jury, in July 1992, found PanAm *guilty of wilful misconduct for their alleged disregard for federal security rules concerning hand-searching unaccompanied baggage.* An airline can receive no worse indictment than this!

Although Lockerbie was the end of PanAm the company was in decline long before that awful bomb blast. A top-heavy executive squandered financial resources in vying to host the most lavish cocktail-party. There were no restrictions – anyone could attend!

Juan Terry Trippe died on April 3, 1981. PanAm died in bankruptcy court in 1991.

Proof material that one could not exist without the other!

APPENDIX 7

THE MOUNT CAMERON MONSTROSITY

1945 (Photo: Sir Denys Roberts)

The Japanese Military Governor of Hong Kong arrived in February 1942 and ordered a War Memorial built on Mount Cameron. Lieutenant-General Rensuke Isogai's edict was *to perpetuate the memory of the heroes who had captured the British Crown Colony*. His *Tower of Triumph* was to stand 480 metres high and be visible from every corner of Hong Kong.

To celebrate December 8, 1942, the first anniversary of Japan's attack on Hong Kong, General Isogai drove to Mount Cameron. He was to witness the ceremonial installation of a sword in the Memorial's foundation. The famous sword expert Kurihara had received the sacred weapon from the hands of Emperor Hirohito. Following the sword ceremony Isogai laid the foundation stone.

Then, using forced labour, they started work on the foundation. Granite for facing the tower came from quarries in the Happy Valley area behind the cemetery. Workmen faced these granite blocks on the sporting grounds of Craigengower and the Police Recreation Club. It was a

APPENDIX 7

Sunday custom for the Japanese to make a pilgrimage to the shrine, each carrying a stone to help in its erection.

To celebrate the surrender of the Colony the Japanese screened *Victory in Hong Kong*. A vestibule card showed *Oscars* dog-fighting with doomed British planes trailing smoke. It was exciting but illusory, for the Royal Air Force never got into the air.

The film screened on December 25, 1942, and the venue that preached this claptrap to the faithful was the old Queen's Theatre on the corner of Queen's Road and D'Aguilar Street.

Several prominent turncoats, occupying the best seats, joined in the *banzais* on queue. The Hong Kong Chinese population merely ignored this propaganda-padded garbage.

In July 1945, Tokyo ordered work stopped on the Memorial on Mount Cameron. A makeshift roof topped a mere 80 feet of pylon. The Japanese surrendered Hong Kong to Sir Cecil Harcourt on 15 September 1945.

February 26, 1947, was the day the Mount Cameron *monstrosity* disappeared from the Hong Kong panorama. The Wah Hing Construction Company, the felling contractors, had removed eight of the Monument's 12 *legs*. They weakened the remaining four legs by acetylene torches and packed them with explosive charges to be fired electrically.

Mr H. W. Forsyth, the PWD engineer in charge, saw Governor Sir Mark Young accompanied by his family arrive on the site. I recalled that Sir Mark's treatment in Japanese hands was harsh and here he stood about to see his tormentors humbled – I wondered what were his thoughts?

Forsyth's signal started a worker pounding a gong for three minutes. An explosion caused a vast cloud of chalky dust to billow into the sky – it was four in the afternoon. A breeze cleared the air, and with other onlookers I cheered unashamedly as that symbol of the "monkey-men" disappeared and our navigational check-point with it.

The demolisher did not expunge every visible memory of that monstrosity. The foundation now supports apartments. I wonder how many residents realise this – it is rumoured that the sacred sword still remains in the bowels of the foundation!

1947 – LEGS WEAKENED FOR DEMOLITION.
(Photo: Sir Denys Roberts)

FEBRUARY 26, 1947
An explosion, a cloud of chalky dust and a Japanese symbol of conquest becomes history. (Photo: Sir Denys Roberts)

APPENDIX 8

THE PENINSULA HOTEL & LEOPOLD GADDI

Almost from the beginning the Peninsula Hotel had an affinity with aviation. Its history goes back to 1924 when James H. Taggart chose his Kowloon site near the docks and the railway station. He began construction in 1925. Two years later, when ready for guests, the Government commandeered it to quarter troops. The Sino-Japanese hostilities had raised concern and Britain shipped several battalions to counteract any expansion of the conflict to Hong Kong.

It was a favourite diversion to hurl bayonets into the beautifully panelled doors. The vandalism of the soldiers meant extensive repairs. Of the battalions quartered there the least destructive was the Scots Guards.

The *Pen* opened for business Tuesday, December 11, 1928. A Carnival Dinner Dance in the Roof Garden attracted a charge of $4.00 for each person. It was a *soup-and-fish affair*, although fancy dress was an acceptable alternative. Even with this splendid addition the Colony's night-life remained provincial, with most activities closed down by 2300 hours. An American standing on the deck of a President Line boat summed it up perfectly – *the best illuminated cemetery in the world*.

In 1946, Cathay Pacific Airways rented two large rooms, 645-6, and covered the floor with camp-beds. Although the beds were comfortable the rooms lacked toilet and shower facilities.

A genial bar snuggled against the west wall of the main lounge. Many of Cathay's early charters reached maturity there. The *ladies-of-the-evening* occupied tables west of the main entrance. The more upstanding patronised the east-side that included a sprinkling of ladies who had bought respectability with wedding rings.

Li Bun, the telephone page, used to locate friends lost in the milling crowd. He chalked the name on a small blackboard, elevated on a broom-stick, with a bicycle bell attached beside his right thumb. We all had messages for him that were mostly reasonable but an overwrought floor-manager intercepted messages too colourful. *Miss Carriage* was one that brought instantaneous suspension.

It was in 1931 that Leopold *Leo* Gaddi *jumped-ship* to join the staff of the Hongkong and Shanghai Hotels Limited (now known as The Peninsula Group). He worked as a chef in

APPENDIX 8

Shanghai, Peking and then Hong Kong. He became manager of The Peninsula in 1952 and lived there until he retired in 1961. He became great friends with all the airlines and their boisterous personnel. We remember him through Gaddi's. He launched his internationally famous restaurant at Christmas 1953.

Leo was a repository of local historical anecdotes. He declared that he owned car registered number two. He stated that the first automobile arrived in Hong Kong in October 1910. The automobile proved unpopular and by the early twenties they were still a rarity. He revealed Governor Sir Henry May became a car user more from necessity than enthusiasm. In July 1912, a failed assassination attack prompted a shift from sedan-chair to motorised transport.

Leo thought these cars operated before the introduction of formal registration. About 1930, the authorities issued the first plate to an American domiciled on the Island. This was Dr J. W. Noble, a dental surgeon, who housed it in a small green shed next to the Lower Peak Tram Terminus. Besides a profitable professional income he was the main share-holder of the *South China Morning Post*.

Leo Gaddi never tired of telling stories about animals. His favourites involved a camel, a tiger, and a plane load of day-old chicks.

One very eccentric member of the Belilios family loved animals. He brought a camel back to Hong Kong and used to ride up and down Old Peak Road on it. The camel had good big feet that gripped the winding road. One boisterous night the high wind of a typhoon destroyed its stable and in wandering it slipped over an embankment. The camel suffered severe injuries and had to be shot. The next problem was who should remove the carcass. There was a tremendous argument between the police and sanitary department. The police stated the sanitary department was responsible for its removal – the stench was revolting. The sanitary department retaliated by reminding the police they should remove all obstructions. Eventually, like so many problems, it solved itself by decaying.

Belilios also had a small pet tiger. His mother was very old and never left her rooms in the Hongkong Hotel. One morning he visited her taking his tiger. Belilios decided to have a quiet breakfast downstairs leaving the beast with the old lady. She became agitated and phoned the manager; *Send somebody up, there's a tiger in my room.*

The manager did not take this very seriously and thought she was going the same way as her son. Belilios saw strange creatures when he'd had a bit too much to drink. Finally he sent a boy who took one look at the tiger and bolted. At last Belilios caught his tiger but how was he to get it out of the hotel? At 0900 hours and the busiest time of the day he could hardly walk through the foyer with it. Finally he got hold of a bamboo carrying chair, removed the cushions, tied the tiger in and the coolies calmly carried it away.

One day Captain *Pinky* Wawn, of Cathay Pacific, flew in with a load of day-old chicks. Cathay lacked a place to store them so the *Pen* came to the rescue. The management allowed deKantzow to use the ground-floor store until the next morning. Pinky, Roy Farrell and Syd adjourned to the west-bar to revive their flagging spirits. Then all hell broke loose as the lounge filled with squawking, agitated chicks. The chicks invaded the kitchen, and the ladies' toilets. The occupants ran screaming into the lounge adding to the bedlam. Women, young and not so young, were standing on chairs, holding their skirts up, and screaming with alarm. The men, dragging their eyes from the entrancing underwear, got into the spirit of trapping the wayward chicks.

The final count found dozens missing! This brought alarm and despondency to Syd and Roy Farrell. Leo Gaddi had few doubts that waiters and room-boys dined grandly off the proceeds of that *great escape.*

Later, when PanAm and BOAC stayed there, the management had turned the Grand Ballroom or *Rose Room* into small cubicles. Each room had a private toilet and shower and were known, by the more naive book-in clerks, as crew rooms. Leo Gaddi, with his intimate knowledge of their prime function, unhesitatingly called them *screw rooms*. We always thought he expressed this with a tinge of jealousy.

Cathay crews derived no benefit from this upgrade in accommodation. The management housed the bachelors at 48 Grampian Road, near Kowloon City, with the rest scattered around Kowloon.

On January 24, 1963, Leopold Gaddi died of a heart attack. That day he was driving on a back road in Switzerland and rounding a bend saw a school-bus stalled across a train line. As he hurried towards the bus he heard the whistle of an approaching train. The children in the bus began to scream with terror. Leo alone pushed the bus from the crossing seconds before the train thundered by. Shaking with the effort he sank on to the grass verge. The bus driver rushed to express his thanks but found him dead.

Leo had died as he had lived – helping others!

MY FIRST AERIAL VIEW FROM *BETSY* 1946

Salisbury Road (foreground) divides the Kowloon Canton Railway complex from the YMCA (left border) and the Peninsula Hotel. Moving right, across Nathan Road, is a vacant area for exhibitions, bounded by Middle Road. On the northern side of Middle Road is Far East Motors with the circular Chung King Arcade (now Chung King Mansion) behind. Middle Road abuts Signal Hill at right border. Street parking was ample – life was easy-paced – also there was oxygen in the air! (Photo: Peter Gautschi)

APPENDIX 8

SEPTEMBER 23, 1983 – *BETSY* COMES HOME
The same view 37 years later. The Pen hasn't changed much – the Sheraton Hotel occupies the exhibition area – the Space Museum (Planetarium) occupies part of the old Kowloon Railway complex and the road traffic has increased.

(Photo: Captain Martin Willing)

APPENDIX 9

PIRACY – SCOURGE OF THE CHINA COAST

The China Coast and piracy are synonymous. Long before the establishment of the Crown Colony of Hong Kong this barbarous profession has cursed its waters. Probably the most infamous was Chui Ah-poh who operated from near Stanley. Chui also obtained a licence to manufacture gunpowder in the Colony then used it to terrorise and murder. Neither were all pirate leaders Chinese men. Several women led large fleets of sampans and proved even more savage than their male counterparts. Nor were all the pirate leaders Chinese – Englishman William Fenton and American Eli Boggs vied for the coast's rich plunder and pickings.

A shocking attack on the Douglas Line's S.S. *Namoa* occurred on December 10, 1890. Earlier the *Namoa* had left Hong Kong for Swatow. The ship's position was Ping Hui Island when 50 screaming pirates wielding cutlasses took control. They murdered Captain Pocock and shackled the officers. They then raped, looted and killed as the whim took them. The low yield of their loot enraged them and they tortured with brutality. One tactic was to jam a carpenter's file between a victim's teeth and work it with both hands. This proved effective and it yielded HK$55,000 – a fortune in those days.

Turning the ship back towards Hong Kong they transferred their plunder to junks and disabled the ship. The *Namoa* struggled back to Hong Kong.

On April 17, 1891, the executioner beheaded 16 pirates who had attacked the *Namoa*. The blood-letting took place on a beach near modern Kai Tak Airport.

In 1929 a small pirate force captured the Japanese S.S. *Deli Maru*. This piracy was notable for its efficiency. They shot an Indian guard without a chance to surrender. The operation was over within a few minutes. The gang of 12 took their orders from a leader less than 20 years old – a slip of a girl.

The ship owners enclosed the officers' quarters, bridge, and engine room with iron bars and gates. For a time these grilles deterred attacks yet pirate ingenuity prevailed.

Today, in spite of an efficient and vigilant police force, supported by air sweeps, pirate raids still abound in Bias Bay. No vessel or person can be sanguine. Shortly after coming to Hong Kong I befriended a local who had trained to be a pilot. Fred Melbye owned property on a hillside overlooking Castle Peak Bay. He showed me his untenanted house

APPENDIX 9

and I made him an offer to purchase. We had come to terms when suddenly he withdrew from the deal. Some months later he disclosed the reason. A few days before my offer a pirate gang raided the home of his neighbour, a Portuguese. In the melee his neighbour lost his tongue, his wife and daughters. How could he expose me to this danger?

In April 1948, an UNRRA official, Mr. A. Hutchinson, arrived at Mascot on a Cathay Pacific charter plane. He warned that pirates operated with impunity on the China coast. In a recent raid they had stolen 50 drums of kerosene from a lighthouse. It was at the mouth of the Yangtze River, 120 miles from Shanghai. The leader left enough in the lamp to negotiate his escape through the dangerous reefs. He warned the keeper to keep his light burning. If it went out he would kill the man's wife he had abducted. The pirates sold the spoils on the black market.

My anecdotes have only scratched the surface of piracy on the China coast. Yet, they are sufficient to show the extent of this perilous menace.

On April 17, 1891, the Chinese authorities brought the Namoa pirates to a beach at Kowloon City. This was near where Sir Kai Ho Kai and Mr Au Tak later reclaimed land for their housing estate that failed and created Kai Tak Airport. A group of Europeans crossed from the Island to witness the executions. (Photos: Ian Diamond – Hong Kong Archivist)

APPENDIX 10

THE SECOND & THIRD OPIUM WARS – 1856-60

Thomas Bruce was the 7th Earl of Elgin and 11th of Kincardine. He was a representative peer for Scotland and a General in the Army. Thomas was a collector of Grecian antiquities, with his greatest treasure gleaned from the rubble of the Parthenon, Athens. He presented this rarity to the British Museum where it is on display as *The Elgin Marbles*. This generous gift has assured his everlasting fame.

George Charles Constantine was his eldest son and heir to the earldom. George never married and died the year before that of his father. The 7th Earl's second son, James, became the 8th Earl of Elgin and 12th Earl of Kincardine in 1841.

James, although possessing a strong face with a determined mouth, was short and portly. He was not a commanding figure and at 46 he looked twice his age. His aloofness was beguiling for it covered a sensitive nature. It was no secret that he preferred the company of his large and beloved family, and the serenity of his streams and glens, to gallivanting around the globe.

Against his better judgment he accepted Prime Minister Lord Palmerston's offer to go to Hong Kong. He was to untangle the mess that the Colony's governor had gotten himself into over the *Arrow* incident. On July 2, 1857, he arrived in Hong Kong aboard the frigate *Shannon*. Governor Bowring's greeting was civil but their mutual dislike was obvious. In a letter to his wife Elgin wrote that Sir John Bowring was a *dangerous person*.

The Indian Mutiny then took a turn for the worst. Lord Elgin redirected the force assigned to the *Arrow* incident to support the hard-pressed British general. There is little doubt that Elgin's timely help saved the sub-continent of India for the Crown. He also rushed to Calcutta where he put himself at the disposal of the Viceroy.

During Elgin's absence in Calcutta, Yeh Ming-chen, Viceroy of Kwangsi and Kwangtung, the province that Canton is the capital of, took control of the *Arrow* controversy. He stated he wanted no dealings with the British and rescinded their trading rights. He further declared that all other nationals could trade using Canton as their entry port. The British merchants were loud in their condemnation of Yeh's unilateral action. They found a ready ear in Bowring. An angry Bowring ordered his admiral, Sir Michael Seymour, to mount a shipping blockade of the Pearl River. The blockade had only limited

JAMES BRUCE – 1860
The 8th Earl of Elgin and 12th Earl of Kincardine.
(Photo: Ian Diamond – Hong Kong Archivist)

SIR JOHN BOWRING – 1854-1859
Governor of the Crown Colony of Hong Kong.
(Photo: Ian Diamond – Hong Kong Archivist)

success, for the shallow water approaches prevented the deep-draft British warships from being effective.

In Calcutta Lord Elgin received word a further force of 1,500 marines was on the way to Hong Kong. He left the Indian delta port aboard the P. & O. Steam Navigation Company's ship the *Ava*. She dropped anchor in Hong Kong Harbour on September 20, 1857.

Elgin's already morbid mood deepened when he learned that Bowring had undermined his authority. Sir John's military force was still under strength so he had prepared an attack on Canton with just his navy. Lord Elgin saw the weakness of the plan, for strong military support was essential to success. Elgin was furious and vetoed Bowring's plan. His Lordship then had an aberrant loss of common sense. He rudely refused the invitation to enjoy the comforts of Government House and instead chose the cramped quarters of the *Ava*. His discomfort increased when boils erupted in some sensitive body areas.

At the beginning of December three shiploads of marines arrived from England. Elgin's military strength was now strong enough to attack Canton. Elgin, and Baron Gros, the French representative, sent a communique to Commissioner Yeh. The communique was moderate in tone and made only two demands. The Chinese should honour the treaty, and compensation for damage incurred when they burned the British *factories* (trading posts) at Canton. Commissioner Yeh had 10 days to accept the terms. Yeh misread the calm tone of the communique as conciliatory and lacking in determination. His reply was tersely negative.

On December 15, 1857, the British and French fleets took station opposite Canton. On the 17th he and Gros, from aboard Her Majesty's ship *Furious*, ordered the capture of Canton.

Twelve days later, the Allied force moved against Canton's east wall. The French positioned their scaling ladders and they were first up the wall. Elgin had made a rare miscalculation. The Chinese willpower to fight was less than he had expected. As the afternoon light faded into darkness the whole wall was in Allied hands. A small Allied force of fewer than 6,000 troops had overwhelmed a garrison of 30,000 men positioned behind a wall 25 feet high and 20 feet wide. This was a tremendous victory for thousands of battle-hardened Manchu troops supported the garrison.

AIRPORT OF THE NINE DRAGONS, KAI TAK, KOWLOON

On January 5, 1858, a roving platoon captured Yeh and his entire military staff. Elgin and Gros had a problem – how to deal with an unregenerate Yeh? They exiled him to Calcutta where his health deteriorated and he died in little more than a year.

Elgin and Gros moved their operational base to Shanghai. Admiral Seymour was tardy in obeying Elgin's instruction to bring his fleet north. Elgin suspected Bowring, his old adversary, was exerting pressure on the slow-witted sailor. Letters received by Elgin from the Imperial Court were becoming arrogantly less courteous. The Chinese reverted to their old ways, and their sham of equality was so transparent that Elgin's irritation was becoming obvious to all.

Finally, with his fleet in position, he ordered his admirals to attack the Taku forts. The bombardment began on May 19 and subdued the fort the following day. Three days later Seymour's naval force moved on Tientsin and met no opposition. The Peking Imperial Court was in turmoil and quickly agreed to all the Allied demands. The battle was little more than a walkover and bred an over-confidence that would bring disaster a year later.

On June 4, Elgin travelled to the temple of *Supreme Felicity*, the venue for his first meeting with the Chinese Commissioners, the authorised negotiators. His escort was 150 scarlet-clad marines marching in impressive precision to the band of H.M.S. *Calcutta*. Elgin, not usually a rude man, stormed from the meeting when the Chinese negotiators forgot to bring a special seal. He assigned his brother Frederick to handle British negotiations. Frederick's assistants were Thomas Wade and Horatio Lay.

Lay, at 27 years-of-age, was the stronger character of the trio and lectured, bullied and thoroughly terrified the elderly Commissioners. There was irony in Lay's outbursts. He lacked connection with the British Government and worked for the Chinese Customs. He was castigating his employer. Yet, he did more than anyone else in securing the Treaty of Tientsin. Lord Elgin did not meet the Commissioners again until June 26, the day he signed the treaty.

TREATY OF TIENTSIN – 26 JUNE, 1858
Lord Elgin, seated centre, signing the Treaty. Admiral Seymour sits at the right table with Imperial Commissioner Gui Liang. Seated at the left table is Hua Shang, Senior Commissioner. (Photos: Ian Diamond – Hong Kong Archivist)

APPENDIX 10

Lord Elgin spent January and February of 1859 between Hong Kong and Canton. The treaty entitled the British to stay in Canton until the Chinese had paid their reparations. On March 4, 1859, he left China with few regrets, and hoping that he would never set foot again in the land he now thoroughly detested. This was not to be!

At Ceylon he spent several days with his younger brother. Sir Frederick Bruce was returning to China as the first British Minister accredited to the Chinese Empire. Sir Frederick was to exchange the now British ratified Treaty with his Peking counterpart.

Some miles from Peking Sir Frederick's delegation came under heavy cannon fire from the Taku forts that forced him to retire. In that deadly action three British gunboats went to the bottom with a heavy loss of life. It was now clear the Chinese did not intend to ratify the treaty. Their attack on Sir Frederick's flag-of-truce proved their treachery.

A few days later, the Taku fort repulsed another British naval attack. It was an ill-conceived plan made from over-confidence. Again they gave a mauling to the British Navy. Rumour was rife that Russians had manned the Taku guns.

*

Lord Elgin again allowed himself to be talked into returning to China. His formal instructions were ratification of the treaty, an apology for the attack on Sir Frederick's delegation, and reparations for the losses that had resulted. He was also to annex the peninsula of Kowloon, opposite Hong Kong Island.

So Elgin sailed east again, but his passage was wrought with unwanted adventure. Just after leaving Ceylon his steamship, the *Malabar*, entered thunderstorm conditions. She struck a rock and her captain had to run her on to a beach. His travelling companion was his old diplomatic partner the Baron Gros.

AUGUST 1860

The North Taku fort after the battle.

(Photos: Signor Beato)

AIRPORT OF THE NINE DRAGONS, KAI TAK, KOWLOON

The shipwreck of the *Malabar* is the subject of a delightful sketch. Its caption reads – *An amicable altercation takes place between their Excellencies whether France or England shall leave the sinking vessel first.* The sketch shows the tall, gaunt Baron Gros, and short, portly Lord Elgin solemnly bowing. Each is offering the other right-of-way. Standing in the background is the bearded ship's captain. No doubt he is wondering why they didn't leave together, surely that would satisfy protocol. The scene expresses no hint of hysteria, more of complete composure. The steady strokes and the detail captured by the artist, Colonel Crealock, show he was not in awe of the occasion!

The loss of their ship delayed their arrival in Hong Kong but the British and French continued assembling their expeditionary forces. There was no space for 17,000 troops on the island, so the British rented the waterfront of Kowloon for £160 a year. The camp occupied the area where the Peninsula Hotel stands today.

The one bright spot on Elgin's morbid horizon was the knowledge that Sir John Bowring had completed his term. The new Governor was the gentlemanlike Sir Hercules Robinson (1859-1865).

*

The **Third Opium War** was about to begin. The Allies occupied Chusan, the island at the mouth of the Yangtze. Meanwhile, during May, the commanders moved their forces from Hong Kong to Shanghai. On June 16, the military commanders and the two Ambassadors formulated their plan of attack. The French forces were to land south of the Taku forts, and the British to the East. The plan was to outflank and take the guns from the rear. Further minor but irritating delays occurred until, on August 1, the Allied troops landed.

The first military reconnaissance met with accurate sniper fire. Using the cover of darkness the 2,000 men retreated. This victory elated the Chinese. The French General de Montauban refused to make further incursions until he had unloaded his stores. The weather appeared to be siding with the Chinese for the torrential rain turned paths into mud and a shortage of small boats added to the delay. The Allies lost 10 crucial days.

On August 14, the Allies had a change of fortune. They captured a small town that cleared the way for a rear attack on the weakest of the four forts comprising the Taku complex. The advance halted when the British General Sir Hope Grant and his French counterpart differed on the next phase of attack. Sir Hope realised that the northern fort was not only the weakest it held the key position. The British General, losing patience with the Frenchman, told him he was attacking, de Montauban could come along or stay as he pleased.

On August 21, a combined attack carried the day against a determined Chinese defence. The generals received reports of Chinese gunners tied to their guns. That day in 1860 five men and a 15-year-old boy won Britain's highest award for valour – the Victoria Cross.

Confusion was evident at the other forts but white flags soon appeared and the Allies took possession. Two days later the British Admiral Sir James Hope took his gunboats up to Tientsin and found it undefended.

The Chinese negotiators followed their ageless tactics of delay. This did not concern Elgin for Grant had consolidated his forces within reach. On September 9, the Allied forces advanced on Peking. Meanwhile a delegation headed by Harry Parkes (British Consul at Canton) and Henry Loch (Elgin's private secretary) left the Allied lines to negotiate with the Chinese.

On looking back, Parkes saw a strong force of Chinese cavalry had moved between him and the Allied lines. The British and French routed this determined attack. The army then pushed forward to rescue their negotiators but it was too late – they were in enemy hands.

APPENDIX 10

ANDREW FITZGIBBON, VC
Hospital Apprentice (later Apothecary). Attached to the Indian Medical Establishment and the 67th Regiment – later the Hampshire Regiment.
Place & Date of Birth: Gogerat, India – 13 May 1846.
Account of Deed: On 21 August, 1860, at the capture of the North Taku Fort, China, Hospital Apprentice Fitzgibbon, aged 15 years 3 months, accompanied a wing of the 67th Regiment when it took position within 500 yards of the fort. He then proceeded, under heavy fire, to attend a dhoolie-bearer, whose wound he had been directed to bind up, and while the Regiment was advancing under the heavy enemy fire, he ran across the open ground to attend another wounded man. In so doing he was himself severely wounded.
Place & Date of Death: Delhi, India – 7 March 1883.

(Photo: Courtesy Imperial War Museum)

On September 21, a sharp engagement brought glory to the French infantry. They carried a Chinese battery at bayonet point. Their gallantry brought nobility to their general. Napoleon III later bestowed upon him the title of *Count Paliko*, named after the bridge that his men had stormed.

Meanwhile, the Emperor had left Peking. Prince Kung, his younger brother, remained to negotiate with the enemy. They made no progress for Parkes and the others were in enemy hands. Prince Kung guaranteed Elgin that if he pulled back his forces he would release his prisoners. Any attack would bring their death. Elgin's problem was great, should he abandon his expedition to save the lives of 37 men, who already might be dead, or continue his expedition.

The dungeon entombing Parkes and Loch was foul and ridden with maggots, yet they remained undaunted. Parkes wrote a letter to Elgin praising Prince Kung's qualifications and suggested a conference. Loch scribbled a message in Hindustani that he hid in the text. It stated that Parkes wrote the letter under duress. The Chinese then allowed the prisoners to receive a parcel containing a change of clothes and some personal effects. Among the clothing was a beautifully embroidered handkerchief. Hidden in the embroidery was the message, in Hindustani, that – *bombardment of Peking will begin in three days' time.*

On October 6, the French occupied the Imperial Summer Palace that lay outside the northern city wall. The Summer Palace was not a single building, but a huge park crowded with pavilions, gardens and lakes. It extended over 80 square miles. The great riches scattered around proved too much for the French soldiers. They began sacking the pavilions. Later that day some British officers arrived on the scene and joined in the looting. A grave problem of discipline existed.

On October 8, Prince Kung ordered the release of Parkes and Loch. After their escort left they found some of their friends fettered to a nearby cart. They reached the Allied camp without further trouble. Prince Kung had freed them not from sympathy; his concern was their murder would bring greater vengeance to his city. Parkes and Loch had endured 20 days of hell – every minute expecting to be executed. Other members of Parkes' delegation were not as fortunate. Some had died of infected wounds.

The snowy ridges of the Western Hills began to prey on Elgin's mind. Hope Grant did little to ease his fears, for with the fighting over he wanted to be back in Tientsin before the beginning of November and the onset of winter. Elgin and Gros lacked the time for subtle diplomacy. They must hammer Prince Kung into submission without delay. An ultimatum gave Prince Kung until noon on October 13 to surrender his city.

The walls of Peking were 40 feet high and 60 feet wide and undamaged. The Prince had several options for its defence and delay was his best weapon. Later years would show that Kung was more the diplomat than the warrior. Kung tried to water down the Allied terms, but just before the deadline he ordered the surrender of the *Anting* gate. Allied troops poured into Peking.

The murder of some of his negotiators kept Elgin in a state of morbid depression. How could he avenge them? Only a spectacular act of redress would atone for the atrocity. The surrender of the *Anting* gate meant that he should bring no further burden on the Peking population. Elgin's spectacular proposal to destroy the Summer Palace was not a blow against the people but against the prestige of the Emperor. The British received his decision with acclaim but it appalled the French that such beauty should be destroyed. They conveniently forgot their loutish looting a few days earlier. On October 18, Allied troops burnt the Imperial Summer Palace.

On October 24, Lord Elgin arrived in State. Prince Kung paid Elgin homage in the Hall of Audience. They signed the Convention of Peking and finally ratified the Treaty of Tientsin. Lord Elgin stayed in Peking for a fortnight to introduce his brother to the Prince. With the installation of Sir Frederick William Adolphus Bruce G.C.B., the Chinese had accredited their first British Minister. Elgin's work was at an end.

Elgin enjoyed a long rest in Shanghai and arrived back in Hong Kong soon after the New Year of 1861. On January 19, he formally annexed the Kowloon Peninsula and Stonecutters Island. This was a simple but moving ceremony. Harry Parkes scooped up a handful of soil and wrapped it in the proclamation. This he offered to the senior Mandarin who returned it, symbolising the transfer of Chinese land to the British Crown.

Two days later, James Bruce, the 8th Earl of Elgin and 12th Earl of Kincardine, left the Colony never to return. On January 21, 1862, he became Viceroy and Governor-General of India. This great statesman died at Dhurmsala, in India, on November 20, 1863. In his 52 years of life he had done momentous deeds. Yet many historians spurn those deeds and remember him as a vandal and fire-bug.

*

Elgin Hill was named for Lord Elgin. The hill supports the Royal Observatory complex. Entry is by a secured lane immediately south of St Andrew's Church on Nathan Road.

Governor Bowring is remembered by Bowring Street. This is one street further north along Nathan Road of that traffic nightmare – Austin Road. Austin Road is the northern boundary of the old Whitfield Barracks now called Kowloon Park.

PRINCE KUNG – 1860
The chief negotiator signed the Convention of Peking and finally ratified the Treaty of Tientsin that formally annexed the Kowloon Peninsula and Stonecutters Island. (Lithograph published 1862 by J. Hogarth)

APPENDIX 11

THE SACRED HILL – SUNG WONG TOI

The *Sacred Hill* of the Sung Wong Toi played a part in the growth of Kai Tak Airport. First during the Japanese Occupation and later when the airfield came of age.

The dynasty of the Sung family began in 960 AD. It would endure for 319 years and end in anguish. Here is the story of its fall.

The House of Sung defeated by the terrible Kublai Khan was in disarray. To preserve the dynasty a hastily organised fleet sailed south hugging the coast. Day after day storms of severe magnitude whipped the sea to a frenzy. A break in the weather found many ships wallowing dangerously and barely afloat. While still far off, the captain of the leading vessel sighted a mountain that resembled a crouching lion. He considered this a good omen and the fleet sailed towards this mountain – now called Lion Rock.

The poor villagers who lived where Kowloon City now stands grew alarmed when they saw the fleet anchoring. Their faces showed amazement when a grand gentleman came ashore and announced that their young Emperor was aboard. He said that their Emperor needed shelter and food for himself and his retinue. He also needed men to repair his damaged ships.

Some say the grand gentleman was Counsellor Lok So-fu. Turning away he saw a great boulder at the crest of a hillock. Against the boulder rested some large rock slabs that protected the entrance to a cave. Here the 11-year-old Emperor spent many restful days. It became the Terrace of the Sung Dynasty Emperor or Sung Wong Toi. One day while gazing at the hills he saw in them the semblance of dragons, his symbol, the Royal of the Dragon Throne.

He counted the dragon shapes and made the number eight. He turned to his Counsellor and said: "Here are eight dragons."

"Nay, there are nine, your Majesty."

"Nine! I count only eight."

The Counsellor looked at the young emperor. "Truly your Majesty counts but eight, but seeing that your Majesty is in their midst, surely there are nine."

So, according to verbal legend, the district became known as Kau Lung meaning Nine Dragons, or, as the English tongue has it, Kowloon.

AIRPORT OF THE NINE DRAGONS, KAI TAK, KOWLOON

LAST OF THE SUNG DYNASTY
Cheung Hing Bing – The Boy Emperor.
(Photo: Chui Clansmen, Hong Kong)

COUNSELLOR LOK SO-FU
Drowned with the Boy Emperor.
(Photo: Chui Clansmen, Hong Kong)

SUNG HUANG TERRACE (SUNG WONG TOI)
AUTUMN by Wu Tak Yee (artist).
(Photo: Chui Clansmen, Hong Kong)

THE SACRED STONE OF THE SUNG c1923
(Photo: Chui Clansmen, Hong Kong)

APPENDIX 11

MY 1947 VISIT TO SUNG WONG TOI

(Photo: Author)

The story ends sadly. The fleet sailed out to give battle to the war-junks of Kublai Khan. They met disaster at the mouth of the Pearl River. With all lost, the faithful minister took the boy Emperor upon his back and leapt into the water. So, in the year of our Lord 1279 the House of Sung ceased to exist.

There is a variation on how Kau Lung, or Nine Dragons, got its name. The peaks from east to west are Razor Hill, Hebe Hill, Kau Lung Peak, Temple Hill, Crown Point, Lion Rock, Beacon Hill, Eagle's Nest, and Tai Mo Shan. From his Terrace the boy Emperor could see only eight of these peaks. Tai Mo Shan, the ninth, although the highest remained hidden by the others when seen from the ground.

During the Yuan Dynasty (1260-1368) an artisan engraved three characters Sung Wong Toi horizontally upon the western face of the rock. Later another engraver added seven characters vertically. These recorded repairs were carried out in 1807 AD in the Ting Mau Year of the Ching Emperor Ka Hing.

Hong Kong born Cliff Large played in the area in 1929. He recalled traces of the encircling stone balustrade. He also recalls the stone's characters were weathering. When I visited the Sacred Hill in 1947 I found it strewn with boulders of varying size and without grass. An elderly Clansman swept the base of the Toi while a capricious wind eddied dust wantonly. No trace remained of the stone balustrade built by Mr. Li Sui-Kam in 1915.

The Toi towered stark and lonely into an overcast sky with its once deeply etched characters crammed with mossy green mud. Here was a bleak reminder of a conqueror's reckless destruction.

In 1915, Professor Lai Chai-Hei (better known as Lai Sui-Hsi) of the University of Hong Kong petitioned the Government to preserve this ancient monument. In 1958, the Hong Kong Government acceded to his entreaty. As the perimeter of the new runway overlapped the Sacred Hill, they created a park W.S.W. of the airport, about 300 feet from the original site. Workmen dressed and there enshrined the Toi. On December 28, 1959, a moving ceremony confirmed this modern setting for an ancient artifact. This satisfied the Chui Clansmen, the ancient guardians of the Sung Wong Toi.

AIRPORT OF THE NINE DRAGONS, KAI TAK, KOWLOON

THE GARDEN OF THE SUNG – 1957
Looking towards the checker-board, unpainted, and the Kowloon roundabout at mid-right. Next-door to the Trinity School I had my uniforms and shirts laundered. Ma Tau Chung Road, which passed in front of Trinity, carried little traffic. A vacant tract of land is seen to the right of Trinity. Olympic Avenue (in right foreground) is merely a dusty track. The whole atmosphere is without stress. How different today?
(Photo: Author)

THE GARDEN OF THE SUNG – 1972
Looking east across the Sung Garden with the Pioneer Concrete plant, for the Tunnel, at centre left. The splendid Terminal building stands at top left.
(Photo: Author)

240

APPENDIX 12

THE LOCKHEED ELECTRA L188 – PROBLEMS & RECTIFICATION

In ancient legend, Electra was the daughter of Agamemnon and Clytemnestra. With her brother, Orestes, she planned to kill the mother she blamed for her father's death. Electra translates from the Greek as the *bright one*.

The Lockheed employee who suggested the Electra name had a prophetic insight that brought his company close to bankruptcy. The Electra L188 was a *bright one* with the unfortunate vengeful trait of her mythological ancestor.

The Electra's reliability continued to disappoint Cathay Pacific. Most of the breakdowns occurred to the complex electrical system. Then disturbing gossip spread from the States. In March, rumour became confirmation when the Federal Aviation Agency (FAA) issued this advice:

> *The Tell City crash is now sufficiently similar to a previous accident of the same type aircraft last September near Buffalo, Texas, to justify operating restrictions pending further investigation. With immediate effect restrict speed to 275 knots at or below 15,000 feet, and to 260 knots above.*
> General Elwood L. Quesada, Administrator, FAA.

Sixty-three persons perished in a Northwest Airlines crash near Tell City, Indiana, on March 7, 1959. In September, a crash near Buffalo cost 34 lives. Eye-witness reports said the Electra, owned by Braniff International, disintegrated in flight. In each crash the investigators found one wing several miles from the impact site, suggesting separation at altitude.

The cause seemed to suggest *clear air turbulence*. This can occur near jet streams and in regions where hot and cold air masses meet. It is possibly the most serious weather condition the aviator can encounter, for radar cannot detect it. The only warning is a sudden change of temperature. When the pilot interprets this there is no time to reduce airspeed, the only safe method of negotiating this phenomenon.

Senator Vance Hartke charged General Quesada with rejecting the Civil Aeronautics Board's proposal that all uninspected Electras should be grounded. His argument: *When a type flies only ten per cent of the total hours and accounts for 76 per cent of the deaths its safety record is not good!*

The engineers investigating the Buffalo crash found hair-line cracks in the small tabs that connect the outer wing surface to its inner framework. The investigators returned to the Tell City wreckage where they found similar cracks. Still Quesada resisted grounding the type. He ordered a further reduction in speed to 225 knots and prohibiting auto-pilot operation pending modifications. His department had learned some Electra auto-pilots had malfunctioned, producing porpoising of noticeable magnitude.

AIRPORT OF THE NINE DRAGONS, KAI TAK, KOWLOON

The *Daily Telegraph* of May 5 continued to speculate. The reporter coupled the clear-air turbulence theory with a *strange harmonic* coming from the outboard engines that, at certain speeds, produced wing vibration. This reporter had a good grasp of aerodynamics – his theory came close to the mark!

Lockheed spent US$25 million solving the problems. One test included testing to destruction a new Electra worth US$1,750,000. The defect was a weakness in the mounts that held the engines in their nacelles. Investigations proved a hard landing or extreme turbulence could damage these mounts, causing the engine to shift. At a certain speed vibration caused more strain on the mounts and a chain reaction transmitted engine movement to the wing. The culmination of this reaction was a flutter so violent that the wing separated from the fuselage.

The modifications added 1,400 lbs of metal reinforcement to key areas. A further suggestion was to install flight recorders. The previous *black box* requirement excluded planes operating below 25,000 feet, so it then applied only to pure jets.

The Lockheed vice-president asked the 13 airlines operating 136 Electras to share in modification costs. When only two agreed Lockheed decided to bear the full cost of modification. The only stipulation was the airlines must be responsible for ferry costs to and from Burbank.

Cathay Pacific had an additional problem when inspection found organic fungus growing in the fuel tanks, filters and pumps. A closer check found the spore on the wing's inner skin and planks – resulting in corrosion. Not all operators had experienced this problem. It seemed to occur only in Electras operating in humid climates.

On December 4, in an operation called *Leap*, Captain Phil Blown flew Electra VR-HFN to Burbank through Tokyo, Wake Island and Honolulu. VR-HFO followed three days later commanded by Pat Armstrong.

In command of the return flight was Tony Rignall I was his co-pilot with F/O Brian Floyd, F/E's Stan Pain and Len Hawkes completing the crew. The passengers were Harry Smith of HAEC and Alan Pratt of the Department of Civil Aviation. The flight got off to a less than promising start. Strong head-winds forced us to turn back at the *November Ocean* weather ship. These adverse winds kept us grounded for nine days before they eased. My part in *Leap* ended on February 4, 1961, when I landed VR-HFN at Kai Tak.

During the Electra modifications Cathay wet-leased a Bristol Britannia 102 from BOAC. G-ANBO operated 79 round trips, 16 of them on the Hong Kong to Sydney route.

The Electra never again gave the company cause to regret having chosen them. There were, however, a couple of incidents.

On February 28, between Sydney and Darwin, Captain Lawrie King, in severe turbulence, took a heavy lightning strike. On descent into Darwin the ray dome collapsed producing violent vibration. Lawrie reduced the speed and landed without difficulty.

At the height of the Vietnamese confrontation Tan Son Nhut Airport, Saigon, handled a movement at 20-second intevals. Captain Leonard *Len* Cowper's Electra touched down in this controlled confusion. A malfunctioning reserve caused an asymmetric condition that veered his plane from the runway's centre line. His plane stopped with the nose and left wheels in the soft grass. A United States Air Force colonel arrived in a jeep accompanied by a bulldozer. He gave Len 30 seconds to get his plane off the runway and signalled his *dozer* into position. Len beat the deadline!

When QANTAS introduced the 707 Cathay Pacific Airways could not compete. Cathay withdrew the type and leased their Australian traffic rights to BOAC. On November 3, the final Electra service left Sydney under my command.

APPENDIX 13

AFTERMATH OF MURDER ON THE WING, 23 JULY, 1954

The crew and passengers were:
Survived: Captain Philip Blown, Captain Cedric Carlton, Stewardess Esther Law, Mrs P. M. Thorburn, Mrs F. Parrish, Miss Valerie Parrish (6), Mr Peter S. Thatcher, Mr Lui Luen-fong.
Died: Flight Engineer George Cattanach, Radio Officer Steven Wong, Stewardess Rose Chen, Miss Rita Chen, Mr Leonard L. Parrish, Master Laurence Parrish (4), Master Phillip Parrish (2), Mr Tie Tian-chuang, Mrs Findlay, Mr Paul Yong Nam-ying.

Cathay Pacific bought a replacement Skymaster from Canadian Pacific Air Lines. CX had it running to a schedule within three weeks of the disaster. The Company submitted a claim for UK£251,400 to the Chinese Government, who paid Her Majesty's Government in November (1954). *Jock Swire's Diary* lamented that Cathay received £175,000 on account *but can expect a stiff fight with the Claims Commissioner for the balance.*

The Foreign Office allayed his fears on August 25, 1955. The Company received a final cheque for £57,000 – exceeding the submitted claim by £7,000.

Cathay Pacific remembered Captain Woodyard at Christmas 1954 by presenting him with a salver engraved:
   To Captain Jack Thompson Woodyard, USAF. *In grateful recognition of his gallantry in*
      SA-16, No. AF1009 off Hainan Island, July 23, 1954.

In February 1955, The Director of Civil Aviation, Mr Muspratt-Williams, presented a silver cigar case to the US 31st Air Rescue Squadron. His presentation came from the Government and people of Hong Kong for their courageous rescue of the Cathay survivors.

On August 26, 1955, at Clark AFB, Major General John W. Sessumus, Jr, decorated Captain Woodyard and his crew with the Distinguished Flying Cross (DFC). He also decorated Captain Baker and Captain Veith, commander and co-pilot of the second Grumman, with the DFC, and their crew with the Air Medal.

Captain Woodyard's commanding officer brought his bold action to the notice of a prestigious committee. The Cheney Award is for an act of valour, or self-sacrifice in a humanitarian interest, associated with aircraft, but not necessarily of a military nature. The mother and sister of Lieutenant William H. Cheney established the Award in 1927. William Cheney died in an air collision over Foggia, Italy, on January 20, 1918. The selection panel did not choose Captain Woodyard.

Mr Julian F. Harrington, the US Consul-General in Hong Kong, expressed regret at the paucity of credit for the Skymaster crew. His words were loud and clear – without the skilful ditching there would have been nobody to rescue!

On June 15, 1955, Captain Philip Blown and Captain Cedric Windas Carlton stood before his Excellency the Governor, Sir Alexander Grantham. Mr M. C. Illingworth, the Governor's ADC, read an account of the deed. Then Sir Alexander decorated them with the silver badge of the Queen's Commendation For Valuable Service in the Air.

Many tributes praised the action of Woodyard and his men. Of those, to my mind, this was the sincerest. John Thorburn, husband of a survivor, wrote to General Sessumus. He began by praising the crew of the Skymaster and ended with his heartfelt thanks to Woodyard and his men for *bringing my wife back to her babies and me.*

APPENDIX 14

CHEK LAP KOK – THE ULTIMATE AIRPORT

When Hong Kong reverts to China in 1997 the new Airport on Chek Lap Kok Island will be far from finished. Will this imaginative project begun by a far-sighted Hong Kong Government reach fruition? I have reservations, but the Hong Kong Airport Core Programme seems to harbour few doubts!

Here is the ACP's splendid impression for the airport in the year 2040.

This photograph shows the progress in January 1994. The island of Chek Lap Kok is an entire building scar. What a contrast to when we flew our Catalina on the clear-weather route, north of Lantau, to and from Macau. Then the island's main cottage industry was mining black marble. Some of these magnificent slabs formed the massive doors of their monastery and others were used to face portions of the old Hong Kong & Shanghai Bank in Central.

GLOSSARY OF ABBREVIATIONS & MEANING OF WORDS

AF – Air France.
AFB – Air Force Base (American usage).
ANA – Australian National Airways.
ARB – Air Registration Board.
ATA – Actual Time of Arrival.
AVG – American Volunteer Group (Flying Tigers).

BA – British Airways (Imperial Airways, BOAC).
BCPA – British Commonwealth Pacific Airways.
BOAC – British Overseas Airways Corporation (now BA).
B&S – Butterfield and Swire.

CAD – Civil Aviation Department.
Capt. – Captain.
CAT – Civil Air Transport Inc.
CATC – Central Air Transport Corporation.
CATHAY – Cathay Pacific Airways (CPA).
CFI – Chief Flying Instructor.
CHUTAI – Squadron – Japanese flying term.
CNAC – China National Aviation Corporation.
CPAL – Canadian Pacific Air Lines.

DCA – Director or Department of Civil Aviation.
DFC – Distinguished Flying Cross.
DSC – Distinguished Service Cross.
DSO – Distinguished Service Order.

ETA – Estimated Time of Arrival.

FAA – Fleet Air Arm.
F/E – Flight Engineer or *flying spanner*.
FEFTS – Far East Flying Training School Limited.
fei gei – Cantonese for aeroplane.
F/O – First Officer.

GC – George Cross.
george – Aeroplane auto-pilot.
Gimo – Generalissimo Chiang Kai-Shek.
GMT – Greenwich Mean Time (also written Z).
GoC – General Officer Commanding.

HAEC (*HAECO*) – Kong Kong Aircraft Engineering Company.
HKA – Hong Kong Airways.
HKAAF – Hong Kong Auxiliary Air Force.
HMS – His/Her Majesty's Ship
HONG – the word implies big company – a house of foreign trade – it has no relation to the name Hong Kong.

AIRPORT OF THE NINE DRAGONS, KAI TAK, KOWLOON

HKVDC – Hong Kong Volunteer Defence Corps.

ICAO – International Civil Aviation Organisation.
IFR – Instrument Flying Rules (flight on instruments).
ILS/PAR – Instrument Landing System/Precision Approach Radar.

JAL – Japan Air Lines Co. Ltd.
JAMCo – Jardine Aircraft Maintenance Company Limited.
JS&S – John Swire and Sons Limited.

KBE – Knight Commander of the [Most Excellent Order of the] British Empire.
KEMPEITAI – Japanese secret police.
KMT – KUOMINTANG – The National Government of Generalissimo Chiang Kai-Sek.

LORCHA (lor'cha) n. a light vessel of European build, but rigged like a Chinese junk.
LST – Local Standard Time.

MAL – Malayan Airways.
MATCO – Macau (Macao) Air Transport Company.
MC – Military Cross.
minima – aviation term – minimum operating conditions for a specific company.

NDB – Non-Directional Beacon (navigation aid).
NULLAH – (nul'a) n. a water-course or open storm-water drain.

OBE – Officer of the (Most Excellent Order of the) British Empire.
OSS – Office of Strategic Services (USA).

PAL – Philippine Air Lines.
PAMAS (*PAMCo*) – Pacific Air Maintenance & Supply Company Limited.
PANAGRA – Pan American-Grace Airways.
PanAm – Pan American World Airways.
pax – Aviation parlance for passengers.
P&O – Peninsula and Orient (shipping line).
props – Propellers.
PWD – Public Works Department.

QANTAS – Qantas Empire Airways (Queensland & Northern Territory Aerial Services Limited.
RAAF – Royal Australian Air Force.
RAF – Royal Air Force.
RAN – Royal Australian Navy.
RFEIC – Roy Farrell Export-Import Company.
RN – Royal Navy.
R/O – Radio Officer or *sparks*.
rpm – revs-per-minute (engine operation).

SENTAI – Group – Japanese flying term.
SCMP – *South China Morning Post* – Hong Kong newspaper – first issued November 1903.
Sgt. – Sergeant (rank).

tael – Chinese weight (a tael of gold weighs 1.3 ozs)
TAIPAN – the chairman of a *HONG* literally means *big boss*.
THAI – Thai International Airways.
TI – Time Interval.

UNRRA – United Nations Relief and Rehabilitation Administration.
USAF – United States Air Force.
USN – United States Navy.

VC – Victoria Cross.

WEI-HAI-WEI – a city at the entrance of the Gulf of Chihli and north of Shanghai and south-east of Port Arthur. Its position is 37.40N: 122.15E.

PRINCIPAL WORKS CONSULTED

A Brief History Of Hong Kong by Winifred A. Wood (1940).
A History of Hong Kong by G.B. Endacott (1958).
A History of Hong Kong by Frank Welsh.
American Heritage History Of Flight, The, by the editors of *American Heritage – The Magazine of History.*
A Million Miles In the Air by Captain Gordon P. Olley.
A Nation of Flyers (German Aviation) by Peter Fritzsche.
An Illustrated History of Hong Kong by Nigel Cameron.
Arrow War, The – An Anglo-Chinese Confusion 1856-60 by Douglas Hurd.
Bloody Shambles, Vols. 1 & 2, by Christopher Shores & Brian Cull with Yasuho Izawa.
British Trade and The Opening of China 1800-42 by Michael Greenberg (1951)
Burke's Peerage – Baronetage & Knightage – 1956 – 101st Edition.
Chinese Creeds and Customs, by V. R. Burkhardt. Three volumes.
Civil Aeronautics Board, Docket Nos: 1499, 1706. Brief of Pan American Airways, Inc. Henry J. Friendly, John H. Slate, Jr. Attorneys for Pan American Airways, Inc. February 17, 1947.
Colony in Conflict, by John Cooper.
Conquest Of the Air, The, by Frank Howard and Bill Gunston.
Dragon's Wings, The, by William M. Leary, Jr.
Early Aviation, by Sir Robert Saundby 1971.
Encyclopaedia Britannica 1970.
Fall of Hong Kong, The, by Tim Carew.
Government and People in Hong Kong 1841-1962. A Constitutional History by G.B. Endacott (1964)
Great Planes, The, by James Gilbert 1970.
Guinness Book Of Records – 19th Edition 1972. Edited and complied by Norris and Ross McWhirter.
Harry S. Truman, by Margaret Truman 1972.
Hong Kong Airport – booklet produced by HKG. DCA 1962/63
Hongkong Around and About by S. H. Peplow & M. Barker (1931).
Hong Kong Annual Report 1951.
Hong Kong – Borrowed Place – Borrowed Time, by Richard Hughes.
Hong Hong – The Colony That Never Was by Alan Birch.
Hong Kong 100 Years Ago – a Picture-story of Hong Kong in 1870. Text by John Warner.
Hong Kong the Formative Years 1842 – 1912. The Shell Company of Hong Kong.
Hump Pilots Association, Inc. (China – Burma – India) U.S.A.
I Flew for China, by Captain Royal Leonard (1942).
In the Mouth Of the Dragon, by Philip Geddes.
John Samuel Swire 1825-98, Senior, The, by Sheila Marriner and Francis E. Hyde.

Magic Stone, The . . . a legend from Hong Kong.
Myths and Legends of China by E. T. C. Werner.
Peninsula Group Magazine, The – April 1974.
Pow Mah Precious Horse by Henry Ching, O.B.E.
Prelude To Hong Kong by Austin Coates (*The Asian Magazine, The Japanese Times* – June 19, 1966.)
Second World War, The – by Winston S. Churchill 1952.
   VOL: 3 – The Grand Alliance.
   VOL: 5 – Closing the Ring.
Sung Wong Toi – A Commemorative Volume, Complied & Edited by Jen Yu-Wen (Kan Yau-Man). Published by the Chiu Clansmen's Association of Hong Kong.
Syd's Pirates by Captain Charles (Chic) Eather (1983).
Taikoo by Charles Drage.
Taipans, The – Hong Kong's Merchant Princes by Colin N. Crisswell.
Triad Societies In Hong Kong by W. P. Morgan.
War Monthly Magazine (a parts series) Issue 41 – page 26. "Hong Kong 1941" by Nigel Bagnall. An account of the Japs overrunning the Crown Colony.
Wings (An Encyclopedia of Aviation in weekly parts.)
World Book Encyclopedia, The. "H" Vol: 9. (Article contributed by Richard Harris.)

NEWSPAPERS

Hong Kong:
   China Mail.
   Hong Kong Telegraph.
   Sing Tao Man Pao.
   South China Morning Post.
   Tiger Standard, The.
   Wah Kiu Man Po.

Australia:
   Daily Mirror, Sydney.
   Daily Telegraph, Sydney.
   Sydney Morning Herald, Sydney.

INDEX

Bold type page numbers refer to illustrations/photographs.

A

Abbott, Lt.Col. Harry W: first tenant, Kowloon Aviation Field, founded Commercial Air Company, 7; bought Lim On's derelict Jenny, 7; Curtiss Jenny JN-4, **7**; wing walking – dubbed *Crazy Harry*, 7; Curtiss Oriole, **8**.
Ader, Clement: flew Armainvilliers, France, October 9, 1890, not confirmed, 2.
Air Asia Limited: brief Corporate notes, 192.
Aircraft on Hong Kong Register: 179-189.
Air France: HKG service, 37; last service 1940, 37; suspends HKG service, 42.
Air India International: bomb aboard *Kashmir Princess*, 110 H.M.S. *Dampier* recovers bodies and survivors, 110; 707, collapsed undercarriage, 169.
Allan, Captain G.U. *Scotty*: Australian pioneer aviator, 146.
American Round-the-World Fliers, The: resume, 199, **201**.
Amphibian Airways, Inc.: brief Corporate notes, 192.
Anderson, Vyvyan Henry: joins CAD, 85.
Andrews, Flight Sergeant: British pioneer engineer, 9; **10**.
Ano, K.: Japanese pioneer pilot, 26.
Armstrong, A.B. *Pat*: arrives with 96 Squadron, 54; joins Cathay Pacific, 65; Electra ferry, 141; commercial jet record Singapore to HKG, 150.
Armstrong, Captain William: Imperial Airways surveyor, 27; arrives in HKG and waxes lyrical, 30.
Arnold, Geoff: Cathay Pacific ground engineer, 76.
Arnold, Leslie P.: American round-the-world flight, 199, **201**.
Arozamen, Joaquin: Spanish pioneer mechanic, 12; 206.
Aylward, Eric: PAMAS staff engineer, telephone & bomb, 92.

B

Baker, Captain Dale R.: 31st Air Rescue Squadron, 109; Grumman Albatross, 109; CPA DC-4 shot down, 109; 243.
Baldwin, Thomas: arrived in HKG 1891, parachute descent, 1; 1910 returned, 1.
Ballantyne, R.G.: HKG Airways Captain, hydraulics fail on take-off, 85.
Barton, Hugh: Jardine Chairman, seat on Cathay Board, 118.
Bell, *Dinger*: Royal Observatory, heavy rainfall, 126.
Bell, J.H.D.: new Airport Fire Officer, 116.
Beltrame: Argentine pioneer engineer, **18**.
Bennett, A.D. *Don*: BOAC Captain, Kai Tak service, retires, 162.
Birch, Timothy: Radio HKG's – the Miracle Strip, 127.
Bixby, Harold M.: PanAm negotiator, 23; postal agreement with China, 32.
Blown, Captain Phil: Cathay DC-4 shot down, 109; decorated, 113, 243; Electra ferry, 141.
Bohm, Capt. Ross Sandford: pilot, Catalina VR-HEV, **96**; Communists capture, 95; accused of smuggling, 95; jailed, 97; released, 97, **96**; died, 97.
Bond, William Langhorne.: CNAC's ops. manager assesses the *Hump*, 42; PanAm Captain Fred S. Ralph phones, 44; rushes to Kai Tak, 44; finds half his fleet in ashes, 45; PanAm's *Hong Kong Clipper* sunk, 44; after dark, dodging craters, his pilots evacuate people, 45; awake for 53 hours, 45; *Papa Moss* advises Kai Tak's demolition, 45; Captain Moon Chin flies him to Chungking, 45.
Bowring, Sir John: Governor, a troubled period, xiii; poisoned bread, wife dies, xiii; resume, 230, **231**.
Bowring, Sister Aloyisa (Emily): remained in HKG, xiii; takes the veil, xiii; Headmistress Canossian School, xiii; dies, xiii.
Bowring, The Hon. Theodore Louis: HKG – Director of Public Works, explains building the Miracle Strip, 124; rubble from the Kowloon Hills & Sacred Hill, 124.
Boxer Uprising: 1900 – Peking besieged, 4.
Bremer, Captain: pioneer pilot, 23.
Bremer, Sir Gordon: proclaimed British sovereignty, xi.
Brennan, Leo: CPA flight engineer, DC-6B ferry, 128.
Bridgeman, Bill: CPA's DC-6B instructor, 128.
British East India Company: permanent base at Canton, viii.
British Overseas Airways Corporation (BOAC): took over from Imperial Airways, 42; suspends HKG service, 42; returns with Hythe and Plymouth flying-boats, 56; continues stirring, 63; align with Jardine Matheson to form Hong Kong Airways, 63; flying boat diverted to Hainan, 64; China bi-lateral agreement, UK nomination, 65; extends service to Iwakuni, Japan, 73; introduce Argonaut type, **85**; last HKG *Plymouth* flight, 86; a regional carrier?, 105; Argonaut coolant leak, 105; MAL interest, 118; regionals lose money, 118; dumps HKG Airways, 118; inspects new runway proposal, 122; mockup of curved approach, 122; favourable report, 122; Comet at opening ceremony, 129; Comet 1Vs service, 142; Comet collision, 154; Corbett Report, 154; Don Bennett retires, 162; Jumbo introduced, 164.
British World Flight: resume, 202, **204**.
Broadbent, R.: author of Broadbent Report, 98; **99**.
Broadhead, Ray: CPA navigator, 707 ferry flight, 169.
Brock, William: American pioneer pilot, 14; *Pride of Detroit*, 14; **18**.
Brown Black, The Hon. Robert: HKG – Colonial Secretary, 124; opens Miracle Strip (then Governor Sir Robert), 129; rides in BOAC Comet, 129; opens Terminal 148, **149**; retires, 152.
Brown, Don: CPA – F/E, nose-wheel stuck, emergency landing, 152, 153.
Brutin (Burlin): French pioneer pilot, 21; **21**.
Burman, Walter: HKG Airways, Chief Pilot Viscount fleet, 117.
Bush, Henry Peter: bizarre rescue adventure?, 119.
Butterfield & Swire: segment of John Swire & Sons, 73.

C

Caldecott, Governor Sir Andrew (1935-37): meets first Imperial service, 31.
Callaghan, Leo: CPA flight engineer, Skymaster inaugural flight to Singapore, 90; insists friend lives, 95.
Calvo, Pedro Mariano: Spanish pioneer mechanic, 12; in desert, 12; 206.
Canadian Pacific Air Lines: HKG service, 86; Britannia 314 service, 142.
Cannon, George S.R.: takes control of Aradio Services, 66; resigns, 116.
Cannon, Major A.S. *John*: the Midnight-flit, 71.
Capern, R.J. *Ron*: CAD, Briefing Officer, 116.
Carlton, Captain Cedric *Ced*: Cathay DC-4 shot down, 109; decorated, 113, 243.
Carrington, John: CPA Captain, on DC-6B ferry, 128.
Cathay Holdings Limited: complicated take-over of HKG Airways, 118; brief Corporate notes, 193.
Cathay Pacific Airways (CPA): evolved from RFEIC, 58; Farrell and de Kantzow original subscribers, 58; begins Macau non-schedules, 62; *Nikki* damaged, 62; advised to reduce American ownership, 73; Swire retained original name, 73; opens Catalina service to Macau, 73, **74, 75**; first engineering store, 76; first *hangar*, 76; located southern side of runway 07/25, 77; sold Quonset for HK$5,717,777; Cathay supported by Government, 79; Catalina *Miss Macao* pirated, 79; DC-3s, **82**; Shanghai charters, 84; Kunming charters, 86; buys Skymaster, 86; Skymaster inaugural Singapore flight, 90; carries *Gimo's* silver bullion to HKG, 90; Skymaster inaugural Saigon flight, 90; routes south of HKG, 91; Hainan battery fires on DC-3, 92; let-down charts, 97; Skymaster dry-charter, 100; a regional carrier?, 105; buys DC-6, 106; DC-4 shot down, 108, **108**; resume, 243; dry-charters Korean National Airways DC-4, 117; unimpressed with HKG Airways return, 117; refuses NWA approach, 118; rejects regional company status, 118; *Jock Swire* wins the *Battle of HKG Airways*, 119; DC-6B arrives, Bill Bridgeman instructor, 128; first civilian plane off Miracle Strip, 128;

249

AIRPORT OF THE NINE DRAGONS, KAI TAK, KOWLOON

Electra service, 141; passenger removed, 145; Convair 880 arrives, 146; plane arrested in Manila, 152; Convair emergency landing, 152, **153**; buys 2nd Convair, 154; lost BOAC friends, 154; Convair into sea, 157, **157**; simulator from nose section, 157, **157**; *hand-me-downs*, 164; Convair, death of worker, 164; Convair bombed over Vietnam, 165, **166**; Lockheed L-1011 type and simulator, 168, 169; balloon, 169; 707 emergency landing, 169; brief Corporate notes, 193, *Betsy* comes home, **227**.
Cathay Pacific Airways (1948) Ltd.: brief Corporate notes, 193.
Cathay Pacific Holdings Limited: holding company during sale of American shareholdings, 73; brief Corporate notes, 193.
Cattanach, George: engineer, uninjured in Catalina crash, 95; Cathay DC-4 shot down, killed, 109, 243.
Cave-Brown-Cave, Group Captain H.M.: led Far East Flight, 14; 18; **19**.
Central Air Transport Corporation (CATC): share bi-lateral agreement, China nomination, 65.
Chek Lap Kok: new airport site, 174; **244**.
Chen, Stewardess Rose: Cathay, DC-4 shot down, killed, 109.
Chennault, Major General Claire L.: orders Leonard fly to Kweilin, 41; Chennault, Major General Claire L.: claims ownership of defected planes, 90; interest in CNAC planes, 91; brings legal action, led by *Wild Bill* Donovan, 91; Communist claim upheld, 91; Privy Council favours him, 101; winches planes on to L.S.T. *Chung* and leaves, 101; CAT, pax. division suspended, 161.
Cheong-Leen, R. J. *Remy*: Act. Asst. DCA (Ops), inspects bombed Convair, 165, **166**.
Chiang Kai-shek, Generalissimo *Gimo*: nearly captured, 39; questions HKG's future, 50; troops unpaid, 86; shifts capital to Taiwan, 90; Hainan falls, 92; transfers CNAC interest to Chennault, 91; dies, 171.
China National Aviation Corporation (CNAC): PanAm control, 23; the *Hump*, 23; helped evacuate HKG, 23; HKG service, 32; DC-2 shot down, 37; night service to Chungking, 37; stormy weather a blessing, 37; evacuates Hangkow, 39; first airline back in Colony, 54; restores air mail to China, 54; share bi-lateral agreement, China nomination, 65; Skymaster crashes on Basalt Island, CNAC vice-president Quentin Roosevelt killed, 77.
Chinese Air Force: deserters, 31; returned to China, 31.
Chir, Yung-Mur, Johann: CPA Senior Purser, Convair 880 aborted take-off, awarded, 157, **157**.
Civil Aviation Department (CAD): located beside Supreme Court, 56, 60; *Papa* Moss becomes Director, 56; advises CPA to reduce American ownership, 73; move to New Secretariat, 108.
Civil Air Transport (CAT): Boeing 727 crash, 160; pilots charged manslaughter, 160; IALPA threaten boycott, 160; Chennault's airline pax. division suspended, 161.
Clarke, Tony: HKG Air International pilot, 163; disagreement, Licensing Authority, 164.
Clarke, W.V.: ATCO Grade II, 127.
Clifford, Bert: ARB Surveyor, retired, 152.
Communist: advance southwards, charterers thrive, 84; support North Korea, 94; capture Catalina, 95; gunboat shells British launch, 80 Squadron rescue, 103; shoot down Cathay DC-4, 109; warn rescue planes away, 109; resume wx. broadcasts, 115.
CONTROL TOWER – Locations: **190**, 191.
Cole, R.: CAD-ATCO, 150.
Convention of Chuenpi – 1840: ceded HKG Island and Harbour to Britain, x.
Cooper, R.K. *Reg*: CAD-ATCO, 150.
Cox, *Squire* **John Henry**: singsongs, ix.
Cramer, Dale: Captain of pirated *Miss Macao*, killed, 79.
Cumine, Eric C.: Terminal drawings, 140, **141**.
Cunningham, Group Captain John *Cat's Eyes*: Comet at Miracle Strip opening, 129; pilots Vice-Regal party, 129.

D

da Costa, Delca: Cathay air hostess dies on pirated *Miss Macau*, 79.
da Cruz, Lieutenant: Portuguese pioneer pilot, 25.
Davidson Trading Company: owners Lancelot and Wilkinson Dent, xi.
Davis, John Francis: succeeded Lord Napier, ix.
Day, Mr & Mrs: honeymoon flyers, 21; resume, 211.
de Beires (Brito) Pais: Portuguese pioneer pilot, 9; Breguet 14, *Patria*, 9; crashed in HKG, 11.
de Kantzow, Captain Sydney *Syd*: the *Hump*, 23; Generalissimo Chiang's personal pilot, 23; RFEIC director, 57; Cathay Pacific Airways original subscriber, 58; Kai-shek's pilot, 23; a hard negotiator, 73.
Delaney, Don: CPA Asst. Chief Engineer, Convair ferry, 146; radio instructions, stuck nose-wheel, 153, **153**.
de Leuil, Harry: RFEIC Sydney manager, 57.
DEPARTMENT OF CIVIL AVIATION:
    Directors of Air Services: 178.
    Directors of Civil Aviation: 178.
    CAD – Controllers of Kai Tak Airport: 178.
    Locations: **191**, 191.
de Ricou (Recoux), Capt. Charles E.W.: French World War I aviator, 6; established Macau Aerial Transport Company, 6; HKG Government set harsh restrictions, disbanded, 7.
de Sibour, Viscount: French pioneer pilot, 23; resume, 218.
Dew, Stuart E.: CAT captain, 160; manslaughter charge, 160; Taipei boycott, 160; acquitted, 161.
Dhabher, Buji: Partner, Dragonfly Helicopters, 160; insurance withheld, later paid, 160.
Dickson, Captain: pioneer pilot, 23.
Dobson, Bill: CPA Public Relations, 59; fired on at Macau, 63.
d'Oisy (Doisy), Lieutenant Georges Pelletier: French pioneer pilot, 9; resume, 198.
Donovan, Major General William *Wild Bill*: wartime head of OSS, leads Chennault's CNAC claim, 91; Communist claim upheld, 91.
Donovan Robert *Bob*: RFEIC captain, 57; Shanghai evacuation, 84; electrical storm, 84; guided by fire-beacons, 84; Kunming evacuation, 86.
Douglas-Hamilton, Lord Malcolm: FEFTS – CFI, 24.
Downing, Roy Evans: arrives as ATCO, Grade II, 66; on duty, 83, 84; gates on runway extension, 93; the funeral procession, 93; *Kashmir Princess* bomb, 110; becomes DCA, 166.
Dragonfly Helicopters Ltd.: Bell 47G-5 crashes, 158, **159**; insurance withheld, later paid, 160.
Dudman, William Forrest *Bill*: reactivates FEFTS, 59; retires, 145.

E

Earnshaw, Reginald *Reg*: *Crazy Harry's* mechanic, drowned, 8.
Eather, Charles *Chic*: CPA pilot, 59; de Kantzow gives Kai Tak briefing, 61; the gold charters, 72, **72**; chased by black snake, 77; I instruct for FEFTS, 77; Ryan ST M, **78**; at FEFTS when Cathay Dakota crashes, 84; Taiwan unfriendly, 91; *honey-truck* on extension, 93; diverts to Manila, lands at Clark AFB, unwelcome, 100; FEFTS link trainer, 116; Korean National Airways DC-4, 117; commercial jet record HKG to Singapore, 150; nose-wheel stuck, emergency landing, 152, **153**; diverted to Taipei, 169; bird-strikes, 169; looks back, 174, looks ahead, 175.
Elgin, Earl (James Bruce): resume, 230, **231**.
Elliot, Captain Charles: replaces Sir George Robinson, ix; defied Commissioner Lin, ix; historical birth of HKG, ix; imprisons seaman, ix; x; nominates HKG Island, x; angers Lord Palmerston, x; negotiating Convention of Chuenpi, 1840, **xi**; Queenstown building boom, xi; caught in typhoon, xii; price on head, xii; a wasted life? xii.
Esteve, Rafael Martinez: Spanish pioneer pilot, 12; **13**; in desert, 12, 206.
Eurasia Aviation Corporation: contract between China and Lufthansa, 26; Soviets prohibit overfly rights, 26; inaugural HKG service, tri-motor Junkers Ju52s, 30; serves HKG, 34; **38**; Junkers Ju52, **38**; Japanese fighters intercept, 37; sacks German staff, 43.

F

Falgate, D: CAD, ATCO Grade II, 116.
Falkenthul, F/E C.J. *Chuck*: Convair instructor, 146.
Far East Aviation Co. Ltd. The: brief Corporate notes, 194.
Far Eastern Air Transport: Skymaster ditches off Philippines, 66, 70.
Far East Flight: Southampton flying-boats, 14.
Far East Flying Training School (FEFTS): incorporated 1933, 24; W.F. Murray, Commandant, Lord Malcolm Douglas-Hamilton, Chief Instructor, 24; instructors mobilised, 41; strafing destroys planes, 44; reactivated by Bill Dudman, 59; Chinese fire on trainer, Sel Halls, CFI, & Bill Dobson aboard, 63, **63**; loses Piper L4J, pilot rescued, 77; I begin instructing, 77; installation, **78**; Airspeed Oxford, fiendish traits, 100; Link trainer, 116; pupil nicks Stinson L-5, 127; new premises, 141; Dudman retires, W/C Scales his successor, 145; brief Corporate notes, 194.

INDEX

Far East Flying & Technical School Ltd.: brief Corporate notes, 195.
Farrell, Roy Clinton: RFEIC partner, 57; Cathay Pacific Airways original subscriber, 58; establishes PAMAS with spares from Manila dump, 77; he shoots snake chasing me, 77.
Fawdon, John: HKG Airways, Captain, 117.
First World War: began August 4, 1914, 4.
Foi Malikhao: prosecutor, bombed Cathay Convair, 165; *not guilty* verdict, 165.
Fokker, Mijnheer Anthony: 18.
Forte, Woody: CATC captain, boxes of Mexican dollars, 86.
Francis, Flt Lt George *Kiwi*: Vampire F-3 adventure, 82.
Frost, Robert Lowich *Bob*: Cathay Sales & Traffic Manager dies on pirated *Miss Macau*, 79.
Funk, Michael A.: Asst. Airport Manager, 140.
Furley, John: CPA captain, Hainan battery fires on plane, 92.

G

Gaddi, Leopold (Leo): resume, 224.
Gallarza, Eduardo Gonzalez: Spanish pioneer pilot, 12, **13**; landed in tree, 12; reached Manila, 12; 206.
Garuda Indonesian Airways: Convair 990A, 152.
Gauntlett, Squadron Leader E.J.G.: HKAAF, dies in Spitfire, 105; B&S employee, 105.
Gouveia, Manuel: Portuguese pioneer mechanic, 9.
Grantham, Governor Sir Alexander: on defected planes, 91; early architect of Miracle Strip, 124.
Gray, Flying Officer H.B. *Dolly*: scheme to bomb Canton refused, 45; in charge of Kai Tak work party, 47.
Green, Capt. Geoff: 1970s Cathay Pacific Airways' balloon, 2, 169.
Green Island Cement Co: installs precipitator, 108.
Gunn, Captain Tom: 1915 hydroplane exhibition Shatin, 4.

H

Hainan Island: BOAC flying boat diverted, 64; CPA DC-4 shot down, 108; Douglas *Sky Raiders* shoot down Communist planes, 110.
Hall, Nev: HKG Airways, Viscount F/O, 117; later with CPA, 117.
Hallam, John Anthony Tony: ATC Class II, 101; retired, 101.
Halls, Sel: FEFTS CFI fired on at Macau, 63, **63**.
Hamilton, Owen FitzWilliam (*Hammy*): arrives, 37; becomes Assistant Superintendent of Airport, 43; interned in Stanley, 47; becomes Oxford's assistant, 56; retires, 146, **146**; missed Terminal opening, 148; Xavier Cugat's chihuahua, 156.
Harcourt, Rear Admiral Sir Cecil: accepts Japanese surrender, 50, **50**.
Harris, Bill *Hokum*: RFEIC Chief Engineer, 57; engineering store, 76; bombs in defected planes, 92.
Hemsworth, Neville Gerald *Nev*: RFEIC captain, 57.
Henderson, A. S. *Steve*: foam expert, becomes Airport Fire Officer, 106; retires, 116.
Hernandez, Senor: balloon exploded North Point, 1.
Heron, R.G. *Reg*: CAD, Signals, 116.
Hewson, Ernest Sunley *Ben*: arrives as ATCO, Grade I, 66; takes over RAF Control Tower, 66.
Hicks, Captain: CAT, 727 crash, 160; wife killed, 160; manslaughter charge, 160; Taipei boycott, 160; acquitted, 161.
Higgs, Frank L.: CNAC captain, evacuates people from Kai Tak, 45; *Terry & the Pirates* cartoon, 45; on return, British gunners fire on him, 45.
Hill, Flight Lieutenant D.S. *Sammy*: scheme to bomb Canton refused, 45.
Hilsz, Maryse: French pioneer aviatrix, 23; resume, 216.
HMS Flycatcher: replaces HMS *Nabcatcher*, 64; site drawing, **67**; HMS *Nabcatcher*: becomes HMS *Flycatcher*, 64; *Tiger* on base-leg, 68; withdraws from Kai Tak, 73; site bought by two aircraft maintenance companies, 73.
HMS Nabcatcher: Naval repair depot, Kai Tak, 50; damaged in 1946 typhoon, 55, 56.
HMS Pegasus: arrived HKG 3 November, 1924, 11; equipped Fairey 111D seaplanes, 11; survey cameras, 11; leaves HKG, 12.
Hole, Commander George Francis: Director of Harbour Department, directed HKG Air Services 1930, 20; report, 21; meets first Imperial service, 31.
Holland, Geoff: HAEC engineer, injured in Catalina crash, 95.
Hong Kong: Harbour & Kowloon Peninsula 1859-1865, **xvii**; Victoria c1855, **xvii**; conscription, 40; Sir Mark Young and General Maltby arrive, 43; Christmas Day surrender to Japan, 46; British surrender force arrives, 50; Roosevelt loath to return HKG to Britain, 50; Truman agrees Colony's return, 50; HMS *Swiftsure* enters harbour, 50; Red Guards mass on border, 90; demonstrations, 91; CNAC & CATC offices pickets, 91; Communists support North Korea, 94; heavy rain, 156; 1992 aerial view, **173**.
Hong Kong Aircraft Engineering Company (HAEC/HAECO): merge of JAMCO & PAMCO, 95; overhauled Catalina crashes, 94; aerial view of complex, **94**; amalgamation PAMAS & JAMCO, 95; embargo on spares, 102; BOAC Argonaut repaired, 102; repairs land-mined Burmese Dakota, 102; repairs Taiwan medium bomber, 127; new hangar, 150; 1959 installation, **151**, 1966 view, **156**; assembles Bell 47G-5, 158, **159**; largest hangar in Far East, 161; worker killed, 164; overhauls Chinese Viscount, 169; installation view, **170**.
Hong Kong Air International: helicopter services, 163.
Hong Kong Airways: formed, 63; China bi-lateral agreement, UK nomination, 65; obtain schedule routes, 65; purchases 2 Dakotas, 65; begin two daily services to Canton, 65; rights to Manila, 79; timed let-down, 84; wet-charter BOAC Plymouth, 85; hydraulics fail on take-off, 85; routes north of HKG, 91; Communist planes fire on DC-3, 94; Bamboo Curtain closed, 98; sold Dakota fleet, 98; wet-charter DC-4, 106; reactivated, Viscount, 117; suggests a regional company, 118; brief Corporate notes, 195.
Hong Kong Auxiliary Air Force (HKAAF): Spitfire ditched in Kowloon Bay, 103; Spitfire belly landed, 104; Gauntlett dies in Spitfire, 105; Harvard trainer crashes, 106; fly-past, 111; Harvards guide launch, 111; Spitfire lost, 111; Harvard lost, 114; helicopter force lands, 155; Auster ditches, 155; Musketeer crash, 166.
Hong Kong Flying Club: suspends operations, 23; Government backs Vaughan Fowler, 23; reactivated, 24; name changed to FEFTS, manager Vere Harvey, 24; shared RAF area, 15; 16; Governor Sir Cecil Clementi supporter, 17; Legislature votes $60,000, 17; reactivated, 77; loses Piper Cub, 85; Musketeer accident, 154; Beechcraft *Musketeer*, 158; *Musketeer* accident, 162.
Hoskins, George Peter: RFEIC/CPA captain, 58.
Howell, Bob, DFC: Convair 880 aborted take-off, 157, **157**.
Howqua – Co-hong: **xv**; fixed prices, viii; Canton Factories, **xv** delegation tactless, ix; Co-hong abolished, xii.
Hunt, Dick: Cathay Pacific captain, Catalina, carries Ex-Emperor Bao Dai to Annam, 76; Skymaster ferry flight, 86.

I

Imperial Airways: used DH86A *Dorado*, 27; begins service, 31; *Dorado*, 32; revised Bangkok routing, 35; Japanese advances cause nervousness, 35; Union Jacks on DH86A's wings, 35; *Delphinus*, 36; becomes BOAC, 42.
Indge-Buckingham, Police Inspector Frank: remembers *tent-city*, 56, **59**.

J

Jackson-Smith, Ron *Jacko*: CPA Captain, Convair 880 aborted take-off, 157, **156**.
James Robertson & Company, Glasgow: sheeting for hangar, 22.
James, William Michael *Bill*: radio officer, Catalina VR-HEV, **96**; captured by Communists, 95; accused of smuggling, 95; jailed, 97; released, 97; **96**.
Japan Air Lines (JAL): DC-8 emergency, 154; Jumbo introduced, 164.
Japanese: bomb Bias Bay, 35; cruiser bombs Canton, city falls 39; troops occupy HKG border, 39; civilians killed at Lo Wu, 40; 84th Chutai at Canton, 41; appreciate HKG met. reports, 41; Major Kato commands 64th Sentai, 43; *Climb Mt. Niitaka*, 43; HKG bombed, 43; Wang Ching Wei-ites blaze-trail, 44; Tai Mo Shan radar, 48; Mt. Cameron Memorial, **50**; resume, 222, **222**, 223; demolish CAD complex for runway, 48; spirits exorcised from Sacred Hill, 48; Great East Asia Co-Prosperity Sphere in tatters, 48; Kamikaze pilots, 49; crashed Zeke fighter, **52**; atomic bomb, 49; Japan surrender, 50, 52.
Jardine, Matheson: peer of British trading companies, xi; founded on opium trade, xi; with BOAC forms Hong Kong Airways, 63; BOAC buys HKG Airways shares, 118; offers to Cathay, 118; intrigue rife, 119.
Jardine, Dr William: *Iron-headed Old Rat*, xi.
Jardine Aircraft Maintenance Company (JAMCO): establishes maintenance company, 65, **66**; expands on area of HMS *Flycatcher*, 75; Zigmund *Sol* Soldinsky in charge of overhaul shop, 75; brief Corporate notes, 196.
Jenvey, Mike: ATCO 1, promoted, 171.

AIRPORT OF THE NINE DRAGONS, KAI TAK, KOWLOON

Johnson, Captain E.S. *Sherm*: Convair instructor, 146.
John Swire & Sons: parent company of Butterfield & Swire, 73; show interest in American shareholdings, 73.
Jolly, James: Director of Air Services 1940, 20.

K

Kai Tak Airport: backdrop a range of serrated hills, the Nine Dragons of Kau Lung (Kowloon), 5; civilian flying began there in 1924, 7; first service aircraft, 12; called RAF Base Kai Tak, 12; matsheds beside nullah, 12; crane lifted planes, 12, **15**; lard factory, 14; Far East Flight arrive, **14**; Government takes control, 14; drought, 15, **16**; 1929 area 205 acres, 17; matshed fire, 22, **22**; another matshed fire, 22; 1934, **24**; **25**; modern civil hangar, 25; Sunderlands again visit, 26; 1934-1935, **27**; came of age, 31; Imperial service, 31; hangar, 32; over-run, 46; POW runway builders, weak surface, 47; filling from Diamond & Sacred hills, 48; American air attack, **49**; aerial photo, **51**; crashed *Zeke*, **52**; 1945 field area 376 acres, 53; problem of weak runways, 53; *tent-city* terminal, 53; Police Inspector Frank Indge-Buckingham remembers *tent-city*, 56, **59**, 61; Sea-wall Terminal commissioned, 64, **64**; night operation restricted, 65; Privateer lands after dark, 65; panorama, **67**; Runway 07 view, **68**; aerial view, **69**; 6,000 foot view, **69**; schedule and non-schedule carriers, 70; becoming a busy place, 70; new premises, 75; new Control Tower, roof of Jardine building, 76; Skymasters on tarmac, **85**; CNAC & CATC defected planes, 90, **86**; defected planes immobilised, **88**; aerial view, **89**; Nationalist Ministers discuss defected planes, 90; Chennault claims ownership, 90; extension runway 13, 93, **92**; expansions, **93**; possible airport sites, 98; the Broadbent Report, 98, **99**; planes using, 100; Privy Council favours Chennault, 101; Airport closed unless passenger, 101; restrictions removed, 101; control of aviation fuel, 101; USAF C54 (Skymaster) crashes and burns, 102; DH Dove visits, 102; extension a disappointment, closed, strengthened, 102; Airport 1952, 103; Spitfire belly landed, 104; Vampire veered off runway, 104; appoints foam expert, 106; minor work on sea-wall terminal, 106, **107**; 108; Cathay DC-4 shot down, 108, 109, 112; update of planes using airport, 110; bomb on *Kashmir Princess*, 110; air show, 114; accidents – passim, 115; seaman charters, Suez, 116; VIP lounge, 116; Thai Airways hydraulic failure, 116; Air Laos DC-3 fire, 116; NWA DC-7C, 117; Vickers Viscount 760, 117; Taiwan P4Y medium bomber force landed, HAEC rectifies, 127; quietly closed old runways, 140; lighting contract, 142; night flying, 142, **142**; USAF C-47 crashes, 144; *Venom* hydraulics fail, 145; props. and jets bad mix, 145; entry visa refused, attempts suicide, 147; 24 hour operation, 150; reverts to Freight, 150; Airport 1962/63, **151**; Garuda's Convair 990A, 152; Thai Airway's Caravelle, 152; Auster crashes, 152; Lufthansa emergency landing, 152; Cathay emergency landing, 152, **153**; planes collide in high wind, 154; *Musketeer* accident, 154; JAL DC-8 emergency, 154; wall-to-wall humanity, 155; Canadair accident, 155; Hercules C-130 crash, 155; DC-8 lands heavy, 155; Caravelle undershoots, 156; stabbing incident, 156; Cathay Convair into sea, 157, **157**; PanAm Jumbo, 162, **163**; grooving, 163; acrimony over clearance, 163; tunnel, 164; link taxiway, 165; Cricket autogyro accident, 165; IGS for Runway 13, 166; China Air Lines 707 accident, 166; another PAL hijack, 166; aerial photo 1973, **167**; seagulls, 169; Singapore Airlines 707 emergency, 171; 1975 aerial view, **172**; 1993 aerial view; **173**.
Kai Ho Kai, Doctor: – medical degree at Aberdeen University, called to the Bar at Lincoln's Inn, 5; with Au Tak reclaimed portion of Kowloon Harbour, became nucleus of Kai Tak Airport, 6; Knighted 1912, **6**.
Kau-kuen Wong: Act. Marshalling Supervisor, 140.
Kessler: CNAC captain, assists in evacuation, 45.
Kestrel: makes strange catch, 155.
Kilburn, R.S.: Partner, Dragonfly Helicopters, 160; insurance withheld, later paid, 160.
King, L.G. Lawrie: HKG Airways F/O (later CPA), fired on by Communist planes, 94; nose-wheel stuck, emergency landing, 152, **153**.
Kishen, Mandarin: negotiating Convention of Chuenpi, 1840, xi; disgraced, xi.
Knowles, *Bill*: Cathay's Managing Director, rejects regional company scheme, 118.

L

Lampard, Dave: HKG Airways captain, gives Donovan Kunming let-down, 86; HKG Airways, Viscount captain, 117.

Law, Stewardess Esther: Cathay, DC-4 shot down, rescued, 109; 243.
Leonard, Captain Royal: CNAC pilot, 23; Generalissimo Chiang Kai-shek's pilot, 23; helped evacuate HKG, 23; *Papa Moss & Flying Palace*, 34-35; last plane out of Hangkow, overloaded, 39; bullion to Kunming, 41; the spies, 41.
Leslie, *Vic*: RFEIC/CPA pilot, 57.
Lillywhite, Frederick Richard John *Fred*: reports for duty, 73; Airport Manager, 146; conducts Vice-Regals around Terminal, **149**; retires, died 1990, 165.
Lim On: HKG pioneer aviator, Happy Valley Racecourse, 4.
Lin Tse-hsu: arrived in Canton in 1839, edict to surrender opium, ix; in a rage occupies Macau, x.
Livock, Flight Lieutenant *Gerry*: first RAF flight in HKG, 11; surveyed from Tolo, 11; 2i/c Far East Flight, 14.
Liu Ching Yi, Colonel: escapes with 9 defected planes, 90; **88**; immigrated to Australia, dies, 90.
Lockheed Electra L188 – Problems & Rectification: resume, 241.
Lobo, Rogerio Hyndman (now Sir): associates with CPA, 58; tells of the gold charter tribulations, 71.
Lock, Captain: first regular Imperial service, 31; first passenger, Ong Eee-lim, 31.
Lok, Peter K.N.: CAD, ATC cadet, 116; qualified ATCO, 150; DCA HKG. 1988 – 1995, vi; on the first plane landing on the Miracle Strip, 128; spent a night beneath flight path, 123.
Loriga (Loringa), Joaquin (Taboada): Spanish pioneer pilot, 12; **13**; at Macau, 12; reached Manila, 12; 206.
Loring, Fernando Rein: Spanish pioneer pilot, 23; second trip to HKG, 23; **28**; resume, 211, **213**.
Louttit, Lyell William *Mum*: RFEIC radio officer, 57; Skymaster ferry flight, 86.
L.S.T. Chung: Chennault's floating workshop, 101; Shanghai escape, 101; in business at Canton, 101; winches defected planes aboard, 101.
Lufthansa: HKG service, 40; Ju52 stranded at Bangkok, 41; emergency landing, 152; Jumbo introduced, 164.
Lum, Cheong A.: a Chinese baker, poisons bread, xiii; police raid bakery, xiii; extradited from Macau, xiii; trial, xvi; discharged lack of evidence, xiii; the E. Sing Bakery, xvi.

M

Macau: Portuguese Enclave, about 40 miles west of HKG, viii; Portuguese discovered the direct sea route to China, viii; bombed by Americans, 49; Cathay non-schedule flights, 62; *Nikki* damaged, 62; the gold charters, 71.
Macau Air Transport Co. (HKG) Ltd. (MATCO): brief Corporate notes, 196.
Maclaren, Squadron Leader: led British round-the-world flight, 9; Vickers-Napier Vulture, 9; **10**; landed Kowloon, 9.
Maltby, Major General Christopher M.: arrives in HKG, 43; appoints Max Oxford liaison officer, 43; refuses RAF plan to bomb Canton, 45; orders Sullivan to destroy *Vildebeestes*, 45; orders Kai Tak evacuated, 45.
Marshall, Alan: Australian author *I Can Jump Puddles* decides not to board *Miss Macau*, 79.
Matheson, James: the dangerous thinker, xi.
McDonald, William: CNAC captain, assists in evacuation, 45.
McDuff, Keith Stewart *Ken*: Cathay first officer dies on pirated *Miss Macau*, 79.
McIllree, Eric: ferried 2 Ansons to HKG, 71; demonstrates at Macau, 71; closes deal and ferries to Rangoon, 71.
Miss Macau: Cathay Catalina chartered by MATCO's, 79, 80; pirated near Macau, one survivor, 79; Dale Cramer captain, 79; wreckage, 80.
Moench: French pioneer pilot, 21; **21**.
Morgan W.J. *Bill*: Lillywhite's replacement, dies, 165.
Morrison, H. Neil: Pilot Officer, RAF, 141; joins CPA, 141; dies in bombed Convair, 141, 165, **166**.
Morrison, J.R.: Chinese Secretary, xii.
Mose, H.L. *Lou*: HKAAF Spitfire ditched, 103; joins Cathay, killed in UK, 103.
Moss, Albert James Robert *Papa*: Aerodrome Superintendent, 20; Director of Civil Aviation, 20; Royal Leonard & *Flying Palace*, 34; interned in Stanley, 47; becomes Director of Civil Aviation, 64; immobilises defected planes, 90, **88**, retires, 101.

INDEX

Moxham, John (Mox the Ox): Cathay captain, Shanghai evacuation, 84; severe electrical storm, 84; guided by fire-beacons, 84.
Mt Cameron Memorial: 50; briefing, 61.
Mukden: Japanese occupy, 21; riots in Kowloon, 21.
Murray, Capt. Lee: injured in Catalina crash, 95.
Murray, W.F.: Commandant FEFTS, 23.
Muspratt-Williams, Mervyn Jackson: DCA, 101, service background, 101; *Kashmir Princess* investigation, 111; new runway plans to London, luke-warm reception, 123; greets Governor for Runway opening ceremony, 128; Terminal Opening, 148, **149**; retired, 101, 117, 156; dies in Malta, 101, 161.

N

Napier, Lord: first superintendent of British trade in Canton – 1834, ix; died in Macau, ix.
Nelson, Erik: 1st Ass. Aerodrome Superintendent, 25.
New Runway: farsighted decisions, 121; possible airport sites, 121, 122; UK offers loan, 122; Broadbent Report suggestions, 122; Scott & Wilson, Kirkpatrick & Partners, London consultants, modify Broadbent's report, 122; design comparison, **130**; mock-up, **129**; boring disclosed POW weak areas, 122; suggested a new reclamation, 122; flats and high ground for demolition, 122, 130, **131**; cost beyond Colony's means, 123; modified scheme accepted, 125; a separate taxiway necessary, 124; reduced length attracts criticism, 125; contract awarded to French company, 125; sub-contract to Gammon, 126; building progress, **131**; access road, **132**; building progress, **134**, **135**; heavy rain and typhoons take toll, 126; dredged cannon, 126, **136**; finished strip, **137**; USAF Skymaster crash opens Miracle Strip, 128, **137**; first plane to land Albatross, 128; first plane off a RAF Venom, 128; first civilian plane off Cathay's DC-6, 128; Official Opening, 128; helicopter cuts ribbon, 128, **138**; Governor opens runway, 128, **138**; Venoms lead fly-past, 129, **139**; FEFTS's *Tiger scratched*, 129; civilian planes fly-past, 129; Police Band *beat the retreat*, 129; Miracle Strip from altitude, **139**; further extension, 161, **161**; work starts, 162; acrimony over clearance, 163; Channel Rock swallowed, 164; extension open, **170**.
New Terminal Building: to supplement new strip, 140; Freight Building standby Terminal, 140, **144**; Eric Cumine & Co. drawings, 140, **141**; Technical sub-committee, 145; completion date passes, 148; opens, 148, **148**, **149**; hydraulic operated bridges, 161; finance for next phase, 164; building programme, 171.
New Territories: leased to Britain in 1897, xiv.
Nogues, Maurice: French pioneer pilot, 23; carried first air-mail to/from HKG, 23; resume, 215.
Norquay, Neil: repairs *Nikki* at Macau, 62.
North West Airlines: survey HKG route, 84; DC-7C arrives, 117, **117**.

O

Opium: British blamed for introducing opium, ix; addicts called hippies, ix.
Opium Wars:
  First Opium War – 1839: begins over trading practices, x; British forces overrun Canton, x; Convention of Chuenpi ceded HKG and harbour to Britain, x.
  Second Opium War (Arrow War) – 1856: began over flag violation, xiv; British and French captured Canton, xiv; Treaty of Tientsin (1858) initialled, xiv, **232**; resume, 230.
  Third Opium War – 1860: China refused to ratify Treaty of Tientsin, xiv; summer palace burnt and destroyed the Taku forts, xiv; China ratifies Treaty of Tientsin, ceded Kowloon Peninsula (to Boundary Street) and Stonecutter's Island to Britain, xiv; resume, 234, VC winner, **235**, Taku fort, **233**; Prince Kung, **236**.
Owen, Bessie: flies in, 34; resume, 214.
Oxford, Maxwell Norman *(Max)*: second assistant to *Papa Moss*, 37; liaison officer, 43; escapes by sea, 46; Act. Director of Air Services, 54; transfers to Malaya, 93.

P

Pacific Air Maintenance & Supply Company Limited (PAMAS): establishes on HMS *Flycatcher* site, 75, **75**; spares from Manila dump, 77; brief Corporate notes, 197.
Pacific Overseas Airlines (Siam): Skymaster crashes, no survivors, 98.

Paish, John, DFC: Cathay captain, crashes Braemar Reservoir, 84; track to oblivion, 87; smouldering wreck, 87.
Palmerston, Lord: British Prime Minister, x; China ignores ultimatum, x; Britain dispatches warships and troops, x; recalls Elliot, xii.
Pan American Airways System (PanAm): control of CNAC, 23; *Philippine Clipper* Kowloon Bay, Juan Terry Trippe pilot, 32, **219**; refused rights, 32; establishes terminal Macau, 32; extends service to HKG, 33; Sikorsky S-42B, **33**; returns to HKG, 65; sells interest in CNAC to National Government, 91; replaces *Connie* with DC-6B, 100; Jumbo arrives, 162, **163**; seagulls on landing, 169; resume, 219, **220**.
Peninsula Hotel: temporary RAF quarters, 12; Transport Command check-in point, 52; Cathay crew accommodation, 61; resume, 224, **226**, **227**.
Perez, Eugenio: Spanish pioneer mechanic, 12; 206.
Philippine Airlines (PAL): Dakota crashes, 62; hijacked, 164; another hijack, 166.
Pickering, James Fleming *Pip*: reports for duty, 73; Cathay DC-4 shot down, 109; scrambles Hornets, advises Rescue Squadron at Clark AFB, 109.
Pickering, F/O W.R.: killed, 85.
Pirates: anti-piracy patrols resume, 52; attack fishing fleet, 54; Catalina *Miss Macao*, 79; Wong Yu pirate survivor, 81; Madame Wong pirate leader, 83; resume, executions, 228, **229**.
Plenderleith, Flying Officer: pilot British round-the-world flight, 9; **10**.
Polo Brothers: Nicolo and Maffeo probably first traders to Cathay (China), viii; Marco accompanied next expedition, viii; jailed in Venice on return and wrote *Description of the World*, viii.
Pottinger, Sir Henry: first governor of HKG, xii; changes name from Queenstown to Victoria, xii.
Presgrave, John: ANA captain, ferries CPA Skymaster, 86.

Q

QANTAS: Skymaster service, 85, **85**.

R

Ralph, Fred S.: PanAm captain of Hong Kong Clipper, 44.
RAF's Far East Flight – 1927/28: resume 209, **210**.
RAF Kai Tak: becomes RAF Station Kai Tak, 26; Sunderlands again visit, 26; Hawker Horsley replaced by Vildebeeste, 33; Fairey Swordfish, 36; hangar stockpiled, 42; Walrus patrols, 42; Station's aerial strength 5 planes, 43; Wing Commander H.G. *Ginger* Sullivan arrives, 43; Maltby refuses permission to bomb Canton, 45; ordered to destroy *Vildebeestes*, 45; interned at Sham Shui Po, 47; Marines reoccupy Kai Tak, 50; Wing Commander R.C. Haine takes command, 50; HMS *Nabcatcher* repair depot, 50; Transport Command, Peninsula Hotel check-in, 52; anti-piracy patrols resume, 52; Flight Lieutenant Handle ditches near Hainan, 53; post-war control tower, **54**; responds to pirate attack, 54; 96 Squadron arrives, 54; Dakota crashes near Kowloon Tong, 58; 88. Squadron arrives, 90; 80 Squadron get Hornets, ferry problems, 100, 101; Sunderland loses wing-float, 102; Vampire crashes in Port Shelter, 102; Hastings lands short, burns, 102; Hornets rescue launch under Communist attack, 103; future patrols armed, 104; Vampire veered off runway, 104; Hornet crashes in sea, 105; Vampire aquaplanes, 114; training Vampire crashes, 114, Harvard undercarriage collapse, 114; Vampire nose-wheel unsafe, 114; Venoms lead Opening Ceremony fly-past, 129, **139**; Duke of Edinburgh parade, 141; Venom pilot awarded AFC, 145; *Canberra* in sea, 154; *Whirlwind* in sea, 162; *Whirlwind* hi-rise rescue, 162; *Whirlwind* strikes power cable, 162; mercy dash, 164.
Richmond, John Francis *Dick*: flight engineer, Catalina VR-HEV, 96; captured by Communists, 95; accused of smuggling, 95; jailed, 97; released, 97, **96**.
Robinson, Sir George: replaced John Francis Davis, ix.
Roy Farrell Export-Import Company (RFEIC): *Betsy* arrives, 57, **57**; Bill *Hokum* Harris, Chief Engineer, 57; BOAC shows interest, 58; evolves into Cathay Pacific Airways, 58.
Russell, Robert Stanley *Bob*: RFEIC partner, 57.

S

Sacred Hill/Sung Wong Toi: marked for demolition, 124; supply sea-wall pitching blocks, 126; dressing Sung Wong Toi (Stone), **133**; under demolition, **133**; Stone erected in special park, **240**; resume, 237, **238**, **239**.
Saunders, John Kingsley: ATCO Grade II, 127; retired as Act. Deputy Director, 127.

Scaroni, Commander: delivered a Savoia Machetti to Generalissimo Chiang Kai-shek, 16.
Schlee, Edward: American pioneer pilot, 14; *Pride of Detroit*, 14; 18; resume, 208, **208**.
Shaw Brothers: buy PAMAS hangar, film studio, 162.
Siamese Airways: diverts to Tainan, returns to Kai Tak, crashes into sea, 100; mystery solved, 155.
Smith, *Bob*: CPA – Chief Flight Engineer, on DC-6B ferry, 128; Electra ferry, 141.
Smith, E.B. *Bernie*: CPA Captain, passenger removed, 145; Director of Flight Operations, ferry Lockheed L1011, 171, **171**.
Smith, Dave: CPA captain, assesses planes, recommends Electra L188, 118; Electra ferry, 141; Sydney service, 141; Convair 880 ferry, 146.
Smith, F.C.: co-founder HKG Flying Club, **16**.
Smith, Frank, DFC: CPA captain, Skymaster inagural Singapore flight, 90.
Smith, Harry: HAEC executive, 75; tells of *Sol* Soldinsky's engineers, 75.
Smith-Reynolds: pioneer pilot, 23.
Soldinsky, Zigmund *Sol*: in charge of JAMCO's overhaul shop, 75; famous for the DC2 & 1/2 repairs, 75.
Somchai Chaiyasut, Lieutenant: charged, Convair bombing, 165, **166**; trial begins, father defends, 165; found *not guilty*, 165; insurance paid, 165.
Spanish Flight (Raid): resume, 206.
Stanley, Major Harry: heads HKG Tourist Association, 127.
Steele, Captain Ken: Cathay, assessed planes, recommends Electra L188, 118.
Stewart, Alex William: RFEIC/CPA radio officer, 58.
St. John Fischer, R.T.: pilot of crashed Bell helicopter, 158, **159**; insurance withheld, later paid, 160.
Stubbs, Sir Reginald KCMG: governor (1919-1925), 9; pirate hide-outs, 12; first Governor to make air survey, 12.
Sun, Chung-liang: owner, Catalina VR-HEV, **96**; captured by Communists, 95; accused of smuggling, 95; jailed, 97.
Sunby, Charles: CNAC captain, crashes on Basalt Island, no survivors, 77.
Sweet, Harold: CNAC captain, evacuates people from Kai Tak, 45; engine trouble at Namyung, 45; flew wing to Suifu for *Sol* Soldinsky to repair, 75; Captain Sweet died in 1948, 75.
Swire, John Kidston *Jock*: negotiates to purchase American shareholdings, 73; Cathay Pacific Airways (1948) Limited formed, 73; Swire retained the Burma operation but not the gold-charters, 73; matches wits with BOAC, 118; wins the Battle of HKG Airways, 119.

T

Taaffe, Ron: CPA, F/E – CPA balloon, 169.
Tai Mo Shan: highest point in the Colony, 5; air defence radar moved, 92.
Tak, Au: owned photographic business, 5; with Doctor Ho Kai reclaimed portion of Kowloon Harbour, development failed, became nucleus of Kai Tak Airport, 6.
Teeters, *Don*: Cathay Catalina captain, 72.
TERMINALS – PASSENGER – Locations: **190**, **191**.
Thai International: introduce Caravelle, 152; Caravelle undershoots, 157.
Thomson, Lord: Air Minister, **10**.
Thomson, Thomas Russell: CAD, Airport Commandant, 117; replaces Winship, 150; DCA, 156.
Thorpe, John Trevor: CAD-ATCO 11, later DCA, 155.
Tomkins, Ronald Stanley *Tommy*: reports for duty, 73.
Treaties of Washington 1921-22: controlled military bases, 12.
Treaty of Nanking: signed 1842, xii; treaty unsatisfactory, xiii.
Treaty of the Bogue: opened five *Treaty Ports*, xii.
Treaty of Tientsin: initialled 1858, xiv; China refused to ratify, xiv.
Trench, Sir David: HKG Governor, 152.
Trippe, Juan Terry: lands *Philippine Clipper* HKG, 32; resume, 219, **219**.
Truman, President Harry S.: agrees to return HKG to Britain, 50.
Turner, Colin O.: ARB Surveyor, 152.
Typhoons: 1841 – slammed Colony, xii. 1927 – destroyed natsheds, 12, **13**, **14**; 1937 – 11,000 killed, 34; 1946-Pat Armstrong's experience, 54; damaged C-47 & Sunderland, **55**; *Alice*, 144; *Olga*, 144; *Wanda*, 147; *Tilda*, 154; *Anita*, 157; *Irma*, 169.

U

USAF: C-54 (Skymaster) crashes and burns, 102; Skymaster crash, early opening of Miracle Strip, 128; C-47 Mt Parker crash, 144, C-54 collision, 154.
US Marine Corps: Hercules C-130 crashes, 155.
US Navy: Privateer lands after dark, 65; Neptune heavy landing, fire destroys, 104; Neptune landing accident, 106; Albatross – first plane to land on Miracle Strip, 128.

V

Van den Born, Charles: Belgian's Farman biplane, **3**; Governor late, 4; Colony's first heavier-than-air flight March 18, 1911, 2.
Van der Sluis, Alan: HAEC, Musketeer accident, 162.
Vaughan Fowler, Wing Commander R.: co-founder HKG Flying Club, 15, **16**; overbearing attitude, 23; Government backing, 24.
von Erzdorf, Marga: German pioneer aviatrix, 23; **29**, resume, 210, **210**.
von Gronau, Wolfgang: German pioneer pilot, 23; **28**; **29**; resume, 213.

W

Wakeford, *Tony*: HAEC GM on largest hangar, 161.
Waldron, E.: Chief Engineer, FEFTS, 24.
Wales, Alex: CPA captain – ferry's DC-6B, 128.
Wallace, John: Radio HKG's – the Miracle Strip, 127; confuses Governor's helicopter, 128.
Wang Ching Wei-ites: HKG Fifth Column, 44.
Ward, Flight Lieutenant A.R.: RAF, killed, 17.
Warne, John: resigns from ATC, 98.
Wawn, John Aubrey *Pinky*: RFEIC/CPA captain, 57.
Weller, Tony: runway builder, weak surface, 47; American bombers, 47, **49**.
Weston, Len: CPA F/E, Electra ferry, 141.
Whiteaad, R.: CAD-ATCO, 150.
Wilcocks, W.: Ground Instructor, FEFTS, 24.
Williams, Jack *Pouch*: repairs *Nikki* at Macau, 62; dies, 146.
Wills, Frank E.N.: Asst. Airport Manager, 140; Airport Manager, 146, **146**.
Winship, Ralph: Deputy DCA, HKG, 101; joins ICAO, 101.
Wolfkill, Grant: released, 147.
Wolinski, Ken: Cathay radio officer, gold charters, **72**; Shanghai evacuation, 84; severe electrical storm, 84; Kunming evacuation, 86.
Wong, Herbie: Electra Sydney service, 141; Dinkum Aussie, 142.
Wong, Madame (Chung Lo-Yu): pirate leader, 83.
Wong, Radio Officer *Steve*: Cathay, DC-4 shot down, killed, 109; 243.
Wong Yu: *Miss Macau* pirate, 80; released, contrived death?, 94.
Wood, *Phil*: CAD, Signals, 116; dies, 161.
Woods, Capt. Hugh L. *Woody*: CNAC DC-2 shot down, 37; assesses the *Hump*, 42.
Woodyard, Captain Jack Thompson: 31st Air Rescue Squadron, 109; French Privateer sights dinghy, 109; Grumman Albatross lands, **112**; Grumman at Kai Tak, **112**; decorated, **113**; 243.
Wray, Cyril E.L.: ARB Surveyor, 152.
Wright, Wilbur: failed to make first flight, 2.
Wright, Orville: world's first controlled flight, 2.

Y

Young, Sir Mark: wartime Governor, 43.

Z

Zanni, Major Pedro: Argentine pioneer pilot, 9; landed HKG 1924, 11; **17**; **18**; resume, 204, **205**.

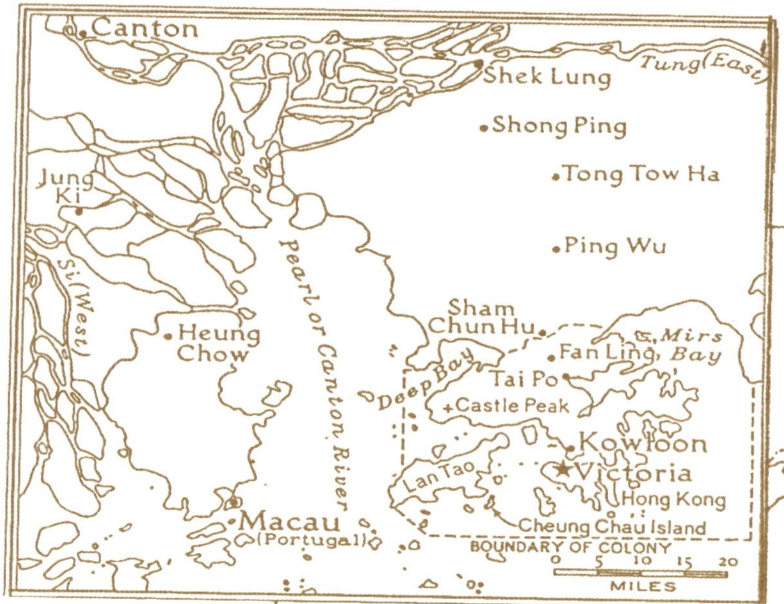
Canton
Shek Lung
Tung (East)
Shong Ping
Tong Tow Ha
Ping Wu
Jung Ki
Si (West)
Pearl or Canton River
Heung Chow
Sham Chun Hu
Mirs Bay
Fan Ling
Tai Po
Deep Bay
Castle Peak
Kowloon
Victoria
Lan Tao
Hong Kong
Cheung Chau Island
Macau
(Portugal)
BOUNDARY OF COLONY
0 5 10 15 20
MILES

SHUM CHUN RIVER
FAN LING
UN LONG
KAM TIN
CASTLE PEAK
TSUEN WA
22°20
STONEC ISLA
GREEN ISLAND
LANTAU ISLAND
TAI O
CHEUNG CHAU
LAMMA ISLAND
SCALE
22°10
114°00